AIN AT WAR

Spain at War

The Spanish Civil War in Context, 1931–1939

George Esenwein and Adrian Shubert

Longman
London and New York

Addison Wesley Longman Limited
Edinburgh Gate
Harlow, Essex CM20 2JE, England

and Associated Companies throughout the world

Published in the United States of America
by Addison Wesley Longman, New York

First published 1995
Second impression 1997

ISBN 0 582 25943 6 CSD
ISBN 0 582 55272 9 PPR

British Library Cataloguing-in-Publication Data

A catalogue record for this book is
available from the British Library

Library of Congress Cataloging-in-Publication Data
  Esenwein, George Richard.
    Spain at war : the Spanish Civil War in historical perspective /
  George Esenwein, Adrian Shubert.
      p.   cm.
    Includes bibliographical references and index.
    ISBN 0–582–25943–6. — ISBN 0–582–55272–9 (pbk.)
    1. Spain—History—Civil War, 1936–1939. I. Shubert, Adrian,
  1953– . II. Title.
  DP269.E74 1995
  946. 081—dc20   94–22117
                                                    CIP

Set in 10/12pt V-I-P Bembo by 20B
Produced by Longman Singapore Publishers (Pte) Ltd,
Printed in Singapore

Contents

List of Maps

4 maps after: Burnett Bolloten, *The Spanish Civil War: Revolution and Counterrevolution.* Chapel Hill, University of North Carolina, 1991.

Acknowledgements

George Esenwein:

In many ways this text is the product of my seven-year personal and scholarly relationship with the renowned Civil War scholar, Burnett Bolloten. Burnett's abiding passion for telling the truth caused him to devote nearly fifty years to unravelling the complexities surrounding that tragic event. My own interest in the subject was aroused and sustained by our frequent (and often) marathon discussions of civil war topics. His wide reading of primary and secondary sources as well as his profound respect for accuracy served as a model of historical scholarship that I have both admired and sought to emulate. Above all, I found Burnett to be a warm and generous person, and I am immensely grateful to him for having shared with me his knowledge and personal reminiscences of the war.

During the time I was at Stanford University, several friends and colleagues were particularly supportive of my work on the civil war and revolution. For their friendship and encouragement over the years I want to thank Paul Avrich, Betty Bolloten, Elena Poniatowska, Helen Solanum, Peter Stansky, and Ella Wolfe. At the Hoover Institution Sondra Bierre, Hilja Kukk, Rebecca J. Mead, Agnes Peterson, Bill Ratliff and other members of the staff of the Library and Archives assisted my researches in various ways. I should also like to thank Andy Norton, David Jacobs, Michael Ballard, Deborah Bundy, and others at the Green Library, Stanford University for their many bibliographical contributions.

My students at Florida Atlantic University also deserve recognition for raising some of the questions which I have tried to elucidate in the following pages.

Acknowledgements

Adrian Shubert:

I want to thank all my colleagues in the Department of History at York University and the students I have taught in History 3391, whose questions have compelled me to think more clearly about the Second Republic and the Spanish Civil War and to become, I hope, a better teacher.

Both authors would like to acknowledge the contributions of the following people. Thanks to staff at Longman for their useful suggestions, for their faith in our abilities to finish the project, and for having rescued the manuscript from infelicities of grammar and style. Thanks to Antonio Cazovla for doing the index. Burnett Bolloten, Noam Chomsky, Stanley G. Payne, and Paul Preston were kind enough to read and comment on parts of the manuscript. Though the book has benefitted from their observations, the authors bear full responsibility for any errors or oversights that appear in the text.

For my love and inspiration, Ana
George Esenwein

and

To the memory of Burnett Bolloten
George Esenwein
and Adrian Shubert

Introduction

The term 'civil war' conjures up the image of a country divided in two: Roundheads and Cavaliers in England in the 1640s; North and South in the United States between 1861 and 1865; Reds and Whites in Russia between 1918 and 1921; and Republicans and Nationalists in Spain from July 1936 to April 1939. But is this picture an accurate one? Does it, for example, come close to conveying the true nature of the causes and consequences of the internecine struggle it purports to describe? In the case of the Spanish Civil War the answer to both of these questions is clearly no: while there was indeed a domestic conflict in which two contending sides called Republicans and Nationalists (or Loyalists and Rebels) fought each other for nearly three years and in the course of which several hundred thousand people were killed, the civil war obviously amounted to much more than just a two-sided struggle.

For many years, however, the complexities underlying Spain's war were obscured by controversy. In retrospect it is easy to see why this was the case. Few historical events in the twentieth century have stirred political passions as deeply or have sparked as many acrimonious debates as the Spanish Civil War. The truth of this claim is most obviously borne out by the thousands of monographs, biographies, memoirs and literary works that it has inspired in the past fifty years. A quick survey of the titles and themes of this enormous body of literature makes clear that there are scarcely any issues associated with the Civil War that are not open to dispute.[1]

What was it about the Spanish Civil War that made it such a controversial

---

1. Even the vocabulary employed by historians has reflected the controversial nature of the war: pro-Republicans have been variously referred to as Loyalists, Republicans, anti-Nationalists, etc. Likewise, the rebelling side has been dubbed the Insurgents, the Nationalists, fascists, etc.

subject? First and foremost is the fact that it is arguably the first modern European war where propaganda played a central role both in defining the aims and overall objectives of the opposing sides and in shaping our understanding of its historical significance.[2] Most contemporary accounts of events in Spain tended to be two-dimensional, reflecting the real, even lethal, ideological differences that were then framing the boundaries of international politics. No doubt this is what George Orwell had in mind when he wrote in 1943 that 'History had stopped in 1936.'[3] What struck Orwell, and indeed many others at the time, was not just the seemingly endless stream of propaganda emanating from both sides during the Civil War but what he referred to as the 'deliberate conspiracy' outside the country 'to prevent the Spanish situation from being understood.'[4] Thus, even if they happened to be poles apart politically, both pro-Republicans and pro-Nationalists shared common ground in presenting the war as a Manichean struggle, characterized on the left as an encounter between the forces of fascism and democracy and on the right as one between Christian civilization and communist barbarism.

Following the outbreak of general war in Europe, the distinguishing features of the Spanish imbroglio became even further blurred against the broader canvas of world war. In addition to the distorting influences of ideology and propaganda, the timing of Spain's epic struggle contributed to the widely-held view, then and subsequently, that it should be regarded as a dress rehearsal for the Second World War.

If, with the benefit of hindsight, we can now see that early interpretations of the Spanish Civil War were being refracted through a clouded lens, the question arises as to why this distorted picture persisted for nearly fifty years. A major reason has been that very few of the histories about the Civil War have managed to surmount the ideological barriers and transcend the highly-charged political atmosphere of the 1930s and 1940s. This was especially true inside Franco's Spain, where for nearly forty years official accounts of the war categorically insisted that it had been a national crusade (*la cruzada*) which involved a struggle between Jewish-Bolshevik-Masonic elements on the one side and the forces of Christianity and law and order on the other. More surprising is the fact that the mostly pro-Republican works produced outside Spain during the post-war period also failed in many instances to overcome these obstacles. Even scholarly studies,

---

2. This is not to deny the important role propaganda played in the First World War (political posters and the like) and the Bolshevik Revolution of 1917. See below, Chapter 12.
3. George Orwell, 'Looking Back on the Spanish Civil War', reprinted in *Homage to Catalonia* (Harmondsworth, 1970), pp. 233–4.
4. George Orwell, 'Spilling the Spanish Beans', in *An Age Like This: 1920–1940* (London/ New York, 1968), p. 276.

which represented a variety of viewpoints and on the whole offered a far more sophisticated analysis of the war than the propagandistic tracts being churned out in Spain, were so preoccupied with the universal issues and problems that had been raised in the aftermath of the Second World War that they tended to overlook the fact that the Spanish Civil War was fundamentally a domestic conflict which could be properly understood only within the context of that country's history.[5] The significance of Spain's tragic war, according to nearly all of the pro-Republican histories written during the 1950s and 1960s, lay in the fact that it was the opening act of a much larger political drama that unfolded on the world stage soon after the Civil War had ended, a view summed up by the liberal American historian Gabriel Jackson when he wrote, 'the majority [of Republican Spaniards] fought to preserve Spain, and Europe, from tyranny'.[6]

As time passed, some historians were slow to abandon this point of view and embrace new perspectives. For example, the author of a recent book on the war put Stalin at the head of principal figures on the Republican side, followed by Hemingway, Orwell, and André Malraux, while on the Nationalist side Hitler was second only to General Franco himself.[7] Film is another medium that has kept alive the moral dualisms, the black and white simplicities characteristic of the 1930s. The fact that as late as the mid-1980s a documentary produced about the Abraham Lincoln Battalion could be entitled 'The Good Fight' speaks volumes about how foreigners still see Spain's civil war experience.

Yet the period following Franco's death in 1975 and continuing up through the last stages of the Cold War has also seen a dramatic change in the political and intellectual climate, not only in Spain but throughout the West. One of the positive by-products of this has been the proliferation of studies that seek to demythologize the Spanish Civil War and thereby situate it in its proper historical context.[8] In keeping with this latest trend our principal objective in writing this book has been to provide a short,

5. For further discussion on this see below, Chapter 12. A fuller treatment of this topic can be found in Paul Preston's insightful essay, 'War of Words. The Spanish Civil War and the historians', in *Revolution and War in Spain, 1931–1939* ed. by Paul Preston (London, 1984), pp. 1–13.
6. The veracity of these commonly shared assumptions was reinforced first by the outcome of the Second World War and later by the peculiar dynamics of the Cold War. In the former case, the defeat of the Axis powers seemed to justify the left's total condemnation of the Franco regime: the Spanish government's friendly associations with Italy and Germany during the war gave credence to the idea that the civil war was a Manichean struggle between democracy and fascism. Not surprisingly this interpretation of events proved to be just as popular in the polarized political world of the 1950s and 1960s.
7. Peter Wyden, *The Passionate War* (New York, 1983), p. 13.
8. In Spain, some of the leading civil war historians in this movement are Juan Pablo Fusi, Ángel Viñas, and Santos Juliá.

analytical narrative which throws light on a significant historical event but at the same time restores to the Spanish Civil War the sense of the complexities which we believe make it such a fascinating subject. Throughout we have tried to emphasize both the deeply-rooted indigenous origins of the war as well as the interplay between domestic and international forces.

To capture the multifaceted features of the war as well as to highlight the distinctions of two periods in Spanish history we have maintained a division of labour. Since Adrian Shubert's previous research projects have concentrated on the era of the Second Republic, it was logical for him to edit Part 1. Likewise, we concluded that, given his extensive work on Civil War topics, George Esenwein was well-suited to write Parts 2 and 3. But though our accounts of the Republic and civil war represent two viewpoints, the project has from the beginning been a collaborative effort. Drafts of every chapter were read and edited by both authors and the completed book represents a distillation of our numerous exchanges of ideas and mutual criticisms.

Part 1, called 'The Second Republic and the Origins of the Civil War', describes the four most important problems with which the various governments of the Republic came to grips, their attempts to resolve them and the resistance generated by these reform efforts. The second part, 'Civil War and Revolution', opens with a description of the social and political consequences of the July 1936 military rebellion. The theme of popular revolution, and particularly its impact on the daily lives of men and women in the Republican zone, is taken up in the next chapter. The dissensions among the Republican forces over how the war was to be conducted are the subject of Chapter 8. Subsequent chapters examine the role of foreign intervention and developments in the Nationalist and Republican zones. The book concludes with a brief epilogue which explains why, until very recently, the bitter legacies of the Civil War continued to exercise a profound influence over Spanish society.

PART ONE

The Second Republic and the Origins of the Civil War

CHAPTER ONE

The Course of Politics

The immediate roots of the Second Republic lay in the dictatorship of General Miguel Primo de Rivera (September 1923 to January 1930). For the previous half century, ever since the short-lived and chaotic First Republic (1873–74), republicanism had been an incoherent and marginal political force in Spain. Only in Barcelona after 1907, when Alejandro Lerroux's radicals developed an anti-clerical and anti-regionalist programme directed at the working class, did it have any mass support. However, by resorting to a dictatorship attempt to resolve the crisis which had begun in 1917, Alfonso XIII discredited the liberal, constitutional monarchy which had existed since 1876. At the same time he revived republicanism as a significant political force, turning formerly staunch monarchists such as Niceto Alcalá Zamora and Miguel Maura into republicans and alienating much of the military.

The monarchy had tied its fate to a non–democratic solution to a major political and social crisis and when that solution failed it brought with it the end of the monarchy. The process was similar to that in Italy, where the collapse of the Fascist regime during the Second World War was quickly followed by the abolition of the monarchy and the creation of a Republic. In Italy, however, Mussolini was able to stave off the crisis for twenty years and the Republic, which was created in the context of military defeat and the Cold War, took on a conservative tone. In Spain, on the other hand, Primo de Rivera failed in his attempt to create a corporatist state with a mass base on the Italian model, and remained in power for only seven years. He was replaced first by General Berenguer (January 1930 – February 1931) and then by Admiral Aznar (February – April 1931), both of whom sought a way to return to constitutional government. This was obstructed by both the lack of unity among the monarchist political forces and the increasing unity of the opposition which, backed by a growing political

7

mobilization among the population, was determined to prevent any return to the situation before Primo de Rivera's coup. In this context the Second Republic came into existence dedicated to reform but facing a set of elites who identified their interests with those of 'Spain' and who intransigently sought to oppose any significant change.

THE BIRTH OF THE REPUBLIC

The disparate republican forces had begun a process of expansion and cohesion in 1926 which was completed on 17 August 1930 with the signing of the so-called Pact of San Sebastián. At that meeting representatives of seven Republican parties agreed to set up a Republic with autonomy for Catalonia, Galicia and the Basque Provinces so long as it was consonant with 'the liberal and democratic spirit of the revolution'. They also established a revolutionary committee and liaison groups to deal with the military and the labour left. The participants did not discuss specific programmes as 'the representatives of the parties gathered there differed on any issue that was not a vague affirmation of the need to establish a Republic'.[1]

The San Sebastián coalition presented itself as socially moderate. The Provisional Government which was named in October 1930 was headed by a former monarchist minister and practising Catholic, Niceto Alcalá Zamora, and had another former monarchist, Miguel Maura, as Minister of the Interior. It also included the aged and increasingly conservative former demagogue, Alejandro Lerroux. While the coalition sought to bring the labour left – anarchosyndicalists and socialists – into the movement these forces were to have a clearly supporting role, calling a general strike to back up a military rising by sympathetic officers.

Of all the groups that the coalition brought into the movement the Socialists proved the most elusive, refusing to commit themselves until October 1930. The Socialists' prevarication stemmed from the dispute which had arisen within the party over the strategy of cooperating with the Primo de Rivera regime which it had adopted in 1923. This strategy was supported by two of the three wings of the PSOE, those led by Julián Besteiro and Francisco Largo Caballero, while only Indalecio Prieto and his small group of supporters advocated co-operation with middle-class Republicans. By 1927, however, rank-and-file discontent with the party's policy led Largo Caballero, who was always sensitive to the temperament of the base, to change his mind. Even so, this did not lead to immediate

---

1. Shlomo Ben-Ami, *The Origins of the Second Republic in Spain* (Oxford, 1978), p. 80.

acceptance of the idea of collaborating with the Republicans as Largo Caballero did not commit himself to this position until the autumn of 1930. In return for the support of the Socialists the Republicans agreed to institute legislation to introduce workers' control and set up a labour arbitration system, and offered them three posts in the Provisional Government.

The Republicans initially expected to topple the monarchy by a military coup but they proved to be ineffectual revolutionaries. Risings planned for October and November were both aborted and a December revolt misfired when two officers in Jaca moved two days early and the Socialists then failed to call a general strike. After these failures the Republicans announced that they would abstain from any elections called by the government, a position which was supported by the Socialists and, for their own reasons, by the monarchist liberals as well. The government had hoped to use general elections as a way of returning to the status quo ante, but this tactic was rejected by both the opposition and some monarchist elements. The Republicans demanded that municipal elections be held before general elections and that the latter must lead to a Constituent Cortes. When municipal elections were called first, for 12 April 1931, they agreed to take part and effectively turned them into a referendum on the political future of the country.

The right acquiesced in this interpretation and undertook a defensive campaign extolling the superiority of the monarchy over a republic. As Shlomo Ben-Ami describes it, 'Everywhere the topics of the communist threat, the quest for preservation of the social order, the warnings of imminent economic chaos, a clear attempt to play on the fears of the well-to-do classes and the defence of the king were frequently used . . . The general tendency . . . was that of reluctantly accepting the challenge that the elections were political in character, and, therefore, praise for the Monarchy and defamation of the Republic were commonplace'.[2] The Church called on Catholics to vote for the monarchy. Both sides made use of modern techniques of political campaigning, a clear indication that the apathy and *caciquismo* on which the Restoration political system had been based were largely things of the past.

The monarchists won a majority of the town councils but most of their victories were in the smaller, rural centres where electoral manipulation could still be effective. On the other hand, they lost forty-five of the fifty-two provincial capitals and most of the other larger towns and cities. The results were taken by most members of the government as a rejection of the monarchy and only one, Juan de la Cierva, was prepared to use force

2. Ibid., pp. 225–6.

to defend it. On 13 April negotiations began between the Count of Romanones and Alcalá Zamora for a transition, during which the Republican leader issued his famous ultimatum demanding that the King leave the country 'before sunset'. While these negotiations were taking place there were numerous and imposing street demonstrations in favour of the Republic and the new regime was being declared in town halls across the country. In the afternoon of 14 April, General Sanjurjo, the commander of the Guardia Civil, went over to the Provisional Government, driving the last nail in the monarchy's coffin. At 5 p.m. the Republican flag was raised at the Madrid city hall and two hours later at the Ministry of the Interior. At 8 p.m. Alcalá Zamora declared the Republic from the balcony of the Ministry amidst what Santos Juliá calls a 'spontaneous fiesta popular' in which a broad spectrum of the city's social groups participated.[3]

THE PROVISIONAL GOVERNMENT

On 14 April the San Sebastián coalition became the Provisional Government of the Second Republic. The composition of the cabinet was a faithful reflection of the heterogeneity of the political forces which had fathered the new regime, ranging from Alcalá Zamora and Maura of Derecha Republicana, through Lerroux of the Radicals, liberal republicans Marcelino Domingo and Manuel Azaña to Socialists Francisco Largo Caballero, Indalecio Prieto and Fernando de los Ríos. These groups had been able to remain united so long as their objective was to install the Republic. Once this had been achieved and it came time to determine the nature of that Republic, to fight elections and please electorates, this unity was not likely to endure. The Socialists, whose rank and file had invested such high hopes in the Republic and who faced a major challenge to their left from the CNT, were particularly vulnerable to such pressures. With hindsight it would appear that the coalition was doomed to divide; the only question being along what lines. Would it be the Socialists or the right, Derecha Republicana and the Radicals, who would leave? Would the Republic turn out to be conservative or progressive?

It did not take long for the first cracks to appear. The church burnings of 10 May posed questions of public order and religious policy which alienated Maura and, to a lesser degree, Alcalá Zamora. Their party took in many former monarchists and caciques who opposed the labour decrees of Largo Caballero and de los Ríos and gave Derecha Republicana a more markedly conservative tone. These divisions widened in the run-up to the

3. Santos Juliá, *Madrid, 1931–1934* (Madrid, 1984), pp. 8–15.

June elections to the Constituent Cortes as each party sought to stake out its political territory. Lerroux, who twenty years earlier had plotted with the anarchists to assassinate Alfonso XIII and had called his 'young barbarians' to violent revolt, now presented himself as the 'champion of moderation and gradualism' and emerged as the hero of the right.[4] On the other side, Marcelino Domingo's Radical Socialists took an emphatically progressive, even revolutionary, tone while Azaña's Acción Republicana distanced itself from the Radicals, its erstwhile partners in Alianza Republicana. For their part, the Socialists, while counselling moderation, emphasized the 'social' nature of the Republic.

Although the coalition had not been officially disbanded at the national level it had fallen apart in many parts of the country. The Radical Socialists refused to form part of any slate which included the Derecha Republicana, the Socialists recommended but did not insist that their regional associations form alliances and in some places the Radicals stood alone. The fragmentation of the coalition was most complete in Toledo, where there were three separate slates: Socialists, Radical Socialists-Acción Republicana and Radicals-Derecha Republicana. Despite a strong showing by the Radicals, who took eighty-nine seats, with Lerroux being elected in five capitals, including Madrid, the Constituent Cortes had a definite left-wing flavour. The PSOE had 117 seats, the Radical Socialists 59, Acción Republicana 27 and Esquerra 33. Derecha Republicana elected only 27 deputies, an ominously low figure given that the non-republican, and in many cases anti-republican, right had a larger number of seats: 24 for the Agrarian Minority, 9 for the Basque-Navarrese coalition, 4 for the Basque Nationalist Party and 2 each for the Lliga Regionalista, the Traditionalist Communion and the monarchists.

The Provisional Government remained in office after the elections, more than anything else because there was no feasible alternative. The coalition finally broke up during the debates on the Constitution, which lasted from August to December 1931, and during which the nature of the Republic was determined. The breakup came over Article 26, which severely limited the place of the Church in Spanish life. Alcalá Zamora and Maura resigned immediately following its passage on 13 October and a new cabinet headed by Azaña and including the remaining members of the coalition saw the Constitution through the final two months of debate.

The document which was approved by the Cortes on 9 December 1931 declared Spain to be a 'Republic of workers of all categories' with separation of Church and state and all education to be controlled by the state. The right to hold private property was not absolute as property could be

---

4. Ben-Ami, *Origins*, p. 287.

expropriated, with indemnity, for reasons of social utility. The possibility of regional autonomy was recognized. Spain was, at least on paper, 'a thoroughly democratic, laic and potentially decentralized republic'.[5]

THE AZAÑA GOVERNMENT AND THE FAILURE OF REFORM

Once the Constitution had been approved Alcalá Zamora was elected the Republic's first President. Azaña remained Prime Minister, a position he would hold until September 1933. However in forming his new cabinet, Azaña was forced to choose which of the two largest parties, Radicals and Socialists, he wished to include, as the antipathy between the two and their diametrically opposed visions of the nature of the Republic prevented them from working together. He chose the Socialists who, for their part, made it clear that they expected the reformist potential of the Constitution to be realized, especially with regard to the land.

By opting for an alliance with the PSOE Azaña showed that he was disposed to continue with reforms. The question then became: Could his government move far enough swiftly enough to satisfy the Socialist rank and file, whose expectations for the Republic were great, possibly excessive? And even if it could, would the right allow those reforms to be effective? The Socialist Party had invested a great deal of political capital in the Republic, as much as anyone, but it was a highly risky investment. If the Republic proved unable to deliver a satisfactory degree of reform they exposed themselves to the danger of losing rank-and-file support to the forces on their left (the anarchists and communists), who had no committment to the regime and engaged in repeated attacks on it. As Preston states: 'The difficulty of the Socialist position can be easily imagined. In order to justify appeals for rank and file patience and to counter Communist accusations of "social fascism" some visible reforms were essential. Yet the economic situation and the hostility of the employers made it almost impossible to translate paper reform into practice.'[6]

In some areas the government acted vigorously. In January 1932 it passed the first pieces of legislation to realize Article 26 of the Constitution, legalizing divorce, secularizing the cemeteries and dissolving the Jesuits. The completion of the Republic's religious policy did not come until May 1933 with the passage of the Law of Congregations. The school-building programme initiated by the Provisional Government was continued so that

---

5. Gabriel Jackson, *The Second Republic and the Civil War* (Princeton, 1966), p. 45.
6. Paul Preston, *The Coming of the Spanish Civil War* (London, 1983), p. 72.

in March 1932 Education Minister de los Ríos could announce that in one year the Republic had built 7,000 public schools. However budgetary problems forced the virtual paralysis of this programme at the end of 1932. In 1933 the government undertook an unusual experiment in cultural policy with the *misiones pedagógicas*, in which university students showed movies and reproductions of great works of art and performed the classic works of the Spanish theatre in the most isolated and backward villages of the country.

In the spring of 1932 the Catalan autonomy statute and the agrarian reform bill were presented to the Cortes for discussion. In both cases the right was able to use obstructionist tactics to prolong the debates for months and might have continued its filibuster for many more had it not been for an attempted military coup on 10 August. Led by General José Sanjurjo, the former Civil Guard commander who had been fired by Azaña, the rising was poorly planned and easily put down by the government. The *sanjurjada* served to revive the reformist energies of the government, which pushed through both the autonomy and agrarian reform bills in a few weeks.

For the Socialists the most important piece of legislation was the Agrarian Reform Law and this proved to be a major disappointment. But even this moderate reform led the landowners, with the encouragement of Gil Robles, to declare 'all-out war on the Republic'.[7] They ignored the rulings of the mixed juries, failed to pay wages owed to workers and began a lock-out by refusing to cultivate their land. As the inefficacy of reform became evident it led to a growing radicalization of the Socialist rank and file, especially among the agricultural labourers (who now made up the largest single federation in the UGT), the Asturian miners and the construction workers of Madrid. In turn, the Socialist leadership and its policy of support for the Republic came under increasing pressure.

The most important result of the pressure from below was the change wrought in the position of Largo Caballero. Beginning in late 1932 and culminating during the election campaign of October and November 1933, Largo underwent a rapid radicalization which took him from being one of the strongest supporters of the Republic to the open advocacy of revolution. Largo Caballero's radicalization was further encouraged by the rise of fascism in Europe, and especially the accession to power of Hitler in January 1933. The admiration for Mussolini and Hitler expressed by Gil Robles, the leader of the newly-created CEDA, led some Socialists, Largo among them, to fear that he embodied the Spanish variant of fascism.

If many Socialists, and especially their leaders, were disappointed with

7. Ibid., p. 74.

the achievements of the first two years of the Republic, to a great extent they had only themselves to blame. Their schematic and unsophisticated Marxism led them to see in Azaña and the Republican left the agents of the bourgeois and democratic revolution which would pave the way for socialism. But this was a serious misreading. For the most part the Spanish bourgeoisie supported much more conservative options, such as Lerroux and Gil Robles. The Republican left had minimal contacts with these powerful economic forces; its support came from white-collar workers, the professional middle class and, to a certain extent, small farmers. As Juan Avilés Farré comments, 'all this explains the ease with which these "bourgeois parties" could ally themselves with socialism'.[8]

The Socialist dilemma was most vividly illustrated at the beginning of 1933. On 8 January the CNT launched a revolutionary rising. It was easily repressed but in the Andalucian village of Casas Viejas the repression included the burning alive of a number of people who had barricaded themselves in a hut and the shooting of a dozen more. The right played up charges by the police commander that Azaña had given him orders to shoot to kill and forced the government to spend a great deal of energy in clearing itself. Casas Viejas emphasized more than ever that, in order to defend a bourgeois Republic, the Socialists were sacrificing their credibility with the Socialist masses. That sacrifice may have seemed worthwhile in 1931, when the new regime's reforms were visibly benefiting the working class. In 1933, however, with legislation in the Cortes paralysed by the Radicals and the Agrarians and in the rural areas by the employers' boycott, only the conviction that things would be worse if they left persuaded the Socialists to stay on in the government.

After Casas Viejas the days of the Republican-Socialist coalition were numbered but it soon became clear that with or without the Socialists Azaña and the left-Republicans would soon be out of office. In April 1933 elections were held to replace those municipal officials who had won by acclamation two years earlier. Parties which supported the Republic took 9,800 positions, but of those almost 2,500 went to the increasingly conservative Radicals. The accidentalist and monarchist right took almost 5,000. These results were taken by President Alcalá Zamora as the pretext to dismiss the Azaña cabinet and ask Lerroux to form a government. When Lerroux proved unable to do so Azaña was recalled and his Socialist ministers returned with him.

In September, elections to the Court of Constitutional Guarantees returned a right-wing majority which included such notorious anti-Republicans as José Calvo Sotelo and Juan March, the millionaire financier

---

8. Juan Avilés Farré, *La izquierda burguesa en la IIa República* (Madrid, 1985), p. 346.

who had been convicted of smuggling. At this point Azaña was dismissed once again and Lerroux formed a government. Lerroux's cabinet lasted less than a month but that was enough for him to effectively abandon the social legislation of the Azaña period. On 2 October the Socialists announced that they would no longer cooperate with the Republicans and the next day the government fell. On 8 October Diego Martínez Barrio formed a caretaker administration whose principal task was to organize elections. These were called for 19 November.

THE REORGANIZATION OF THE RIGHT

The political landscape was now very much different from what it had been in June 1931. Then the left had been united and riding the wave of euphoria stemming from the creation of the Republic; the right had been discredited and in disarray. Now the alliance of the left had disintegrated while the right had a well-organized and well-financed party with a charismatic leader prepared to make the necessary political deals to assure success.

The traditional monarchist parties – liberals and conservatives – had been strongly persecuted by Primo de Rivera, who blamed them for the sad state of the country and tried to replace them with his own political vehicle, the Unión Patriótica. By 1930 they were in an advanced state of disarray which was completed by the election of 12 April and the creation of the Republic. The two parties were formally dissolved shortly thereafter. The right thus confronted the Republic without any established political parties but was able to regroup quickly. It began by converting other organizations which espoused its values, the CNCA and the ACNP, to overtly political uses. The strategy around which the right coalesced was known as accidentalism: accepting the rules of the democratic game in order to defend property, the Church and national unity. Although these organizations advocated a Catholic social programme, in practice accidentalism came to mean intransigent opposition to any social reform, however moderate.

The right's first new political organization, Acción Nacional, was established on 26 April 1931 as an umbrella group to coordinate the campaign for the elections to the Constituent Cortes, held in June. It drew support from a variety of conservative and monarchist forces but its most important component was Acción Castellana, which had inherited the support of the deeply-Catholic smallholders of northern Castile who had belonged to the agrarian syndicates organized by the CNCA. Acción Nacional's campaign was strident, even hysterical, playing on fears of communism and revolution. It also revealed once again the intimate connection between the defence of religion and the defence of property. Twenty-four Acción Nacional candidates were elected and sat in the Constituent Cortes as the Agrarian Minority.

The right came to define itself in opposition to the reformist content of the Republic and the key element in this process of definition was the debate over the Constitution, above all the approval of Article 26, which restricted the role of the Church, and Article 44, which authorized the expropriation of property, making agrarian reform a possibility. The Agrarians abandoned the Cortes following the approval of Article 26 on 13 October and undertook an impressive – and inflammatory – campaign for constitutional revision. In one of his many speeches José María Gil Robles, who emerged as the leading figure on the right, accused the government of 'trampling on poor nuns'. The Agrarians returned to parliament in the spring of 1932 to fight the Catalan autonomy statute and the agrarian reform bill. They were remarkably successful in using parliamentary tactics, including 143 amendments, to block agrarian reform: after four months of debate only four of twenty-four articles had been approved.

The failure of the attempted coup by General Sanjurjo in August 1932 and the subsequent revitalization of the government, which pushed through both the Catalan statute and agrarian reform in short order, strengthened Gil Robles in his belief that legalism was the most effective way of fighting reform. At a congress held in October 1932, Acción Popular approved the legalist tactic although it refused to make any profession of republicanism. The growth of Acción Popular, which had forty-six affiliated organizations by the end of 1932, as well as the logic of legalism led to the creation of a Catholic political party. In February 1933 representatives of forty-two groups with almost three-quarters of a million members met in Madrid and agreed to form the Confederación Española de Derechas Autónomas (CEDA). The party's stated goals were the revision of the Constitution and 'the defence of the principles of Christian civilization'. Addressing the final session of the congress, Gil Robles left no doubt that 'Christian civilization' meant the socio-economic status quo: 'When the social order is threatened, Catholics should unite to defend it . . . We will go united into the struggle, no matter what it costs . . . We are faced with a social revolution. In the political panorama of Europe I can see only the formation of Marxist and anti-Marxist groups. This is what is happening in Germany and in Spain also.'[9]

Both the anti-Marxist theme and the sympathy for fascism carried over into the party's campaign for the November 1933 elections. Gil Robles

9. Cited in Preston, *Coming*, p. 43.

advocated, and achieved, a broad 'anti-revolutionary' front which included the Alfonsine monarchists of Renovación Española, which had been created shortly after the CEDA, and the Comunión Tradicionalista (Traditionalist Communion) as well as local alliances with other conservative groups, including the Radicals in some places. The programme of the alliance emphasized an amnesty for those involved in the Sanjurjo revolt, the revision of the religious and social legislation and the defence of the 'interests of the national economy'. With a well-financed campaign modelled on the propaganda techniques of the Nazis, which Gil Robles had studied at first-hand, the CEDA could expect to do well.

The elections were a triumph for the right, a disaster for the left. The CEDA, fighting its first election, emerged as the single largest party with 115 seats and the Radicals improved from 89 to 104. The PSOE saw its 117 deputies reduced to 58 while the left-Republicans were all but wiped out. The Radical Socialists, who had split into three factions before the election, disappeared and Azaña's party took only half a dozen seats. Azaña himself was elected only because Prieto had included him on the Socialist slate in Vizcaya.

The reasons for this outcome are clear. The most important was that the left went into the elections divided while the right was united. The electoral law was designed to prevent parliamentary fragmentation and favour coalitions: in each province the slate with the majority of votes would receive 80 per cent of the seats. This meant that a relatively small difference in votes, 3,385,000 for the right to a total of about 3,000,000 for the left, was transformed into a massive difference in seats. The Socialists' decision to go it alone flew in the face of an electoral law for which they themselves had voted, and proved costly. Their 1,600,000 votes won them 58 seats compared to the 104 the Radicals took with only 800,000 votes. But the Socialists were not the only force of disunity. The candidacies were determined at the provincial level and this gave rise to a great variety of alliances. Azaña's party, for example, allied with the Socialists in thirteen provinces, with other left-Republicans in sixteen, and with right-Republicans in seven. In six it stood by itself.

A second, and less important, factor was the abstention of the anarchists. In 1931 they had voted; in 1933, having learned that Republican repression differed little from its monarchist counterpart and with thousands of its militants in prison, the CNT organized a vigorous and effective campaign around the slogan ¡no votad! In all areas where the CNT was strong the abstention rate was well above the national average.

THE RIGHT IN POWER

Gil Robles found himself the leader of the largest party in the Cortes but the right did not have enough seats to form a government. The CEDA leader adopted the tactic of supporting a Radical cabinet which would have to annul the reform legislation of the first two years of the Republic. Gil Robles' basic demands were an amnesty for those convicted following the *sanjurjada*, the revision of religious legislation and the emasculation of the labour and agrarian reform laws.

The all-Radical cabinet which Lerroux formed after the election undertook to meet these demands. It ignored legislation such as the Law of Congregations, slowed the agrarian reform to a virtual halt and appointed as presidents of the mixed juries men favourable to the employers. The Law of Municipal Boundaries was repealed on a provisional basis in January and defintively in May. New, conservative civil governors were appointed and the Civil Guard used more freely against workers.

But even this was not enough for Gil Robles. In March he forced the dismissal of three of the most moderate members of the government, including Interior Minister Diego Martínez Barrio who then abandoned the Radicals to set up his own party, Unión Republicana. Martínez Barrio was replaced by Rafael Salazar Alonso whose approach to labour matters was to treat any strike as a threat to public order and incipient subversion. Southern landowners responded by cutting wages by as much as 50 per cent, organizing a boycott of unionized labour and revealing their Catholic social conscience by telling unemployed labourers that they should ¡comed Republica!

It was developments such as these which gave the period of centre-right government the name *bienio negro*. However things were not black everywhere in Spain. In Madrid at least, 1934 was a relatively good year for the workers as the Radical government, lacking any strategy for preventing strikes, repeatedly settled them in favour of the workers, much to the chagrin of the capital's employers. According to Santos Juliá, 'for the workers of Madrid 1934 was . . . the year of their greatest and broadest conquests'.[10]

In April the government proposed an amnesty for General Sanjurjo and the others convicted for their roles in the abortive coup of August 1932. Alcalá Zamora opposed the amnesty but refused to make use of his veto power. Instead he signed the law while declaring his disagreement. Lerroux resigned but was replaced by a similar cabinet headed by fellow Radical Ricardo Samper. Almost immediately the new government became

10. Santos Juliá, *Madrid*, p. 332.

involved in a conflict with the Generalitat over its Law of Agricultural Contracts.

The new government, in which Salazar Alonso continued as Minister of the Interior, also had to face a general strike which the Socialist agricultural labourers' union FNTT called for June. This strike was the first substantial symptom of the radicalization being experienced by the Socialist rank and file, and of the socialist leadership's increasing inability to restrain its followers. The strike call came after the union executive had repeatedly, and without any success, appealed to the government to enforce the labour laws still on the books. It also came in the face of opposition from the UGT, which considered it ill-advised and a certain failure. Even so, FNTT President Ricardo Zabalza felt he could not ask his members to endure any further.

The goals of the strike were moderate but Salazar Alonso declared it to be revolutionary and brought the full force of the state to bear. There were massive arrests and deportations of strikers, and even of four Socialist deputies; the labour press was closed down, as were union halls; and a number of left-wing town councils deposed.

Through the summer of 1934 Gil Robles made it clear that even the Samper government was not tough enough and on 26 September he withdrew his support, demanding that the CEDA be represented in any new cabinet. Leading Socialists and even such moderate Republicans as Martínez Barrio and Felipe Sánchez Román advised President Alcalá Zamora to dissolve the Cortes and hold new elections. Instead, he called on Lerroux to form yet another cabinet. Lerroux announced his new government on 4 October. It included members of the CEDA in the Ministries of Justice, Labour and Agriculture.

This announcement was the occasion for the Socialists to launch their much heralded rising against the fascist threat. It was a total failure everywhere in the country except Asturias, where the radicalism of the miners carried the movement far beyond what the socialist leadership had intended and turned it into a full-scale social revolution. The Asturian insurrection was immediately followed by a fierce and wide-ranging repression. At least 30,000 people were imprisoned, awaiting trial before military courts, and hundreds of municipal governments controlled by the left suspended. These arrests and suspensions were extended to those parts of the country in which nothing had happened, as the right took advantage of the opportunity to throttle the labour movement. The Socialist press was banned and did not reappear until the beginning of 1936. In Asturias itself prisoners were tortured and Luís Sirval, a distinguished journalist who dared report on this subject, was killed by a soldier. Two leading Asturian Socialists, Ramón González Peña, the alleged leader of the revolt, and Teodomiro

Menéndez, were sentenced to death, although these sentences were commuted by Prime Minister Lerroux. Largo Caballero was also brought to trial, as was Manuel Azaña, who had been in Barcelona the day of the revolt there but was not at all involved with it.

After the October revolution the pattern of politics returned to what it had been before. The new Lerroux administration continued to undo the work of the Azaña governments, stopping the school-building programme and returning to the Jesuits the properties which had been taken from them. Even the attempt by the Minister of Agriculture Manuel Giménez Fernández to act on the CEDA's stated social Catholic beliefs (by introducing legislation to give long-term tenants the opportunity to buy the land they worked) was torpedoed by his fellow *cedistas*. As Blinkhorn describes him, Giménez Fernández was 'the sincere social-Catholic who . . . was politically martyred by the conservative backwoodsmen of his own party'.[11] It was, apparently, these backwoodsmen who called the shots within the CEDA. In March 1935 Gil Robles withdrew his support from the government when Lerroux agreed to commute the death sentences passed on González Peña and Teodomiro Menéndez.

At first Alcalá Zamora refused to accept Gil Robles' demands for six cabinet posts including the War Ministry and called on Lerroux to put together another Radical government. That cabinet was replaced on 6 May by another, this time with five *cedistas* including Gil Robles himself as Minister of War. The too liberal Giménez Fernández was replaced at Agriculture by the conservative former monarchist Nicasio Velayos y Velayos. During his tenure wages cuts, firings and evictions took place at an increased pace and in July the already timid Agrarian Reform Law was revised so as to make it virtually meaningless.

The resignation of two ministers in September led to another change of government. Joaquín Chapaprieta put together a new cabinet in which Gil Robles stayed on at the War Ministry and Lerroux moved over to Foreign Affairs. However at the end of October Lerroux and fellow Radical Rocha were forced to resign because of their involvement in a scandal over the granting of gambling licences. At the same time Chapaprieta had introduced a tax reform bill which would have increased inheritance taxes. CEDA deputies obstructed it in the Cortes by presenting numerous amendments and when Gil Robles refused to impose party discipline on them Chapaprieta resigned.

This time Alcalá Zamora could not resort to his old standby, Lerroux. Already badly tainted by the *straperlo* affair which had forced him out of

11. Martin Blinkhorn, 'Anglo-American Historians and the Second Spanish Republic: the Emergence of a New Orthodoxy', *European Studies Review*, 1973, p. 83.

the cabinet in October, two months later he and his party saw whatever credibility they had left disappear in the Nombela affair which involved the misappropriation of public funds. The President was left with only two options; call on Gil Robles to form a government or dissolve the Cortes and hold elections. This was just what Gil Robles wanted, as he assumed that the President would not expose himself to possible impeachment by dissolving the Cortes a second time during his term of office. Alcalá Zamora surprised him by calling on Portela Valladares to form a caretaker government to oversee elections.

Chapaprieta had resigned on 9 December. On 11 December Gil Robles met with Alcalá Zamora and learned that he would not be made Prime Minister. That night Gil Robles discussed the possibility of a coup with General Fanjul but when he sounded out other generals, among them Francisco Franco, the consensus was that the time was not ripe. Gil Robles' legalist approach would have to undergo one more, this time decisive, test.

THE POPULAR FRONT

In the aftermath of the Asturian insurrection and the subsequent repression there was a widespread realization among Republicans and all left-wing political forces of the need for some form of unity. Azaña had recognized the need to re-establish the alliance with the Socialists well before the events of October but was unable to do so until afterwards. But Azaña's plan was only one of a number of competing formulae for the unity of the left. One other was the Popular Front as designed by the Comintern, but the Spanish communists were an insignificant force and their proposal did not get much of a hearing. More important was the Alianza Obrera (Workers' Alliance): a revolutionary, anti-fascist workers' front, put forward by dissident communist Joaquín Maurín. This diversity of proposals was a product of the fragmentation of the Spanish left, a 'mosaic of political tendencies and projects'.[12]

The manifesto announcing the coalition which came to be known as the Popular Front was published on 16 January 1936 but the process which had led to its formation had begun over a year and a half before and grew out of Azaña's intitiative and the support of Indalecio Prieto. It was an attempt to revive the coalition between Republicans and Socialists which had marked the first two years of the Second Republic; its aims being to return the coalition to power, grant an amnesty to those imprisoned

12. Santos Juliá, *Los Orígenes del Frente Popular* (Madrid, 1979), p. 137.

following the events of October 1934 and resume, with a greater sense of urgency, the reformist trajectory of the first Azaña government. The first step was the consolidation of the fragmented Republican forces. This began in April 1934 when Azaña's Acción Republicana, Marcelino Domingo's Partido Radical Socialista and Santiago Casares Quiroga's liberal Republicans from Galicia formed Izquierda Republicana; although even this modest advance was accompanied by mutual jealousies. Five months later, in September, two other small Republican groups formed the Unión Republicana created by Martínez Barrio when he broke with the Radicals in March (once Gil Robles had succeeded in having him forced from the cabinet). Republican unity was completed in April 1935 when Izquierda Republicana, Unión Republicana and the tiny Partido Nacional Republicano led by Felipe Sánchez Román issued a joint manifesto calling for the immediate restoration of civil liberties, guarantees of legal treatment of political prisoners, an amnesty covering people's roles in the events of October 1934, readmission of all workers fired after October, revision of the punishment of public officials, permission for unions to function again and restoration of municipal governments dismissed by Madrid.

Martínez Barrio and Sánchez Román saw the agreement among Republicans as a way of stabilizing the regime and re-establishing 'the spiritual peace of the nation by passing an amnesty bill'. This required the successful 'channelling of the aspirations of the proletariat'. The price of failure would be 'to launch it outside the constitutional consensus on an angry journey on the road to revolution'. For Martínez Barrio the situation was clear: the 'Republican Front was the only way to avoid the solution to the problems of the regime from becoming either a coup or a revolution'.[13]

These conservative Republicans did not want the agreement to extend any further to the left. They opposed any return to a coalition with the Socialists, whom Martínez Barrio called a 'danger to the life of the regime', but they were forced to yield to Azaña on this point. They certainly did not want any contact with parties to the left of the PSOE, especially the Communists. Sánchez Román withdrew his party from the coalition on the eve of the completion of the manifesto – which he had largely drafted – and although no reason was given it was generally agreed at the time that this was a protest against the inclusion of the Communists. Azaña was insistent that the Socialists be included in the coalition. In fact he had been in contact with PSOE leaders since the summer of 1934. In September he coincided with Prieto in Barcelona at the funeral of a former cabinet

13. Diego Martínez Barrio, *Páginas para la historia del Frente Popular* (Madrid, 1937), p. 13; *Orígenes del Frente Popular Español* (Buenos Aires, n.d), p. 89.

colleague and took the opportunity to remind him that they needed to revive the coalition if the left were ever to return to power.

Azaña and Martínez Barrio may have disagreed over opening the alliance to the left to include the PSOE but there was no difference in their conception of the purpose of the alliance: to put into office a Republican administration which would consolidate the Republic. This was what Azaña proposed to Prieto when they resumed contact following the October insurrection. Prieto, who had always considered it a mistake to have broken the alliance with the Republicans, had been advocating just such an approach since the summer of 1933 and in November he acted on his concern by including Azaña and Marcelino Domingo on the Socialist slate for his home turf of Vizcaya.

Prieto's belief in the need for cooperation between Socialists and Republicans was only strengthened by the failure of the October insurrection and in the spring of 1935 he began to make his views known in the party. He stated his position publicly in an article which was published in *El Liberal* of Bilbao on the fourth anniversary of the Republic. The 'electoral isolation' of 1933 was an error, but one which could be easily corrected. The Socialists could not win any future election on their own and needed to work with other groups 'as a means of defence'. The alliance should extend to both the left and right of the party and should have a 'clear and simple programme' which did not fail to address the agrarian question.[14]

However, Prieto's belief in a return to the alliance with the Republicans was not held by all Socialists and in the aftermath of October 1934 he and Largo Caballero, who had accentuated his revolutionary rhetoric, engaged in a bitter struggle for control of the party. Largo's most fervent supporters were in the Socialist Youth, who were moving closer to the Communists and advocated expelling the moderates from the PSOE. For his part Prieto could count on some of the most important names in Spanish Socialism, among them the hero of the Asturian insurrection, Ramón González Peña, and the leader of the powerful Asturian miners' union, Amador Fernández.

While Prieto and his supporters were engaged in their struggle against Largo Caballero within the PSOE, Azaña had begun to work up popular support for the as yet undefined electoral alliance of the left in a series of three speeches he gave between May and November 1935. These 'open air speeches' attracted a total audience of nearly 700,000 people and were, in reality, the start of the electoral campaign of the Popular Front, even though no alliance as yet existed and no election had been called.

Azaña emphasized the reformist goal of the alliance. He invoked the

14. Indalecio Prieto, *Posiciones Socialistas* (Madrid, 1935), pp. 98–110.

spirit of the first six months of the Republic, but also promised that the new coalition of the left would go far beyond those reforms. At the same time, he acknowledged that these reforms would be directed as much against the spectre of revolution as against the right: 'What we must do is change the condition of politics so that popular exasperation does not reappear, so that the masses do not continue in the state they were in during 1934 . . . Let us convert them to democracy. This is the true formula for the salvation of the Republic and the prosperity of the Spanish people'.[15]

Azaña's campaign culminated on 20 November in the outskirts of Madrid before a crowd estimated at 500,000 people. He promised to restore the social legislation of the first *bienio*, thereby restoring to 'the working class the hope that in the innovating and democratic Republic they would find a peaceful way of improving their situation'. Once again the need to head off revolution was very much on his mind. He stated that agrarian reform was 'the backbone' of the Republic but aside from the abolition of the Tenancy Law passed in 1934, and which had undermined the position of tenants of the land, he made no specific proposals. All this required the broadest possible electoral front. Once the elections had been won it would be necessary to carry out the programme and for this task the government of Republicans would need the continued support of masses 'organized and disciplined in democratic forms'.[16]

Azaña concluded by stating that he was not afraid of the masses and that he knew how to direct 'the popular torrent'. But Azaña was not the man to lead the masses and this rally itself revealed his very real limitations as a popular leader as well as the limitations and contradictions of the emergent Popular Front. One incident symbolized his dilemma; that of a moderate liberal politician attempting to lead an increasingly radicalized working class. When Azaña finished speaking the audience saluted him with the clenched fist. He did not return the salute.

The principal Republican leaders had been meeting during the summer of 1935 to work on the programme for the coalition. Azaña had visited Prieto in Belgium in September, and in November he wrote to the Socialist Party formally inviting it to join the alliance. At the urging of Largo Caballero the Socialist executive decided to accept the invitation but only so long as any workers' party or union prepared to back the coalition would also be accepted. This was a major change of position for Largo Caballero, who until then had firmly opposed a return to the coalition, and one which was caused by his on-going struggle with Prieto for control

15. Manuel Azaña, *Obras*, vol. III, pp. 252–65
16. Ibid., pp. 287, 290–1.

of the PSOE. Fearing that Prieto's advocacy of the coalition with the Republicans was winning him influence, Largo Caballero decided to preserve his position by including the Communists in the alliance. However, the Republicans refused to include the Communists on the committee and Largo Caballero refused to accept the compromise proposed by Martínez Barrio: that the Socialists represent the Communists and any other working-class groups interested in supporting the coalition. At a crucial meeting of the PSOE executive on 16 December he withdrew from the negotiations and resigned as president of the party, although he did set up a parallel committee composed of the UGT, the Socialist Youth, PCE and the Partido Sindicalista; this group was kept informed of the proceedings of the Electoral Committee by the two Socialist representatives.

Largo Caballero's change of heart and his resignation as PSOE president brought to an end the possibility that one of the alternative versions of the unity of the left which were being proposed would be realized. The Communists were the most severely affected. Ever since October 1934 the PCE had been attempting to establish some type of 'organic bond' with the Socialists by means of formal agreements at the top and the creation of local joint activities among the rank and file. This would lead to the formation of the Popular Anti-fascist Bloc, the goal of which was to establish a 'Provisional Revolutionary Government'. This proposal was abandoned after the VII Comintern Congress in the summer of 1935 and the official Popular Front line was adopted instead. As described by José Díaz after his return from Moscow, this was more than a return to the original spirit of the Second Republic envisaged by Azaña and Prieto; it had to be specifically anti-fascist, by which he meant the destruction of the social and economic base of fascism. This required expropriation of the land, the purge of the armed forces and self-determination for the oppressed nationalities. In the end, however, the PCE did sign the electoral manifesto of the left (in the formulation of which it had not had any participation) which was not anti-fascist and which represented very much a return to the Republic of 14 April. The alliance came to be known as the Popular Front, but the name was all the Communists contributed to it.

The principal alternative to the Popular Front as it emerged was the Alianza Obrera (Workers' Alliance), which was invented by Joaquín Maurín, leader of the Partido Obrero de Unificación Marxista (POUM). As early as 1932 Maurín was calling for a united movement of the working class, peasantry and Catalan regionalists in order to complete the democratic revolution. His calls for the unity of the country's progressive forces took on greater urgency following Hitler's accession to power. Anti-fascism now became the immediate goal but not the only one. The Alianza was not just a defensive measure but also a tool of revolution.

The events of October 1934 only confirmed Maurín in his belief that the Alianza was the most advantageous form of organization for the working class. October had marked the beginning of the Spanish revolution; it was the Spanish version of July 1917 in Russia. If a Spanish October were to follow, the working class had to forge its revolutionary instruments: the Alianza Obrera and a single, revolutionary Marxist party. The Alianza was clearly the more important of the two and as advocated by Maurín in 1935 it was a strictly working-class and revolutionary alternative to the Popular Front, either in the form proposed by the Communists or that in which it was emerging in Spain.

This coincided with Largo Caballero's rhetoric, but after October 1934 the Socialists abandoned the idea of the Alianza. Faced with the Socialists' lack of interest and the increasing support for some sort of electoral alliance, in November 1935 Maurín proposed a strictly working-class electoral front which could then make a temporary alliance with the Republicans. The Socialists showed no interest in this idea either, but they did invite the POUM to join Largo's parallel committee. Although the POUM executive continued to favour a strictly workers' electoral front it was forced to join the Popular Front because of overwhelming popular sentiment for it. On 15 January 1936 Juan Andrade signed the manifesto despite the POUM's lack of any say in its formulation. The revolutionary approach to unity had failed.

The Popular Front Committee (with two representatives of the PSOE and one each from Izquierda Republicana, Unión Republicana and the Partido Nacional Republicano) began to meet shortly after 16 December. The Socialists presented one draft programme, the Republicans another, but the final version was little changed from the initial Republican draft. The programme was long and complex. It was divided into eight sections and the most important points were: amnesty for all 'social and political crimes' committed before 15 November 1935, defence of the Constitution, agricultural reform, industrial protection, intensification of public works, reform of the banking system and taxation, the passage of social legislation, defence of agricultural wages and educational reform. The measures proposed for the crucial area of agrarian reform were modest: more credit and lower taxes, a new tenancy law and a settlement policy. The manifesto also stated that there were a number of things, all demanded by the Socialists, which 'the Republican parties do not accept' and which were not part of the programme: nationalization of the land and the banks, worker control of industry and the creation of unemployment insurance. The programme was to be carried out by a government composed solely of Republicans.

Once the manifesto was published on 16 January 1936 the Electoral

Committee took charge of candidate selection. The candidacies were divided between the Republicans on the one hand and the Socialists on the other. The candidates of the other working-class parties which had signed the manifesto (the PCE, Partido Sindicalista and the POUM) were to come from the Socialists' share. The Committee's role was to approve decisions taken at the local level. Surprisingly few problems arose; the most common was finding places for the candidates of the parties to the left of the PSOE. In León the Unión Republicana vetoed the presence of a Communist on the Popular Front ticket while in Seville the Communist candidate withdrew only three days before the election under pressure from the Unión Republicana. That party's two candidates (one a former deputy under the monarchy and a practising Catholic, and the other a wealthy landowner) felt understandably uncomfortable sharing a platform and a ballot with the PCE. The final distribution of candidates was: PSOE, 126; Izquierda (IR), 106; Unión Republicana (UR) 46; PCE, 19; others, 14.

The Popular Front did not cover the entire country. Catalonia produced its own alliance of the left, the Front d'Esquerres, which was announced only two weeks before the election. Like the Popular Front it included both working-class and middle-class parties although the weight of the working class was much less than in the rest of the country, due to the refusal of the CNT to have any relations with political parties. Its manifesto was much less detailed than that of the Popular Front and made even fewer commitments to reform. The main points were amnesty, restoration of the autonomy statute, restoration of the social legislation of 1931 and 1932 and of the Law of Agricultural Contracts. The Esquerra got twenty-two of the forty-one places on the ticket, the labour organizations eleven.

The election campaign revealed once again the essential moderation of the alliance, although there were some local discrepancies. The regional organizations were not always just transmission belts for the national Popular Front. In Asturias, for example, the local Popular Front ran a campaign much more directed to the concerns of the working class and with a much more radical rhetoric than the Popular Front's organizers would have liked.

Largo Caballero bore the brunt of the Socialist campaign, as Prieto was still officially in exile. His speeches were full of revolutionary talk, but now it was talk of a revolution somewhere far in the future. Repeatedly he emphasized that the Socialists would stand by their commitment to Azaña. But it was Azaña who once again best expressed the meaning of the Popular Front: 'Ours will not be a Socialist nor a Communist mandate but a Republican mandate.'

By contrast, the campaign of the right claimed that a Popular Front victory would lead to revolution. Its tone was nothing short of apocalyptic.

Some of the right's pamphlets in Seville claimed that 'the revolution wants to take away your children and destroy your family' and if 'marxism' won the result would be 'dissolution of the army, destruction of the Civil Guard, arming of the canaille, burning of banks and private homes . . . the distribution of your women. RUIN! RUIN! RUIN!' Another described the Popular Front as 'marxism, masonry and the anti-Spain'.[17] Gil Robles' campaign was blatantly counter-revolutionary, but the revolution against which he inveighed was more his creation than that of his opponents on the left. Using electoral techniques learned from the Nazis, the right flooded the country with printed propaganda and made use of the radio. The right had not been able to put together a single electoral alliance at the national level to match the Popular Front, but alliances were made at the local level with their exact composition dictated by local conditions.

The Popular Front won a narrow victory on 16 February. The results have given rise to heated debate but the most widely accepted calculations of the voting, those of Javier Tusell, give the left 4.65 million votes, the right 4.5 million and the centre 526,000. Both Gabriel Jackson's and Gerald Brenan's accounts are more favourable to the Popular Front, which is credited with 4.7 million compared to 4 million for the right.[18]

The right had increased its absolute vote by more than 750,000 over 1933 but the left had improved by about one million. In large part this was due to the position of the CNT which, while still refusing to join, or even formally support, the Popular Front and the Front d'Esquerres did urge its members to vote for the left so that the prisoners of October 1934 could be amnestied. The victory of the Popular Front, as narrow as it may have been, was achieved under unfavourable circumstances. The civil governors had all been appointed by the right and in some places they harassed the left, prohibiting Popular Front meetings, blocking the distribution of its propaganda and arresting militants. The small difference in votes was translated by the electoral law into a large majority of seats. The results announced on 20 February gave the Popular Front 257, the right 139 and the centre 57. A run-off election was needed for over twenty other seats but the Popular Front had already won an absolute majority.

---

17. Preston, *Coming*, p. 172; Javier Tusell, *Las Elecciones del Frente Popular* (Madrid, 1971), vol. II, pp. 371.
18. Ibid., pp. 13–15; Jackson, *The Second Republic*, p. 193; Gerald Brenan, *The Spanish Labyrinth* (Cambridge, 1960), p. 298.

THE ROAD TO CIVIL WAR

The Popular Front never had more organizational structure than the election committee which had negotiated the programme and then refereed the selection of candidates. Only the Socialists and Republicans had been represented on this committee but once the election was over both lost interest in it. For Prieto it was 'now the political parties and the parliamentary caucuses which count'. Azaña too wanted to return to normal political instruments, in his case cabinet and parliament. In his first speech to the Cortes after the elections he repeated his intention of carrying out the election programme 'without changing a single comma' and announced that this would be done by the government alone.[19] Despite the concern of Azaña and Prieto to return to politics as usual, after the election politics moved increasingly out of the normal fora of parties and parliament and into the streets.

Immediately after the results of the election were announced Prime Minister Portela Valladares, thrown into a panic by rumours of a military coup, resigned and Azaña reluctantly assumed office at the head of a government composed solely of Republicans. The new administration acted quickly to carry out the Popular Front programme. On 22 February the political prisoners were freed; the next day a moratorium was declared on the payment of agricultural rents in the south and on 29 February the eviction of tenants was prohibited. The government also promised a rapid agrarian reform but in this it found itself reacting to events, as labourers in the south, and especially Badajoz, occupied landed estates.

On 7 April President Alcalá Zamora was impeached on the grounds that he had exceeded his authority by dissolving the Cortes twice in one term. The only acceptable replacement turned out to be Azaña and on 8 May he was chosen by the Cortes in a vote which the CEDA and the monarchists boycotted. The new president asked Prieto to form a government but it was at this point that the struggle within the Socialist Party had its most unfortunate effects. Prieto had a programme for energetic reform and the neutralization of the threat of a coup but Largo Caballero, who continued to talk about revolution without doing anything to prepare for it, blocked Prieto from becoming Prime Minister. Largo Caballero was acting as the proverbial 'perro del hortelano' (gardener's dog), 'que ni come ni deja comer' (who neither eats nor lets anyone else eat). His position is well described by Preston:

> he opposed any interim Socialist participation in the government and continued to talk of revolutionary social change as being imminent. In doing so, he fell

19. Juan Simeon Vidarte, *Todos fuimos culpables*, (Mexico, 1978), p. 99.

between two stools. The threat of a right-wing military or fascist coup might have been averted by revolutionary action, although the objective conditions were hardly conducive. Equally, a strong Socialist presence in the government might have curtailed fascist provocation before it created the necessary context for a coup. Largo's policy prevented either.[20]

The struggle for control of the PSOE continued after the left's veto of Prieto in May and was still going on when the civil war began. Ironically, as social and political tensions heightened in June and July – and as the CNT was making inroads among Socialist workers in Madrid – Largo Caballero moderated his position rapidly. While 100,000 workers were on strike in the capital he left to attend an international labour conference in London. On 18 July his newspaper, *Claridad*, responded to the military revolt by calling on the workers to defend the Republic and 'the democratic revolution'.

From March 1936 on there was an upsurge of political violence. The first important incidents took place in Madrid: an assassination attempt against a leading Socialist, Luís Jiménez de Asúa, and the firing of shots at the home of Largo Caballero. Both left and right were involved although it is impossible to determine where the initiative lay. However, while the leftist press urged its readers not to retaliate, the rightist press harped on and exaggerated the degree of violence and disorder, which it blamed on the left alone.

It was in this context of political violence and growing fear among the middle classes of anarchy and social revolution that a political realignment took place on the right. Once its legalist tactic had failed to protect the interests of the established elites from reform, the CEDA disintegrated. Gil Robles did little to prevent this. He was fully aware of the military conspiracy which had begun immediately after the election, helped finance it and in June ordered party members to put themselves at the service of the military revolt.

As it had in Italy between 1920 and 1922, the fear that normal politics could no longer stave off revolution provided the opportunity for an explicitly Fascist party to grow. As the CEDA fell apart in the spring of 1936 thousands of members of its youth wing, JAP, joined the Falange Española. While this did not turn the Falange into a major political force it did represent the first thing approximating success that the party had ever enjoyed.

The Falange was created in the autumn of 1933. Its leader, José Antonio Primo de Rivera – the son of the former dictator – and another member were on the electoral list of the right in November 1933 and José Antonio was elected for Cádiz, although neither was identified as a representative of the Falange. At the end of 1933 the party was in '. . . critical condition.' The total lack of funds reduced to virtually zero its chances to carry out

20. Preston, *Coming*, p. 179.

propaganda and even made the maintenance of party offices difficult.'[21] In February 1934 the Falange merged with another fascist group based in Valladolid, the Juntas de Ofensiva Nacional Sindicalista (JONS), to form the Falange Española y de las JONS. This gave the party a stronger organization and some support in the provinces but it did not lay the basis for significant growth or financial security. At the beginning of 1935, the party had fewer than 5,000 members.

In August 1934 José Antonio, who quickly emerged as the leader of the new party, signed an agreement with the monarchist party Renovación Española which effectively turned the Falange into the shock troops of the monarchists in return for a monthly subsidy. José Antonio put the party at the service of the Minister of the Interior in October 1934 and the Falange participated in the repression. It was already clear that the Falange's nationalism, Catholicism and anti-Marxism were much more important than its proclaimed anti-capitalism and this trend was accentuated as José Antonio strengthened his control and Ramiro Ledesma Ramos, one of the founders of the JONS, abandoned the party at the beginning of 1935 to protest against its increasing conservatism. In June 1935 José Antonio put his party at the service of the Italian government, from which he received a monthly subsidy until June 1936. He also tried to establish ties with the Nazis, but the German government did not feel that the Falange was worth supporting. At the same time the party began to move towards the army and attempted to become the political mentor of the military conspiracy. It failed in this, although some officers did join the party.

The Falange was not included in the electoral coalition of the right in February 1936. Standing for the party in Cádiz, José Antonio lost his seat and received only four per cent of the vote. As bad a showing as this was, it was the best the party could manage: in only three other provinces did it receive as much as one per cent.

In March 1936, just when the influx of new members began, José Antonio and most of the Falange leadership were arrested and the party's offices and newspapers closed down, leaving it totally disorganized. From prison José Antonio called on the army to revolt. Any ambivalence he might have felt about the Falange becoming involved with the military centred around its choosing to support the right kind of conspiracy, one that would lead to the party achieving a more important role in political life. This he felt he had found in the small group headed by General Emilio Mola, the military governor of Pamplona.

The conspiracy began almost immediately after the elections of February 1936. General Sanjurjo, from his exile in Portugal, and General Goded

---

21. Sheelagh Ellwood, *Prietas las Filas* (Barcelona, 1984), p. 42.

became the nominal head of the movement, were the high-profile officers who joined. Francisco Franco proved much more elusive, and avoided committing himself until very late in the day. Another key figure was Lieutenant Colonel Valentín Galarza. He led the Unión Militar Española, a semi-clandestine organization founded in 1933, which by March 1936 claimed to have some 3,500 members, about 45 per cent of all officers on active duty. The military conspirators also established ties with various right-wing civilian political groups, including the authoritarian monarchists of Renovación Española, the Carlists and, after May, the Falange.

The government was well aware of the conspiracy but, either from over-confidence or from fear, failed to take energetic measures to stop it. Officers suspected of involvement were sent to remote postings: Franco to the Canaries, Goded to the Balearics and Mola to Pamplona, but nothing more was done.

By the spring, the pieces were pretty much in place; all that remained was to find the right moment to launch the coup. This was eventually provided by the increasing spiral of political violence after the elections. According to the best estimates, there were 269 political killings from February to mid-July 1936. This was considerably more than the 207 killings at the peak of the Fascist offensive in Italy, in the first five months of 1921.

On 13 April, a judge who had just sentenced a Falangist to 30 years in prison for killing a Socialist newsboy was murdered in the streets of Madrid. The next day, some Socialists retaliated by killing a Civil Guard lieutenant during a Republic Day parade. On 12 July, a pro-Republican officer in the Assault Guards was murdered by Falangists on his way to work. Later that night a group of policemen arrested José Calvo Sotelo, murdered him and dumped his body in a nearby cemetery. The right claimed that this was a crime of the state, and singled out La Pasionaria, who it claimed, but never proved, had threatened Calvo Sotelo's life in the Cortes in June. This was the catalyst: four days later the military revolt that became a civil war began.

FROM REPUBLIC TO CIVIL WAR

Why did the Republican experiment, which had begun so hopefully, end so disastrously? Was the Spanish Civil War the product of some failure of the Second Republic and its leaders? Could more skilled political leadership have avoided the catastrophe?

It is by now a well-established axiom that the origins of the Spanish Civil War lay in the Second Republic. The Civil War took place during the Republic and brought it to an end; surely it also produced the causes of the war? This is at best a half truth, and only then if the relation between the two is properly understood. It is true to the extent that the reformist policies of the centre-left governments of the Republic provoked reactions which eventually led to civil war. It is not true to the extent that the conditions which those governments sought to change had long historical roots. The policies were the product of the Republic, the problems the product of the past, especially the nineteenth and early twentieth centuries.

Yet even this reduced connection between the Republic and the Civil War must be put in its proper context. The Civil War was not, as has often been claimed, the product of any 'failure' of the Republic. Such interpretations usually blame parties of the left, and especially the Socialists, for putting their own partisan goals ahead of the rules of democracy, thereby killing the Republican legitimacy they claimed to value. This point has been made most bluntly by Richard Robinson when he writes that 'given that the future of the Republic depended on the Socialist movement and the Catholic party, it is important to recognise that it was the former and not the latter which abandoned democratic methods and appealed to violence'.[22]

Juan Linz has put forward a more sophisticated version of this argument. Linz argues that the Republican-Socialist coalition failed because it gave priority to non-structural problems, such as the army and the Church, which created resentments but did not satisfy the demands of its own rank and file: 'The specific formulation of policies and the failures of their implementation . . . left an unfortunate heritage: the mobilization of opponents, the disillusionment of a key supporter, the Socialist Party, and the continuing and intensified hostility of the anarchosyndicalists.'[23] These dissatisfactions led to the breakdown of the regime, a breakdown of which the Socialists were 'a major, if not decisive factor' and which was already substantially complete by the time of the military revolt of 17 July 1936.

Linz concludes that the military revolt was not the main cause of the breakdown of the Republic. Perhaps. But it was the main cause of the civil war and that is what is most important. The Civil War was the result of the failure of a military rising against a legitimately-elected democratic government, not the failure of the Republic. As Santos Juliá has written in a perceptive essay, 'the Civil War did not originate in any presumed failure of the Republic but in the failure of a coup d'état whose goal was to cause the failure of some of the initiatives taken by the Republic to

---

22. Richard Robinson, *The Origins of Franco's Spain* (Newton Abbot, 1970), p. 12.
23. Juan Linz, 'From Great Hopes to Civil War. The Breakdown of Democracy in Spain', in *The Breakdown of Democratic Regimes*, ed. by J. Linz and A. Stepan (Baltimore, 1978), pp. 155, 195.

33

restructure social and political relations in Spain . . . The Republic did not fail; rather it was made to fail.'[24]

What prompted the military rising was not the Republic's failure, but quite the opposite: the possibility that it would succeed. But succeed in what? The military revolt was motivated by fears that the Republic would be successful in its programme of wide-ranging reform, the end result of which would have been to replace one economic, social and political formation – or one vision of 'Spain' – with another. The progressive governments of the Republic aspired to more than just a change in political forms and, as Edward Malefakis has suggested, this is what distinguished it from the roughly contemporaneous republics in Portugal, Greece and even Germany. 'The [Spanish] Republic differs clearly from all the others in that in its first two years it was capable of defining itself as a regime which aspired to carry out a much more complete and idealistic program of national regeneration. The reforms postulated by the San Sebastián and Azaña coalitions between April 1931 and September 1933 touched more important aspects of life and were carried out more satisfactorily than in any of the other new republics.'[25]

The men who governed the Second Republic between April 1931 and September 1933, and again after February 1936, did not form a monolithic bloc with a single, shared programme. Between Socialists and Republicans, and between different kinds of Socialists and different kinds of Republicans, there were very real differences. Even so, it is possible to see something of a shared vision, albeit one which was not articulated as such: they sought to build a democratic state in which the army ceased to make and unmake governments and in which regional aspirations for home rule were recognized; they sought a society in which the role of the Church was limited to worship, and the worst social inequities, especially those on the land, were eliminated. And they sought to do so through democratic, reformist methods. This was a view of the problem, and a vision of the objective, in which distinctions between structural and non-structural issues had no place. It also constituted a challenge to the major Spanish elites – the owners of large landed estates, the Church and the army – as well as an attack on the vision shared by these groups and many ordinary Spaniards of a unitary, centralized and Catholic nation in which existing social hierarchies were eternal.

Republican reforms can be seen in another way: they constituted the first serious attempt to revise the outcome of the liberal revolution of

---

24. Santos Juliá, 'El Fracaso de la República', in *Revista de Occidente*, November, 1981, pp. 199–200.
25. Edward Malefakis, 'Peculiaridad de la República Española', in ibid., pp. 25–6.

the early nineteenth century. They also represented a major assertion of the power of the State at the expense of the private power of the Church and the landholders and the inadequately-controlled power of the military. As a result, the hostility they generated was not directed against individual policies but against the Republican project itself.

The chapters that follow will discuss the four central areas of reform: the Church, the military, the regional question and the social question. They will sketch the long-term historical roots to show how it was that they became 'problems' the leaders of the Republic sought to solve, and then describe the solutions they attempted and the responses they provoked. Within this complex of confrontations, the social question, and in particular the question of agrarian reform, was, as Preston has argued, 'the most crucial of those several component confrontations within the civil war which broke out in 1936'.[26]

The leaders of the centre-left governments responsible for the reforms certainly made mistakes. This was particularly so in the case of religious reforms, which put even more restrictions on the Church than full separation of Church and State required. But it is highly unlikely that a more skilful handling of that issue, or of the restructuring of the army, or of any serious attempt to alleviate the misery of the rural proletariat of the south, would have prevented an assault on the regime. To the extent that the Second Republic was meant as not just a new form for political life, not just an alternative to the monarchy, but as the vehicle for effecting significant changes in the life of the nation, the resistance of the elites was virtually a given.

Stanley Payne sees this 'patrimonial' concept, which privileged specific content over 'the basic rules of the game', as crucial to the failure of the Republic's democratic experiment. He contrasts this weakness of political leadership, and especially on the part of Manuel Azaña, to the much more 'able, adroit and prudent leadership' of the politicians responsible for the democratic transition of the 1970s.[27] This is true, but the political attitudes of Azaña and the others were as much a part of the legacy of Spain's recent past as were the social question and the place of the Church. In the same way, the undeniable and laudable prudence of the architects of the transition, and especially of the leaders of the left, was in no small part a by-product of the Civil War and the Franco regime.

This process was not unique to Spain. In his book *The Persistence of the Ancien Regime*, Arno Mayer has argued that the First World War was 'an

---

26. Paul Preston, 'The Agrarian War in the South', in *Revolution and War*, ed. by Paul Preston (London, 1989), p. 159.
27. Stanley Payne, *Spain's First Democracy* (Madison, 1993), p. 384.

expression of the decline and fall of the old order fighting to prolong its life', that the old order's elites 'proceeded to reaffirm and tighten their political hold in order to bolster their material, social and cultural preeminence' and that in this struggle for survival war became 'an instrument of domestic politics'.[28] A similar process was at work in Republican Spain, although under different circumstances. The old elites had already lost political power and then found their 'material, social and cultural preeminence' at risk. When the electoral victory of the Popular Front in February 1936 showed that conventional political action had failed to stave off this threat they turned to violence, and although they had planned on a coup they did not step back from civil war.

28. Arno Mayer, *The Persistence of the Ancien Regime* (London, 1981), pp. 4, 15, 305.

CHAPTER TWO
The Church

In October 1931 Prime Minister Manuel Azaña outraged Catholic opinion when he told the Cortes that 'Spain is no longer Catholic'. For all the furore his remark provoked it was not inaccurate; that millions of Spaniards wanted nothing to do with the Church was recognized even by some clergymen. In 1936 Father J. Ordóñez Márquez published a book on religious practice in Huelva, entitled *La Apostasia de las Masas*, in which he asked whether Spain was Catholic and was forced to answer that it was not. Three years later Father Sarabia, a famous missionary priest, wrote a book whose title ominously echoed Azaña's comment, *¿España, es católica?*.

Such a willingness to pose the question of the real position of Catholicism in Spanish society was rare in the Spanish Church of the 1930s; rarer still was the willingness to publicly admit that the majority of Spaniards had little more than a nominal allegiance to the Church – and that a great many held a positive hatred for it. Rarest of all was the admission that the Church itself shared some responsibility for this situation. Instead of asking itself what it could do to recapture the faith of those Spaniards who had abandoned it, the Church demanded that the State make the country safe for Catholicism. During the Second Republic and for a long time before, the Church, with only few and minor exceptions, had refused to come to terms with reality. Ever since the end of the Old Regime and the implantation of a liberal political system in Spain, the Church had insisted that the State allow it a monopoly on religion and a privileged position as arbiter of moral and educational standards for the whole country. And, for the most part, the State had been willing to do this so long as the Church preached acceptance of the socio-economic status quo as part of its religious message.

In the Second Republic, and especially in the governments of 1931 to 1933, the Church encountered a regime which was no longer prepared to enter into such an arrangement but which wanted to reduce the role of the Church to one more congruent with its actual place within Spanish society. The Church's response was to claim that the Republic was attacking the Church, religion and the very core of Spain itself. These arguments were used by landed interests to generate a mass base among the still practising smallholders of northern Spain for opposition to the reformist Republic and, when it came, for the Nationalist revolt against the Republic. The Spanish hierarchy, with only five exceptions, embraced the Nationalist revolt and legitimized it as a Crusade. (Only in the Basque Provinces, where religion was closely identified with regional nationalism, was there any significant dissent from this interpretation.) In their *Joint Letter of the Spanish Bishops to the Bishops of the Whole World* the leaders of the Spanish Church painted the civil war as a struggle between religion and atheism. The war was 'an armed plebiscite . . . The one side attempting to suppress God, whose work must be accomplished by the Church in the world, and the Church herself was suffering immense harm . . . such as perhaps no other institution has ever suffered in history; the other side . . . was striving to keep alive the old spirit, both Spanish and Christian'.[1] Religion, or rather the place of the institutional Church, was one of the issues which contributed to the poisoning of the political atmosphere of the Republic, but the civil war was not, as the bishops claimed, a religious war, except to the degree that religion could be used to provide ideological cover for less exalted interests.

THE CHURCH IN LIBERAL SPAIN

During the Old Regime the Catholic Church was an institution impressive in its wealth, social power and political influence. However, during the crisis of the Old Regime and the emergence of the new liberal political system, which took place fitfully between the Napoleonic invasion of 1808 and the end of the Carlist War in 1840, the Church found its institutional power greatly reduced. The Church had great difficulty in coming to terms with the liberal state, which had very different ideas about the role of the Church in Spain than did religious leaders. In the first fifty years of the nineteenth century the place and nature of the Church was a major political question.

The reshaping of the Church began with the Cortes of Cádiz, which abolished the Inquisition and declared freedom of expression and of the press, measures which were strongly opposed by the hierarchy. During

---

1. *Joint Letter of the Spanish Bishops to the Bishops of the Whole World* (London, 1937), p. 15.

the liberal triennium of 1820 to 1823 further reform proposals, such as the closure of purely monastic religious orders, strengthened the Church's opposition to liberalism. The most concerted attack on the role of the Church was launched by the progressives between 1835 and 1843. Between October 1835 and July 1837 the monasteries were suppressed, their properties sold and the male orders abolished. In 1841 the property of the secular clergy was put up for sale and the government proposed a major reorganization of the parish and diocesan structure as well as limiting the Church's contacts with Rome.

The sale of the lands of the regular clergy was undoubtedly the major blow to the wealth and power of the Church, even though its material position had been in steady decline since the beginning of the century, under attack by liberals and the reactionary monarch Ferdinand VII alike. There was also popular opposition to the Church's financial position voiced through a growing resistance to the payment of the tithe. Spanish liberals were not enemies of religion or even of the Church. Both branches of Spanish liberalism, the moderates and the progressives, considered religion absolutely essential to the stability of the social order and both wanted to give the Church a role in line with that belief. They questioned the size and wealth of the Church but they did not question its monopoly of spiritual affairs. Catholicism was declared the religion of the state in all liberal constitutions, even the progressive Constitution of 1837, which also provided for state support for the Church and its ministers. The most important secular function the Church could perform, especially for the moderates, was to preserve the social order. As *El Guardia Nacional* wrote in March 1838, the role of the clergy was 'to inspire the obedience of the masses towards the classification of society. It is essential that religion teach people that without obedience there is no society.' Any social problems could be resolved through charity, with 'the voice of the clergy counselling the wealthy'.[2]

When the moderates returned to power in 1843 they were determined to improve relations with the Church. The Constitution of 1845 declared that Catholicism was 'the religion of the Spanish nation' and that the state would provide economic support. In 1848 the government and the Vatican initiated negotiations for a Concordat, which was finally proclaimed in 1851.

The Concordat gave the Catholic Church a religious monopoly: 'The Apostolic Roman Catholic religion . . . continues to be the only religion of the Spanish nation; all other cults are excluded.' The state was to provide

---

2. Cited in J. Longares Alonso, *Política y religión en Barcelona, 1833–1843* (Madrid, 1979), p. 243.

financial support for the secular clergy and the religious budget, *clero y culto*, was set at one seventh of total government expenditures. In addition, the government would support seminaries, allow the Church to own property and assure that education conformed to Catholic doctrine. The male orders were allowed to return on a limited basis, although the ambiguity of the wording allowed the Church to ignore the intended limitation. For its part, the Church recognized the land sales that had already taken place and reaffirmed the right of the Crown to appoint bishops.

The Concordat was briefly set aside by the governments of the revolutionary interlude of 1868 to 1874, when governments suppressed religious communities, barred religious orders from owning property, eliminated the ecclesiastical legal jurisdiction (*fuero*) and introduced civil marriage and civil registries for birth and death. The government of the First Republic (1873–74) even proposed the separation of Church and State but this never came into effect. The Restoration's Constitution of 1876 returned to compliance with the Concordat, but with one minor change. The architect of the new constitution, Antonio Cánovas del Castillo, was determined to create a system acceptable to the widest range of liberal opinion so that Article 11, which regulated religious matters, allowed the private practice of other faiths although Catholicism remained the religion of the state. In return, nineteen bishops were given seats in the Senate.

The Concordat succeeded in settling the issue of Church-State relations, but left open the equally important issue of the influence and position of the Church in Spanish society. It created what William Callahan has called 'a legal framework allowing the Church to function normally for the first time since 1834 . . . but laid the groundwork for a continuing struggle over the Church's determination to install its vision of the Kingdom of God on earth in a secular and economically changing society'.[3] From 1851 until the declaration of the Second Republic, the Church continually pushed its claims for a predominant role in education, censorship and public morality.

Despite the regulation of relations between Church and the liberal State, the Spanish Church was never comfortable with liberalism, especially when it suggested that the actual strength of Catholicism among the Spanish people was less than that claimed. After analysing a number of pastorals by Restoration bishops, García de Cortázar concluded that the Spanish hierarchy was afraid of liberalism, which it saw as 'to blame for everything wrong with society'.[4]

---

3. William J. Callahan, *Church, Society and Politics in Spain, 1750–1874* (Cambridge, Massachusetts, 1984), pp. 192–3.
4. F. García de Cortázar, 'La Iglesia Española de la Restauración: Definición de Objetivos y Prácticas Religiosas', in *Cuadernos de Deusto*, 1982, p. 76.

If the elite of the Church was incapable of coming to terms with liberalism, the ecclesiastical rank and file was even less able to do so. The parish clergy had always been poorly trained and badly paid, and this did not change in the nineteenth century. The Concordat had called for the creation of central seminaries, but the education they provided was considered inadequate. However, not all priests had the benefit of a seminary education. In 1852 the new training programme instituted a special abbreviated education of three years (compared to the normal fourteen) for priests destined for rural parishes. Frances Lannon has studied one seminary, in Vitoria, and pointed out how it contributed to the weakness of the clergy of late nineteenth and early twentieth century Spain, especially its alienation from the society to which its members had to relate. It was:

> a Catholic educational institution deliberately enclosed within its own moral and intellectual, as well as physical boundaries. The pedagogical stress lay on as total a separation from outside influences, regarded more often than not as inherently pernicious. As one student wrote as late as 1930 . . . 'the seminary was a nursery where tender shoots are preserved from the suffocating atmosphere of an unhealthy world'.

An attempt to broaden the curriculum and relate it to social questions was made in the 1920s and 1930s but was short-lived.[5]

Parish life reflected the shortcomings of clerical training. Sarabia described the poverty of parish life in the Asturian town where he grew up at the turn of the century. 'In a healthy and moral traditional atmosphere there was a routine and lifeless Christianity . . . Frequently no one took communion . . . there were one or two sermons per year . . . We children never had catechism class. I never heard an explanation of the catechism, either at school or in church. All we had was rote learning of the Astete [catchecism].'[6]

The situation was much worse elsewhere. There were very few clergy at all in the rural south. At a time when the average size of a parish in Spain was 729 people it was 3,667 in Málaga and 7,493 in Cádiz. This was a pattern inherited from the Old Regime Church, but in the nineteenth century the Catholic Church faced a new problem of its own making in the cities. The Church did not deploy its manpower and resources in response to urbanization and the growth of populous working-class suburbs. The parish structure of Barcelona was not changed after 1877 and in 1907 some parishes had over 50,000 residents. The Madrid working-

---

5. Frances Lannon, 'A Basque Challenge to the Pre-Civil War Spanish Church', in *European Studies Review*, January, 1979, pp. 31–35.
6. P.R. Santidrián, *El Padre Sarabia Escribe su Historia* (Madrid, 1963), pp. 31–2.

class parish of Puente de Vallecas had five priests for 80,000 people in 1930 while one central parish had sixteen for 20,000 people.

There were some attempts to develop a Spanish version of social Catholicism based on Leo XIII's encyclical of 1893, *Rerum Novarum*, but they did not achieve very much. The attempts to create genuine Catholic unions, like those of the Asturian priest Maximiliano Arboleya, were undermined by the hostility of the employers, for whom the overriding purpose of Catholic unions was to serve as a prophylactic against the labour movement.

With this conservative social message and its abandonment of both the rural and urban working classes in favour of a strategy of capturing the elites, it is not surprising that observable signs of religious belief, and those that the Church most valued, attendance at religious services, had declined sharply in many regions of the country well before the Second Republic. The regional patterns of religiosity in Spain had been set as early as the middle of the nineteenth century and changed little thereafter:

> The Church was strongest in areas of large peasant populations who had a reasonable security of land tenure and lived in numerous small villages with a strong sense of communal life. It was weakest in the great latifundia lands of Extremadura, La Mancha and Andalucía, where a rural proletariat lived in desperate circumstances. And already by 1869 the weakness of the Church in the metropolitan areas was becoming evident.[7]

In the socially polarized agrarian south and in the major urban centres and industrial zones, religion had taken on clear class connotations. Observance in the south ranged from very low to almost non-existent and the class division between observance and non-observance was clear to everyone. Agricultural labourers saw religion as the property of the ruling class. In the village of Casas Viejas, which in 1933 became notorious for a massacre carried out by the police, 'religious observance . . . was sharply circumscribed. The masses said on Saturday night and Sunday morning were attended by men and women of the upper classes . . . by those dependent on them . . . and by the defenders of the social order. Few campesinos [peasants] ever attended mass.'[8]

The situation was similar in the cities. In the Madrid working-class suburb of San Ramón de Vallecas only seven per cent of the parishioners attended mass and only six per cent fulfilled their Easter obligation. Just a quarter of the children were baptized and only ten per cent of the dying received the last rites. In the Asturian coalfields the situation was little better. Father Maximiliano Arboleya wrote in 1922 that 'the most educated

7. Callahan, *Church*, p. 244.
8. Jerome Mintz, *The Anarchists of Casas Viejas* (Chicago, 1983), pp. 68–70.

of the workers in the coalfields and the large manufacturing centres, as well as in many of the smaller ones, are irreligious, while the rest are anti-religious'.[9]

Anti-clerical sentiment was widespread among the lower classes in Spain and while it was most frequently contained in popular sayings and beliefs focussing on the supposed immorality of the clergy it would, on occasion, find more violent modes of expression. In 1834 monasteries were stoned in Barcelona and the following year seventy-eight monks were killed in Madrid in riots caused by rumours that the Jesuits had poisoned the city's wells. Violence surfaced once again in the Tragic Week (26 July–1 August 1909) in Barcelona when over fifty churches and convents as well as church schools and welfare institutions were burned. These outbursts coincided with moments of political tension and may have owed something to political agitators, but it is clear that it did not take much to make the urban lower classes turn on the visible symbols of the Church.

THE SECOND REPUBLIC AND THE CHURCH

Less than one month after the declaration of the Republic in April 1931 there was another outbreak of anti-clerical violence. It began in Madrid on 11 May, apparently triggered by the opening of a monarchist political club and the publication on 7 May of a pastoral letter. In this letter the Archbishop of Toledo praised the monarchy – and Alfonso XIII in particular – and suggested by analogy that the Second Republic was similar to the short-lived Communist regime in Bavaria in 1919. Six convents were burned in the capital and fifteen more in various southern cities. José Sánchez says 107 buildings were sacked and other estimates were as high as 170. Despite the insistence on the part of Interior Minister Miguel Maura, a conservative Republican and practising Catholic, that the Civil Guard be called in to restore order the government waited two days to do so.

It has been argued that this episode discredited the government in the eyes of the Church and showed Catholics that their religion was not secure under the Republic.[10] The Church had indeed been prepared to deal with the new regime. On 15 April the papal Nuncio began negotiations with the government directed towards reaching some agreement on the status of the Church and the initial pastorals of the bishops had called for obedience

9. Cited in D. Benavides, *El Fracaso Social del Catolicismo Español* (Barcelona, 1973), p. 530.
10. José Sánchez, *Reform and Reaction: the politico-religious background to the Spanish Civil War* (Chapel Hill, 1964), p. 96.

to the established authorities. However, one cannot conclude from this that had the government acted strongly to show its good faith on 11–12 May the Church's attitude to the Republic might have been more favourable. This initial acceptance of the Republic was the product of 'a cautious attitude motivated by fear, rather than as a positive acclamation'[11] and, in any case, Cardinal Tedeschini's diplomatic approach was far from being universally shared by the country's bishops.

The leaders of the Republican–Socialist coalition were determined to separate Church and State and reduce religious influence in society, especially in education. For the left-Republicans in particular, this was central to their programme. The Spanish Church could never have accepted it. As Frances Lannon has written, 'The crusade had been waged for a long time by the Church for its own institutional interests, for survival. The cost of its survival was the destruction of the Republic.'[12]

The Provisional Government and the government led by Manuel Azaña acted in a number of ways to circumscribe the role and activities of the Church to a degree unprecedented in the country's history. On 6 May the Provisional Government issued a decree ending compulsory religious education; on 21 May it required that all elementary school teachers have a university education, a measure which most affected the nuns who taught in Church schools; and the next day it announced freedom of religion. In June public processions for Corpus Christi were prohibited.

Taken together, the convent burnings and the decrees of May and June broke the fragile tolerance for the Republic within the Church. The Bishop of Vitoria was expelled from the country and following the declaration of freedom of religion the Primate, Cardinal Segura, left for Rome where he publicly denounced the government's religious policy. When he tried to return to Spain he was arrested and immediately deported. With bishops and parish clergy attacking the decrees on religion through the summer of 1931, Ben-Ami is correct when he says that 'the precarious coexistence of Church and Republic was definitely shattered long before October 1931 when the anti-religious clauses were introduced into the Constitution'.[13]

The Constitution defined the new, limited place of the Church in Republican Spain. Article 3 stated that Spain had no official religion, the first such declaration in the country's history. However, even this was less controversial than Article 26 which placed a number of restrictions on the activities of the Church and especially the religious orders. The article was approved by the Cortes in October 1931 after a lengthy and heated debate

11. Ben-Ami, *Origins of the Second Republic in Spain* (Oxford, 1978), pp. 255–6.
12. Frances Lannon, 'The Church's Crusade Against the Republic', in *Revolution and War*, ed. by Paul Preston (London, 1989), p. 54.
13. Ben-Ami, *Origins*, pp. 259–60.

which included Azaña's remark about Spain no longer being Catholic, and led to the resignation from the government of Maura and Niceto Alcalá Zamora as well as the withdrawal of Basque and Agrarian deputies from parliament. There can be no doubt that Article 26 confirmed Catholics in their already established suspicion of the Republic.

Article 26 ended government financial support of the Church. The activities of the religious orders were to be closely regulated; they would be prohibited from owning 'more property than is necessary for their living needs or for the direct completion of their special goals' and from being involved in education, industry or commerce. They would have to inform the government of all their investments and pay taxes. Any order which 'imposed a vow of obedience to an authority distinct from the State' – which meant the Jesuits – was to be disbanded and its property seized by the state to be used for education and charity.

The Constitution stated the principles of the new regime but it was left to subsequent enabling legislation to give these principles legal force. The first law was that dissolving the Jesuits on 23 January 1932. Banks and companies in which the order had a financial interest were required to inform the government of this within ten days so that the property could then be nationalized. Jesuit educational institutions were closed down, a move which touched some 7,000 students in the order's twenty-one secondary schools and six post-secondary institutions. January also saw legislation secularizing the cemeteries and instituting civil divorce. In November the government announced that all financial support for the clergy would be ended within a year. (The real weakness of the Church was revealed in the apathetic response to the appeal made by the Archbishop of Seville for donations of one peseta per family per month in order to help the Church make up for the ending of state financing.)

The most important piece of legislation was the Law of Congregations, which was submitted to the Cortes in October 1932, passed in May 1933 after months of debate and obstruction by the right, and finally signed into law on 2 June 1933. The law carried out the provisions of Article 26 of the Constitution. Its most important aspect was the prohibition on the religious orders being involved in education and the requirement that they withdraw from secondary teaching by 1 October 1933 and from primary education by the end of the year.

With the Law of Congregations the religious legislation of the Republican-Socialist government was complete. The day after the President signed it into law the hierarchy issued a collective declaration. This stated that the law was not binding on Catholics as it forced them to violate the laws of the Church (in particular the obligation to have their children educated in Catholic schools) and implied that Catholic deputies who had voted for the bill were in danger of being excommunicated. The next day, 4 June, the Pope made his first official statement on the situation in Spain. His encyclical *Dilectissima nobis* repeated that the Church put little weight on the form of governments, only their treatment of the Church, and roundly condemned the Spanish government's religious legislation.

The centre-right governments which were in power following the election of November 1933 diluted the religious laws as much as possible. In April 1934 parliament passed a bill introduced by José María Gil Robles which circumvented the ban on state support of the clergy by giving all priests over the age of forty pensions as retired civil servants at two-thirds of their salary in 1931. The provisions of the Law of Congregations prohibiting the religious orders from teaching were suspended in December 1933 and virtually all its other provisions were ignored. Public processions on the major holidays were allowed and many holy days were made school holidays once again. The government also initiated discussions with the Papacy towards a new Concordat but these made little progress.

The pendulum swung back to enforcement of the law, which had never been repealed, following the election of February 1936 which brought the Popular Front to office. The Minister of Education immediately ordered a survey of the school system so that the religious orders could be removed from the classrooms as quickly as possible. By the late spring the government was announcing the closure of religious schools throughout the country. Jesuit property was ordered to be confiscated but a Socialist bill that would have ended the payment of pensions to the clergy did not become law.

There can be no doubt that the role the Republicans and Socialists legislated for the Church was much more in line with its actual place in society than the universal influence it claimed for itself. However, the vehemence and comprehensiveness with which they limited the place of the Church were both a contravention of genuine democratic principles and a disastrous political error. Important measures (such as banning the clergy from teaching) and lesser ones (such as prohibiting public religious processions), as well as harassment at the local level (including such things as a tax on the ringing of church bells), exceeded what was required by any genuine separation of Church and State. More dangerously, they also gave the impression that the Republic was persecuting the Church and in this way provided the right with an issue which it could use to create mass support, first for an electoral crusade and then for a military one.

The right very quickly seized on the religious issue and used it as an umbrella under which its other interests huddled for protection. As early as 21 April 1931, that is one week after the declaration of the Republic, *El Debate* (the main Catholic newspaper) was attempting to unite all those opposed to the new regime under the slogan 'Religion, Fatherland, Order, Family and Property' and the next week it declared that 'we must all defend Spain and ourselves and our material and spiritual goods'. After the right withdrew from the Cortes in protest against the approval of Article 26 it undertook a massive propaganda campaign demanding revision of the Constitution. The religious provisions were presented as a total assault not only on the Church but also on property and the family. The conflation of religion with the material interests which the right defended was well illustrated by José María Gil Robles in his closing speech at the founding congress of the CEDA in February 1933: 'When the social order is threatened, Catholics should unite to defend it and safeguard the principles of Christian civilization . . . We will go united into struggle no matter what it costs . . . We are faced with a social revolution.'[14] This was a very precise preview of the rationale the Church hierarchy would use in baptizing Franco's revolt against the Republic a crusade.

The use of such rhetoric allowed the right to develop a mass base through what Preston and Sevilla-Guzmán have called the 'instrumentalization' of the Catholic smallholding peasantry of northern Spain, especially in Old Castile. This strategy took institutional form in the Confederación Nacional Católico-Agraria (CNCA), a federation of confessional and anti-Socialist rural syndicates which had been created in 1917. The syndicates were most numerous in Palencia, León, Old Castile and Navarre and had as their aim 'to prevent impoverished farmers turning to the left by offering them credit facilities, agronomic expertise, warehousing and machinery' while at the same time defending the interests of all agriculturalists, small and large.[15]

Although the CNCA claimed to be apolitical it produced the leaders of the CEDA (Gil Robles was the most outstanding example) and it exulted in the electoral victory of the right in November 1933. It was from those areas in which the CNCA was strongest that the CEDA drew its greatest electoral strength and that the military rebellion of July 1936 would draw its mass support.

Nowhere was this truer than in Navarre which provided 10,000 Carlist volunteers for the Franco rebellion. There the Republic had come to be synonymous with anti-clericalism and the religious issue was 'skillfully exploited by press and pulpit' to generate increasing support for Carlism. However, the growing strength of Carlism could be used to defend interests beyond the strictly religious. As Blinkhorn describes, 'the particular significance of the Navarrese Carlists' unanimity and combativeness on the

14. Cited in Paul Preston, *The Coming of the Spanish Civil War* (London, 1983), pp. 29–30, 43.
15. Preston, 'The Agrarian War in the South', in Preston, ed., *Revolution and War*, p. 161.

religious question was the manner in which they were carried over into other issues:

> specifically . . . that of the land. For, within the framework of an ostensibly religious crusade against a 'Godless' Republic, the Navarrese Carlist elite began to show an increasing preoccupation with more material affairs, and in particular with the attempts of successive Republican governments to modify the distribution and use of various forms of landed property'.[16]

However, it was not inevitable that Catholicism would be used as a rallying point for anti-Republican forces. The Basque Provinces, which rivalled Navarre as the most religious region in Spain, supported the Republic, not Franco. There the desire to achieve regional autonomy outweighed any hostility generated by the Republic's religious legislation, even among the clergy. The granting of autonomy and the constitution of a regional government controlled by the Catholic Basque Nationalist Party (PNV) in October 1936, after the civil war had already begun, kept the region on the Republican side. Events in the Basque Provinces after they fell to Franco in June 1937 revealed that the defence of religion and the clergy was little more than rhetorical cover for other concerns: when the Nationalists executed fifteen priests the Church, which had condemned Basque Catholics' support for the Republic, made no complaint.

16. Martin Blinkhorn, 'Politics and Society in Navarre, 1931–1936', in ibid., pp. 73–4.

CHAPTER THREE
The Regional Question

Following the Restoration of 1876 and the imposition of political stability Spanish industry experienced a period of prosperity. The leading industrial areas in the country were on the geographic periphery; Catalonia for textiles, and the Basque Provinces, especially Vizcaya, for iron, steel and shipbuilding. Ironically, as these regions experienced economic growth they also gave rise to regional nationalist movements which expressed dissatisfaction with their position within the Spanish state. At first these movements had a cultural orientation, based on the fact that both regions had an indigenous language other than Spanish. These cultural movements then became political, voicing demands for autonomy (home rule) or even separation.

However, Catalan and Basque nationalism did not share similar political, social or economic orientations. Catalan nationalism was initially dominated by the industrial bourgeoisie which aspired to advance industrial development by reshaping all of Spain in the image of Catalonia. By the time of the Republic, though, this elite movement had given way to a more broadly based political force concerned as much with social reform as with regionalism. By contrast, Basque nationalism emerged as a reaction against the rapid industrialization of Vizcaya which was seen as threatening the region's social system, its conservative Catholic values and the integrity of the Basque race; and although its original virulence was soon moderated it remained both strongly Catholic and socially conservative.

Both regional nationalisms did share one thing in common, and for the fate of the Second Republic this would be the most important point about them: they provoked incomprehension, fear and even hatred from the Spanish right, which saw regionalism as a threat to the existence of the unified nation-state which had existed, in their minds, since the eighteenth century, if not since the time of the Catholic Kings. (They also saw regionalism, and the Catalan brand in particular, as a threat to their own economic and political hegemony.) This visceral reaction was most intense and immediate within the officer corps, few of whose members came from these regions, who shared a rigidly centralist view of the state and one of whose stated tasks was the defence of the territorial integrity of the nation. That the Second Republic had granted broad autonomy to Catalonia in 1932 and was about to do so to the Basque Provinces in the spring of 1936 touched off their fears of 'separatism'. In yet another respect the conservative vision of Spain was being dismantled and this contributed to the military rebellion of 17 July. Just how important a factor this was is perhaps revealed in the motto of the Franco regime: *Una, Grande, Libre* (One, Great and Free).

THE EMERGENCE OF CATALAN NATIONALISM

Catalan nationalism emerged in the last quarter of the nineteenth century from two distinct intellectual traditions. The first was a conservative, Catholic tradition which looked back to the glories of medieval Catalonia, seeking to recreate a natural, hierarchical state informed by the teachings of the Church. This strand of nationalism was best expressed by the Bishop of Vic, Josep Torras i Bages in his book *La Tradició Catalana* (1892). The second evolved out of Federal Republicanism and found its best exponent in Valentí Almirall. Almirall proposed a democratic and secular nationalism in which Catalonia would aspire to lead Spain. He wanted the Catalan bourgeoisie to transcend its concern with tariff protection and aspire to national political power.

> The modernization of the country requires that hegemony pass from the agrarian oligarchy of the south and centre and its unitary political structure to the bourgeoisie of the periphery, but on the condition that these, and especially the Catalans, know how to live up to their historical responsibilities and present the country with ideals which oppose the traditional values of the agrarian oligarchy.[1]

Almirall had a radical political background, having been a Federal Republican, and this stood in the way of his attracting much support from the Catalan elite. His objective of a broad, inter-class Catalan front to reform Spain was given a more conservative, and acceptable, formulation by Enric Prat de la Riba in his *La Nacionalitat Catalana* (1906).

Catalan nationalism remained a largely intellectual and cultural movement until the loss of the American colonies to the United States in 1898.

---

1. J. Trías Vejarano, *Almirall y los orígenes del Catalanismo* (Madrid, 1975), p. 360.

This, and the subsequent refusal of the state to support a series of ideas designed to compensate for the loss of the crucial colonial market for Catalan textiles, led the industrial bourgeoisie, which had fully supported the Restoration and profited from it, to turn to regionalism. In 1901 four nationalists, three of them representatives of big business, were elected to the Cortes for Barcelona and shortly thereafter the Lliga Regionalista was formed. The Lliga was socially conservative and business oriented, the political expression of the bourgeoisie, 'a class which aspired to the leadership of a state', in Pierre Vilar's words.[2] It was led by the lawyer and financier Francesc Cambó, arguably the most able Spanish politician of the early twentieth century.

Catalan nationalism very quickly angered the army. A series of anti-military cartoons led officers to attack the offices of the satirical magazine *Cu-Cut* and the conservative nationalist paper *La Veu de Catalunya*. This incident led to the passage of the Law of Jurisdictions in 1906. The response in Catalonia was the formation of a broad electoral alliance, Solidaridad Catalana, under the leadership of the Lliga, to contest the elections of 1907 in which it swept forty-one of the forty-four parliamentary seats for the region. However this alliance, which included Carlists and Republicans, very quickly broke down in the face of the widely differing objectives of the various parties.

The Lliga pressured Madrid for Catalan home rule on the one hand and economic policies favourable to industry on the other. It achieved much of the former goal in 1914 when the four provincial Diputaciones were merged into the Mancomunitat, which acted vigorously to improve the region's infrastructure and promote culture. The second goal was much more elusive. In 1916 the government announced a tax on wartime industrial profits. This angered the Lliga which, the next year, attempted to lead a coalition of Republicans, Socialists and disgruntled army officers in a political revolution against the monarchy.

The events of 1917, which ended with the army putting down a general strike organized by Republicans and Socialists, sent Cambó and his party scuttling back behind the shield of the central government. The Lliga's brand of conservative regionalism had always contained a basic flaw: it did not take into account the Catalan working class which, after 1917, was flocking to the anarchosyndicalist CNT. Barcelona was at the centre of an upsurge in labour militancy which turned into full-scale class war between 1919 and 1923, and this led the Lliga to realize that they needed the central government, and more particularly the army, to preserve their

2. Pierre Vilar, 'Spain and Catalonia', *Review of the Fernand Braudel Center* (Spring, 1980), p. 546.

socio-economic position against revolution. This, in turn, led to the virtual abandonment of their regionalist demands.

Between 1920 and 1922 General Martínez Anido satisfied the Catalan bourgeoisie's demands for tough measures against the CNT but the appointment of more conciliatory civil governors in 1923 marked their final alienation from the Restoration system. In September 1923 a 'panic stricken high Catalan bourgeoisie' strongly backed Primo de Rivera's coup. 'Under the stress of class warfare and the dangers to its vital interests, the Lliga accelerated its drive to strengthen its links with a "strong", counter-revolutionary Spanish state while relegating its autonomist aspirations to a secondary position.'[3]

Primo had promised to preserve social peace and grant autonomy. He achieved the first but totally reneged on the second and in 1924 he abolished the Mancomunitat. The Lliga had been losing electoral strength to more radical nationalist groups since 1919 but its support for Primo put paid to its pretensions as a regionalist party. Even though Cambó withdrew his support for the regime in 1926 the Lliga never recovered its position of political dominance. Rather, it was pushed aside by Republican regionalists with close ties to the working class and the peasantry. When full regional autonomy was achieved, under the Second Republic, it was due not to the Lliga but to these other groups, united into the Esquerra Republicana de Catalunya (Catalan Republican Left).

THE EMERGENCE OF BASQUE NATIONALISM

Basque nationalism was very different from its Catalan counterpart, in terms of both its ideology and its social constituency. It too emerged in a context of industrialization but as a reaction against the effects of that industrialization, especially urbanization and immigration. Far from being led by the industrial bourgeoisie, it was directed against it and towards a largely self-sufficient peasantry and the artisanate and petty bourgeoisie. Basque nationalism was created and was always most vital in Vizcaya, 'where rapid industrialization and massive immigration broke the stability and the traditional forms of Basque social life, where traditional culture and identity were seen as seriously threatened'.[4] In those provinces less touched by industrialization Basque nationalism proved unable to displace Carlism, a more traditional and deeply rooted conservatism.

3. Shlomo Ben-Ami, *Fascism from Above: the dictatorship of Primo de Rivera in Spain* (Oxford, 1983), p. 42.
4. Juan Pablo Fusi, *El País Vasco: Pluralismo y Nacionalidad* (Madrid, 1984), pp. 43–4.

Perhaps no single thing reveals the profound rejection of the modern world that lay behind Basque nationalism better than the obituary offered by Sabino Arana Goiri for Victor Chávarri, the very personification of Basque industry, who died in 1900. While the rest of the Basque press praised Chávarri fulsomely and even the Socialists admitted his contributions, Arana called him 'a disastrous man for Vizcaya. Vizcaya is congratulating itself because its cruelest enemy has disappeared. The good sons of Vizcaya are celebrating too because they realize what his disappearance means.'

It is no exaggeration to say that Basque nationalism was Arana's creation. Arana came from a Carlist family and carried the theocratic orientation of Carlism into the new nationalism. In 1894 he founded the Centro Vasco and the next year the Vizcayan Provincial Council, which would be the forerunner of the Basque Nationalist Party (PNV). The main points of Arana's nationalist programme were independence for Vizcaya, which would be 'Roman, apostolic and Catholic in every manifestation of its internal life and relations with other peoples' and in which the state would be subordinated to the Church. It would also join with the other Basque regions, in both Spain and France, to form a Basque confederation which would be called Euskalerria, a name Arana had to invent himself as no single independent Basque state had ever existed.

At first Arana's nationalism was blatantly racist. His definition of the Basque nation was based on five components: race, language, laws, customs and historical personality, but the last four were clearly subordinate to the first. Potential members of the first nationalist society had to have four Basque surnames (that is have four Basque grandparents) and all candidates were carefully screened. Arana personally warned against intermarriage with non-Basques. He was particularly concerned to defend the purity of the race against the *maketo* (a pejorative word for non-Basque Spaniards) invasion which had been stimulated by industrialization.

As it had in Catalonia, the disaster of 1898 provided a political impetus for Basque nationalism. Arana himself was elected to the Vizcaya Diputación in 1898 but nationalism made little electoral progress thereafter. One major reason for this was that it did not receive the support of the region's industrial bourgeoisie. Unlike their Catalan counterparts, most leading Basque industrialists and financiers remained loyal to the constitutional monarchy and controlled the regional branches of the two dynastic parties. Indeed, following an upsurge in PNV electoral strength in 1917 and 1918 the two parties joined together in the Liga de Acción Monárquica, which successfully restored their political dominance.

There was, however, one segment of the bourgeoisie which did join the nationalists. This group, which was tied predominantly to the shipbuilding industry, came to nationalism between 1898 and 1902 and brought to it a more liberal orientation. Thereafter Basque nationalism was marked by a continual struggle between these liberal nationalists, 'who wanted to achieve a party organization which would let them direct a nationalist program which was compatible with the Constitution, and therefore which dropped independence as a goal', and the intransigent supporters of Arana's initial vision.[5]

Arana himself was increasingly influenced by the liberals and in 1902 stated that autonomy within the Spanish state was also an acceptable goal. However Arana died before he could make the definitive restatement of policy which he had promised and thus left a legacy of ambiguity which the PNV never resolved. As Corcuera Atienza notes, 'the fusion between the two sectors made possible the appearance of a mass party although it would always be possible to distinguish two blocs within it: the "radical nationalists" and the bourgeois regionalists. The history of nationalism . . . would be the history of the confrontations, separations and reunifications of these two blocs'.[6]

The nationalists were not totally deaf to the concerns of the Basque working class, or at least that part of it which was racially Basque, and in 1911 the Solidaridad de Obreros Vascos, SOV, a trade union close to the PNV, was founded. The SOV was based on the principles of nationalism, explicit anti-socialism and Catholic social doctrines. It did function as a genuine trade union although it tried to avoid strikes whenever possible. It grew slowly and by 1921 had only 2,200 members, many of them white-collar workers.

In 1921 the PNV, which had been renamed the Comunión Nacional Vasco (CNV), split. The younger members demanded a more radical stance and a greater concern for social questions and left to form a new party which they called the Partido Nacionalista Vasco (PNV). The Primo de Rivera regime banned all nationalist political activity although there was an important upsurge in cultural activity. In April 1930 the two nationalist parties patched up their differences and reunited as the PNV, and during the rest of the year nationalism was able to make some breakthroughs in the province of Guipúzcoa. However the PNV was very much a party of the right and did not get involved with the Republicans who were conspiring against the monarchy. As a result, despite its unprecedented strength, Basque nationalism entered the Republic politically isolated.

---

5. J. Corcuera Atienza, *Orígenes, Ideología y Organización del Nacionalismo Vasco, 1876–1904* (Madrid, 1979), pp. 586–7.
6. Ibid., p. 591.

THE SECOND REPUBLIC AND CATALONIA

During the Primo de Rivera regime Catalan republicanism gained strength at the expense of the Lliga. The most visible and popular of the numerous left-wing regionalist organizations was the separatist Estat Català led by a former army colonel, Francesc Macià. In exile in France he conspired with the CNT and in 1926 led an abortive invasion of Catalonia, for which he was put on public trial in Paris. Catalan Republicans were in touch with the Republican revolutionary committee in San Sebastián and in August 1930 committed themselves to the Republic in return for the promise that once a statute had been drafted and approved in a plebiscite it would be authorized by the Constituent Cortes. Despite this commitment, autonomy did not come swiftly nor did it enjoy an untroubled existence.

Macià returned to Spain in February 1931 and the next month chaired a 'Conference of the Left'. This brought together into the Esquerra Republicana Catalana, his own party, Lluis Companys' Partit Republica (with its base of support among the region's tenant farmers, the *rabassaires*), and a small group of social democrats around Joan Lluhí. The Esquerra won the municipal elections of April 1931 with 36 per cent of the vote, compared to 24 per cent each for the Lliga and the Radicals. On 14 April Companys proclaimed the Second Republic but an hour later Macià announced the creation of the 'Catalan State and Republic'. The Provisional Government in Madrid sent three ministers, two Catalan Republicans and a Socialist, by plane to Barcelona where they got Macià to agree to hold to the San Sebastián agreement in return for recognition of him as head of a provisional regional government, the Generalitat.

The Generalitat called an assembly of town councils which created a committee to draft a statute. The draft was put to a plebiscite on 2 August and received 99 per cent support. Two weeks later it was presented to Alcalá Zamora who introduced it to the Constituent Cortes as a government bill. However, debate did not start until May 1932 and then it proceeded slowly as the right filibustered and presented hundreds of amendments inside the Cortes and organized anti-Catalan demonstrations outside. It took four months to approve the eighteen articles and would have taken longer had not the failure of the Sanjurjo revolt on 10 August provided fresh impetus for all reform measures.

The autonomy statute which the Cortes approved was more limited than the draft it had received, especially in the key areas of education and finance. The regional government was granted authority over municipal government, local courts, civil law, public works, law and order, local finance and roads and bridges, and Catalan was recognized as an official language. However, Madrid retained control of the schools and instruction in Spanish remained obligatory. The Generalitat was free to set up its own schools in which instruction was in Catalan but its precarious financial base precluded this. The financial arrangement contained in the original draft would have given the Generalitat a budget of 233 million *pesetas* in 1931 but the actual statute gave it a budget of only 66 million. To make matters worse, the central government was very slow to actually transfer powers to the regional government. Still, despite these drawbacks, when Azaña went to Barcelona to present the statute he was given a hero's welcome.

The first elections for the regional government were held in November 1932. The Esquerra won a sweeping victory, taking sixty-seven of the eighty-five seats, although the 46 per cent of the vote it won was much less than it had received in the parliamentary elections of June 1931. As the Esquerra continued to govern Catalonia after the right came to power in Madrid in November 1933 the scene was set for a conflict. The transfer of powers took place at an even slower pace than it had under Azaña but the situation came to a head when the Generalitat passed its own agrarian reform law, the Law of Agricultural Contracts, in April 1934. The conflict over this law revealed that regional autonomy could not be separated from the other questions facing the Republic, especially the social question. As Albert Balcells comments:

> The *rabassaire* question was the nucleus of the crisis of the autonomous regime because the financial and landowning oligarchy considered it vital to smother agrarian reform in Catalonia at a time when it was being stopped in the rest of the country. It was essential to do away with an autonomy that allowed Catalonia to continue the reformist policies which the Spanish right wanted to end. The struggle for autonomy and the class struggle appeared to be clearly linked and the most intransigent Catalan landowners were forced to become centralists.[7]

The law was designed to allow the *rabassaires*, the Esquerra's single most important constituency, to buy any land they had been leasing for at least eighteen years. It was anticipated that some 70,000 would have been able to do so. Under pressure from the landowners' lobby, the Institut Agrari de San Isidre, the Lliga requested the central government to challenge the constitutionality of the law and on 8 June the Court of Constitutional Guarantees made a controversial finding against the Generalitat on the grounds that it had no authority to legislate on agrarian matters. Companys, who had become head of the Catalan government after the death of Maciá in December 1933, responded by having the law passed again. At this

7. Albert Balcells, *Historia Contemporánea de Cataluña* (Barcelona, 1983), pp. 277–8.

point Prime Minister Samper was prepared to compromise, as was the Lliga. However, the hardliners among the landowners were not and they abandoned the Lliga to set up a Catalan branch of the CEDA, which had been demanding that the Court's decision be enforced. The issue was settled in September when the Generalitat revised the law to the satisfaction of the central government.

This peace did not last long. When a new government which included three members of the CEDA was announced on 4 October Companys found himself in a difficult position. Facing a general strike which was spreading through the region and under pressure from the intransigent nationalists in his own party, Companys declared the Catalan state of the Federal Spanish Republic and called on the Spanish left to establish a provisional government in Barcelona. Companys did not arm the workers or call out the *escamots*, the Esquerra militia, and he and his government surrendered within a few hours.

The events of October allowed the Spanish right and its Catalan allies to take their revenge. The autonomy statute was suspended indefinitely and most town councils were deposed. The Law of Agricultural Contracts was annulled and some 1,400 tenants evicted. Companys and his ministers were tried by a military court and sentenced to thirty years. In May 1935 martial law was lifted and the Generalitat was allowed to function, although under the control of a series of governors-general appointed by Madrid.

As in the rest of the country, the election of February 1936 was contested in Catalonia by two blocs: the Frent d'Ordre (Order Front) headed by the Lliga, and the Frent d'Esquerra headed by the Esquerra and including a number of nationalist and working-class parties, although not the CNT.

The programme of the left emphasized the restoration of the statute and full democratic rights, amnesty for political prisoners and the return to their land of the *rabassaires* evicted after 6 October 1934. The left won forty-one of the fifty-four seats; the Lliga took twelve but its partners of the Spanish right got none. The statute was restored on 1 March and the Law of Agricultural Contracts immediately afterwards. At the beginning of July the Generalitat once again took over responsibility for public order. Police officials appointed by the right were replaced by men loyal to the government who designed a plan to control a potential military revolt. Their preparations were well made: when the military uprising did come it was defeated in Barcelona by the combination of a loyal police force and the workers' militias. Ironically, though, that same revolt, which claimed to be intended to prevent revolution, triggered a sweeping revolution whose epicentre was in Catalonia.

THE SECOND REPUBLIC AND THE BASQUE COUNTRY

The achievement of autonomy for the Basque region proved to be much slower and more difficult than it had been for Catalonia. Although Basque autonomy was an issue more or less continually during the Republic – and was taken up by the left as well as by the PNV – a statute was not granted until October 1936, almost three months after the civil war had begun. This delay was due to uncertainties over the meaning of Basque autonomy, what Juan Pablo Fusi calls 'the absence of a consensus over what constituted the "Basque difference", of a consensus over the political and territorial idea of Euzkadi', complicated by the ideological differences and competing interests of the main political forces in the region.[8]

In Catalonia the right was regionalist and the dominant force on the left, the anarchosyndicalists, did not participate in electoral politics and thus did not represent a political threat to regionalism. Neither of these conditions held in the Basque Provinces. There the right, in both its monarchist and Carlist variants, opposed regional autonomy while the left, Socialists and Republicans, had a strong, if geographically concentrated, electoral presence and supported autonomy but only so long as it was consistent with their own beliefs.

Unlike the Catalan Esquerra, the PNV did not participate in the conspiracy against the monarchy or form part of the San Sebastián coalition. (A non-Catholic and avowedly democratic minority which had split off from the PNV at the end of 1930 to form Acción Nacionalista Vasca did take part but it never amounted to much.) This meant that the Provisional Government had no committment to the Basques, although Indalecio Prieto had raised the question at San Sebastián. Both the Socialists and the Republicans perceived the PNV as right-wing and clerical, that is fundamentally opposed to the laic, democratic republic they were trying to create, although by 1931 this perception was no longer accurate. Under a new generation of leaders, of whom José Antonio de Aguirre was the most important, the PNV had become a 'multi-dimensional party' whose policies were approaching those of Christian Democracy.[9]

---

8. Fusi, *El País Vasco*, p. 171. Fusi, 'The Basque Question, 1931–1939', in *Revolution and War in Spain*, ed. by Paul Preston (London, 1989), p. 189.
9. Fusi, 'The Basque Question, 1931–1939', in P. Preston, ed., *Revolution and War*, p. 189.

At a more down-to-earth level, neither the Republicans and Socialists on the one hand nor the PNV on the other were prepared to accept autonomy in a form which left the other in control of the region. At the same time, the Carlists were opposed to the autonomy demanded by the PNV and advocated instead a return to the traditional autonomy of the *fueros*.

The first draft statute was written at the initiative of the PNV. Their idea was to bypass national politics by putting the process in the hands of the town councils, most of which were controlled by the nationalists. The draft, which was completed by May, called for the government of the 'Basque state' to have jurisdiction over a wide range of matters, including control over the police and the army in the region. This provoked political tensions which were only exacerbated when, on 7 June, the PNV made two changes to the draft: the residence requirement for Basque citizenship was raised from two to seven years and relations with the Vatican were added to the powers of the regional government.

The revised draft was discussed and approved at a meeting of the region's mayors on 14 June, although the mayors of the four capitals – which represented 30 per cent of the population – and of other large centres such as Eibar did not attend. On 22 September the 427 mayors who had voted for the draft presented it to Prime Minister Alcalá Zamora but three days later it was rendered unconstitutional by an amendment to the Constitution, presented by Alcalá Zamora himself, which reserved relations with the Vatican for the central government. That the PNV had fought the June 1931 elections in alliance with the Carlists and had included the draft statute as part of their platform only convinced an already sceptical left that the statute was decidedly anti-Republican.

But the left was not the enemy of Basque autonomy. On 8 December the government had announced that the initiative for developing a statute lay with the administrative committees of the provincial Deputations, which were controlled by the Republicans and Socialists. A committee was formed which included representatives of the four Deputations plus four Republicans, three Socialists, one nationalist, one traditionalist and one independent Catholic; and by late March a new draft had been produced. This draft provided a more limited authority for the regional government than had the first and it contained an explicit statement of conformity to the principles of the Constitution of the Republic. By the end of April the draft had been approved by both the mayors and the Deputations but at an assembly called for 19 June in Pamplona a new problem arose: 123 of the 267 towns in Navarre, accounting for 55 per cent of the population of the province, voted against it.

This paralysed the process until September 1932 when, in the enthusiasm generated by the passage of the Catalan statute, it was relaunched by Prieto. However the draft was not put to a plebiscite of the town councils until August 1933, when it was approved by 234 of 282, and to a referendum until November. The delay was due to political reasons. The left wanted 'an autonomy similar to that of Catalonia: identified with the Republic and in their hands', not those of the PNV.[10] The committee which drafted the new statute did not include any nationalists and the new civil governors appointed to the region began to harass the PNV. Tensions between the PNV and the left reached the point of violent street clashes.

The left paid for this strategy. On 5 November, 84 per cent voted yes in the autonomy referendum and in the national election held two weeks later the PNV took 13 of 17 seats in Vizcaya, Guipúzcoa and Alava while the left was reduced to two. (At the same time, the Carlists won ten seats in the region.) The statute was presented to the Cortes on 21 December 1933 and a parliamentary committee, chaired by Aguirre, began to consider it three weeks later. At this point the process ran into a new obstacle. A traditionalist deputy from Alava claimed that since only 46 per cent of the electorate in his province had voted for the draft in the referendum, consideration of the statute could not proceed. This led to prolonged debate and a decision that a new referendum was required in Alava.

More important than this specific decision, however, was the revelation of the hostility of both the local traditionalist right and the Spanish national right to Basque autonomy. This revelation was greatest with regard to the CEDA: its policy on the issue had never been clearly defined but it now showed itself to be uncompromisingly hostile to nationalist aspirations. This meant that the Radicals, who depended on the CEDA to remain in power, could no longer court the PNV and the statute was not brought to a vote during the life of the second Cortes.

Even though the PNV was not involved in the insurrection of October 1934 and voted confidence in the Lerroux government immediately afterwards, the autonomy process remained stalled. In the autumn of 1935 the two principal leaders of the right made their opposition to Basque autonomy clear. Gil Robles stated his support for a traditionalist solution while José Calvo Sotelo attacked nationalism head on, claiming that it was based on a hatred of Spain and Spaniards and making his famous remark that he preferred a red Spain to a broken one ('roja antes que rota').

The PNV found itself isolated in the election of February 1936. The Popular Front attacked its clericalism and its support of Lerroux while the right criticized its 'separatism'. Facing a challenge for its Catholic constitu-

---

10. Juan Pablo Fusi, *El Problema Vasco en la Segunda República* (Madrid, 1979), p. 94.

ency, the PNV responded with a campaign which emphasized its Catholic and conservative nature. The nationalists lost votes but managed to hold on to nine seats, compared to seven for the Popular Front and eight for the right.

At the urging of Prieto, who hoped to steal the issue for the left, the Popular Front had included autonomy in its programme. After the election Prieto once again pushed the issue, but this time in cooperation with the PNV. He personally chaired the parliamentary committee which was created on 16 April – and on which Aguirre sat – and urged that the 1933 draft statute be simplified in order to expedite its passage. Even so, problems arose over financial issues and the question was handed to a team of experts who reported early in July. The statute was almost completely ready when the civil war broke out; the only important change that was made before Basque autonomy was finally proclaimed on 1 October 1936 was the creation of a Provisional Government to remain in office while the war lasted. The government was headed by Aguirre and nationalists held the most important posts as the exigencies of war forced the Republic to accept a Basque autonomy controlled by the PNV.

NAVARRE

The defection of Navarre from the Basque autonomy process in 1932 revealed the complexities and ambiguities of Basque regionalism, ambiguities which extended to the very definition of the boundaries of Euzkadi. Although the northern part of the province was culturally Basque, less than a quarter of the population was Basque speaking. The weakness of Basque feeling was revealed in the weakness of the PNV in Navarre during the Republic. It received no more than 10 per cent of the vote compared to 70 per cent for the backward-looking supporters of the Catholic monarchy and the ancient regional charter, the Carlists.

More important, though, the changing relation of Carlism to Basque autonomy revealed the interrelationship of the major issues during the Republic and the primacy of the social question. The Navarrese Carlists initially supported the inclusion of their province in the proposed autonomous Basque region and, as we have mentioned, formed an electoral alliance with the PNV in the spring of 1931. However, once it became clear that regional autonomy could not be used to defend the position of the Church the Carlists withdrew their support. As Martin Blinkhorn observes:

The position of the Navarrese Carlist notables in 1932 is easily understood. Most of the notables, plus a considerable proportion of the rank and file, were becoming daily more involved in other, wider issues for which autonomy seemed to offer no solution. Whether the abandonment of the autonomy statute's religious clauses was the reason or merely the pretext for the Navarrese Carlists' breach with the Basque Nationalists their concern for the Church was sincere and their growing preference for conducting its defence in the national arena quite logical.[11]

Religion was not the only issue with which the province's elite was concerned and which could best – and perhaps only – be pursued at the national level. The other was land. Both legislation on rural leases and the growth of the FNTT (the Socialist agricultural workers' union) in the southern region of the province were cause for concern, and the Carlists reacted in two ways. The first was to carry the struggle, ideological and otherwise, against 'Marxism' into the *ribera* itself. The second was to cooperate more closely with groups in other parts of the country which shared these concerns. In turn, the new primacy of social issues changed the tone of Carlism itself, which 'came to embrace a social conservatism of a flavour not previously characteristic of [it]'.[12]

This led the Carlists of Navarre to cooperate eagerly with the military conspiracy being organized by General Emilio Mola who, after February 1936, was stationed in the provincial capital of Pamplona. It also led them to rebel against the national leadership of the movement in order to do so. The national leader, Fal Conde, insisted that Mola accept Carlist demands as the condition for Carlist support of the rising. These demands were extensive and included the use of the Carlist flag, the immediate abolition of the Republican Constitution and of Republican religious legislation, and the creation of a corporatist state. Mola refused to accede to these demands but the deadlock was broken by an initiative of the Navarrese Junta which indicated its willingness to arrive at a separate agreement with the generals and did so on 12 July.

In effect, the Carlists in Navarre did a deal with the leaders of the military revolt. They abandoned their nominal goal of a decentralized Catholic monarchy in return for control over affairs in the province and the opportunity to create the harmonious and Catholic society of which they spoke. However, as Blinkhorn has observed, this

> exposed the contradictory nature of the social-Catholicism to which most leading Carlists subscribed. For social harmony had been restored not by attack-

---

11. Martin Blinkhorn, 'War on Two Fronts: Politics and Society in Navarre, 1931–1936', in P. Preston, ed., *Revolution and War*, p. 73.
12. Ibid., p. 75.

ing the disease of social and economic inequality but by eliminating its symptoms; it was based not upon the religiously inspired consensus of which social-Catholics fruitlessly dreamed, but on the shedding of blood and the silencing of opposition; and it was protected not within a framework of decentralization such as Carlists advocated but under the auspices of an authoritarian, centralizing and oppressive state.[13]

Contradiction there was, but this should be little surprise. The Navarrese elite, as had its Catalan counterpart, found itself in the position of having to weigh its desire for home rule against its concern to maintain the social and economic status quo. For the Navarrese, as for the Catalans, the priorities were clear.

13. Ibid., p. 81.

CHAPTER FOUR
The Military

The Spanish Civil War began with the failure of a carefully planned military revolt. The conspirators expected the government to collapse immediately; they certainly had not anticipated the massive popular resistance which turned a military coup into a civil war. Neither their actions nor their expectations were unusual, for military intervention in politics had been one of the characteristic features of Spanish political history ever since 1814. Spain's contributions to the political vocabulary in the nineteenth century – *guerrilla, caudillo* and *pronunciamiento* – reflect this quite clearly.

However, it is essential to keep in mind that the rising of 17 July was far from receiving the unanimous support of the military and the para-military forces of public order, the Civil Guard and the Assault Guard. A large number of officers, including many senior generals and the commander of the Civil Guard, remained loyal to the government and in some places, of which Barcelona was the most important, this loyalty was crucial in the initial defeat of the rebellion.

Military reform had been one of the most important areas of activity of the governments of the Republic in 1931 and 1932 and the decrees, for which Manuel Azaña was responsible, generated a considerable amount of anger and discontent within the officer corps. However, the rising of 17 July 1936 cannot realistically be seen as a corporate response to this perceived attack on military rights, rather, the revolt must be analysed as the work of a minority of officers connected with right wing political elements who used the fear of the breakdown of public order, social revolution and separatism to mobilize broad segments of the officer corps behind a coup. The actual military reforms were much less important than the rhetoric about them which centred on the graphic language, this time taken out of context and distorted, of Manuel Azaña.

A HISTORY OF INTERVENTION

The most characteristic form of military intervention in politics in the nineteenth century was the *pronunciamiento*, in which individual officers rose against the existing government on behalf of an opposing ideological principle: absolutism, moderate or progressive liberalism, or republicanism. Julio Busquets has documented forty-one such risings between 1814 and 1875, of which twenty-seven were liberal. The goal was not to replace civilian rule by military rule, but one ideological system with another. Individual officers did assume positions of power but there were no military dictatorships in nineteenth-century Spain. Even during the regency of General Espartero (1840–43) there was always an elected civilian government. The army was the final arbiter of political disputes; it was not yet the guardian of the national identity.

The frequency of these military risings was due to three factors, one having to do with the conditions of military life, the other two with the nature of political life. Career prospects for officers were dismal throughout most of the nineteenth century. The wars of the early years of the century: Napoleonic Wars, colonial wars of independence and the Carlist War, created a huge officer corps, not all of whose members could be kept on full pay at all times. The officer corps was further expanded after each important political crisis: in 1843, 1854–56, 1868 and 1873–75. Between 1868 and 1875 it doubled in size. By 1874 there was one officer to every ten soldiers, compared to ratios of one to between seventeen and twenty-four in other European armies. Wages were low, and often in arrears, and promotion was slow unless speeded up by favouritism. The quickest way to move up the hierarchy was through being on the winning side in a military revolt.

The army was particularly oversupplied with generals. Between 1827 and 1875 there were never fewer than 436 and from 1844 to 1857 there were at least 600. In 1862, 308 of the 550 generals on active service lacked a command and some critics pointed out that Spain had enough generals to staff all the armies of the continent. Even in 1896, the year in which the number of generals was at its lowest at 296, the Spanish army had more generals than those of Britain, Germany, Italy or Austria-Hungary.

This explains why officers were attracted to insurrections but not why these took place so frequently. The large number of coups and attempted coups was basically due to the two major weaknesses of constitutional government in Spain. The first was that the threat to liberalism represented by the Carlist War (1833–40) meant that the survival of constitutionalism depended on the success of the generals. Men like Espartero and Narváez were, in a literal sense, the protectors and guarantors of the system. Second, the limited franchise instituted by the moderates and their widespread use of electoral fraud, as well as Isabella II's dislike of the progressives, meant that this group was continually out of power and left without any constitutional means of achieving it.

The Restoration of the Bourbons in 1875 began a new period. Until the First Republic the Spanish military had been liberal but the chaos of 1873–74 – the abolition of military service, the purges of monarchist officers and the disintegration of discipline which had bred mutiny and desertion, led to a new conservatism. There was a new generation of leading generals which was especially sensitive to the dangers of disorder, more so once the organized labour movement got underway.

Cánovas del Castillo was determined to bring the military into the new system as the defender of the social order: 'The army will remain for a long time, perhaps forever, the robust support of the social order and an invincible dike against the illegal attempts of the proletariat, which achieves nothing by violence but the useless shedding of its own blood'. Cánovas achieved his goal by institutionalizing the influence of the military: leading officers received promotions and titles, the captains–general became senators by right and other officers by royal appointment. The Ministry of War was left to military men and military affairs remained outside the control of civilian political leaders. Cánovas also invented the soldier-king, something new for Spain, in order to provide a leadership figure. Alfonso XIII in particular saw himself as a military man and gave officers a prominent role at court during his reign.

At the same time the officer corps became ever more self-contained and homogeneous as the sons of officers were favoured and the social base became more restricted. Spanish officers found themselves isolated from – and often in conflict with – the society they were supposed to protect. The cadet's experience was similar to that of the seminarian:

> The age of entry into the military academy was usually below eighteen and many had entered much younger. Much of their previous time had been devoted to cramming for the entrance examination. They had neither served in the ranks nor enjoyed any liberal education . . . the army officer was out of sympathy with modern trends, though he had no reason to be so; was afraid of working class and regionalist manifestations of progressivism . . . and because the army was all he had, was often forced into undisciplined defence of his personal career interests.[1]

This situation was exacerbated by the experiences of the 1890s in which

---

1. Michael Alpert, 'Soldiers, Politics and War', in *Revolution and War*, ed. by Paul Preston (London, 1989), p. 204.

the army fought two colonial wars – in Cuba and the Philippines – and was totally humiliated by the United States in the Spanish-American War of 1898. The military turned in on itself even more, blaming the corruption of politicians and their interference in military affairs for the defeats, resenting the press for criticizing its failures and feeling abandoned by public opinion. A new military ideology emerged which presented the army as the custodian of the basic values of the state and the arbiter of national life. It carried with it a highly charged nationalism and a radical rejection of regionalist demands. (That there were very few Catalan officers only intensified this distrust of regionalism.)

After 1898 the army began to intervene in politics once again, but in a new way. Instead of revolts in favour of one political group or another, officers acted to apply pressure on the government in the name of military interests. As Gabriel Cardona puts it, 'In the twentieth century when the bayonets played politics it was a corporate act of the officer corps.'[2] As early as 1895 a group of uniformed officers attacked the offices of two newspapers which had published criticisms of the army, forcing the government to resign, but the first significant episode came in 1905. In November 200 officers destroyed the print shops of the satirical paper *Cu-Cut*, for which they were congratulated by comrades across the country, including the Captain-General of Seville. The government resigned and its successor gave in to the pressure of military opinion and passed the Law of Jurisdictions which made 'insults' against the army offences to be tried in military courts.

The most important instance of this new military intervention came with the Juntas de Defensa movement in 1917. The juntas, trade union-type organizations of junior officers in provincial garrisons, were first set up in 1916 in response to the announcement of a military reform programme. The reforms would have eliminated 3,000 officers through early retirements, and imposed aptitude tests for promotions. Junior infantry officers, whose careers depended on the strict functioning of the closed scale of promotion by seniority alone, organized themselves to protest against these tests as well as to demand pay increases and an end to the merit promotions enjoyed by those officers fighting in Morocco, known as the *africanistas*. Many of these officers had made lightning careers in the Moroccan war as battlefield heroics, usually at the head of specially formed native units, allowed them to circumvent the seniority system. Franco, who became the youngest general in Europe since Napoleon, jumped 2,438

---

2. Gabriel Cardona, *El Poder militar en la España contemporánea hasta la guerra civil* (Madrid, 1983), p. 50.

places. These *africanista* officers would play the leading roles on the Nationalist side during the civil war.

In May 1917 the government ordered the juntas to disband but they refused and in the showdown the government retreated and legalized them. For the next three years the juntas acted as a virtual parallel power, their influence enhanced by the upsurge of social conflict in Barcelona and the rural south between 1917 and 1921. The triumph of the juntas came, in Boyd's words, 'because the King and his government were fearful of losing military support at a moment of political and social crisis'.[3]

The splits within the army surfaced frequently during the Primo de Rivera dictatorship. Primo had never been a supporter of the Moroccan War and at first he withdrew troops from the colony. This reluctance to prosecute the war was strongly criticized by the *africanistas*, who were not at all shy in letting Primo know their views and some of whom were engaged in plotting a coup. Their misgivings were assuaged when, in cooperation with the French, Primo ordered an offensive which culminated in the victorious landing at Alhucemas and a round of promotions.

But the *africanistas* were not Primo's only problem. From the beginning of the dictatorship he had manipulated senior promotions and this antagonized many officers. Then his attempt to impose an open scale of promotions, or at least keep a number of positions at each rank open for specially selected officers, brought him into direct conflict with the artillery corps. The Artillery was the closest knit of all the corps and had very strong traditions which included absolute adherence to the closed scale. In February 1926 Primo tried to make special promotions inside the corps which responded by going on strike. Primo suspended all the officers although they were later reinstated. Artillery officers were active in the February 1928 coup attempt organized by former Prime Minister Sánchez Guerra and in response Primo dissolved the corps.

Primo was finally forced to resign in January 1930, faced by the loss of confidence of senior commanders and a growing conspiracy in which artillery officers were once again active. In the fifteen months between Primo's resignation and the declaration of the Republic, the governments of General Berenguer and Admiral Aznar attempted to pacify the military opinion Primo had antagonized, but to little effect. The restoration of the closed scale did succeed in drawing artillery officers out of the Republican Military Association which was being organized by Ramón Franco, but the whole experience of the dictatorship had cost the monarchy dearly, contributing decisively to what Gabriel Maura would call the 'loss of

---

3. Carolyn Boyd, *Praetorian Politics in Liberal Spain* (Chapel Hill, North Carolina, 1979), p. 64.

monarchist cohesion in the army'.[4] When the results of the election of 12 April 1931 became known the King found that only a minority of officers were prepared to support him and this convinced Alfonso to stand aside for the Republic.

THE SECOND REPUBLIC AND THE MILITARY

The first governments of the Republic were more active in prosecuting military reform than any of their predecessors. These reforms were the work of Manuel Azaña, who was Minister of War from 14 April 1931 to 12 September 1933. Azaña had long been a student of military affairs: he had observed the First World War from the French and Italian fronts and in 1919 had published a major study of French military policy, *Estudios de política militar francesa*. For Azaña the French experience had tremendous relevance to Spain for it showed that in a democracy the military and civil society could enjoy a beneficial relationship, in which a militarily effective army was under civilian control and respectful of civilian rights and in which the officer corps was not a closed caste. This was a total contrast to the situation in Spain, where the army was not an efficient military machine and an officer corps which was isolated from society freely intervened in politics. As War Minister, Azaña set out to reshape the Spanish military according to the French model and although he was able to make some improvements, especially in reducing the size of the officer corps, he did not manage to realize his overall objective. Along the way, however, he antagonized a good section of military opinion. As Ben-Ami has commented, 'the army he created was neither revolutionary nor Republican . . . it was the style of Azaña, rather than the content of his reforms, which was new and revolutionary'.[5]

Azaña began to act immediately on becoming Minister, declaring an amnesty for those officers involved in the attempted Republican insurrection of December 1930. On 21 April he issued a decree which required all officers to take an oath of loyalty to the Republic within four days. Those who chose not to would be retired. Although no exact figures are available it appears that virtually all officers took the oath; Michael Alpert has found only six who refused.

Azaña also made a number of changes in key commands, although there was not a widespread purge. Azaña was no revolutionary and always took

4. Gabriel Maura, *Así cayó Alfonso XIII* (Madrid, 1948), p. 395.
5. Shlomo Ben-Ami, *The Origins of the Second Republic* (Oxford, 1978), p. 235.

a legalistic approach, 'preferring to deal with the generals than with the most fervent Republicans who were usually captains and majors'. Indeed, the ardently pro-Republican airman Ramón Franco (younger brother of the future *caudillo*) was arrested in the summer of 1931 for wanting to make the air force the military bulwark of the new regime and Azaña was relieved to be rid of him. Five of the generals in charge of military regions were replaced by others who had been victimized by Primo de Rivera and Mola was replaced as Director-General of Security. Sanjurjo was kept on as commander of the Guardia Civil and was given the additional posts of High Commissioner in Morocco and Commander-in-Chief in Africa. It was precisely the failure to purge the officer corps which obliged Azaña to rely on this tactic of 'combinations of generals' in order to maintain a 'precarious control' over the military.[6]

What proved to be the most controversial of Azaña's reforms was the one directed at the most intractable problem of the Spanish military, the excessive number of officers. This had been the perpetual but illusive goal of many Spanish war ministers. It was 'a necessary prerequisite for the restructuring of the country's armed forces'.[7] The decree was published on 25 April 1931. The prologue declared that the reforms consisted of two parts: a long-term reform of the entire military structure which would be carried out by the Cortes; and immediate, urgently needed actions. The most pressing was a reduction in the number of officers from the existing level of 21,996 plus 258 generals.

Officers were given the opportunity of retiring on full pay within thirty days and all generals on active duty could pass to the reserve, also on full pay. The officers who did retire would continue to receive any special pay to which they were entitled for holding General Staff diplomas or certain medals. All the positions left vacant would be amortized. Finally, if after thirty days the number of retirements was not sufficient the Ministry of War would undertake any necessary forced retirements. The decree was a generous one but its overall generosity was undermined by the final article. Even worse, this proved to have been unnecessary as the period for requesting voluntary retirement was extended a number of times and in the end no one was forcibly retired.

What were the results of the decree? The first retirements were announced at the end of May and new announcements were made regularly thereafter. By the beginning of July, when the first extension to the period for requesting retirement had ended, 7,613 officers (37 per cent of those on active duty) had put in their request. These included half of the generals,

---

6. Cardona, *El Poder*, pp. 175, 186.
7. Michael Alpert, *La Reforma militar de Manuel Azaña* (Madrid, 1982), p. 133.

two-thirds of the colonels and lieutenant colonels, half the majors, 40 per cent of the captains, 37 per cent of the lieutenants and almost half the junior lieutenants. The infantry and cavalry, where the excess of officers had been greatest, lost about half their officers, compared to some 40 per cent for the artillery, engineers and technical arms.

The retirement law was undoubtedly a success. The officer corps was reduced by 40 per cent to 12,373 and the number was kept at around 13,000 throughout 1935. However the decree provoked controversy and complaint from both right and left. The main criticism from the left was that Azaña had not purged monarchist and other potentially disloyal elements. The complaints of the right and of the military press were of a different order. The first was that the law was a decree and not an act of parliament and that the limited period officers were given to make their decision forced them to do so without knowing the nature of the overall military reform. Once it became clear that large numbers of officers were prepared to take early retirement the criticisms changed to focus on the possible problems that such massive and indiscriminate reforms might occasion.

One of the other main thrusts of Azaña's military policy was the democratization of the officer corps. It was possible to become an officer by being promoted through the ranks but the Spanish army was unique in Europe in that it maintained two distinct classes of officer; those trained at the academies and those promoted through the ranks. Azaña ended this in August with a law which converted the latter into fully-fledged officers, and in September 1932 complemented it with the Ley de Reclutamientos y Ascensos de la Oficialidad (Law on Recruitment and Promotion to Officers) which reserved 60 per cent of the places in the military academies for NCOs and required that those who filled the remaining places serve six months in the ranks.

Azaña was also concerned to reshape military education, to reduce the time spent in the academies while improving the general education of the cadets. The first step was to restrict access to the academies, as fewer officers would be needed in the new, streamlined army. On 30 June 1931 he closed the General Military Academy in Saragossa; dismissed its director, General Franco; and reorganized the five other academies into three: one for infantry and cavalry, one for artillery and one for the medical branch. All cadets would take all except specialized corps courses together. This was intended to reduce the inter-corps rivalries which had caused so many problems in the past.

Azaña also acted in the conflictual and treacherous matter of promotions, and in the process earned himself the enmity of a number of officers. His policy was based on the 1918 law and on 5 June 1931 he issued a decree which revised all promotions for wartime merit which did not meet the requirements of that law. The result of the revision was announced in January 1933: 148 promotions were recognized, 365 annulled. Among the losers were Goded and Franco: the latter was dropped from the top to two-thirds of the way down the list of brigadiers although neither he nor anyone else was actually demoted. In November 1932 the government passed the Recruitment and Promotion Law which eliminated promotions by merit and selection, although the rigidities of strict seniority were mitigated somewhat by the institution of exams to move from lieutenant to captain and from colonel to general.

The last major area in which the government acted was to assert civilian control over the military and remove the army from non-military affairs. Only three days after the declaration of the Republic the Law of Jurisdictions was repealed, a move which was welcomed by the military press. In May Azaña issued a decree which ended the jurisdiction of military courts over offences committed by soldiers in the civilian sphere and crimes committed by civilians against military men. The decree also dissolved the Supreme Military Council and transferred its responsibilities to a special branch of the Supreme Court. On 16 June 1931, one last step in this area was the abolition by decree of the position of Captain-General. The Captain General had been the supreme military official in each of the eight military regions and was also superior to the civilian officials. On numerous occasions these officers had used their authority to bring a military solution to political or social conflicts.

However, these measures to demilitarize the enforcement of public order were not really effective. As Manuel Ballbé has observed, from the beginning of the nineteenth century on the civilian administration was very weak and political leaders, 'unable to provide a minimally efficient organization of their own to sustain the state', had constructed a 'specific authoritarian state structure' which was characterized by 'the preponderance of military judicial institutions and methods in the administration . . . specifically with regard to security and the police'.[8]

All the governments of the Second Republic retained this proclivity to use the military, and the militarized police forces, to maintain public order instead of working to create a professional, non-military police. The Guardia de Asalto, which was created in October 1931 and intended as a loyally Republican force, shared the military character of the Guardia Civil. Military men continued to dominate important police posts, such as Commander of the Carabineros, Director-General of Security and even

---

8. Manual Ballbé, *Orden público y militarismo en la España constitucional, 1812–1983* (Madrid, 1983), pp. 21–2.

some Civil Governorships. And although the Law of Jurisdictions had been repealed its spirit remained very much a presence: offences such as insulting the military or the Guardia Civil and acts committed by military men on active duty, including killing citizens, remained under military jurisdiction and in instances of conflict between civil and military jurisdictions the Supreme Court often ruled in favour of the latter.

The Public Order Law, the work of the Republican-Socialist coalition, contributed in a major way to continuing the militarization of policing and, consequently, the politicization of the military. The law gave the government the authority to declare any of three stages of alert under which it could deport people up to 250 kilometres from their homes, demand prior censorship of the press and special permission for meetings, and make arrests freely. Under a state of war the military assumed supreme authority. From virtually the very day of the law's passage, in October 1933, until January 1936 there was an almost permanent state of alert, alarm or war. 'As in all previous periods, the maintenance of public order was given over to purely military techniques. This meant that the Army was in the forefront of internal civil disputes. Neither the government nor the opposition was prepared to abandon this dynamic to which they had become so accustomed.'[9] A state of alarm was declared on 17 February 1936 after the victory of the Popular Front. It was retained by Azaña when he came to power two days later and remained constantly in effect until the civil war began on 17 July.

Under the centre-right governments in power from November 1933 to November 1935 military reform came to a virtual halt, while some of Azaña's measures were watered down or reversed. Lerroux's war minister after January 1934 was Diego Hidalgo, a notary with little interest in military matters. He immediately restored a quarter of the positions which Azaña had eliminated, but did little else. The most active war minister of the period was Gil Robles, who came to the office in May 1935. Shocked by the events of October 1934 and disappointed by the refusal of Franco and other generals to consider a coup afterwards, he devoted his efforts to making the army an effective instrument of domestic repression. Liberal officers were replaced by *africanistas* while anti-Republican officers were brought into the highest posts: Mola as Commander in Morocco, Goded as Inspector General, the fervent monarchist Fanjul as Under-Secretary and Franco as Chief of the General Staff. Gil Robles also initiated a major rearmament programme and restored the General Military Academy. Preston concludes that 'it would be reasonable to suggest that, not least in

9. Ibid., pp. 363–4.

73

his choice of staff, Gil Robles did as much as possible to prepare the army for a potential rising'.[10]

Following the victory of the Popular Front in February 1936 Azaña appointed his long time collaborator General Masquelet as Minister of War. Masquelet continued the policy of moving suspected conspirators out of key posts, so that Mola was sent to Pamplona and Franco to the Canary Islands, while Goded was left in the Balearics. That, however, was as far as the government was prepared to go and it was certainly much less than Gil Robles had done to shape the army to his liking. The Republican officers' organization, UMRA, presented the government with a list of over 300 officers to be displaced but no action was taken. The government showed no inclination to act against a possible coup and no important conspirator was ever stripped of his command. Perhaps, as Cardona suggests, Azaña 'was convinced that three years of "the supremacy of the civil power" had neutralized a historical problem and that his reforms had transformed the military. The government preferred to believe the excuses and promises of loyalty of Yagüe, Franco and Mola.'[11]

MILITARY POLITICS

If that is what Azaña believed he was dead wrong. It does, however, reveal the crucial difference between Azaña and Gil Robles: 'Azaña's whole object was to distance the military from government policy and party politics. The Radicals and the CEDA sought to associate the Army with a specific government policy by presenting it as the only one which respected the interests of the Army.'[12] Azaña was too much the legalist to approach the army from a partisan position, even when he had the information to have done so, whereas the right was quick to turn to the military to act against the Republic. This can be seen in the distortion and manipulation of the speech Azaña gave on 6 June 1931 in Valencia. In describing the new Constitution, which was then being prepared, he said that those interest groups which had controlled the state would be destroyed:

> We must smash the personal, economic and other conspiracies which have monopolized the resources of the nation for their own benefit; the government must dismantle them and I assure you that if I at any time form part of the government I will apply to this task the same energy and resolution I have already given to smashing other things equally threatening to the Republic.

10. Paul Preston, *The Coming of the Spanish Civil War* (London, 1983), p. 158.
11. Cardona, *El Poder*, p. 239.
12. E. Espín, 'El Panorama militar', in *Revista del Occidente*, 1981, p. 54.

Almost two months later the military press began to cite this speech as an attack on the army as an institution and in August General Fanjul mentioned it in the Cortes. This became the basis of a campaign of personal defamation against Azaña, who was accused, among other things, of being a homosexual and having been thrown out of the military academy for being one. Azaña's remark about smashing other dangers to the Republic was, perhaps, ambiguous – surely he was talking about removing the military as a political actor – but the idea of smashing the army was inconsistent with all his ideas and actions.

Some monarchist generals began conspiring almost immediately after the declaration of the Republic and by the late summer of 1931 there were also rumours that Radical leader Alejandro Lerroux was plotting with Sanjurjo. In February 1932 Sanjurjo, who had been angered by the brutal killing of four of his Civil Guards in the village of Castilblanco on 31 December 1931, was transferred to the Carabineros. Military discontent grew during the debates over the Catalan autonomy statute which was presented to the army by the right as an assault on the unity of the Fatherland. Sanjurjo's plot was a poorly organized blending of a number of conspiracies and this was reflected in the lack of clarity in its aims: some wanted to restore the monarchy, others wanted a conservative Republic run by men such as Lerroux and Gabriel Maura. When the coup was launched on 10 August it was a total failure as very few officers answered the call, although many more were involved in the conspiracy than showed their hand.

The failure of the *sanjurjada* did nothing to discourage further conspiracies although it did make clear the need for more careful arrangements. Late in 1933 the Unión Militar Español (UME) was set up with the aim of putting together such a well planned movement. One of its primary goals, but one which remained elusive, was to attract the support of prestigious generals such as Franco. At first the UME was neither a well organized nor a politically coherent body. According to Stanley Payne:

> The UME's structure was decentralized, even anarchic and its members drawn almost entirely from junior and middle rank officers. There was no precise agreement on aims, which seem to have varied from cell to cell. Some UME groups were concerned about professional perquisites and others about protecting the Fatherland from leftist revolution, while a few established close contact with monarchist conspirators.[13]

The Asturian insurrection marked a turning point. Social revolution had become more than a bogeyman and many officers who had been

13. Stanley Payne, *Politics and the Military in Modern Spain* (Stanford, 1967), p. 243.

willing, albeit unenthusiastically, to go along with the Republic were now prepared to turn against it. At the same time, 'nearly all the groups in the centre and on the right competed directly for the favour of the military'. The first to do so was Gil Robles: on 18 October 1934 he attempted to get a number of generals to act but they refused. Gil Robles was persistent in his efforts to instigate a military coup. In November 1935 he canvassed General Fanjul for a coup to prevent a dissolution of the Cortes and immediately following the election of 18 February 1936 he urged a declaration of martial law.

The UME grew rapidly after the Asturias rising and it entered into contact with a variety of anti-Republican political groups: the Falange, the Carlists and the Alfonsine monarchists, who themselves were in touch with Mussolini and Hitler. In the end, however, it would not be the UME which would organize the coup. Rather, it was General Mola, with the backing of Sanjurjo (who was in exile in Portugal), who brought the various strands together and attracted the leading generals who had been reluctant to associate themselves with the UME.

The conspiracy coalesced when it did under the impact of the electoral victory of the Popular Front and the incendiary exaggeration by the right of the disorder which followed it. Any concern over Azaña's military reforms paled before the perceived threat of impending revolution. During the election campaign the right had portrayed the quite moderate Popular Front as the harbinger of Communist revolution. The right presented the elections in terms of an apocalyptic struggle between good and evil, survival and destruction. In Seville, for instance, pamphlets distributed to women claimed that the Republic intended to take away their children and destroy their families. Another pamphlet alleged that if the left won the elections the consequences would be 'the arming of the rabble; burnings of private houses and banks; distribution of private goods and lands, the common ownership of women'.[14]

After the election the right-wing press and politicians such as Gil Robles and Calvo Sotelo did everything they could to generate the belief that the nation was disintegrating and that social revolution was around the corner. Key generals, including Franco, had met in Madrid on 20 February, the day after Azaña returned to office. Contacts continued thereafter and right wing political leaders were kept informed. Gil Robles, for one, ordered his party's provincial organizations to put themselves at the service of the rising when it should occur. Mola worked carefully and sought to have groups in all the key garrisons. He was frustrated by the extreme caution

14. Preston, *The Coming*, p. 172.

shown by Franco, who did not commit himself until early July, as well as by the competing – and incompatible – demands of the various political forces with which he was in contact; but by early July the plans were laid. Projected dates were set for the middle of the month but the catalyst for launching the coup was the assassination of Calvo Sotelo by Assault Guards on 12 July. Five days later, on the afternoon of the 17 July, the rising, and the Civil War, began.

CHAPTER FIVE
Social Conflicts

The manner in which the reformist governments of the Second Republic dealt with the position of the Church, the regional question and the role of the military contributed in a substantial way to generating the resentments and fears which led the traditional Spanish elites to seek an extra-legal form of resistance, specifically through a military coup. However, this recourse to violence was provoked essentially by the threat that left-wing governments, impelled by the mobilization of the working class, would institute fundamental social reforms, and especially reform of the system of landholding in those regions where large estates and a landless proletariat predominated. It was in defence of property that the right organized itself politically during the Republic, although the significant popular support enjoyed by the most important right-wing party, the CEDA, was based on the manipulation of other themes: the defence of 'agriculture', the defence of national unity and especially the defence of religion and traditional values. These were themes which resonated widely in the more conservative parts of the country.

While agrarian reform was by far the most pressing social question facing the Republic it was not the only one. Industrial workers, although numerically a much smaller group than agricultural workers, also had demands which they expected the Republic to meet and problems they expected it to solve. The situation facing the new regime was best summed up by José Heredia, a coalminer from Riosa in Asturias, in a letter printed in the local Socialist newspaper, *Aurora Social*, only five months after the creation of the Republic: 'The workers saw the Republic as their saviour. If these thoughts had not existed the workers of this town would now be caught up in the whirlwind of a new struggle.' These expectations meant high levels of social conflict would be more or less inevitable during the Republic, especially given the radical temper of the anarchist trade unions.

Surprisingly, it would be in the coalfields of Asturias and not the landed estates of the south where the product of these frustrated hopes would first be made evident, in the insurrection of October 1934. But as high as they were these levels of social conflict did not in themselves generate civil war or revolution. These were the product of the military rising of 17 July.

ANARCHISM

After 1870 labour protest in both agricultural and industrial areas was increasingly expressed within the framework of the organized labour movement. In this respect the Spanish experience was no different from that of other European nations. However the Spanish labour movement stood out in one major way: from the beginning it was divided ideologically between socialists and anarchists, and until the Second Republic the anarchists were the more numerous.

Anarchism was introduced into Spain in 1868 by one of Bakunin's disciples, Giuseppe Fanelli; and at the first national labour congress, held in Barcelona in 1870, the Spanish branch of the First International, Federation of the Spanish Region (FRE) accepted Bakunin's apoliticism. By 1874 the FRE had 30,000 members, mostly in Catalonia and Andalucía, but it was then banned and its membership plummeted. In 1881 it reformed as the Federation of Workers of the Spanish Region (FTRE) which had 58,000 members by 1882. However the FTRE was racked by doctrinal disputes which led to its dissolution in 1888. At the ideological level the disputes were between anarchocollectivism, which derived from Bakunin and advocated that the product of collective labour was to be divided according to the work done by each individual, and anarchocommunism, which was based on the writings of Kropotkin and Malatesta and advocated that the product of labour be distributed according to individual need. These disputes also had a geographical basis: the collectivists were mostly from Catalonia while the communists were mostly from Andalucía. This breach first emerged in a serious form in 1882 when the FTRE disowned the victims of the government's repression of an alleged anarchist terrorist organization in the south known as the Black Hand; as a result the Andalusian group known as Los Desheredados, the Disinherited, left the organization.

For almost twenty years after the disappearance of the FTRE anarchism lacked any real organizational basis. It increasingly lost contact with the labour movement and degenerated into a series of loosely associated cells, which would later be known as affinity groups. This period was marked by the rise of 'propaganda by the deed': assassinations and bombings, most of which took place in Barcelona. Antonio Cánovas, the Prime Minister, was assassinated in 1897 and there were attempts to kill Antonio Maura in 1904 and King Alfonso XIII in 1905 and 1906. After 1902 anarchists in Barcelona did make some attempt to relate to the unions but were unable to establish a strong relationship. As Joaquín Romero Maura has observed, 'the anarcho-communist tactic of not caring about the unions at all, or else of infiltrating them only to blow them up in an attempt to throw them into the revolutionary battle without giving the least thought to the daily struggle of the members had, together with the adverse economic situation, destroyed the Barcelona craft unions'.[1]

Anarchism succeeded in becoming a mass movement firmly rooted in the working class only during the First World War and then only under the label of anarchosyndicalism. This new revolutionary formula was achieved by grafting anarchist objectives onto the tactics and organizational structures of French revolutionary syndicalism. Unions were central and were given a dual function: to carry out the class struggle on a daily basis through direct action (strikes, boycotts and sabotage), and to serve as the basis of the future society which was to be created through the revolutionary general strike. The new approach was given organizational form in 1910 with the creation of the Confederación Nacional del Trabajo (CNT).

The CNT was declared illegal in 1911. It began to rebuild in 1913 and then grew extremely rapidly during the First World War. By the end of 1919 it had over 700,000 members, of whom the vast majority came from Catalonia and Andalucía. At the Sans congress, in 1918, the Catalan Regional Federation abandoned craft unions in favour of industrial unions, *sindicatos únicos*, which brought together all the workers of a single industry and this form of organization was adopted by the CNT as a whole the following year. In the context of the World War, which caused spiralling inflation in Spain, the new form of organization contributed to the radicalization of the class struggle, especially in Catalonia. Between 1919 and 1923 Barcelona was the scene of all-out class war which featured massive general strikes, lockouts, the rise of company unions (*sindicatos libres*), and the emergence of *pistolerismo*: gang warfare which resulted in numerous deaths, among them that of the CNT's most outstanding leader, Salvador Seguí, in March 1923.

The CNT was never ideologically homogeneous. Initially its statutes made no reference to anarchism but by 1919 it had formally become an anarchosyndicalist organization, even though there was strong opposition from influential members, such as the Asturian Eleuterio Quintanilla. After

---

1. Joaquín Romero Maura, 'The Spanish Case', in *Anarchism Today*, ed. by D. Apter and J. Joll (London, 1971), p. 71.

the Russian Revolution there emerged another faction, known as the anarchobolsheviks, who adopted the concept of the dictatorship of the proletariat and succeeded in getting the CNT to adhere provisionally to the Communist International. The CNT was banned by the Primo de Rivera dictatorship and during the period of illegality, September 1923 to May 1930, a new radical faction appeared – the Iberian Anarchist Federation (FAI) – which challenged the established leadership of Ángel Pestaña.

The FAI was founded in July 1927 by ultra-radicals who opposed the increasingly reformist position taken by Pestaña. It was organized on the basis of affinity groups of no more than twelve members and took as its prime objective the preservation of the anarchist character and revolutionary spirit of the CNT. When the CNT was once again legalized the FAI at first had little influence but by working within local CNT unions as a unit it was able to exert considerable influence over the tactics and strategy of the organization during the Republic, influence which contributed to a considerable degree to the levels of social conflict after 1931. The FAI also undertook a highly successful propaganda campaign, which included educational work at the *ateneos* as well as newspapers and magazines, the purpose of which was to infuse the workers with revolutionary fervour.

FAIistas believed strongly in the value of action, a belief expressed in the slogan 'one act equals one thousand pamphlets', and consistently sought to overthrow the government of the Republic, which it saw as no different from that of the monarchy, through a series of strikes and insurrections. This tactic, known as revolutionary gymnastics, was based on the theory that these revolts would strengthen the revolutionary instincts of the workers and hasten the revolution. There were three such insurrections in the first two-and-a-half years of the Republic: January 1932 and January and December 1933. All were failures and provoked government repression which weakened the CNT. Even so the FAI remained the dominant force in the CNT. The only important opposition group, known as the *treintistas* (from the anti-FAI manifesto issued in 1931 by thirty leading *cenetistas* including Pestaña), was forced from positions of influence, such as the editorship of *Solidaridad Obrera*, and then out of the CNT itself. In January 1933 they created the Sindicatos de Oposición, which had about 40,000 members by 1936 when they were readmitted to the CNT. But for all its anarchist purity, the FAI was unprepared to deal with the situation of civil war and revolution which emerged after July 1936 and ended up cooperating with and then forming part of the government.

ASTURIAS

Asturias was one of the most important industrial regions in the country. But even so, the 25,000 or so miners were a tiny part of the national working class, especially when compared to the rural proletariat. However, in October 1934 the Asturian coalfields were the site of a major working-class insurrection against the government of the Republic. The Asturian revolution was the most substantial revolutionary episode in twentieth-century Europe after the Russian Revolution. It was also the central event in the history of the Second Republic. As the first major outbreak of class war in Spain it revealed that the Republic was proving incapable of satisfying the expectations of rank-and-file workers and, as a result, was beginning to lose their support. In this and a number of other ways it foreshadowed the civil war which lay less than two years in the future.

The Asturian revolution was the work of a deeply radicalized working class which had invested its hopes for change in the Republic and then seen those hopes dashed. Traditionally the region's miners were Socialists, belonging overwhelmingly to the Sindicato Minero Asturiano (SMA). In the 1920s the mining industry was subject to a prolonged crisis which the union had attempted to deal with by appealing to the government, even though the government was a military dictatorship under General Primo de Rivera. The union's docility lost it the support of thousands of miners, many of whom joined the anarchist and Communist Sindicato Único Minero (SUM). However the enthusiasm generated by the creation of the Republic and the prestige which attached to the Socialists from their identification with it allowed the SMA to regain its hegemonic position in the coalfields.

During the first two years of the Republic the SMA leadership consistently called on the rank and file to avoid strikes and trust in the Republican government to deal with the on-going crisis of the mining industry. National conferences to deal with the industry's problems were held in 1931 and 1933 but produced no solutions as the mine owners refused to make any concessions to the workers. Even though the union executive felt that labour conflict could only undermine the Republic, wage cuts, layoffs and short weeks and the subsequent rising militancy of its rank and file forced it into calling general strikes in the industry in November 1932 and February–March 1933. The situation was deteriorating to such an extent that at the beginning of 1933 the Socialist press was reporting the miners' restiveness with great concern. On 3 January *El Socialista* described the social climate in the coalfields as 'charged with passion and madness; only our comrades are holding the lid on'. In spite of the union's reluctance to call strikes Asturias led all Spanish provinces in the number of strikes in

1932 and 1933; in the number of strikers it was first in 1932 and second the next year.

Following the victory of the right in the elections of November 1933 the union had even more difficulty than before in controlling the rank and file. Although the union leadership began to speak of the government as fascist and announced that it was time for the working class to take power, it also called on the miners to show restraint and not dissipate their energy before the moment for revolution came.

However the beginning of direct repression by the Lerroux and Samper governments – arms searches, an anti-strike bill and increasing use of the Civil Guard and Assault Guard to break up strikes and meetings – shattered the republican illusion the workers had held. After November 1933 strikes became increasingly politicized as the miners came to reject the legitimacy of the Republic in which they had invested so much hope. In the first two-and-a-half years of the Republic there was only one mining strike which could be called political in the sense of challenging or protesting against the actions of the state or its agents; in the first nine months of 1934 alone there were eight such strikes. The first, in February, was a 24-hour strike in solidarity with the Austrian Socialists which effectively paralysed all mining operations. Five were in protest against police actions, such as arms searches and the arrest of militants. The other two were protests against rallies organized by the CEDA.

The radicalization of the miners also led to a sort of unification of the labour movement which, in Asturias as in the rest of Spain, was divided among Socialists, anarchosyndicalists and Communists. This new solidarity was embodied in the Alianza Obrera (Workers' Alliance) which was formed in March 1934. The idea of the Alianza had been developed in 1933 by Joaquín Maurín, leader of the dissident Communist organization Bloc Obrer i Camperol (BOC). Maurín proposed a united movement of the working class, peasantry and Catalan republicans to fight against fascism and then to make the revolution. But Maurín's idea was received without interest by both the CNT and the Socialists. The former did not see fascism as different from any other political form and refused to have anything to do with the Alianza; the latter feared that the Alianza would usurp their role as the leaders of the working class. However, in Asturias both the Socialist and anarchosyndicalist regional leaderships were impelled by the militancy of their rank and file to ignore the position of their national organizations and sign (on 31 March 1934) the Workers' Alliance pact which called for the creation of a 'federalist, Socialist regime'.

Although the Asturian rising was the product of the radicalization of the region's workers it was not totally spontaneous. Rather, it was intended as part of a nationwide rising planned by the Socialists to keep the CEDA from coming to power. The national Socialist leadership began discussing such an insurrection immediately after the elections of November 1933. A committee of the PSOE, UGT and Socialist Youth was set up in February 1934 to plan the revolt. Arms were gathered and contacts with army officers made. The programme for the movement was drafted by Prieto and called for a number of reforms, the most important of which were land reform and the dissolution of the Civil Guard.

After November 1933 the Socialists used the threat of revolution in an attempt to dissuade the government from dismantling the reforms of the Republican-Socialist coalition. Largo Caballero in particular took on an increasingly revolutionary tone as the desperation of the rank and file increased the pressure on the Socialist leadership to act. They were also concerned to keep the CEDA, which they saw as a fascist party, from coming to power. As Preston states, 'in 1933 the full extent of Nazi horrors was as yet unknown. In the light of what was known of Nazi and Fascist persecution of leftists, the CEDA's broadcast intention to smash Socialism, Gil Robles' corporativist ambitions and CEDA-encouraged employers' attacks on unionized labour were, to most Spanish leftists, indistinguishable from contemporary fascism.'[2]

The Socialists had often repeated their threats of revolution. The announcement of the new Lerroux cabinet, which included three members of the CEDA, on 3 October decided them to act on their threats, but even then only reluctantly. Here was the scene in Socialist headquarters in Madrid:

> Caballero, Prieto, Zugazagoitia, de Francisco, Carrillo were there, among others. The news was followed by a tremendous silence. Caballero and Prieto were on their feet, ready to leave when the two messengers arrived. Hats in hand they looked at each other as if to ask 'What do we do?'. Someone broke the silence by saying that they had to give the word to launch the strike and begin the movement. Silence followed. Largo spoke. With considerable dignity he said 'I won't believe it until I see it in the *Gazette*'.[3]

The rising was a disaster. The plans were not yet complete, the leadership was arrested or forced to flee and the anticipated support from the army and the police did not materialize. The general strike in Madrid was halted after a few days and in Catalonia Companys surrendered only a few hours after having declared the independent Catalan republic.

In Asturias things were very different however, and also very different from what the national Socialist leadership had been planning. The miners subdued the Civil Guard posts in the coalfields, often only after prolonged

---

2. Paul Preston, *The Coming of the Spanish Civil War* (London, 1983), p. 100.
3. Amaro del Rosal, *1934: La Revolución de octubre* (Madrid, 1984), p. 260.

and bloody sieges, and marched on the provincial capital, Oviedo. It took five days of street-fighting for them to capture the centre of the city and even then the cathedral, the barracks and the Civil Government building remained in the hands of the military. At the southern end of the coalfield a couple of thousand miners were able to encircle the military column marching north from León and hold it up for six days before the arrival of reinforcements allowed it to retreat. In all the government concentrated 26,000 troops, including the Foreign Legion, in Asturias with the operation being coordinated by Francisco Franco, but it still took two weeks for the rising to be subjugated.

More important than the length of the armed struggle in Asturias was the fact that while it was going on an incipient social revolution was taking place in those parts of the region controlled by the workers. The reformist objectives of the national rising planned by the Socialists were left far behind as local revolutionary committees composed of delegates of the various working-class organizations emerged and took control at the municipal level, creating a series of mini-communes. In Mieres the committee included Socialists, anarchists, the PCE and the non-official Communists of the Bloque Obrero y Campesino; in Sama de Langreo it comprised Socialists, Communists and anarchists; and in La Felguera it was composed solely of anarchists. These committees organized militias and the production of military equipment. They also took charge of numerous aspects of civilian life, imposing food rationing, organizing medical services and police forces and keeping essential public services operating.

These local committees were much more radical than the provincial committee based in Oviedo, which was the Asturian agent of the nation-wide Socialist insurrectionary network. The provincial committee, which was dominated by Socialists, quickly realized that as Asturias had risen alone the movement was doomed and began to consider surrender. The committee fled Oviedo on 11 October and was quickly replaced by another, this time dominated by the PCE, which lasted only a day before being replaced by a third committee made up of six Socialists – including some of the members of the original committee who had returned – and three Communists. The primary consideration of the new committee was to bring to an end a struggle which was lost. The President, Belarmino Tomás, negotiated a surrender with General López Ochoa on condition that the African troops would not enter the coalfields and that there would be no reprisals; promises which were immediately broken. On the night of 18 October Tomás announced the terms of the surrender and called on the workers to lay down their arms.

The shadow of the Asturian revolution hung over Spanish politics after October 1934. The experience of armed insurrection led some elements of the PSOE to call for a bolshevization of the party and the creation of a single, revolutionary working-class party. The failure of the insurrection led other Socialists, such as Indalecio Prieto and key Asturian leaders such as Ramón González Peña and Amador Fernández, to promote a return to the alliance with the left-Republicans which had marked the first two years of the Republic. In this way the Asturian revolution was directly responsible for the creation of the Popular Front at the beginning of 1936. And since the policy of the Popular Front which had most resonance among the working class was amnesty for those 30,000 people imprisoned in the repression which followed October 1934, it was to a significant extent responsible for the electoral victory of the left in February 1936.

The Asturian insurrection foreshadowed the civil war in a number of ways. Militarily, the workers concentrated all their efforts on Oviedo at the expense of other, more important objectives, such as Gijón. During the civil war the military value of the Asturian miners was eliminated by the conduct of Colonel Aranda, the military governor of the province, who told Socialist leaders that he would support the Republic and then declared for Franco once they had led their militias south towards León. This made another siege of the provincial capital necessary, this time lasting until the fall of the northern front in November 1937.[4]

Politically the Alianza Obrera was a forerunner of the close co-operation between the UGT and CNT during the civil war. Likewise, the refusal of the Communists to join and their attempt to convert the workers' militias into a regular army anticipated one of the central conflicts in the Republican camp during the civil war. In October 1934 there was a tendency for central political authority to collapse, symbolized in the predominance of the local committees over the provincial committee. Political authority fractured during the civil war as well, but at the level of regions, not that of municipalities. Political authority was retained by the Republic in the form of the Council of Asturias and León but while the Council theoretically represented the central government it was not totally subordinate to it and, in the last days of the war in the north, even declared itself independent.

Finally, the Asturian revolution signalled the inability of the Republic to resolve the central dilemma which faced it: the threat of social conflict if it did not provide meaningful social reform. Both the Asturian insurrection and the civil war which came shortly afterwards were social conflicts fed by the disappointment of the hopes for a better life that the Second

---

4. See Chapter 6.

Republic had kindled in the Spanish working class; these hopes had been blocked by the right, before October 1934 by intransigence and obstructionism, in July 1936 by the recourse to a military revolt.

THE AGRARIAN PROBLEM

As early as the 1760s Spanish governments recognized that a serious agrarian problem existed in southern and western Spain, regions where landholding was dominated by large estates and where there was, as a consequence, a large population of landless labourers. Some measures were taken to alleviate the miserable conditions of this rural proletariat by making common lands available to them for cultivation but they were short-lived and ineffective. Efforts to distribute land were resumed in the 1790s but with a different motivation; to deal with the soaring debt of the government caused by Spain's participation in the wars initiated by the French Revolution. Thereafter the plight of the rural poor took a back seat to the plight of the treasury.

Through a series of laws which began in 1798 and ended in 1856, land held in entail by the Church and municipalities, and some land under the seigneurial jurisdiction of the nobility, was sold at auction to private individuals. This long process, by which privileged property was converted into private property, is known as disentailment (*desamortización*). The process had two key moments. The first came in the midst of the Carlist War, when the liberal government was desperate for money. Under the leadership of Juan Alvarez Mendizábal two disentailment laws (19 February 1836 and 29 July 1837) placed virtually all the extensive property holdings of the Church in the hands of the State which put them up for sale. The second moment came on 1 May 1855 when Pascual Madoz's Law of General Disentailment put all lands belonging to the municipalities on the auction block. This was the last piece of disentailment legislation, but the sale of land continued until the last years of the century.

The pattern of landholding in Spain varied markedly from region to region, with small farms of less than ten hectares dominating in the north and large estates of more than 100 hectares dominating in the south. In general terms the principal effect of the disentailments of the nineteenth century was:

> to accentuate the pre-existing structure: where latifundia predominated they grew and where property holdings were based on medium farms and minifundia,

the latifundia were diminished. Thus in the south property ownership was concentrated to an even greater degree than before.[5]

The nobility continued to control large amounts of land but since this was no longer protected by entail the less economically adroit noble families could now see their estates shrink or disappear and a number had this happen. The Church and the municipalities disappeared as landowners and their lands were taken over for the most part by a new agrarian bourgeoisie which came from urban merchants and professionals, many of whom had leased large estates from the Church before the disentailments. By the twentieth century most of the large estates were in the hands of non-nobles. The predominance of such estates meant that landholding was more concentrated in the south and west than anywhere else in Spain. This concentration was increased by marriage ties which allowed a very small number of people to effectively control entire towns or districts. In the province of Córdoba, for example, 3 per cent of the landowners held 57 per cent of the land. A group of 459 people, many of whom were related through marriage, controlled 31 per cent of the land.

Many peasants were able to acquire a small amount of land but their purchases represented only a small percentage of the land which changed hands. But their loss was more than just a matter of not purchasing lands available for sale, especially in the south. The Madoz disentailment had converted municipal lands into private property, thereby removing an important component of the economy of the poor while the new land-owners eliminated customary practices such as gleaning.

The agricultural system of the south was based on the *latifundia*. With few exceptions these large units of production were not well managed or progressive. As Malefakis comments, 'Every available standard of measurement suggests that the large domains were managed without initiative or imagination, that their owners failed to apply modern farming techniques and that the rate of capital investment in the land was minimal.'[6] The south had the lowest rates of fertilizer use in the country, it was slow to introduce machinery such as tractors and harvesters, irrigation was not widely used and there was little initiative in introducing new crops for which the region's lands were suited. Absenteeism was widespread, especially among the aristocracy and the bourgeoisie with the most extensive holdings. Their estates were leased intact to tenants who worked them with wage labour or, in turn, subleased them in smaller units.

5. Germán Rueda, *La Desamortización de Mendizábal y Espartero en España*, (Madrid, 1986), p. 136.
6. Edward Malefakis, *Agrarian Reform and Peasant Revolution in Spain* (New Haven, 1970), p. 78.

In these circumstances the wealth of the estate owners or their large tenants was based on the maximum exploitation of the labour force. This was made up of the vast majority of the population which had too little land to provide subsistence or no land at all. Their wages were very low, usually half or less than the national average. In the second half of the nineteenth century rapid population growth led to an increase in the available labour force which kept wages depressed. But even these miserable wages were not available regularly: the limited range of crops, olives and wheat for the most part, did not provide continual employment. Labourers could look forward to a maximum of between 180 and 250 days of work per year or as few as from 130 to 150. Seasonal unemployment was normally between 25 and 30 per cent.

Perhaps even worse than these material conditions was the subordination which was expected from the workers. Since there was not enough work for everyone who wanted it, employers were able to choose freely among the applicants. The *latifundia* had a small number of permanent employees. The vast majority of the workers were hired on a daily basis, often on a very humiliating basis: those seeking work would gather each morning in the town square where the foremen would come to choose the men they wanted. A worker who did not show the expected docility or who joined a union could easily be left without work or not given the opportunity to rent the small plots which landowners often made available.

In these circumstances protest and conflict were endemic, most frequently in the form of robbery, crop burnings and banditry. There were also intermittent revolts: in Seville in 1857, during which Guardia Civil barracks were burnt; in Loja (Granada) in 1861; and in Montilla (Córdoba) in 1873. After it was introduced into Spain in 1868, anarchism found fertile ground in this state of latent revolt and was able to survive periodic waves of repression. Arson and other forms of protest continued: in 1892 there was a major rising in Jerez de la Frontera (Cádiz) and an important strike wave in 1904–5.

The most important outbreak of protest was the *trienio bolchevique* of 1918 to 1920. Triggered by news of the Russian Revolution and encouraged by the CNT, strikes and land occupations swept across Andalucía. This so frightened the landowners that for the first, and last, time they co-operated with the National Catholic Agrarian Confederation (CNCA) in creating Catholic unions and marginally improving the position of agricultural labourers. Order was restored only after troops were sent to the region. The countryside was relatively quiet during the Primo de Rivera dictatorship but this did not mean that the problems of the rural south had disppeared. Disastrous crops in the winter of 1930–31 led to widespread violence; in some places troops had to be used. At the same time the rapid

89

growth of the Socialist National Federation of Land Workers (FNTT), which had been founded in April 1930, brought the plight of the rural labourers to the forefront of concern among Socialist leaders.

AGRARIAN REFORM

The Provisional Government acted quickly in a number of ways to alleviate the sharpest edge of the misery of the agricultural poor while a comprehensive agrarian reform law was being drafted. Between 28 April and 14 July 1931 six decrees were issued dealing with the agrarian situation. Most of the initiative came from the Ministry of Labour headed by the Socialist Francisco Largo Caballero. The first decree was issued on 28 April. Known as the Law of Municipal Boundaries, the decree was intended to fight unemployment by requiring landowners to hire residents of the municipality and prohibiting the employment of workers from elsewhere. This was particularly important in Andalucía where migrant workers, many from Portugal, could be found to work for miserable wages and, when necessary, to break strikes. The next day a second decree prohibited the eviction of tenants except for non-payment of rent or failure to cultivate the land.

Largo Caballero issued two more decrees on 7 May. One created arbitration committees (*jurados mixtos*) for agriculture. Composed of representatives of employers, unions and the state, these committees were empowered to ensure that labour legislation was enforced and could fine employers who broke the law, and also served as a forum for collective bargaining. The second decree was intended to prevent landowners from short-circuiting the new legislation by refusing to cultivate their land. The obligatory cultivation (*laboreo forzoso*) requirement was backed up by the threat of expropriation of those lands which were not exploited according to the 'uses and customs' of the region. The fifth decree, on 19 May, was intended to solve the problem of subleasing by giving preference to registered workers' organizations over individuals when large properties were put up for lease. Finally, on 1 July the eight-hour day was applied to agricultural work. This meant that workers would be paid overtime for the traditional work day of sun-up to sundown or that more workers would have to be hired.

All six decrees, except that on rural leases, were later approved by the Cortes. This burst of legislation certainly raised howls of opposition from landowners and their various federations, which claimed that the decrees would destroy Spanish agriculture. The decrees were impressive on paper but seemed to have been considerably less so in reality. The power of the large landowners and local bosses remained intact and government officials did not act energetically to overcome their ignoring the new laws. In some provinces the Civil Governors cooperated with landowners while in others their attempts to enforce the law were obstructed by the local elites. In Córdoba, for example, Eduardo Varela Valverde, Civil Governor between July 1931 and June 1932, made free use of the Civil Guard to put down strikes and earned the praise of the province's elite and the opprobium of its Socialists.

Whatever the effectiveness of these initial decrees, they were intended as temporary palliatives until an agricultural reform law could be passed. Objectively agrarian reform was the most pressing issue facing the Republic but governments did not act as if this were the case. It took almost a full year for a bill to be presented to the Cortes and another six months for it to become law, and even then the law was far from meeting the needs of the situation.

In May 1931 the Provisional Government set up a technical commission to prepare a draft bill which was submitted to the government on 20 July. The commission designed its bill to provide a quick and simple solution to the problem of the south, with a goal of providing land to between 60,000 and 75,000 families per year. The process was to be completed within fifteen years. Properties of over 300 hectares or those producing more than 10,000 pesetas in income were to be settled by landless peasants who, in return for a low annual rent, would receive permanent use rights. The reform was to be financed by a surtax on large properties and implemented immediately by decree.

The commission's draft had a number of advantages: it was, in Malefakis' words 'technically excellent; it provided a simple, direct and efficient instrument of reform and had the advantage of affecting only a few thousand of the very largest landowners in Spain'.[7] However it was quickly diluted due to political opposition. Of course the right and the landowners' organizations were horrified and mobilized against the draft law. More important, there was widespread opposition within the government coalition. For the Socialists it was too moderate, for the Radicals and conservatives too sweeping. The commission's project was abandoned and Alcalá Zamora put together a ministerial committee to write a new draft. The new, more limited bill was presented to the Cortes on 25 August where it was more or less totally rewritten by the left-Republicans and Socialists on the Agricultural Committee.

This reverse contributed to the resignation of Alcalá Zamora as Prime Minister in October 1931 but his successor, Azaña, also ran into problems in trying to reconcile Socialist aspirations and Radical fears on the land

7. Ibid., p. 176.

issue. Following a cabinet shuffle in December in which the Radicals were dropped from the government, the Minister of Agriculture, Diego Hidalgo, set out to prepare a new draft bill. The Hidalgo bill was introduced in March 1932 and was approved by the Cortes with only minimal changes, even though it took six months of gruelling debate to do so. The opposition to the bill was led by the Agrarian Minority, which carried on a very effective obstruction campaign by introducing numerous amendments to each clause of the bill. Seventy amendments were presented to Article 5 alone. After three months of debate only four of the twenty-four articles had been approved. However the rising by General Sanjurjo on 10 August revitalized the government and a month later, on 9 September, the bill was approved.

The Agrarian Reform Law was very different from the draft initially presented by the Technical Commission. That proposal had been designed to deal as quickly and straightforwardly as possible with the specific problem of large estates and landless labourers. The law which was passed over a year later was much less focussed. Geographically it covered the entire country, not just the south where the problem lay. Socially it was not limited solely to the large landowners but, through the provision that lands which had been leased for twelve or more consecutive years were to be expropriated, the law also targeted small and middling landowners. This greatly – and unnecessarily – multiplied the number of people threatened by the agrarian reform, which could be convincingly portrayed as an attack on all landed property.

Moreover, the law was very complex. Its guiding principle was that:

> no individual might own more than a certain amount of land within a single township; this amount varied according to the type of land owned. The maximum property limit in each municipality for vineyards was set at between 100 and 150 hectares; for orchards from 100 to 200; for olive groves from 150 to 300; for grain lands (which constituted about three-quarters of the tilled land in Spain) from 400 to 600; and for partly cultivated pasture lands, from 400 to 750 hectares.[8]

There were thirteen categories of land which could be expropriated. Four were subject to expropriation in their entirety: lands which had been under seigneurial jurisdiction, lands leased continuously, lands which were badly cultivated, and lands in irrigation zones which had not been irrigated. Lands held in excess of the maximum per township were liable to expropriation. Below these limits land could be expropriated in two sets of circumstances: if a landowner retained enough land to exercise undue social and

8. Ibid., pp. 205–6.

economic influence; or if land within two kilometres of a village belonging to a person with land valued at over 1,000 pesetas was not cultivated.

The law applied to arable land only and functioned so that an individual could own the maximum amount of land in a number of municipalities without being liable to expropriation. Pasture and forests were excluded entirely. Even so 'a very large proportion of the land in Spain came to be included in the Inventory of Expropriable Property, in which estates affected by the reform were registered'.[9] In the *latifundia* provinces of the south about half the cultivated land was included. The reform was to be overseen by the Agrarian Reform Institute (IRA) which was governed by a large council made up of technicians, representatives of government agencies and of landowners, tenants and labourers. This could only be a formula for delay and obstruction, and this was what happened as the council spent months attempting to interpret the law and resolve procedural problems.

Except for the lands of grandees and those lands which had been under seigneurial jurisdiction, compensation had to be paid for all property which was expropriated. In fact, some 90 per cent of expropriated land required compensation and, in addition, the state undertook to pay off any mortgages and reimburse the value of any crops in the ground. This meant that the cost of the reform was very high, especially since the original proposal for a surtax on large estates was dropped and not replaced by a serious alternative, even though the government had envisaged a tougher global income tax as a way of financing the reform. Title to the expropriated land was to remain with the state; the settler enjoyed all the rights of property ownership except the right to mortgage, lease or sell his land.

As complex and cumbersome as it was, the Agrarian Reform Law could have been the vehicle for major changes had it been energetically enforced. Azaña did not do so. The Prime Minister was more concerned with military and religious matters than with agrarian questions. He did not use his full powers to seize lands and his government never gave the IRA more than the minimum budget set out in the law. By the end of 1933 only 4,399 people had been settled by the IRA on only 24,203 hectares of land, a far cry from the pace of at least 60,000 families per year which the Technical Commission had envisaged.

The pace of reform was further slowed by the landowners, who did everything they could to obstruct it. In the autumn of 1932 they began a campaign, supported by leading CEDA politicians, to urge landowners not to cultivate their land. The government responded with a decree on the intensification of cultivation, under which uncultivated parts of large estates

9. Ibid., pp. 209–210.

would be given to landless labourers for two years. After this period the labourers would leave, presumably to receive land elsewhere. At first the decree applied only to the province of Badajoz, where the tenant farmers and sharecroppers (known as *yunteros* because of the team of mules, or *yunta*, which most of them owned), whose position on the land was particularly insecure, had been engaged in land occupations. By December it had been extended to nine other provinces: Cáceres, Cádiz, Ciudad Real, Córdoba, Granada, Málaga, Salamanca, Seville and Toledo. This vigorous action by the government calmed the situation, but only briefly. Across the south landowners locked out workers and vindictively told them to ¡*Comed República*! (literally, 'Eat the Republic'), and also flouted the decisions of the mixed juries on wages and working conditions.

The province of Seville provides an excellent example of the systematic obstruction practised by the landowners. They ignored the obligatory cultivation decrees, refused to limit the use of agricultural machinery as a means of creating employment and managed to get the government to waive the Law of Municipal Boundaries and have the entire province treated as a single unit. They also drastically reduced the amount of land in cultivation: in 1932 there were 35,462 hectares fewer being farmed than in 1931 and in 1933 another 31,000 hectares were withdrawn from cultivation. Landowners also organized to fight the government. In May 1932 they created the Federación Provincial de Asociaciones y Patronales Agrícolas whose principal objectives were to achieve more favourable conditions for agriculture and to bring the right to power. In May 1933, as well as threatening to paralyse work on the land, the Association voted to boycott the mixed juries until procedures were changed and the presidents, appointed by the government, were replaced. Three months later it demanded a series of policies from the government which would have amounted to a repeal of all the Republic's labour and agrarian reform legislation. Three of the Association's leaders were CEDA militants and two were elected to the Cortes in November 1933.

While the centre-left coalition was in power the Socialist Agricultural Workers' Union (FNTT), like the SMA in Asturias, encouraged its members to rely on the government to deal with their problems and to avoid strikes. This approach was the polar opposite of the CNT's, which refused to work through the mixed juries set up by Largo Caballero. The anarchosyndicalists were responsible for a large number of strikes in the first years of the Republic, many of which were expressions of their refusal to work through the state. A good example were the strikes they called in Córdoba in June and July 1931 against the mixed juries and to demand strict application of the Law of Municipal Boundaries, strikes which were 'more a struggle between the unions than a labour conflict'.[10] In the autumn there were more strikes called by the CNT demanding direct dealings with the employers.

Even more important than the numerous strikes called by the CNT were its three attempts at revolutionary insurrection. These forced the government to become involved in repression and allowed the right to identify the Republic with disorder. The insurrection of January 1933 led to the brutal episode in the village of Casas Viejas which contributed significantly to weakening the government coalition and the impetus for reform.

REFORMING THE AGRARIAN REFORM

Although the right had failed to prevent the passage of an agrarian reform law it was successful in emasculating the one piece of supplementary legislation the Azaña government introduced and then, following the elections of November 1933, in watering down the Agrarian Reform Law itself. In July 1933 the government put forward a bill on agricultural leases for central and northern Spain. The bill prohibited subleasing, established controls on rents and strengthened the tenant's position on the land by mandating a minimum lease of six years which was to be renewed automatically unless the landowner decided to cultivate the land directly. In addition, the bill offered tenants the opportunity to become property owners. They were to be given first right to purchase if the land they leased were put on the market, and those tenants who had leased the land for twenty years consecutively could buy that land for twenty times the assessed taxable income whenever they wanted. For six weeks the Agrarians put up a determined resistance to the bill. Their concerns centred on the limitations of rents and the manner of determining the purchase price, and they were able to get their amendments on these crucial points accepted. Consequently, rents were to be set by the courts, which put tenants at a major disadvantage, and when tenants bought land they were to pay full market value.

The emasculation of the leases bill revealed the limits of the right's dedication to its loudly proclaimed 'Catholic' social principles. This was shown even more clearly in the way the reform efforts of CEDA Agriculture Minister Manuel Giménez Fernández were destroyed by his own

10. Manuel Pérez Yruela, *La Conflictividad en la provincia de Córdoba*, (Madrid, 1979), p. 128.

party. Giménez Fernández's genuinely held social Catholicism was apparent in the lease bill he presented to the Cortes in December 1934 which provided for tenants having access to property ownership after having leased land for only twelve years. Debate on the bill spread over thirty sessions, from 5 December 1933 to 14 March 1935; the principal opposition came from within the CEDA itself while party leader Gil Robles did nothing to enforce party discipline. The CEDA right wing succeeded in weakening any provision which threatened landowners' property rights: the length of leases was cut from six years to four, controls of rents were abolished and the concept of 'access to property right', a mainstay of Catholic social thought, was eliminated. They were also able to have included a number of special provisions which allowed landowners to refuse to renew existing leases once they expired. Another of Giménez Fernández's projects, a bill to 'increase small farming areas' by authorizing the IRA to permit those without land to farm a quarter of any estate larger than 300 hectares if this did not interfere with the activities being carried on there, was introduced in February 1935 and met a similar fate.

Giménez Fernández was dismissed in the cabinet shuffle of March 1935 and the Ministry of Agriculture was handed over to the hardline wing of the CEDA. In May 1934 the Law on Municipal Boundaries was repealed and landowners rushed to hire migrant labour from Portugal and Galicia. In many towns elected Socialist mayors were replaced by government appointees. In July the new minister, Nicasio Velayos y Velayos, introduced a new agrarian reform project, known as the Law for the Reform of the Agrarian Reform. The key change was the abolition of the Inventory of Expropriable Property, which meant that the owners of lands possibly subject to expropriation could manipulate them in order to bring their holdings below the maximum allowed, by dividing a large estate among their children, for example. The new law also altered the way compensation for lands taken was to be calculated, much to the benefit of the landowners. As a result, any further agrarian reform became much more expensive. In addition, the 50 million pesetas the Agrarian Reform Law had set as the minimum budget for the IRA was turned into the maximum possible budget.

This legislative revision was accompanied in the countryside by a return to the conditions prevailing before the Republic. Those labour laws which had been left unchanged went unenforced. With the state back firmly on their side landowners reduced wages, blacklisted union workers and blithely ignored the obligatory cultivation decree and the rulings of the mixed juries. In December 1934 the juries themselves ceased to function. Requests that the laws be enforced sent by Socialist union officials to the provincial authorities were ignored. The landowners' response to rising unemployment and increasing misery was charity, taking up collections and opening *cocinas económicas* (soup kitchens). Even when urged by the authorities to take stronger action landowners would not: in the face of particularly severe local unemployment the Civil Governor of Córdoba suggested that landowners in Lucena employ a specified number of workers. They refused.

The repercussions were quickly felt in the FNTT. With the centre-left in power and a Socialist at the Labour Ministry, moderation and trust in the authorities were reasonable policies. Even so, the slow pace of reform and the ease with which landowners evaded labour laws created considerable impatience among the rank and file which forced some provincial leaderships to take more militant action such as the harvest strike called by the Córdoba federation in June 1933. Under the conditions prevailing after November 1933 a moderate approach was suicidal. At the end of January 1934 the leadership of the union was changed; the new president was Ricardo Zabalza, a militant and a supporter of Largo Caballero. Under Zabalza the FNTT took on a more radical tone and under pressure from its rank and file, and against the advice of the UGT leadership, it called a general strike for 5 June. The union's demands were far from revolutionary: the most important were respect for the *bases de trabajo* set by the mixed juries, controls on the use of machinery and non-local workers, that employers hire on a strict rotational basis with no regard for political affiliation, and that the IRA take over lands scheduled for expropriation and lease them on a collective basis to the unemployed.

The workers' response to the strike call varied from province to province but even in those where it was massive landowners were able to import labour and make use of soldiers to operate their machines. The Minister of the Interior, Rafael Salazar Alonso, declared the strike revolutionary and acted unhesitatingly to suppress it, in the process effectively destroying the labour movement in the south. There were numerous arrests, including those of four Socialist deputies, and massive deportations. Socialist town governments were dismissed and the union halls (*casas del pueblo*) closed down, not to reopen until 1936. The effectiveness of his policy was evident: there were few strikes in 1935 (in the province of Córdoba none at all), although the continuing tensions were expressed more furtively, through robberies and break-ins.

THE REVITALIZATION OF REFORM

The right had effectively destroyed the agrarian reform initiated, however tentatively, under Azaña and brought the labour movement under control but it did not enjoy its achievement for long. Within six months the government had fallen and new elections were called. With the victory of the Popular Front agrarian reform was carried out at a much more rapid pace than ever before, but it was not the new government which took the lead. At the beginning of March 1936 a wave of land seizures began in the province of Madrid and spread to a number of other provinces. The situation was most serious in Badajoz where, on 25 March, the provincial federation of the FNTT authorized the seizure of about 3,000 estates in which 60,000 people took part. Three days later the government sanctioned the occupation. *Yunteros* also occupied land in Córdoba and in the face of this pressure the government applied provisions to this province intended for Badajoz alone. There were other problems as well: rain had damaged the olive and wheat crops, making unemployment a major problem in the spring of 1936. This led to a wave of strikes which began in May; according to government statistics there had been 192 by 18 July.

Faced with this massive mobilization the government had no choice but to act. In mid-April the Minister of Agriculture introduced a set of five bills dealing with the land reform and at the beginning of May two more, and some were passed as early as June. At the same time the IRA, which had been reorganized to allow it to function more efficiently, settled 110,921 peasants on 572,055 hectares of land between March and the outbreak of the civil war. This was significantly more land than had been distributed since the beginning of the Republic. The government also took other steps to deal with the situation: reappointing the town councils which had been dismissed after October 1934 and changing the personnel of the mixed juries so that they were more sympathetic to the workers. Meanwhile civil governors dealt with the crisis of unemployment through the practice of *alojamiento*: assigning a number of workers to landowners whether they needed them or not.

The unprecedented energy with which the government acted to distribute land and ensure employment for the landless scared the landowners. Even more worrisome, however, was the new assertiveness of the labourers; what Manuel Pérez Yruela has called 'the new equilibrium in social relations . . . In every respect, economic, religious, political, and especially in everyday relations, the workers wanted to demonstrate the power and support which the electoral victory had given them . . . The attitude, the new tone, was more important than the actual number of violent conflicts which took place compared to other years.'[11] In this new climate many landowners took fright and left their estates for the provincial capital or

11. Ibid., pp. 203, 206.

Madrid. In the town of Bujalance (Córdoba), the local union even had the effrontery to guarantee the safety of the landowners if they stayed. There was no more violence than before, but the rural south was becoming a world turned upside down. Only the arrival of Franco's troops and Falangist militias would 'set it right', and then only with great brutality.

PART TWO
Civil War and Revolution

CHAPTER SIX

Rebellion and Civil War

THE FIRST DAYS

On 17 July 1936, after months of meticulous planning, the moment of truth for the military conspirators finally arrived. The *alzamiento* or rising began at Melilla, the port city on the northeastern coast of Spanish Morocco, and by the following afternoon the rebellion had spread to the Peninsula. When the discontented officers launched what they later referred to as the *Movimiento*, they had high hopes of an early victory. The plotters had devised a simple blueprint for action: the *alzamiento* was to unfold along the lines of a classic *pronunciamiento*. Once the Army of Africa had secured Spanish Morocco, insurgent officers were to seize control of the major military installations on the mainland from which they would declare an *estado de guerra* (state of war). Next they would take over the provincial and national capitals and set up a military directory modelled on Miguel Primo de Rivera's regime, which aimed to suppress the Republic until public order could be restored throughout Spain. The success of the coup d'état hinged on a number of elements, but, above all, timing was of the essence. If their plans were to be realized, then the rebels would have to conquer the major cities in one sweeping stroke, giving their enemies no time to organize a counter-offensive.

On the mainland, the pattern of revolt varied considerably, although there were several factors which usually determined the outcome of events. As Raymond Carr has pointed out, it was generally true that where the Guardia de Asalto and Guardia Civil joined forces with the rebels the rebellion was successful.[1] In areas with large left-wing working-class populations this alliance proved crucial. This was because, except for small

1. Rayond Carr, *The Civil War in Spain* (London, 1986), p. 75.

caches of weapons being hoarded by some unions, the workers themselves were unarmed and therefore powerless to counter-attack. To arm civilians, especially the proletarian militias, was fraught with revolutionary implications, and for this reason the government at first refused to distribute weapons to them. In fact, their principal weapon was the general strike; the reflex action of all leftist unions upon hearing news of the conspiracy. Yet because the general strike was ineffectual against armed troops, it obviously made a difference if the workers themselves possessed weapons. Thus it was also generally true that where the workers were given arms in a timely fashion, the rebellion was successfully put down.

During the first week of the rebellion, the Nationalists achieved several strategic victories in the Andalusian cities of Cádiz, Córdoba, and Seville. Their most surprising success came in Seville, home of a large but ideologically divided proletariat. The head of the conspiracy there was the eccentric General Quiepo de Llano, the commander of the carabineers who was to gain notoriety during the war for delivering bloodthirsty harangues over Radio Seville. Thanks to his audacity and decisive actions, rebel forces quickly gained the upper hand. A chief element of Quiepo de Llano's strategy was his clever use of the radio. By broadcasting an endless stream of misleading news bulletins – his denial that the rising had been put down on the mainland, for example – he managed to sow confusion among his enemies and to make converts of officers and civilians wavering in their political loyalties. Then, after gaining control of the police and military units, he ordered his men (soon reinforced by the highly disciplined Moorish troops, the *regulares*) to sweep through working-class districts and annihilate any proletarian opposition. The response of the workers was confused and badly coordinated – due in part to the bitter rivalry that existed between the anarchosyndicalist and communist unions – and, in any case, they were clearly no match for the well-armed rebels. Over the course of the next few days the soldiers conducted a brutal campaign of executions known euphemistically as 'house cleaning'. One witness estimated that the soldiers massacred around 9,000 workers. Within a few days, the working-class threat had been extinguished, and control of Seville had passed into the hands of the insurgents. Once Seville fell, the garrisons at Cádiz (a naval port) and Córdoba followed suit.

From the very beginning, it was evident that the rebelling segments of the Army could not rely on popular support, which, in the event, was confined to certain cities and regions known for their traditionalism. Thus the insurgents predictably achieved easy victories in the Navarre region of the Basque country and in Burgos, Segovia, and Salamanca. Perhaps the greatest demonstration of popular enthusiasm for the revolt occurred in Pamplona, the heart of the ultraconservative Carlist movement and capital of Navarre. With the backing of the Carlist *requetés*, General Mola, a pivotal figure in the conspiracy, had only to declare a state of war to secure the entire province. Instead of erupting into a discordant clash of opposing forces the rising assumed a festive air. The *requetés*, wearing their distinctive red *boinas* (berets) and shouting ¡*Viva Cristo Rey!* (Long live Christ the King!), were met by tumultuous crowds thronging the streets.[2]

Elsewhere the insurgents subdued areas by capitalizing on the climate of political confusion, partly engendered by the dithering responses from the provincial governments. Such was the case in the Aragonese capital of Saragossa, which was taken without a fierce struggle despite the fact that it was a bastion of anarchosyndicalist strength. This was largely because the commander of the garrison, General Miguel Cabanellas, prevaricated long enough to buy the rebels the time needed to purge the military of any pro-Republican elements and to consolidate their forces with those of the Guardia Civil. Without hesitating, the police proceeded to arrest union leaders before they had a chance to mobilize their unions.

As we have already seen, the Asturian capital city of Oviedo had an even greater reputation as a centre of working-class militancy. Yet, thanks to a strategem employed by the garrison commander, Colonel Aranda, the city was easily conquered by the insurgents. By falsely professing his allegiance to the Republic, Aranda convinced the local residents that Oviedo was under no threat from the rebels. Confident that their city was in safe hands, several columns of miners set off for Madrid, giving Aranda the hoped for opportunity to declare for the rising and seize military control of Oviedo.

In the two cities where rebel victories would have assured the success of the *alzamiento*, Madrid and Barcelona, the insurection was stillborn. While this came as no surprise to the rebels, these defeats proved to be a major setback for the *Movimiento*.

The rebels suffered their most crushing defeat in Barcelona, Spain's largest industrial city, and capital of the semi-autonomous region of Catalonia. There the attempted coup was forcefully suppressed by the working classes who were supported in their efforts by members of the Guardia Civil and Guardia de Asalto. At the outset, the plotters' chances for success in Barcelona were prejudiced when they lost the advantage of surprise. Planning to arrive secretly from Majorca on 19 July, the chief organizer of the plot, General Goded, proposed to occupy Barcelona by mobilizing the

---

2. According to Martin Blinkhorn the preponderance of Carlism in this region led to an anomalous situation. 'Whereas in most of Nationalist Spain military control was almost total, in Navarre the utter dependability of the majority of the population and the warm relations between Mola and the local Carlists made it possible for civilian government to continue alongside the military authorities.' Martin Blinkhorn, *Carlism and Crisis in Spain, 1931–1939* (Cambridge, 1975), p. 268.

12,000 or so soldiers quartered in the garrisons located in the centre and on the outskirts of the city. However, news of his conspiracy reached the Catalan government (Generalitat) the night before. Within hours rumours of the planned attack were running rampant. When Lluis Companys, President of the Generalitat, adamantly refused to issue arms to civilians, the unions decided to take matters into their own hands. The defence committees of the CNT and FAI struck first by seizing (with the assistance of sympathetic guards) several small armouries and by confiscating weapons from some ships in the harbour. They also began, along with members of the Marxist POUM and the Socialist Party, commandeering cars and trucks, a few of which were hastily converted into crudely-shaped armoured vehicles.

Early on 19 July, soldiers from the Pedralbes barracks began marching towards the main square of Barcelona, the Plaça de Catalunya, where their column was to converge with units arriving from other barracks. Much to their surprise, the troops were met by a large and angry mob composed of proletarian militias, Civil Guards, Assault Guards and by members of the city police (Mozos de Escuadra) who also stayed loyal to the Generalitat. Those soldiers who managed to make their way to the prearranged place of rendezvous took refuge in strategic buildings ringing the plaza: the telephone exchange, the Hotel Colón, and the Ritz. After the workers threw up barricades around the city centre, intense fighting broke out everywhere. By the time Goded arrived from Majorca by hydroplane, nearly all the rebel-held fortifications were besieged. Overwhelmed by the sheer numbers of civilians and security forces, the bulk of the rebel positions were subdued by nightfall. Only the Atarazanas and San Andrés barracks held out until the following day.

The next morning the anarchosyndicalists spearheaded the final assault on the Atarazanas barracks. Showing unbridled valour – if little military judgement – the anarchists stormed the barracks in a mass attack. This inevitably achieved victory, but at the cost of many casualties, including the venerated anarchist leader Francisco Ascaso who was mortally wounded in the head during the onslaught. The dramatic event not only produced the civil war's first revolutionary martyr and people's hero, but it also established the anarchosyndicalists as the indisputable victors of Barcelona.

Events in Madrid, the Republican capital, followed a different pattern. Initial word of the rebellion caused no alarm in the government. Over Madrid Radio the Prime Minister, Casares Quiroga, attempted to quiet any fears among the *madrileños* by dismissing the plot as absurd and declaring that the rising was confined to Spanish Morocco. But his communiqué failed to reassure the people, for they swiftly reacted to the news by demanding arms from the inert government. Casares Quiroga stubbornly refused to do this, fearing that an armed populace could not be controlled. Late on 18 July the CNT and UGT organizations gave orders for a general strike and began throwing up barricades throughout the working-class districts of the city. By now events were moving at such a dizzying pace that they were well beyond the government's control. Unable to withstand the mounting demands of the situation, the Prime Minister tendered his government's resignation to President Azaña. He was momentarily replaced by the President of the Cortes, Martínez Barrio, who desperately attempted by telephone to reach a compromise with the insurgent officers and thus prevent the rebellion from getting off the ground. The next day José Giral, a distinguished university professor who was a close friend of Azaña, formed a new government. Under immense pressure from the workers' organizations he immediately took the step his predecessors had baulked at: distributing arms to the proletarian militias. His bold action was to prove decisive for the Republican government.

Meanwhile, the leader of the Madrid insurgents, General Fanjul, had declared a state of siege from his headquarters in the Montana barracks. Next day, 20 July, fighting broke out between the armed workers and the besieged soldiers. By the evening of the following day, the people emerged victorious. There was now no way of averting the coming disaster of civil war.

SPAIN DIVIDED: THE MAP OF CONFLICT

Two weeks after the military rebellion, the country itself was roughly divided into two huge sectors, with approximately 11 million under rebel rule and 13 million in the republican zone. Because the insurgents had conquered many areas where the majority of residents were hostile to them, the line dividing Spain did not represent a true political boundary. Areas that just days before had been strongholds of the left – Saragossa, Seville, and Estremadura, for example – now fell under the umbrella of insurgent rule. Within a few weeks, the insurgents had taken over one-third of Spanish territory, including the food producing regions, while the Republicans controlled the centres of heavy industry and the huge gold reserves of the Bank of Spain.

From a purely military standpoint, the *alzamiento* had been a near disaster. Instead of rapidly achieving control of Spain, the rebels had to be content with far less. Not least of their setbacks was the fact that the Army as a whole had not rallied behind the plotters, with the rebels achieving complete success only in the 6th and 7th military regions. Most senior officers remained loyal to the Republic as did a significant number of the

Republican security forces, the Guardia de Asalto. The rebels suffered another major disappointment in failing to take over the Navy. Thanks largely to the initiative shown by sailors, who seized control of many of the ships commanded by pro-rebel officers, nearly two-thirds of the fleet stayed in Republican hands. As a result, the insurgents were unable to ferry the trained troops of the Africa Army across the Straits of Gibraltar. In fact, it was only because Germany and Italy decided at the end of July to aid the rebel cause by supplying them with much needed transport planes (Savoias and Junkers 52s), that the insurgents managed to keep their military initiative from completely stalling.

Above all else, the military conspirators had failed to realize their major objective, namely to restore calm to a country afflicted with chronic civil disorders. Instead, their rebellion had achieved precisely the opposite: it sparked off a civil war and unleashed a massive popular revolution that quickly spread throughout the Republican zone. The Republican government was the first casualty of the rebellion and revolution. Unable to assert itself effectively and authoritatively when challenged by a mutiny within its own Army, the government instantly lost all credibility in the eyes of the people. This in turn precipitated the sudden collapse of innumerable republican institutions. In countless villages and towns, working-class anti-fascist militias committees sprang up, sometimes completely supplanting the local *ayuntamientos* (municipal governments), which had either been abolished or taken over. The political complexion of these militias or anti-fascist committees varied from region to region, generally reflecting the relative strength of the different political parties. Thus, the socialists were in the ascendancy in Mieres (Asturias) and Santander; the socialists and communists shared power in Málaga (Andalucía); the POUM ruled the committee set up in Lérida (Catalonia); while the anarchosyndicalists controlled committees in much of Catalonia and Aragón. By the end of the first week of the conflict the machinery of the state lay in shambles, and 'power', in the words of the communist politician Dolores Ibarruri, 'lay in the streets'.[3]

Because their passivity in the face of military rebellion had allowed the government to be overtaken by circumstances, the bourgeois republican parties had almost overnight lost not just their credibility but also their *raison d'être*. Generally speaking, they remained, to borrow a metaphor from one pro-republican, in a 'comatose state' for the duration of the civil war.[4] The only notable exceptions to this were in the Basque provinces in the republican zone, where the conservative Basque National Party (PNV)

---

3. Dolores Ibarruri, *Speeches and Articles, 1936–1938* (Moscow, 1938), p. 214.
4. Henry Buckley, *The Life and Death of the Spanish Republic* (London, 1940), p. 402.

was a predominant force until 1937; and in Catalonia, where Lluis Companys' left-republican Party, Esquerra, played an important role in reconstituting the powers of the Generalitat.

Despite the fact that republican institutions had been rendered impotent, the middle-class members of the republican left, Republican Union and Radical-Socialist Parties remained in office as representatives of the Popular Front government for the next several weeks. Above all, the central government owed its continued existence to the fact that it still controlled the diplomatic channels to the outside world. José Giral, the Prime Minister, attempted to salvage what he could of the tottering state apparatus, and Manuel Azaña stayed on as President of the Republic. Both failed, however, to invest the government with any authority. Even their supporters, like the moderate socialist Indalecio Prieto, privately criticized Giral's administration for its blatant incompetency. By the end of August it was apparent that rule by the middle-class parties was no longer tenable. On 4 September, Giral resigned and a new government was formed under the popular left-socialist leader, Francisco Largo Caballero.

Given that the military rising in much of Spain had been defeated principally by the working-class organizations (which then went on to become the driving force of a powerful revolutionary movement), the question arises as to why the workers were unable to crush the remaining rebel forces during the first week of the conflict, the period when the latter were most vulnerable. Part of the answer to this question has to do with the positions of the political forces of the republican side. The bitter interparty rivalries that had been brewing during the Second Republic had, by the eve of civil war, generated an atmosphere of mutual distrust that could not be dissipated by their common opposition to the military rebellion. Thus their individual responses to the coup were conditioned above all by the ideological perspectives that each had evolved over a long period of time.

THE REPUBLICAN POLITICAL CONSTELLATION

At the beginning of the civil war, the anarchosyndicalists of the CNT and FAI emerged as the chief promoters of the revolutionary movement that was engulfing vast areas of republican territory, especially in Aragón, Catalonia, and the Levante. That the anarchosyndicalists were at the forefront of the popular revolution is understandable. Because those institutions traditionally relied on to direct social and economic changes had virtually ceased functioning, most political parties found themselves incapable of effectively responding to the demands of the rapidly evolving and unpredictable circumstances. This was not true for the anarchists, who, although unprepared for a revolution of such massive proportions, were nonetheless conditioned through years of indoctrination and revolutionary practice to act spontaneously and directly.

Now that civil war had broken out and the power of the workers was in the ascendant, the revolutionaries of the CNT and FAI insisted that work begin immediately on laying the foundation for the establishment of their ultimate goal: a stateless form of communism, '*comunismo libertario*'. Their attempts to restructure society were both guided and propelled by their unshakeable faith in the justice of their mission as well as by the belief that Fascism would be defeated only if the revolution and war were waged simultaneously. For the anarchosyndicalists, the first step in making the social revolution was to undertake a thoroughgoing collectivization programme, embracing both land and industry. The general course of anarchist activity in the initial stages of the war is best illustrated by the case of Catalonia, where libertarian strength and influence was preponderant.

Following the defeat of Goded's troops and after the full heat of street-fighting had died down, the anarchosyndicalists were generally recognized as the masters not only of Barcelona but of the whole Catalonian region. Yet, apart from their social and economic projects, they had no strategy for wielding political power. Although for the first time in their seventy-year history they were presented with the opportunity to abolish the state, the anarchosyndicalists refused to seize power. To have done otherwise, according to the FAI leader Abad de Santillán, would have meant establishing a libertarian dictatorship, something which flagrantly violated the most hallowed principles of their anti-authoritarian creed. Perhaps also because they were convinced that they lacked the power to impose their revolutionary programme throughout Catalonia, the anarchosyndicalists decided on 23 July to accept President Lluís Companys' proposal for a dual power sharing scheme, whereby the Generalitat would remain standing alongside a newly created political body: the Central Anti-Fascist Militias Committee, CAMC.

Whatever their reasons for agreeing to Companys' plan, the anarchosyndicalists took the unprecedented step of joining a government body and collaborating with non-anarchist parties. Significantly, among the fifteen representatives comprising the CAMC, the CNT and FAI were given only five seats – although they did control the key posts of war, public order, and transport. The remaining portfolios were distributed among the Esquerra, the UGT, the middle-class Acció Catalana, and the Marxist POUM. The main work of the CAMC lay in maintaining a rearguard and in raising militias for the front, but in addition it soon became the de facto ruling power in the region, overseeing not only the economy but also legislative and judicial functions.

By controlling their own armed forces – such as the *patrullas de control*, the FAI Investigation Groups, and Barrio defence units – the anarchosyndicalists ruled the streets and thus replaced the Guardia Civil as the symbols of public order. They also maintained a strong presence in military affairs. The CNT and FAI were the first to raise a column to be sent to the Aragón front, and they played a central role in establishing military training schools. In the economic sphere, the anarchosyndicalists were able to use the CAMC as a vehicle for conducting their comprehensive collectivization programme. By mid-August, the CNT and FAI had assumed administrative and technical control of a large number of factories, public transport facilities, and agricultural enterprises.

Anarchosyndicalist hegemony was also established in the towns and villages of the countryside. In Aragón, for example, the anarchists dominated the Defence Council of Aragón, which was set up in order to coordinate the revolutionary movement in that region. And, before they were overrun by Franco's troops, many villages in Andalucía enthusiastically went over to anarchism, establishing their own libertarian communes.

Elsewhere, however, it was apparent that the anarchosyndicalists were not in a position to carry through a general revolution. In the Basque region, which had not experienced a social revolution, the voice of the anarchosyndicalists was relatively insignificant; while in the besieged city of Madrid, a socialist stronghold, the main focus was on the war effort.

REFORM, REVOLUTION AND SPANISH SOCIALISM

Earlier we noted that, like anarchosyndicalism, Spanish socialism was a heterogeneous movement, traditionally possessing left, right and centre wings. The period 1931–36 saw the dialectical interplay of three distinct tendencies: a non-revolutionary, orthodox Marxist faction headed by Julián Besteiro; a reformist-parliamentary group (PSOE) led by Indalecio Prieto; and a trade union tendency (UGT), represented by Francisco Largo Caballero. After 1934 Besteiro and his followers retired to the background, and thereafter Largo and Prieto were locked in a bitter power struggle to dominate the movement. Largo himself, who, after forty years of being a reformist, had recently embraced the language and style of a classic Marxist revolutionary, commanded the respect and allegiance of the massive UGT, whose membership had swelled to around one-and-a-half million by the time war broke out. Though the head of a minority faction, Prieto nonetheless presented a formidable challenge to Caballero's leadership, not least because of the control he exercised over the executive apparatus of the PSOE.

By denouncing the Popular Front programme of February 1936 and exhorting the workers to establish a 'dictatorship of the proletariat' by whatever means possible, the *caballeristas* obviously contributed to the tense pre-war political atmosphere. Besides prejudicing the Popular Front government's chances of survival, the ultrarevolutionary stance of the Caballero socialists further exacerbated the fissiparous nature of the socialist movement. In particular, the Caballero/Prieto rivalry – more intense now than ever before – precluded the possibility of establishing socialist unity, for the socialists were hopelessly split into mutually antagonistic camps. Thus, in July 1936, it was a deeply divided socialist movement that confronted the enormous difficulties brought on by a revolution and civil war.

When the generals rose in July, large numbers of rank-and-file socialists took the initiative and joined the revolutionary movement. Many saw the collapse of bourgeois authority as an opportunity to seize control of land and factories and create a proletarian dictatorship. In districts formerly governed by *caciques* and absentee landlords, local branches of the socialist FNTT started collectivizing the land of large estates, and in the Valencian region, socialists established a number of agricultural collectives. They also formed de facto alliances with anarchosyndicalists so that they could jointly administer the operation of such vital services as the railways and other communication facilities.

On the other hand, the socialist leaders were, like the leaders of other proletarian parties, caught unawares. As Burnett Bolloten has pointed out, although there is no written or oral record that any leading socialist made a public declaration urging the establishment of a socialist state, such a proposal would have been consistent with Largo Caballero's pre-war position. Curiously, though, Largo refused to accept a leadership role in the revolutionary process. Apart from his behind the scenes denunciations of the Giral administration, Largo was not actively campaigning for a proletariat dictatorship. What caused him to refrain from openly declaring for revolution at this crucial juncture is hard to say. It is possible that he may have been swayed by the pragmatic arguments of the moderate elements in his party as well as by the communists, who were desperately attempting to shore up Giral's shaky government. In addition, his radical temper may well have been cooled by his fear that the setting up of a socialist regime would have destroyed any chance of securing badly needed war materials from the Western powers.

ORTHODOX MARXISM: THE PCE

Founded in 1921 by several dissident socialist groups as well as by a faction of Leninist-inspired syndicalists from the CNT, the Partido Comunista de España (PCE) remained a minor factor in Spanish politics before the civil war. From its inception, the development of 'orthodox' Spanish communism was conditioned by two major factors: factional strife and foreign intervention. The official party, which maintained headquarters in Madrid, took all its directives from Moscow. Whenever disagreements arose between the PCE leadership and the Comintern, the judgements of the latter were always binding. Thus members who refused to accept the Comintern's infallibility regarding policy and the interpretation of theoretical questions faced certain expulsion from the party. But despite these attempts to impose a strict discipline on the party's cadres, the movement itself remained uncoordinated and fragmented for many years. Moreover, the PCE's Russian style of politics failed to attract the Spanish proletariat, whose sympathies were already divided between the socialists and anarchosyndicalists.

The active participation of foreign agents or 'instructors' in the PCE's internal affairs also had a profound impact on the party's development. This was especially true during the civil war, when the party's political bureau was actually being run by Comintern officials. When the military rising began, several prominent Comintern *apparatchiks* were already operating in Spain, one such being the Argentinian Vittorio Codovila (alias 'Medina') who was, according to one well-informed communist source, the 'real head of the party' before the war. Codovila, who also served as 'Moscow's eye' in Spain after the July military rebellion, received able assistance from such skilled *apparatchiks* as the German Heinz Neumann and the Hungarian Ernö Gerö (alias 'Pedro'), who directed communist affairs in Catalonia during the civil war. Some of the Comintern's best brains and seasoned agents arrived shortly after the war began. Palmiro Togliatti (called 'Ercole', 'Ercoli', and 'Alfredo'), an Italian communist who was a member of the Executive Committee of the Comintern, remained in Spain until the end of the war, as did the Bulgarian, Boris Stepanov. Another important 'instructor' was the Italian Vittorio Vidali (known as Carlos Contreras), who became chief political commissar of the prestigious Fifth Regiment.

Throughout the Second Republic, the communists had been constantly searching for ways to break out of their isolation from the masses. This led them to develop a variety of strategies, ranging from union splitting – practised before 1934 – to forming broad alliances with leftist working-class and liberal bourgeois parties as embodied in the Popular Front Programme. When the Comintern adopted the moderate Popular Front strategy

113

(which called for the collective defence of bourgeois-democratic regimes) in the summer of 1935, the party was obliged to jettison its ultrarevolutionism. Instead of assailing the socialists as 'social fascists' and struggling to overthrow the government in order to establish workers' soviets throughout Spain, the PCE was now laying stress on working-class unity and promoting alliances with the liberal segment of the bourgeoisie. The new strategy also demanded a complete revision of the party's theoretical assumptions: in Spain the objective conditions were no longer considered ripe for a proletariat dictatorship, rather they required that she first pass through the intermediary stage of bourgeois democracy. While the PCE's *volte-face* in no way implied that the communists were abandoning their ultimate goal of establishing a soviet-style government in Spain, it did mean that, at least for the time being, the revolutionary aspirations of the workers would have to be harnessed.

The communists' anti-revolutionary policies appealed strongly to the left-republican parties and especially to the Prietista-wing of the socialist movement. And, as we have already seen, the PCE's strategy found concrete expression in the formation of the Popular Front alliance of 1936, thanks to which the left-wing parties emerged victorious in the February elections. The programme of the Popular Front, however, found little echo among the great masses of workers belonging to the UGT and the CNT-FAI. Thus, although the PCE may have enhanced its standing among the middle classes, it had as yet to acquire a substantial working-class constituency.

In their tireless pursuit before the war both to strengthen the Popular Front alliance and to enlarge their popular base, the communists finally achieved a significant victory in April 1936 when a merger was concluded between the Socialist Youth (FJS) and Communist Youth (JCI). The result of this fusion was an organization of some 150,000 members called the Juventud Socialista Unificada, JSU (Unified Socialist Youth), which provided the orthodox communists with a secure foothold in the socialist movement. Headed by Santiago Carrillo, who emerged as a key communist figure during the civil war, the JSU represented the PCE's first major step towards its professed goal of creating a unified socialist movement under the direction of a single Marxist party.

When confronted by the military uprising of July, the PCE responded by doing all it could to prop up the Popular Front government. For example, in Seville, a communist stronghold since 1930, the PCE had placed its faith in the government – as against the spontaneous and independent actions of the workers – to put down the rebellion. Yet, as we have seen, Seville's governor remained paralysed by fear while Quiepo de Llano took the city with only a few troops. In those regions where the workers refused to wait for the government to take action against the conspirators, the PCE, like most middle-class republican parties, tended to retreat to the background rather than engage in the intense street fighting.

While the pro-government policy adopted by the PCE may have been unpopular and even distanced the party further from the mainstream of the labour movement, it was in keeping with the moderate line being followed by the USSR and its instrument for international politics, the Comintern. At the time, Moscow was endeavouring to improve its diplomatic ties with the Western democracies – especially with France and Great Britain – so it clearly did not want to raise the spectre of communist revolution in a European country. And, as an obedient servant of the Soviet Union, the PCE was obliged to interpret events in Spain according to the prevailing Comintern line. Consequently, the PCE readily promoted the view that the war was being fought not to advance the social revolution but to defend the Republic and preserve democracy in Spain.

Amidst the climate of political dissolution that prevailed during the first weeks of the war, the communists were the only ones who openly challenged the radical agenda that the left-wing organizations were striving to implement. They were the first, for example, to champion the interests of the middle classes: they undertook a spirited defence of the small and medium property owner, the tenant farmer, artisan, and small businessman. The PCE's principal mouthpiece, *Mundo Obrero*, thus appealed to everyone 'to respect the property of small businessmen and industrialists, for they are our brothers'.

Fearful that their movement might be absorbed by their rivals, especially in areas where the CNT and FAI were in the ascendant, the communists moved quickly to consolidate their forces. At their insistence four Catalan organizations were merged towards the end of July, forming the Partit Socialist de Unificat de Catalunya (PSUC). Although the PSUC was nominally socialist – one of the constituent parties was the Catalan Federation of the Socialist Party – it was in fact controlled by the communists. Soon after it was constituted the PSUC adhered to the Comintern, and throughout the war its policies were indistinguishable from those of the PCE.

As the party was at first quite minuscule – its largest component, the Unió Socialista de Catalunya, had a membership of only some 2,500 – it hardly seemed to pose any threat to the revolutionary organizations. Yet, in the following months, the PSUC experienced a spectacular growth and became a decisive political force in Catalonia.

COMMUNIST DISSIDENTS: THE POUM

The left-wing political arena was further complicated by the presence of the highly controversial and independent Marxist party, Partido Obrera de Unificación Marxista (POUM). The party itself never attracted a mass following, although, thanks to the prestige enjoyed by members like Joaquín Maurín, Julián Gorkín, Jordi Arquer, and Andreu Nin, it exerted an influence throughout Spain that was disproportionate to its actual numbers. At its inception, the POUM claimed around 7,000 members: approximately 6,500 coming from the independent communist Bloc Obrer i Camperol (BOC), and 500 from the Trotskyist Izquierda Comunista, (IC). By the time the war broke out, the POUM had grown to around ten thousand members, with its centres of power and influence largely confined to Catalonia.[5]

Branded as Trotskyist by its Stalinist critics in the PCE both before and during the civil war, the POUM was actually an amalgam of mainly Catalan dissident communist groups which never maintained anything but tenuous relations with the Fourth International movement. In fact, from its foundation in September 1935, the POUM had followed an independent course of action that sometimes brought it into conflict with Trotskyists and Stalinists alike. The party's principal leader and co-founder, Joaquín Maurín, was unequivocally opposed to Trotskyism, as were most members of the BOC, the majority current in the POUM. It is essential to note in this connection that, while they no longer swore allegiance to Trotsky, several key members of the ruling cadre, notably Juan Andrade and Andreu Nin, were deeply influenced by Trotskyist ideas. Neither Andrade, at one time a prominent member of the Izquierda Comunista, nor Nin, the former head of the IC and Trotsky's principal contact in Spain between 1930 and 1934 who became political secretary of the POUM during the war, ever renounced their commitment to such fundamental Trotskyist notions as the idea of the 'permanent revolution'. According to this view, which was shared by Maurín and his followers, the Spanish revolution would develop not through distinct stages, as the Stalinist PCE maintained, but as a continuous process, passing directly from the democratic phase to the socialist one. The POUM generally were also in agreement with Trotsky's trenchant critique of Stalinism. Such conceptual differences may have been academic before July 1936, but during the war they were a main source of friction between the various republican political parties.

---

5. The POUM's trade union affiliate, Federación Obrera de Unidad Sindical, (FOUS), claimed a membership of around 60,000 before it merged with the Catalan UGT in July 1936.

Indeed, it was the POUM's understanding of the revolutionary process as well as its virulent anti-Stalinism that later proved to be an enormous liability for the party.

THE NATIONALISTS AT WAR

We have seen that, though the July rebellion had failed in two-thirds of the country, the insurgents pressed hard to achieve a swift victory. From a purely military standpoint this seemed possible, for, in the early weeks of fighting, the insurgents enjoyed several major advantages over their opponents. Above all, they possessed the best-trained and best-equipped sector of the Spanish Army, the famous Army of Africa, which was under General Francisco Franco's command. In addition to these 47,127 men, the rebels counted approximately 35,000 supporters drawn from government para-military organizations like the Guardia de Asalto and Guardia Civil. Second, as we have indicated, the revolution that had been set in motion by the rebellion had left the Republican regular army and other armed government units in shambles. Thus, while the Republican civilian militia initially outnumbered rebel troops their numerical advantage counted for little. Even more important was the fact that the rebels secured military, naval, air and technical support from both Italy and Germany, and this assistance more than compensated for the fact that the republicans controlled Spain's principal resources, including her gold reserves and major industrial and agricultural producing regions.

However, a variety of factors militated against a quick Insurgent triumph. Fate intervened in the opening moments of the conflict: the plane crash that killed General Sanjurjo on 20 July left the conspirators without a leader. While this did not throw the rebel leadership into disarray, it did create the conditions for a power struggle between the members of the ruling junta and the civilian parties on the right. Far more important were the series of technical setbacks that the insurgents suffered at the outset of the rebellion. The Army of Africa's inability to cross the straits in order to form a bridgehead with rebel forces on the mainland, for instance, greatly dissipated the momentum of the rising by upsetting the timing and coordination of the conspirators' actions.

Recognizing that the success of its plans urgently demanded a coordinated military response from every quarter, the rebel army moved quickly to unite its cause. Under Mola's initiative a military junta was set up in Burgos, the Junta de Defensa Nacional, and between 18 July and 1 October 1936 it was staffed by the top nine military leaders in the rebel camp, the most notable being Generals Cabanellas, Franco, Mola, Quiepo de Llano and Kindelán (of the airforce). The purely military composition of the ruling body made it clear that the army was in control of the rebellion and that civilian parties would of necessity be relegated to a subordinate role.

By late September, when a Nationalist victory seemed imminent, another step was taken towards consolidating rebel military authority by establishing a *mando único*. Among the limited field of candidates, Francisco Franco stood out as the most likely figure to assume supreme command. Holding impeccable military credentials – while serving in Morocco he had become Europe's youngest general since Napoleon – Franco commanded the respect of his peers and was widely acknowledged as the best general in Spain. In addition, he outranked his nearest challenger, General Mola (who was only a brigadier general), and the close relations he had established with the rebels' foreign supporters – particularly Germany – made him an indispensable figure in the rebel camp. In the event, on 29 September Franco was appointed as supreme military commander or *generalísimo* of all the armed forces as well as the Head of the Government and of the Spanish State. With the new leader chosen, the process of bringing together all the different bases of rebel operations – such as the Press and Propaganda Office in Salamanca and the administrative branch of the provisional government, Junta Técnica del Estado, operating in Burgos – was set in motion.

The insurgents' swift consolidation of military command greatly facilitated their efforts to build a new army out of the ruins of the old one, with the Army of Africa, Mola's Army of the North and Quiepo de Llano's Army of the South forming the apexes around which a new Nationalist military organization would be built. In the coming months, the rebels revamped their military structures – brigades were reorganized into divisions, for example – and successfully mobilized an ever-increasing number of troops. By the beginning of January 1938, the Nationalist army, with some 500,000 soldiers, was over four times as large as it was at the beginning of the war.

Notwithstanding their vitally important contributions to the initial rebellion, the army leadership was ill at ease with the military role of civilian groups. Thus, for example, when the Junta de Defensa Nacional was set up on 25 July in order to coordinate the political and military activities of the Insurgents, the Falange was left out in the cold. Throughout the autumn of 1936, the Cuartel General took steps to reduce the Falange's and Carlists' control over their own militias. Then, on 20 December, Franco sought to eliminate once and for all the threat of civilian military competition by proclaiming that, henceforth, all voluntary troops would come under the command of the regular army.

PROGRESS OF THE WAR

By early September it appeared as though the Nationalists were at the point of taking the capital: Yagüe's Legionnaires and Moroccan *regulares* had arrived within striking distance of Madrid. And since Madrid was now the last place to retreat to, the disorganized Republican army was forced to make a stand. Yet, at the last minute, instead of marching on the capital, Franco decided to divert his troops in order to save the rebel forces holed-up in the Alcázar.

Towering over Toledo and the Tagus River, the Alcázar was a medieval palace-fortress that had served as a training school for infantry officers since the 1800s. In 1936 it became an island of refuge for some 1,300 insurgents under the command of the military governor, Colonel José Moscardó. Though surrounded by republican militia in the city below, the besieged rebels stubbornly refused to surrender. Thanks to the amazing fortitude and determination shown by its inhabitants – mostly members of the Guardia Civil, Falangists, military officers and cadets – as well as the republicans' repeated failures to take the citadel, the Alcázar siege had achieved legendary status by the time Colonel Varela's column liberated the garrison on 27 September.

While the relief operation held great sentimental importance for the Nationalist cause, it clearly went against the dictates of military strategy. Franco's critics saw it as a serious setback, arguing that, by delaying his advance on Madrid, rebel forces had lost valuable time. In fact, republican reinforcements – such as Durruti's column, Soviet aid and the International Brigades – had arrived in the capital, thereby preventing the Nationalists from achieving an easy victory.

Events of the first months of fighting demonstrated that Franco was not always adhering to conventional military protocols but rather was conducting the war on his own terms. Toledo and Málaga offered the best examples of how his strategy to defeat the republicans was unfolding. In the former case, Franco had willingly stopped short of a certain victory in order to relieve a relatively insignificant military garrison. His gamble had cost him Madrid but it paid off in terms of propaganda: the dramatic rescue of Moscardó and the beleaguered Nationalist forces garnered Franco the kind of international attention he needed to win over foreign opinion for his cause. Later, in Málaga, Franco made it clear to his general staff that he was to be the supreme commander who would take full credit for the Nationalist triumph. Thus when Quiepo de Llano had taken the city and wanted to sweep through eastern Andalucía, delivering a crushing blow to the remaining republican cities in the region, including Almería. Franco told him to hold back. His excessive cautiousness may well have aggravated his commanders, but Franco stood his ground: he wanted to proceed at his own pace. For, as these examples indicate, Franco was not above calculating the symbolic significance of a campaign rather than measuring its success in purely military terms.

CHAPTER SEVEN

Revolution in the Towns and Countryside

In its early stages, the popular revolution provoked by the military rebellion distinguished itself from all others in the twentieth century both by its magnitude and by the dramatic way in which it reshaped the economic and social landscape of rural and industrial areas. As the revolution unfolded in the towns and countryside it became increasingly evident that, although fuelled by popular enthusiasm, it was being propelled and guided in varying degrees by the anarchosyndicalists of the CNT-FAI, the independent Marxists of the POUM, and the left-socialists of the UGT. Yet, despite its impressive dimensions, the revolution itself was for many years either ignored or at best received scant treatment in much of the Civil War literature. This was even true of most fictional accounts. Both André Malraux's *Man's Hope* and Ernest Hemingway's *For Whom the Bell Tolls*, two of the better known novels about the war, ignore the revolutionary side of republican politics. Also curiously silent about this crucial aspect of the Spanish conflict – at least until recently – were the popular media. Such widely-screened films as 'The Spanish Earth' (1938) and Frédéric Rossif's *Mourir à Madrid* (1963) evoke intensely moving and compelling images to convey the tragedy of the war on the republican side.[1] Conspicuously absent from these films, though, are the often stirring episodes

---

1. For a sampling of the various genre of civil war films – ranging from political documentaries to Hollywood commercial productions – see, 'La Guerre D'Espagne vue par le cinéma,' in *Les Cahiers de la Cinémathèque*, no. 21, 1976?, Perpignan, France; and Marjorie A. Valleau, *The Spanish Civil War in American and European Films* (Ann Arbor, Michigan, 1982). Jaime Camino's, *La vieja memoria* (The Old Memory),' produced in the late 1970s, is perhaps the only major documentary film that attempts to present the perspectives of all the major factions involved in the war.

of the hundreds of thousands of people who were engaged in social experiments.[2]

Outside of the anarchist movement, there were very few historians who recognized that in order to understand the Civil War it was crucial to take into account the profound impact of the July revolution on Republican affairs. Two historians who fell into this category were John S. Brademas, who examined the anarchists' role in the Civil War in his Oxford University dissertation (1953); and Burnett Bolloten, whose controversial *The Grand Camouflage* (1961) was one of the first studies to situate the revolution in the broader context of Republican politics. Regrettably, it was not until some years after these groundbreaking histories were published that the revolutionary movement began to receive the attention it rightly deserved in the literature on the Civil War.[3]

Perhaps the principal reason why the popular or July revolution became an historiographical problem is that during the war there was an elaborate attempt by various republican groups to conceal the revolutionary movement. For both political and ideological reasons the communists were impelled to deny that the immense social upheaval which had been unleashed by the military rebellion had fundamentally altered the substructures of the capitalist order. The Spanish Revolution, it was affirmed, like the French Revolution of 1789, had not gone beyond the bourgeois–democratic stage. How they justified this highly questionable interpretation was intimated to Franz Borkenau, an Austrian sociologist and former member of the Comintern who was visiting Spain early on in the war:

> Representative members of the PSUC [i.e., the Communist Party of Catalonia] express the opinion that there is no revolution at all . . . Spain, they explain, is faced with a unique situation: the government is fighting against its own army. And that is all. I hinted at the fact that the workers were armed, that the administration had fallen into the hands of revolutionary committees, that people were being executed without trial in thousands, that both factories and estates were being expropriated and managed by their former hands. What was revolution if it was not that? I was told that I was mistaken; all that had no political significance . . .[4]

As the war progressed, it became ever more difficult for the communists

---

2. Documentary films produced by the right and Nationalist sympathizers outside of Spain were also heavily biased. For examples of this, see, Anthony Aldgate, *Cinema and History: British Newsreels and the Spanish Civil War* (London, 1979).
3. Renewed interest in anarchism and similar revolutionary ideologies during the student unrest of the mid- and late-1960s revived interest in the Spanish Civil War and prompted intellectuals like Noam Chomsky to inquire why the extensive revolutionary movement was virtually ignored in the numerous histories in the war. See his trenchant analysis of 'liberal scholarship' in *American Power and the New Mandarins* (New York, 1969).
4. Franz Borkenau, *The Spanish Cockpit* (Ann Arbor, 1974), p. 110.

to force circumstances to fit their ideological framework. Partly because of this in March 1937 they decided to modify their position. At a plenum of the Central Committee of the PCE, the Party Secretary, José Díaz, proclaimed that the foundations of fascism had been destroyed in Spain. 'In all the provinces dominated by us,' he explained, 'there are no great landowners any more.' He likewise conceded that militarism had disappeared and that the power and influence of the Church, another pillar of the *ancien régime*, had also been shattered. Despite these concessions to reality, though, the communists made it clear in their propaganda that the objective conditions for a social revolution did not exist in Spain. They therefore refused to abandon the view that Spain was in the throes of a bourgeois-democratic revolution, albeit one marked with a profound social content. Thus Díaz went on to declare that the civil war was being fought in order to establish a 'democratic republic of a new type', that is, not one 'like that of France or any other capitalist country' but rather one where the material bases on which fascism and reaction rest had been completely demolished.

There can be little doubt that the communists' persistent refusal to acknowledge the depth and magnitude of the Spanish revolution had more to do with political motives than with their desire to remain consistent with Marxist theory. For at the root of their efforts to deny the class character of the Spanish struggle lay their domestic and foreign policy objectives. Within Spain itself the communists were striving to push through their own programme of nationalization, whereby agricultural and industrial enterprises would be brought under a central authority.

The Spanish communists were also obliged to adhere to an anti-revolutionary position because they recognized the preeminence of the Soviet Union's diplomatic aims. At a time when Russia was herself experiencing a massive domestic programme of social and economic engineering, the USSR's overriding foreign policy concern was to protect herself from outside intervention, especially from the increasingly aggressive fascist countries. In fact, it was the Soviets' fear of German expansion eastwards that had spurred them to abandon their revolutionary political outlook in 1935 in favour of the Popular Front strategy, which promoted closer cooperation with the democratic capitalist powers. Partly because their anti-revolutionary outlook had met with some success in France – with whom Russia signed a pact of mutual assistance in May 1935 – the Soviets did not want anything, including the untimely Spanish conflict, to upset the diplomatic course they were now charting. As far as Moscow was concerned, the workers' revolution in Spain had to be indefinitely postponed so that the Republic could be presented as a democratic regime, one that was potentially an ally to the Western powers.

While the communists and their supporters were attempting to conceal or at the very least minimize the significance of the July revolution, its physical reality was being recorded by numerous eye-witnesses. The German Agustín Souchy, the Austrian Franz Borkenau, and the Englishman George Orwell were among the better known foreigners who managed to capture in their writings the spectacular and often bewildering economic and social changes that unfolded during the first months of war and revolution. In his diary, later published as the *The Spanish Cockpit*, Borkenau recalls his first impression of Barcelona during the high tide of revolutionary transformations: '[As] we turned round the corner of the Ramblas [the chief artery of Barcelona] came a tremendous surprise: before our very eyes, in a flash, unfolded itself the revolution. It was as if we had been landed on a continent different from anything I had seen before.' Indeed, evidence of the revolution was visible from every street corner. Draped over the entrances of countless cafés, shops, and other businesses were large signs, proclaiming with such slogans as *Empresa Obrera* (Proletarian Enterprise) and *Incautado* (Expropriated) that the enterprise was now under worker management. The lexicons of worker control were stamped on the sides of taxis, cars, and public trams, which now bore the initials and identifying colours of the different workers' parties: CNT-FAI, UGT, POUM, PSUC, etc. And, on newspaper kiosks and the walls of nearly every building were plastered huge propaganda posters. Employing forceful language and utilizing the dramatic modernist art symbols characteristic of the period, these visually stunning posters announced a variety of pointed messages: 'Stamp out Fascism!'; 'Anarchist books are our weapons against Fascism'; 'Comrades! Increase production and we will smash Fascism!'; 'The drunkard is a social parasite. Eliminate him!'

What was most astonishing, especially to foreigners, was the way in which the bourgeoisie had 'disappeared' overnight. When people began returning to the streets on 24 July, no man or woman dared appear in a hat or otherwise dress in a bourgeoise style. The anarchist daily *Solidaridad Obrera* (popularly known as 'Soli') defiantly proclaimed: 'Hats have ever been a useless symbol of pride and privilege. Pirates, buccaneers, princes, señoritos, priests – these are the hatted folks of history. What has the free worker to do with this outworn symbol of bourgeois arrogance? No hats, comrades, on the Ramblas and the future will be yours.' Even foreigners, such as the American writer Meagan Laird, felt pressured to adopt the new dress code: 'I am without a hat, and wearing a sleeveless cotton tennis dress. No woman in the whole city dares to go out with a hat on now. It is the symbol of wealth in Spain – the sign and stamp of the hated aristocracy.'[5] Instead of the latest fashions, it appeared as though everyone was donning the *mono azul* (literally, 'blue monkey') or worker overall which was meant to symbolize the new social order.

The British author George Orwell and the United Press reporter Burnett Bolloten were particularly struck by the moral content of the revolution. For underlying the new social and economic order was a morality that was manifesting itself in a multiplicity of ways. Taxi drivers, barbers, waiters, and shoeshine boys refused tips with infinite pride, explaining that the revolution had liberated men forever from moral servitude. Luxury hotels in the major cities were requisitioned by the revolutionaries and put in the service of the revolution: some were converted to barracks for the military, while others – like the famous Ritz hotel in Barcelona – became communal dining halls. As far as the revolutionaries were concerned the days of privilege, egoism, hate, envy and other 'bourgeois values' had been banished forever.

REVOLUTION AND UTOPIANISM

Given the unbridled enthusiasm with which so many people embraced the revolution, it is apparent that the Spanish revolution was above all a movement galvanized by utopian ideals. This is especially evident in the case of the anarchosyndicalists' attempts at revolutionary experimentation. The great Russian anarchist Michael Bakunin's often-quoted dictum that 'the urge to destroy is a creative urge' was applied with apostolic fervour in Spain. Like Bakunin, the Spanish libertarians had long believed that the first step of the revolution was to purify the atmosphere and 'transform completely the milieu in which we live'.[6] Indeed for the Spanish anarchists the early days of the revolution represented a period of 'magnificent disorder – a disorder that makes possible the resurgence of the old regime'. First and foremost this meant liquidating all the existing bourgeois institutions in order to create the conditions for the proverbial *tabula rasa* on which a new society could be erected in accordance with libertarian principles. As one libertarian explained: 'We must carry out a total revolution. Expropriation must also be total . . . If the Spanish worker does not carve out his own liberty, the State will reconstruct the authority of the government, destroying little by little the conquests made at the cost of a thousand sacrifices.'[7] It was vital not to hesitate or delay the revolutionary

---

5. Meagan Laird, *The Atlantic Monthly*, November 1936, p. 528.
6. James Joll, *The Anarchists* (Cambridge, Massachusetts, 1980), p. 69.
7. *Solidaridad Obrera*, 26 August 1936.

process, according to the vast majority of anarchists, for they believed that unless the 'chains of repression' were immediately destroyed the moment for liberation would pass them by.

In contrast to their Marxist counterparts, who held that the revolution required a centralized vanguard party, the anarchosyndicalists believed that the masses would, thanks to years of revolutionary indoctrination and revolutionary practice, know what to do when the day of revolution arrived. It is important to note in this connection that, by 1936, anarchist ideas had filtered down to even the least literate segments of society; for it was customary for the *obrero consciente* or enlightened anarchist to indoctrinate illiterate workers and peasants in cafés and other public gathering spots by reading the libertarian press out loud.

The blueprints for social and economic reconstruction were scattered in dozens of anarchist tracts but they were most coherently and persuasively expressed in the works of such venerated anarchist thinkers as the Italian Errico Malatesta, the Russian Peter Kropotkin, and his leading Spanish interpreter during the 1930s, Dr Isaac Puente. According to Puente's widely-circulated pamphlet, *Comunismo libertario* (1932), which in many respects represented a distillation of seventy years of anarchist thinking in Spain, the free municipality and trade union were to be the social units around which future society would be organized. The emerging libertarian society was to be based on a system of reciprocal pacts, which was to serve as the mechanism for cementing together the new organizations.

Further evidence of the idealism animating the revolutionaries can be found in their collectivization programme. In the economic sphere, the anarchosyndicalists saw the collective as the foundation-stone for a truly emancipated society. The advent of collectivism, predicted the anarchist thinker José Negre, would finally bring about man's liberation from both the economic chaos and the moral corruption engendered by the capitalist system. But under the new system, the innate sense of solidarity and fraternity present in all men and women would prevail, providing the basis of a simple economic exchange that functioned according to the maxim: 'from each according to his abilities to each according to his need'. The abiding optimism of these beliefs suggests that the anarchists themselves were far less concerned with the financial advantages of collectivization than they were with the social and moral arrangements to be found in the new system. To create a society based on justice was their main goal; they had no interest in establishing competitive economic structures which only enriched the community materially. This is not to say that the Spanish revolutionaries were completely oblivious to the practical realities of their movement. For notwithstanding their revolutionary romanticism, the anarchists also held a pragmatic view of what was needed to bring about the social and economic reality they envisaged. In their industrial collectives, for example, some anarchists enthusiastically promoted the ideas of so-called 'scientific management and technology'. In fact, during the war the quality of workmanship and efficiency of production were stressed within each *sindicato* as witnessed by the fact that several anarchist unions adopted the management techniques of Taylorism; this, among other things, sought to measure with mathematical accuracy each step of the production process.[8]

THE NEW SOCIETY: THE CHANGING ROLE OF WOMEN

The social content of the revolution is illustrated by the changed status of women in the republican zone. From a strictly legal standpoint, republican women reaffirmed the political and social rights they were granted during the liberal period of the Second Republic. The legalization of divorce, abortion on demand, and equal status for working women were among the reforms they regarded as fundamental to the Spain they were defending. A small number of women rose to become important and influential figures in public life. Federica Montseny became the first woman in Spain to serve in a government cabinet, while Dolores Ibarruri, Teresa Pàmies, and Margarita Nelken played prominent roles in a variety of political and social activities at the regional and national levels. Perhaps the most dramatic shift in gender relations at this time, however, came about when a certain number of women took up arms and joined the militias. Although few of these *milicianas* were ever combatants at the front, all were prepared to risk their lives in order to defeat fascism.[9]

While republican groups of various political shades promoted women's rights, not all were striving towards the same end. Non-revolutionary parties, such as the Esquerra, advocated a middle-class feminism, whereas for many of those on the left the question of women's liberation was bound up with the revolutionary process. For example, the all-women's group named Mujeres Libres (Free Women) was one of the leading left-wing organizations that was not interested in emancipating women in general. Although it was autonomous from the gigantic CNT-FAI organizations, Mujeres Libres was regarded by its some 20,000 or so members as an integral component of the anarchist movement. Nonetheless, Mujeres

8. On the influence of Taylorism in the anarchist unions see Michael Seidman's study, *Workers Against Work* (Berkeley, 1990).
9. On this fascinating subject, see Mary Nash, 'Women in War: Milicianas and Armed Combat in Revolutionary Spain, 1936–1939', in *The International History Review*, vol. XV, no 2, May 1993.

were above all concerned with the plight of working-class women who, it was argued, suffered in bourgeois society under the twin burdens of capitalist exploitation and male oppression. Thus, for example, while the FAI urged prostitutes to organize themselves and called upon men to treat them with the respect shown to other comrades, members of Mujeres Libres demanded that prostitution be abolished altogether: 'The most pressing task to be realized in the new social order,' exhorted the Mujeres daily, 'is to suppress prostitution. Before we occupy ourselves with the economy and instruction . . . we have radically to put an end to this form of social degradation.'[10]

Other political groups, such as the PCE, PSUC and the POUM, also made great strides towards breaking the age-old mould of gender prejudice. In a society deeply imbued with conservative religious values and dominated by a 'machismo' ethic this was no mean feat. Countless years of female subjugation had left their imprint not only on men but also on most women. The Australian poet and Marxist activist Mary Low observed this phenomenon during the early weeks of the revolutionary movement: 'The Spanish women were anxious to grab their liberty, but they had been closed up and corsetted so long that they didn't know how much of it there was to be had. Often they were content with the little scraps which answered their first call. It seemed so much to them.'[11]

On different levels Spanish women in Republican Spain were liberated from their traditional roles: not only were they permitted to enter the workplace[12] but they were also given the opportunity to participate in areas formerly the exclusive preserve of males. Many worked in jobs vacated by men who had gone off to fight.[13] In unprecedented numbers, women also assumed managerial positions in the trades, service, and manufacturing industries. In some enterprises – especially where women's groups set up new schools, crèches, and collective services – the growing predominance of female labour resulted in a transformation of the workplace environment.

Even at home, the female's status was undergoing radical revision. Young girls were, for the first time, allowed to socialize in restaurants, bars and other public places – although they rarely went out unchaperoned. In some parts of republican Spain formal attempts were made to redefine family relations along revolutionary lines. For example, Andreu Nin, the POUM Minister of Justice in the Generalitat, had inserted in the new marriage code a paragraph which instructed the husband 'to remember that your

10. *Mujeres Libres*, 8 August 1936.
11. Mary Low and Juan Brea, *Red Spanish Notebook* (San Francisco, 1979), p. 184.
12. See Seidman, *Workers Against Work*.
13. Lourdes Beneria, 'Women's Participation in Paid Production Under Capitalism: The Spanish Experience', in *Review of Radical Political Economics*, vol. VIII, no 1, 1975.

wife goes into marriage as your companion, with the same rights and privileges as yourself'.[14]

Although in some respects women's lives were profoundly altered by these revolutionary changes, it is also true that most women in the republican zone were far from being wholly freed from the bonds of traditionalism. In fact, generally speaking, gender relations were not radically transformed in Republican Spain. Even in the libertarian movement, which adopted the most radical women's rights agenda, old ideas and prejudices died hard. The French anarchist Gaston Leval, who witnessed the unfolding of the revolutionary movement in anarchist-dominated regions of the republican zone, observed that only in about half of the libertarian agrarian collectives did women receive the same wages as men, while in the rest women who did the same work as males were paid less, presumably on the grounds that women rarely lived alone. Other pro-libertarian eye-witnesses' testimonies point out that, despite the recognition of their labour, women were frequently assigned to conventionally-defined female tasks, such as cooking and cleaning.[15] The latent sexism of some anarchist males was also evident in their belief that, owing to inherent physical differences, men were expected to retire at age 65 and women at 50. Yet to establish an economic system based on salary differentials and the sexual division of labour clearly violated the spirit of libertarianism. The existence of these economic practices underscores the fact that, however committed the revolutionaries were to the idea of destroying the traditional pattern of sexism in Spain, they nevertheless failed in many instances to remain consistent with their own principles.

REVOLUTIONARY TERROR/REVOLUTIONARY JUSTICE

If the anarchists believed that the initial stages of revolution would reveal man's innate goodness, it was equally true that the act of revolting reflected man's baser instincts for violence. The use of violence against individuals was one of the more repellent forms the revolution took. After the political boundaries separating left from right had been drawn, a wave of bloodshed swept through both sides. Underlying this 'cult of bloodletting' was the belief that for victory to be assured it was necessary to purge the rearguard of undesirable elements. Because it was sometimes difficult

14. Cited in Low and Brea, *Red Spanish Notebook*, pp. 180–1. See also, Francesc Bonamusa, *Andreu Nin y el movimiento comunista en España (1930–1937)*, (Barcelona, 1977), pp. 453–5.
15. See Martha A. Ackelsberg, 'Separate and Equal? Mujeres Libres and Anarchist Strategy for Women's Emancipation', in *Feminist Studies*, vol. XI, 1985.

to determine the loyalty of an individual or group, there can be little doubt that innocent people fell victim to the purges that took place during the first few months of the war and revolution. The principal targets were those who were directly involved in the rebellion itself as well as those who could be identified as 'class enemies', namely the leading representatives of the right. Literally thousands of people were summarily executed in the opening weeks of the conflict. Just how many were killed is difficult to say with any certainty, not least because many deaths were not faithfully recorded in the public registers. But perhaps as many as 80,000 people were assassinated during the republican or 'Red' repression.

The first stages of the reign of terror that occurred in republican territory, though intimately linked to the class hatred that existed before the revolution, were largely spontaneous. One eye-witness, the American anarchist-feminist Emma Goldman, offered an explanation of how the collective rage among the working classes had spawned terrorism: 'Revolution is always coercive and violent – it is always the culminating expression of the accumulated wrong and injustice as well as brutalities caused by our system; to expect therefore that people who have for centuries known every physical and mental torture should during the Revolution deal with their enemies with kid gloves and gentleness, this is expecting the super-human of the individual and the impossible of the mass.'[16] Whatever psychological motives were behind the terror, there can be no question that its horrifying consequences overwhelmed even those who belonged to the revolutionary movement. The anarchist leader Federica Montseny lamented: '. . . the Revolution, in which uncontrolled and uncontrollable forces operate imperiously, is blind and destructive, grandiose, and cruel; that once the first step has been taken and the first dike broken, the people pour like a torrent through the breach, and that it is impossible to dam the flood. How much is wrecked in the heat of the struggle and in the blind fury of the storm!'[17]

After this first wave of violence subsided, however, the executions did not stop. Rather they continued for some weeks and were conducted in a more organized fashion. In the beginning, left political parties or worker organizations would select the victims. Those accused of being fascist or pro-fascist were hastily convicted in 'revolutionary courts' or people's tribunals which had dispensed with the protocols of the traditional Spanish court system. A few days later the doomed prisoners were spirited away and executed in a macabre ritual known as a *paseo* (literally, taking someone

16. Emma Goldman, *Vision on Fire* (Detroit, 1983), p. 227.
17. *La Revista Blanca*, 30 July 1936; also cited in Burnett Bolloten, *The Spanish Civil War: Revolution and Counterrevolution* (Chapel Hill, North Carolina, 1991), p. 52.

for a ride). These trips took place late at night (usually around midnight): a group of men would be taken by car or truck to a nearby location where they were lined up against a wall and shot. Next morning their mutilated bodies, which could be found lying beside the roadside, served as brutal reminders of how pro-Nationalists were dealt with by the forces of the new order.

These politically-motivated reprisals quickly got out of hand. In the absence of formal judicial institutions, the terrorist code was enforced not just by impromptu revolutionary tribunals like the ones described above, but also by armed gangs of delinquent youths or convicted criminals, the latter having been liberated along with genuine political prisoners when the prisons were opened in July. In addition, a certain number of personal vendettas were settled in the name of the revolution. At other times rearguard violence occurred in response to Nationalist atrocities. Suspected fascists – especially those already imprisoned – were most vulnerable after a particularly devasting Nationalist bombing raid or following a widely-publicized republican defeat. When news of the massacre at Badajoz, where an estimated 2,000 workers were slaughtered in the town's bullring, reached Madrid it nearly provoked a mass killing of the pro-Nationalists incarcerated in the city's gaols.[18]

The CNT-FAI leaders were among the first who attempted to halt the spread of arbitrary violence. Among other things, they used their *patrullas de control* to rein in on non-political killings. And throughout the summer, republican authorities did all they could to curtail the executions. It was not until the end of August, however, when Popular Tribunals were set up by the central government in Madrid, that the wave of indiscriminate killing noticeably began to abate.[19]

Another of the tragic consequences of the 'revolutionary excesses' was the vicious assault on the Catholic Church, a grizzly onslaught that resulted in the destruction of countless religious buildings and the deaths of over 6,800 members of the clergy (including some 280 nuns). According to José Sánchez, who has written extensively on the subject, the anticlerical fury of 1936 was the greatest clerical bloodletting in the modern history of the Christian Church. Neither the French Revolution (1789), when perhaps as many as 5,000 clerics were murdered, nor the Russian Revolution, which claimed the lives of some 1,200 Orthodox clerics, approaches the Spanish conflict in terms of the total number of clerics killed. So intense was the revolutionaries' hatred of the Church that they also targeted

18. According to the American journalist Jay Allen, 'Eighteen hundred men – there were women, too – were mowed down' in the central bullring. 30 August 1936, *Chicago Tribune*.
19. The popular Tribunals were officially established on 23 August 1936.

an untold number of lay persons, who were killed because of their known religious affiliation or simply because they dared to profess publicly their faith by wearing a cross or some other religious symbol.

In order to comprehend why the Church had become a chief target of the revolutionaries, one must remember that the clergy was regarded by the extreme left as a pillar of social oppression. As one anarchist trade union newspaper put it, the Church was the symbol of obscurantism, the avid backers of 'God, Country, and the King'.[20] In hundreds of villages and towns, churches, convents and other religious buildings were sacked and then set ablaze by the revolutionaries. Surprisingly, some of the church-burnings took place in an orderly fashion. In these instances the fire brigade would be called in to make certain that adjoining buildings did not catch on fire, and then the revolutionaries would go about the business of confiscating *objets d'art* (which were sometimes appropriated for public museums) and anything else deemed worth saving.

These public acts of immolation undeniably had eschatological overtones, for the anarchists were acting in the belief that by physically destroying churches and their religious symbolism it was possible to eradicate Catholicism. Yet it would be wrong to conclude from this that such acts of violence should be understood simply as millenarian or irrational responses to organized religion. In some cases, church-burnings stemmed from a well-defined political rationale. The fact that the Church openly sided with the military rebellion, for example, doubtlessly fuelled (although it did not necessarily justify) the deeply-rooted popular hatred of Catholicism. In Barcelona, for example, some churches or religious buildings were destroyed because the people truly believed that rightists were seeking refuge there or were even using the churches as fortifications in their attempt to crush the local populace. There is also some evidence supporting the view that, at least in small towns of the southern *latifundia*, the destruction of churches signified a form of class confrontation; a way for the unempowered masses to demonstrate their loathing of and frustration with the ruling classes of the region.[21]

To better understand the rationale behind much of the revolutionary

20. *CNT*, Madrid, 5 August 1936. In fact, the attacks on the Church and the attempts to exterminate its representatives reflected a commitment to a virulent form of anticlericalism which had afflicted the anarchist and other Spanish political movements of the left since at least the turn of the century.
21. Richard Frederick Maddox, 'Religion, Honor and Patronage: A Study of Culture and Power in an Andalusian Town', Ph.D (Stanford University, 1986), pp. 443ff. It has also been suggested that even such horrific acts as the exhumation of the mummified bodies of priests and nuns were complex acts that involved a variety of both irrational and rational impulses. See Bruce Lincoln, 'Revolutionary Exhumations in Spain', *Comparative Studies in Society and History*, vol. XXVII (1985), pp. 241–60.

violence we have described, it must be remembered that the revolutionaries themselves were not defining crimes according to the laws of the Second Republic, which they proclaimed abolished, but rather in accordance with the 'laws' of the revolutionary society they were striving to create. For the left in general – be they anarchist or Marxist – it was no good defining justice from a liberal-bourgeois perspective. Thus, for the Marxist radicals of the POUM this meant setting up a system of justice defined and controlled by the workers. In the view of Andreu Nin, the political-secretary of the party who served as Councillor of Justice in the Generalitat between September and December 1936, a form of 'proletarian justice' was to prevail now that the bourgeois institutions had been rendered impotent and the workers were in the process of building a new moral and political order. 'Nothing of bourgeois justice must remain', declared Nin soon after taking up his new post. 'Everything must be remade from the beginning. For this reason the old Codes are of no use to us, since they are Codes to defend bourgeois property.'[22]

THE ECONOMICS OF REVOLUTION: COLLECTIVIZATION

One of the most potent legacies of the July revolution was the far-reaching agrarian and industrial collectivization programme undertaken in the towns and the countryside. Except for the Basque region, which was largely undisturbed by the convulsions of social revolution, collectivization spread rapidly and spontaneously to nearly every corner of the republican zone. The numbers of those involved in collectives is impressive: some 750,000 in the countryside and a little over a million in industry. Not surprisingly it was most fully developed in those areas dominated by the anarchosyndicalists and left-socialists. Industrial collectives sprang up in all the major urban centres, including Barcelona, Madrid, Valencia, although it was in Catalonia, the centre of Spain's manufacturing industries, that industrial or urban collectivization went the deepest. The peasants of Aragón, the Levante, and Andalucía fervently supported collectivization. And, except for pockets of resistance from independent farmers – such as the ardently individualistic tenant farmers in Catalonia, the *rabassaires*, and small landholders – it encompassed the entire spectrum of agricultural activity.

Like the Russian Revolution of 1917, when many factories were occupied by workers after their owners went into hiding or fled the country, workers of the CNT-FAI and UGT found themselves in control of numer-

22. *Spanish Revolution* (POUM journal) Vol. I, no. 2, 28 October 1936.

ous enterprises of all types. During the course of the war some 2,000 wholesale businesses, factories, restaurants, hotels, barbershops, and countless other concerns were, in varying degrees, collectivized. When compared to the Russian example, it is patent that in Spain the degree of workers' control was far more penetrating and of a greater magnitude. The Spanish workers not only took over the supervision of businesses that had simply been abandoned by their owners – which was generally the case during the Russian Revolution – but in many instances they also completely reorganized the production and trade of industrial and agricultural enterprises.

INDUSTRIAL COLLECTIVES

When the revolutionaries seized the industries of the Republican zone, the economy was at the point of collapsing and thus the first and most pressing problem facing the workers was to keep it running. In the industrial centres this was not easily accomplished. Many of the trained technicians and managers had abandoned the factories: they were either shot, forced underground or into exile, or compulsorily inducted into the revolutionary movement. Perhaps more important, many industries were suddenly deprived of the internal markets (now under Nationalist control) on which they relied. Given that the revolution was in full swing, there was little hope that the worker-controlled enterprises could turn to the markets of the capitalist countries for the foreign exchange required to purchase such badly needed raw materials as cotton and coal. Furthermore, the revolutionaries found that while it was relatively easy to confiscate abandoned factories it was much more complicated to expropriate foreign-owned industrial properties. To avoid unduly antagonizing foreign countries – which might have led to their direct intervention – the revolutionaries were obliged to scale down their economic conquests. At one point the CNT even issued a list of firms belonging to international investors which were declared exempt from collectivization. In fact, however, the revolutionary committees of the CNT-FAI and UGT rarely relinquished their control of many important foreign-owned companies: the British-owned hydroelectric plant, Riegos y Fuerza del Ebro (Barcelona Traction Company), remained under worker control throughout the war.

Another serious problem immediately confronting the revolutionary workers in industry was how to convert the economy to a war basis. Thanks to the initiative and technical skill shown by the unions, this was quickly accomplished in some industries: factories that made lipstick-cases began manufacturing cartridges, and metallurgical plants began producing armour-plated cars and trucks (called tanks) to be sent to combat areas. Also in this regard, a truly remarkable achievement of the revolutionaries was to restore the services of public transport facilities, critically needed to transport troops and supplies to the front. Within weeks of the rising and revolution, the CNT-FAI – usually in collaboration with the UGT – seized control of and then collectivized taxicabs, tramways, buses, and the railways.

From the beginning, the task of collectivization involved balancing ideological principles with the demands of wartime reality. Thus while radical unions began immediately calling for uniform wages and a forty-hour work week, it soon became apparent that such objectives were exceedingly difficult to obtain within the context of a civil war. In a similar way, the revolutionaries had to be content with the fact that, with the exception of certain rural collectives, they were not in a position to exercise complete authority over their collectivization programmes. This was partly due to the fact that key elements of the economy remained in the hands of anti-revolutionary groups. The Madrid government retained possession of the huge gold reserves and also regulated access to foreign markets through their maintenance of commercial treaties. In Catalonia, where the unions had failed to take over the banking system, the revolutionaries were forced to turn to the Generalitat for financial aid. Above all this meant that the government would have a voice in economic planning and decision-making. In subsequent months, the role of government intervention in the economy escalated dramatically. On 24 October 1936, for example, a decree was issued by the Generalitat which legalized collectivized enterprises employing more than one hundred persons. Though this act may have appeared a victory for the radicals, in fact it was an effective way of limiting the spread of collectivization: a large sector of the working population, including artisans and small businessmen, were protected from workers' control.

The incomplete economic revolution gave rise to various categories of 'collectivization', a term that was freely adopted at the time but which was in practice defined according to the degree of worker control within a specific industry. At one end of this spectrum stood the company that was not, strictly speaking, collectivized but rather under union control: *controlada*. In this case, the enterprise remained under private ownership, although its overall operations were supervised and administered by a delegation of CNT and/or UGT members. According to José Peirats, an anarchist historian and civil war participant who has published numerous authoritative studies on the subject, the Control Committees set up in these factories performed a variety of essential tasks, such as assessing what demand there was for the manufactured products and determining the costs of production.

As a rule, if the CNT or UGT unions had been predominant in an industry before the war, then it was relatively easy for them to assume complete control of an industrial concern. When collectivization went beyond a single factory, encompassing all sources of raw materials needed for its manufacturing, the industry was said to be 'socialized'. Limited forms of socialization were realized in the dressmaking, tailoring, and leather goods trades in Valencia, and the cabinetmakers' trade in Madrid and Barcelona. The process of socialization usually entailed transforming the operations of an industry. Plants operating under uneconomic and insalubrious conditions might be shut down and their machinery gathered together in one workshop. In numerous and varied industries resources were consolidated in this manner in order to streamline the production process. Peirats notes with obvious pride how the baking industry in Barcelona improved under socialization:

> As in all of Spain, bread in Barcelona was baked in hundreds of little bakeries, called *tahonas*. These were damp, dark, underground caverns – nurseries for roaches and rats – where the work was done at night. [Under socialization the] bakers abandoned these unhealthy caves and increased production in bakeries that were modern, well-equipped, and well-ventilated.[23]

The socialization of all industries was the ultimate goal of the revolutionaries. Under this system, all collectivized industries were to be interconnected, forming one national network of industries. By instituting socialization, the revolutionaries hoped not only to harmonize the production and distribution of each industry, but also to eliminate what they perceived as the deleterious effects of commercial competition.[24]

RURAL COLLECTIVES

Most of our first hand knowledge of rural collectives comes from the eyewitness accounts of anarchists like Gaston Leval and Agustín Souchy. Nonlibertarians – Franz Borkenau (*The Spanish Cockpit*, 1937) and H. Kaminski (*Ceux de Barcelone*, 1937), for example – have also surveyed the collectivist experiments, although with a more critical eye than their anarchist counterparts. Of all the collectives established, the ones in Aragón and the Levante regions are by far the most thoroughly documented. Apart from recently published secondary literature, the collectives in the central zone (New

---

23. José Peirats, *Los Anarquistas en la crisis política española* (Madrid, 1977), p. 117.
24. For specific examples of socialized industries see Gaston Leval, *Collectives in the Spanish Revolution* (London, 1975). A discussion of the various types of collectivized industries can be found in the correspondence between Burnett Bolloten and Mariano Cardona Rosell, a member of the CNT National Committee during the war, in the Papers of Burnett Bolloten, Hoover Archives, Stanford University.

Castile) and the south (Extremadura and Murcia) have received scant treatment. The character of the collectives varied from region to region, depending partly on the form of land tenure which existed before the war broke out and partly on which group or groups exercised the greatest influence. In the Andalusian province of Jaén, the preponderance of the socialists was reflected in the fact that of the estimated 104 collectives set up there during the civil war, approximately thirty-eight (36.53 per cent) were run by the socialists. On the other hand, in republican-held Aragón anarchosyndicalist influence was so pervasive that nearly all of the 450 or so rural collectives established there were libertarian. The CNT also dominated in Castilla-La Mancha, where they were responsible for the vast majority of 282 collectives set up during the war.[25]

Still other rural collectives were, like those in industry, managed by a coalition of socialist, anarchist, *poumista*, and even communist unions. Irrespective of their political composition, the real power of the collective was wielded by the members of the *consejo de administración*, whose members were elected by a general assembly of the people of each locality. The *consejo* functioned as a coordinating committee whose primary functions were to: (1) direct all work and administrate the means of production; (2) negotiate the exchange of products between the collective and other collectivized enterprises; (3) and make sure that each proposal agreed to by the majority of the collective was properly implemented.

An appreciable number of the rural collectives established in the south and Levante were jointly administered by the UGT and CNT. Commonly held attitudes regarding the fundamental significance of collectivization made this kind of cooperation possible. For example, both groups saw collectivization as the first step towards building a revolutionary society. Even so, it would be misleading to suggest that the anarchosyndicalists and left-socialists were of one mind with regard to the overall aims of the collectivization. For the most part, socialist-inspired land seizures were

25. Several studies on collectivization can be recommended: *The Anarchist Collectives*, ed. by Sam Dolgoff (Montreal, 1974); Walther Bernecker, *Colectividades y Revolución Social* (Barcelona, 1982); Aurora Bosch-Sánchez, *Ugetistas y libertarios* (Valencia, 1983); Julián Casanova, *Anarquismo y revolución en la sociedad rural Aragonesa, 1936–1939* (Barcelona, 1985); Luis Garrido González, *Colectividades agrarias en Andalucía: Jaen, 1931–1939* (Madrid, 1979); José Luís Guitérrez Molina, *Colectividades Libertarias en Castilla*, (Madrid, 1977); Frank Mintz, *La Autogestión en la España Revolucionaria*, (Madrid, 1977); Pérez-Baro, Albert, *30 mesos de Collectivismo a Catalunya, 1936–1939* (Barcelona, 1970); Vernon Richards, *The Lessons of the Spanish Revolution* (London, 1952, 1972 and 1983); Agustín Souchy and P. Folgare, *Colectivizaciones* (a reprint of a study published during the civil war) (Barcelona, 1977); and Hugh Thomas, 'Anarchist Agrarian Collectives in the Spanish Civil War', in *The Republic and Civil War in Spain*, ed. by Raymond Carr (London, 1971).

motivated by their impatience for long overdue land reform and not by their desire to set up a collectivist enterprise as envisaged by the anarchists.

There are a few examples of communist unions participating in collectives, although this practice definitely ran counter to the PCE's stated policy.[26] As we have seen, the Communist Party was rootedly opposed to the revolutionaries' ambitious plans to recast society in a radical framework. Instead, they were seeking to bring about the centralization of the economic and political forces in compliance with their view that the Popular Front government – and not working-class organizations – was to direct both the economic and political life of the republican camp.

Notwithstanding the atmosphere of cooperation which reigned in many collectives and which enabled them to function on a practical level, ideological differences created tensions which persisted throughout the war. In some villages, a modified form of a 'mixed' economy existed, with the CNT and UGT in charge of collectivization projects and so-called individualists (those who opposed collectivization) running their own enterprises. These measures were adopted for a variety of reasons: partly because the anarchists and socialists were not strong enough to impose their will on everyone else, and partly because the revolutionaries thought it best to convert people to their cause rather that resort to coercion. The latter sentiment was echoed during the war by Ricardo Zabalza, the General Secretary of the FNTT, the socialist National Federation of Land Workers: 'I consider that voluntary membership should be the fundamental basis of any collective farm . . . [The] small, well-managed collective will attract the entire peasantry, who are profoundly realistic and practical, whereas forced collectivization would end by discrediting socialized agriculture.'[27] To be sure, individualist enterprises were tolerated only as long as they did not threaten the collectives themselves. In the community of Oliete (Aragón) the administrative council decreed that '. . . individualist comrades shall abstain from working against the collective or they will be judged as counter-revolutionaries'. Moreover, in order to protect the collectivist economy from competition from the individualists and to ensure that they could in no way sabotage the collective's economy, the revolutionaries created watch-dog committees to oversee all aspects of the individualists' farming operations. Restrictions such as these were obviously aimed as

---

26. On early communist participation in the collectivist movement see Fernando Quilis Tauriz, *Revolución y Guerra Civil: Las colectividades obreras en la provincia de Alicante, 1936–1939* (Alicante, 1992).

27. Ricardo Zabalza, *Verdad*, 8 January 1937, cited in Burnett Bolloten, *The Spanish Revolution: The Left and the Struggle for Power during the Civil War* (Chapel Hill, North Carolina, 1979), p. 69.

well at seriously handicapping the anti-collectivist factions, with the hope of eventually rendering them completely ineffectual.

A further source of tension within the collectives can be traced to the fact that force was sometimes used to bring about the economic restructuring of agricultural and industrial enterprises. In their own defence, the anarchists pointed out that anti-fascist militia committees – notably the Council of Aragón – had been established by public assemblies at which members from all republican parties were represented. Yet the truth is that the force was sometimes used to establish collectives, especially in areas where there was considerable peasant resistance to the revolution. Zealous attempts to create collectives in Hospitalet (a suburb of Barcelona), for example, prompted the POUM to complain that the anarchists' strict methods were actually turning some people against the revolution. While the anarchists rarely took drastic measures to enforce their will, there can be no doubt that the ubiquitous presence of armed anarchist militias along the Aragón front brought about conformity among those who would never have freely chosen to install a collectivized economic system.

In its purest form, the collectivist experience represented a complete rupture with the institutions and values of middle-class society. This was especially evident in libertarian collectives. Wherever they arose, they tended to conform to the same procedures of organization. In all libertarian collectives, the first task of the revolutionaries was to set up CNT-FAI committees, which oversaw all aspects of the collectivized community. Next they set about abolishing what they perceived as the main pillars of the capitalist system, particularly religion and money. For the anarchists in Fraga (Aragón) the elimination of money ushered in a new era of equality:

> Here in Fraga . . . you can throw bank notes into the streets and no one will take any notice. Rockefeller, if you were to come to Fraga with your entire bank account you would not be able to buy a cup of coffee. Money, your God and your servant, has been abolished here, and the people are happy.[28]

Social and economic forms that symbolized the *ancien régime* were often completely destroyed or put to different uses. Churches became garages for the local anti-fascist militia, or public dining halls (*comedores*), while others were converted into shelters for the homeless. In the tiny mountain village of Mazaleón (Aragón) the ancient church held a special significance for the peasantry: for years it had served as the focal point of the community, a place where the people could go on Sunday and exchange ideas and share spiritual values. After the revolution, when formal religion had

28. *Die Soziale Revolution*, no 3, January 1937, as cited in Bolloten, *The Spanish Civil War*, p. 66.

been banished, the church continued to be the principal gathering place for the peasants, but, significantly, it was no longer associated with Catholicism:

> The mysticism of the Catholic religion is no longer there. The priests have disappeared. But the peasants do not work to destroy this gothic building that majestically crowns the peak of the mountain. They have transformed it into a cafe and a place for sightseeing . . . They do not meet there Sunday mornings for prayer. Now they meet Sunday afternoons in their collective house under the high gothic roof . . . Belief in nature has taken the place of religion . . . Something more noble has been born: the veneration man has for the collective. This is the religion of the Mazaleón peasants today.[29]

On an economic level, the operations of each collective varied considerably. If money had been abolished, food and supplies were, as much as possible, distributed to the community according to the anarchist communist maxim: 'from each according to his abilities, to each according to his needs'. Usually bread, olive oil, vegetables, fruit and other plentiful items (chocolate and sugar were in abundance in Alcaniz, Teruel, where there was a candy factory) were dispensed free of charge, whereas scarcer commodities, such as milk and meat, had to be rationed by means of a coupon book. In some collectives the wage system was not wholly suppressed. But even if wages were retained, they were restructured in order to reflect the values of the collectivist order. Where money was replaced by a voucher system each family received a weekly wage, which was usually determined by the size of the family and the number of working adults. A family of five, for example, might be given the equivalent of ten pesetas (of the 'old' money), with an increase of approximately one peseta for each additional member. As the national currency had been abandoned, wages themselves were issued as credit vouchers – known as 'people's money' – that were printed by the local union (*sindicato*).

Given the kinds of economic disparities referred to here, it is easy to see how enormously difficult it was for the revolutionaries to expand the trade and production of collectives beyond a local level. Not least of their problems in this regard was the fact there was no functioning unified form of exchange.[30] This obviously posed a serious obstacle to those who thought it expedient to link the economic activities of the different collectives on a regional or national basis. Although there was a regional movement towards coordinating the economies of the different collectives – such as the Aragonese Federation of Collectives founded in January 1937 – a more

29. Agustín Souchy, *Entre los Campesinos de Aragón* (Barcelona, 1937), p. 69.
30. See Bolloten, *The Spanish Revolution*, and Vernon Richards, *The Lessons of the Spanish Civil Revolution* (London, 1983).

broadly-based unifying structure of this kind was never established during the war.[31]

THE LEGACY OF COLLECTIVIZATION

Were the collectives a success? From an economic standpoint this question cannot be answered with an unqualified yes or no. Although some of the failings of the collectives can be attributed to the inherent shortcomings of the revolutionaries' economic planning, their overall performance is impossible to assess for several reasons. First of all, the data are not available to determine conclusively how economically viable the collectives were. No clear pattern of their economic activity emerged during the war, not least because many collectivist experiments were short-lived, lasting only a few months before Franco's troops overran them. Secondly, the collectives were born and developed in a climate of intense economic stress. Faced with chronic shortages of raw materials and other constraints imposed by wartime conditions, the collectives were hardly in a position to realize their full economic potential. And finally, as the defenders of collectivization have argued, the success of the collectives hinged on too many factors beyond their control. As noted above, the opponents of collectivization controlled the banking system, enabling them above all to regulate the flow of credit to collectivized businesses. In practice this meant that poorly managed enterprises were turning to the authorities in vain for financial relief. As Minister of Finance in the central government, the socialist moderate and anti-revolutionary Juan Negrín delighted in the economic deficiencies of the collectives. He reportedly told the American journalist and pro-communist Louis Fischer, 'They are coming to me for running expenses and for raw materials, making it possible for the government to take advantage of their plight to gain control of the factories.'[32]

No less an obstacle to the collectives were the republican factions that violently objected to the revolutionaries' abrupt methods of social and economic reorganization. The communists in particular branded the anarchosyndicalists' and left-socialists' experiments in collectivization and

---

31. Vernon Richards points out that efforts to rationalize the Collectivist system persisted into 1937: 'In June 1937 . . . a National Plenum of Regional Federations of Peasants was held in Valencia to discuss the formation of a National Federation of Peasants for the co-ordination and extension of the collectivist movement . . .' A similar initiative was realized by the peasant federation in Castile in October. See Vernon Richards, *Lessons of the Spanish Revolution*. Second enlarged edition (London, 1983), p. 104.

32. Cited in Bolloten, *The Spanish Revolution*, p. 212–13. A similar view was expressed by Josep Tarradellas, Premier and Finance Minister of the Generalitat. See Mitchell, *The Spanish Civil War* (London, 1983).

socialization as 'premature', and insisted that their continued existence seriously jeopardized the republican war effort.[33] Because the maximalist economic projects being energetically promoted by their political rivals posed an obvious threat to their political agenda, the communists exploited every means possible to sabotage the collectivist movement. They were especially skilful at channelling the anger of the anti-revolutionary elements for their own purposes. In Catalonia, the PSUC organized over 18,000 middle-class tradesmen into the Catalan Federation of Small Businessmen, Manufacturers, and Handicraftsmen (GEPCI). In doing so, they not only provided the middle classes with a vehicle for defending themselves against collectivization, but they also succeeded in greatly expanding their own popular base. The Unió de Rabassaires, a principal ally of the middle-class Esquerra Party, also opposed collectivization and did all it could within the Generalitat to contain the spread of collectives.

Even more decidedly hostile to the collectives was the PCE Minister of Agriculture Vicente Uribe. Soon after taking up his post, Uribe vehemently denounced the excesses of the revolution in the countryside and declared his intention to champion the interests of the peasant proprietors and tenant farmers, who were the most common victims of collectivization. With reference to the collectives established in Valencia he warned the revolutionaries that '. . . the property of the small farmer is sacred and those who attack or attempt to attack this property must be regarded as enemies of the regime'.[34] In order to protect the anti-collectivist forces in the province, the PCE set up the Peasant Federation (FPC) which, according to the official figures, had acquired by March 1937 a membership of 50,000, many of whom had previously belonged to the CEDA affiliate Derecha Republicana Valenciana (DRV). Its opposition to revolutionary organizations was demonstrated early on in the war. When the CNT and UGT established an export agency for citrus fruits, CLUEA, in October 1936, the FPC refused to join. Later, it falsely accused CLUEA of robbing the local farmers, a claim that provoked violence in some areas. In the event, the central government replaced the CLUEA with its own organization, in the direction of which the unions had no say at all.

When measured in terms of their overall impact on peasant society, the collectives can be judged in a more positive light. The collectivist movement, like no other social movement in Spain's history, attempted on a grand scale to overcome not just the material but also the spiritual impoverishment that afflicted the lives of millions of people. Characteristic of most

---

33. As we shall see in a later chapter, the political gravity of this viewpoint was to be explicitly revealed following the notorious May Events of 1937.
34. Raymond Carr, *The Spanish Tragedy* (London, 1977), pp. 102–3.

collectives, for example, was a strong sense of social solidarity: welfare programmes were instituted which provided villages – in many instances for the first time – with medical care and social services for orphans, widows, the infirm, and others in dire need. Another central feature of collectives was their strong commitment to education. One of the first acts of many collectives was to establish schools. In remote hamlets where people had for centuries been deprived of the basic right to be educated this was seen as a momentous step forward. The pursuit of such goals may have appeared to some to be quixotic in the context of civil war. But there can be no doubt that the social idealism of the collectivist movement was largely responsible for raising the morale of the rearguard and giving the dispossessed masses a reason for fighting.

CHAPTER EIGHT

Conflicting Approaches to War: Military Policy in The Republican Camp

Earlier we saw that the July military rebellion had initially been put down in the Republican zone by improvized popular militias or columns that were under the direction of the left-wing trade unions. In the coming weeks the regular Republican army remained in a state of virtual dissolution, and, for this reason, these militias formed both the rearguard and front-line defence of the republican zone. Understandably their early successes generated a great deal of enthusiasm and optimism among the civilian troops. Yet even in these heady moments there were signs that the republicans faced enormous obstacles. For a start it was proving nearly impossible to coordinate military actions against the Insurgents as the militias themselves were operating independently of one another, lacking as they did any central command. Since each trade union maintained its own military headquarters, scant regard was paid to the actions or needs of other units. Thus, for example, in the early days of fighting the anarchosyndicalists raised their own columns and determined their own military priorities. Going against the advice of Colonel Villalba, the commander of Republican forces in the region, and the military leaders of other republican parties, Buenaventura Durruti's column of some 20,000 volunteers set off for Saragossa (Aragón), hoping to liberate one of the principal anarchist strongholds from Nationalist control. Their failure to do so – Durruti's unsupported and inexperienced forces were no match for the rebels ensconced in the Saragossa garrison – pointed to one of the major weaknesses of the independent militia system.

The effectiveness of the popular militias was further undermined by inter-union rivalries. In some areas anarchosyndicalist and Marxist units would often compete with each other rather than combine their efforts to defeat the enemy. When interviewed after the war a a former CNT militiaman on the Aragón front recalled that when the anarchosyndicalists went into action members of the POUM militia 'sat back with their hands in their pockets, laughing'. No doubt the anarchosyndicalists and other critics of the POUM did the same.

Political favouritism also existed in rearguard operations. The supply service or *Intendencia*, transportation section and general staff maintained by each battalion were usually in competition with one another. Some of the damaging consequences of these practices were summarized by one sharp-eyed observer in the following way: '. . . the batallion commissars and quartermasters used political influence in Madrid to obtain what they needed. By packing a department with a staff of its own political faith, a party might switch the precious ammunition, machine guns, rifles, etc., toward its own column out there on the crackling Sierras.'[1]

From the outset, then, it was apparent that competing strategies for prosecuting the war had disastrous implications for the republican units attempting to repel the relentless advances of the Nationalist troops. To resolve this dilemma was no mean feat, not least because the differing responses to civil war and revolution had their roots in the ideological and practical experiences that had long divided the left in Spain.

ANARCHIST THEORY AND MILITARY STRATEGY

The anarchosyndicalists' insurrectionary experiences of the 1930s, particularly the 'revolutionary gymnastics' of the *faistas* that had led to the risings in Figols (Catalonia) in 1932 and in Casas Viejas (Andalucía) the following year, had prepared them for the street fighting and door-to-door skirmishes that characterized the initial stages of the revolution and civil war. But, while the anarchosyndicalists had been introduced to insurrectionary struggle, they were unprepared to conduct a long-term military campaign. Equally important, at least in the eyes of the anarchosyndicalists, was the linkage between warfare and the revolutionary restructuring of society from the base up. Since they saw the two as inseparable, the anarchosyndicalists placed equal emphasis on the war and the collectivization process unfolding behind the front lines. Their early fighting efforts must be viewed in this light, for their initial thinking was that it was possible to overwhelm or at least repel the Nationalists with an intense revolutionary drive. By showing their complete audacity at the beginning, the hope was that the full force of the proletarian revolution could be unleashed, thereby rendering impotent any military threat from the right. This belief was reinforced early on

---

1. Ralph Bates, 'Castilian Drama: An Army is Born', in *The New Republic*, 20 October 1937, p. 287.

by the success of the anarchist militias in skirmishes with isolated groups of pro-Insurgents. In the context of an ever-expanding and increasingly protracted civil war, however, the anarchosyndicalists' concept of revolutionary warfare became more and more difficult to sustain.

In the militias under their command the CNT-FAI insisted that the war be organized in accordance with anarchist principles. Above all this meant creating a people's army where there was no regimentation, no hierarchies, no rituals associated with the regular army. Having abolished the traditional chain of command, each anarchist militia column was led by officers who had been elected by the men themselves. Under this new system, military orders were open to debate, and dissent within a unit could obviously impair the militia's ability to act swiftly and decisively. Still, the anarchists believed that rank-and-file rule served to build solidarity among the troops. In their eyes, it also proved to be a useful means of ferreting out men whose loyalties to the republican cause were suspect.

Following the reorganization of the central government in Madrid in September 1936, some anarchosyndicalists began urgently calling for immediate changes in the militia system, not least because they were growing ever more fearful of losing control over their own military units. Partly in response to the communists' concerted efforts to form a regular people's army under their command and partly in response to Largo Caballero's determination to reorganize or 'militarize' the militias and bring about greater state control over the army, the CNT proposed in September 1936 that a 'war militia' be created on the basis of compulsory service and under the joint supervision of the CNT and UGT.[2] However, none of the anarchosyndicalists' proposals to work outside the official channels came to anything.

Meanwhile, anarchist military leaders such as Buenaventura Durruti and Cipriano Mera were doing what they could to overcome the deficiencies of their militias. Having witnessed the ease with which professionally-trained Nationalist forces slaughtered many of their comrades, they decided that it was necessary to do away with their civilian-based militia system and enforce a stricter code of discipline on anarchist troops. By October 1936, Durruti's column, which was already recognized for its fighting abilities, acceded to certain aspects of militarization. About the same time, Cipriano Mera and other anarchists had also came round to the viewpoint that in order to defeat fascism it was necessary for the anarchosyndicalists to construct their own disciplined and capable army.

The pressing dilemma facing the anarchist military leaders was how to

2. The formal decree declaring the militarization of militias was passed on 30 September 1936.

bring about such changes without flagrantly violating their anti-statist creed. The Russian correspondent Ilya Ehrenburg observed at the time that 'Durruti held firmly to his ideas but he was no dogmatist'. 'War's a bestial thing', Durruti is reported to have said, 'it destroys not only houses but the highest principles.'[3] In fact, as anarchosyndicalists were in principle opposed to wars of all kinds, libertarian leaders could not appeal to their own theory for any theoretical resolution to their thorny predicament. The CNT-FAI leadership also seemed oblivious to the possibility of conducting guerrilla campaigns behind Nationalist lines. For though the exploits of the Ukrainian revolutionary Nestor Makhno were well known within the libertarian community, the lessons of his experiences during the Russian Civil War seemed to have been lost on his Spanish counterparts.[4] Moreover, some anarchists argued that guerrilla tactics, as practised during the Napoleonic wars, were obsolete: '. . . these tactics are no longer effective in modern warfare, unless they are limited to cities and small towns and are directed against a weak and numerically insignificant enemy'.[5]

It is largely because they lacked a concrete plan for military organization that the representatives of the CNT-FAI felt obliged to adopt the more conventional military programme being promoted by their ideological rivals, the socialists, republicans, and, above all, the communists. These doctrinal compromises created serious tensions within the libertarian movement, dividing the leadership from the 'purist' elements in the movement, a certain number of whom steadfastly refused to submit to the process of militarization. No group was more thoroughly representative of this dissident spirit than the notorious Columna de hierro or 'Iron Column', a libertarian militia which occupied a section of the Teruel front during the first months of the war.

Largely composed of militant anarchosyndicalists from the region of Valencia, the Iron Column also included several hundred prisoners from the San Miguel de los Reyes Penitentiary. The fact that some of the latter were hardened criminals – many of the former prisoners merely feigned their conversion to anarchism – led to the widespread notion that the column was nothing more than an army of convicts. Yet the vast majority of its members were dedicated anarchosyndicalists who vigorously defied attempts by CNT-FAI leaders to adopt conventional military measures. As

3. Ilya Ehrenberg, *Eve of War, 1933–1941* (London, 1963), p. 134.
4. Durruti himself, along with his comrade Francisco Ascaso, had personally interviewed Makhno in Paris in 1927. Although Makhno spoke through an interpreter, both Spaniards apparently listened to the veteran's lengthy account of his revolutionary experiences in the Ukraine. See Rai Ferrer, *Durruti*, (Barcelona, 1985), and Abel Paz, *Durruti: The People Armed* (New York, 1977).
5. Alejandro Gilabert, *Tierra y Libertad*, 12 December 1936.

one delegate of the Iron Column attending the CNT congress held in November 1936 put it: 'We accept nothing that runs counter to our anarchist ideas, ideas that must become a reality, because you cannot preach one thing and practice another.'[6]

As the war progressed, however, the Iron Column found it more and more difficult to resist the demands of militarization. By the spring of 1937, the committee of war announced that Column members were to become part of the Eighty-third Brigade of the regular army.[7] From this point on the independence of anarchist militias was drastically curtailed.

THE POUM'S 'RED ARMY'

The Marxist-Leninist POUM also saw the war and revolution as being inseparable. But while they agreed with the anarchosyndicalists that the war was fundamentally a class struggle, they were not prepared to accept the anarchosyndicalists' style of military organization. Instead, they sought to construct an army patterned after the Red Army as it existed during the time it was under the command of Leon Trotsky. According to this, the army would be composed of people's militias which were to be directed by Marxist-dominated soldiers' committees. Like the communists, the POUM began calling for organization and a unified command of the people's army, although the latter made it clear that they did not want to recreate an army of the state. The POUM's English-language weekly, *Spanish Revolution*, put it this way:

> We object to the present measures which create an army other than the Red Army. The combatants of the revolution must not be the headless automatons who so efficiently click their heels and do and die for Hitler and Mussolini. They must be the red army of the workers, fighting under a coordinated military command more capable of winning the war than the independent action of every political party's command. The unified command and the tightening of discipline are necessary, but after the model of Trotsky's army.[8]

Above all, the 'Red' army envisaged by the POUM was to be created and controlled by the trade unions. 'Militant revolutionaries cannot allow themselves to be converted overnight into plain soldiers. They cannot put themselves under a military discipline which has nothing to do with

---

6. See Burnett Bolloten and George Esenwein, 'Anarchists in Government: A Paradox of the Spanish Civil War', in *Elites and Power in Twentieth-Century Spain: Essays in Honour of Sir Raymond Carr*, ed. by Frances Lannon and Paul Preston (Oxford, 1990), p. 166.

7. *Nosotros*, 27 March 1937 as cited in Burnett Bolloten, *The Spanish Civil War: Revolution and Counterrevolution* (Chapel Hill, North Carolina, 1991), p. 342.

8. *Spanish Revolution*, vol. I, no. 2, 28 October 1936.

the revolutionary discipline of the organizations corresponding to their political ideas. . . . The militias cannot be transformed into an army under exclusively military control while the control of the workers' political organizations is discarded. This would mean taking such a backward step that the sacrifices made by the workers in the struggle could scarcely be justified.'[9]

Like the anarchosyndicalists, the style and content of the POUM's military strategy was obviously informed by their ideological perspective: for the *poumistas* it was imperative to picture the civil war in terms of class struggle in which the revolutionary programme of the workers had to be conducted simultaneously with the war effort. Their revolutionary strategy, including their views on military organization, was predicated on this assumption. Thus, for example, if the war was one between bourgeois factions then the workers might align themselves with one of the factions but not to the point of abandoning their organizations (bases of power): '. . . in the case of a bourgeois civil war they [the revolutionary workers] would try by means of their class organizations to pass over and beyond the most advanced bourgeois fraction in order to displace it and themselves take over the direction of the revolution.[10] Significantly, though, the POUM believed that the workers were in the ascendancy in much of Republican Spain – and that especially in Catalonia – it was therefore necessary to conduct the war differently. The assumption was that, in order to ensure that the republican government did not remain within the 'narrow limits of bourgeois democracy', the war itself had to follow a revolutionary trajectory.

Yet, in the critical first months of the war, the *poumistas* failed to create an efficiently-run army that was capable of executing their revolutionary programme. Although there were several reasons for this, including the fact that the POUM never attracted a mass following in the Republican camp, the principal reason for their failure was the immediate success of an alternative military policy being promoted by their arch-rivals, the communists.

FROM REPUBLICAN ARMY TO 'POPULAR ARMY'

The possibility of creating a revolutionary army favoured by the anarch-osyndicalists, the left-socialists and *poumistas* was roundly rejected by the other major factions in the Republican camp. A more traditional stance

9. op. cit.
10. *Spanish Revolution*, vol. I, no. 3, 4 November 1936.

on military matters was held by the republicans, moderate socialists and Spanish communists. Both the *prietista* socialists and liberal left-republicans supported the idea of creating a conventional, non-political army. But it was the last of these three, the communists, who took the lead in developing a military programme that would be universally adopted for the Republican war effort. Like most other anti-revolutionary groups in the anti-fascist camp, the PCE vehemently objected to the radical transformation of the Republican army following the July rebellion. And even though the various left-wing trade unions and political organizations had filled the breach created by the near collapse of the government's armed forces by forming their own military columns or popular militias, these hastily raised militias soon proved unable to check the onslaught of the better trained and better equipped Insurgent troops. It was against this background that the PCE took the initiative in calling both for 'Discipline, Hierarchy, and Organization' in the formation of military units, and for the creation of a government-controlled 'Popular army'. In place of the popular militias, which they saw as the source of the military chaos that reigned in certain quarters of the republican zone, the communists wanted to form army units patterned after their own militia, the celebrated Fifth Regiment. Unlike the militias, many of which practised egalitarianism and therefore discouraged formal rituals characteristic of a traditional army, the Fifth Regiment stressed the need for iron discipline and strict adherence to a hierarchical chain of command.

There were both military and political reasons why the communists were promoting these changes. From a strategic standpoint, they strongly believed that reorganization of the army along conventional lines – that is, where authority was concentrated under a single command (*mando único*) – was the only realistic policy to pursue. At the same time, the communists knew that the consolidation of the militias would be politically advantageous for them. For the implementation of this measure effectively meant divesting their rival political organizations (especially the revolutionaries) of the enormous power they wielded through their own militias. Thus, a shift in the locus of military authority was necessary if the communists were ever to secure a commanding position in the Republican army.

The Fifth Regiment came into being during the early days of the civil war. Drawing upon the organizational framework provided by the communists' Worker and Peasant Anti-Fascist Militia (MOAC) as well as the assistance offered by foreign communist advisors, the Fifth Regiment rapidly evolved into a formidable fighting unit. Under the able leadership of Enrique Líster, who became commander-in-chief of the regiment in September 1936, the efficiency and discipline of the Fifth Regiment as well as its moderate propaganda greatly impressed other groups of the

Popular Front coalition, who were desperately searching for a successful military model. It soon recruited thousands of communists, socialists, republicans as well as non-party workers and peasants. At the peak of its development in December 1936, the Fifth Regiment may well have enlisted over 60,000 men.[11]

Following several disastrous Republican defeats in the autumn of 1936, the pressures to follow the communists' example were immense. In fact, the communists took the first major step in this direction by progressively dissolving the Fifth Regiment, whose battalions were gradually fused into 'mixed brigades' of the 'People's Army', an army of a 'new type' that was only in its embryonic stage at this time.

Behind the communists' slogans calling for unity and organization lay their plan to consolidate all the elements of the Republican army under their own command. Given their lack of popular support in the early months of the war – especially among the working-class organizations – this may have initially appeared as an unrealistic goal. Yet once Soviet arms and supplies began arriving after October 1936, the communists' voice in military affairs was not only heard but listened to. And, considering that the Soviet Union was, except for Mexico, the only foreign power willing to offer such aid, the communist Party could virtually monopolize the supply and distribution of arms, something which they did throughout the war. With the power and prestige they acquired from Soviet aid, the communists were better positioned than any other group to realize their plans to forge the disparate republican forces into a 'People's Army' under a unified command.

Apart from the influence they derived from Soviet aid, the communists' military strategy benefited from several other key factors working in their favour. One had to do with the threatening circumstances in which the republicans found themselves. In the face of mounting Republican defeats and the rapidly advancing Nationalist troops, it was apparent that something had to be done urgently to coordinate and direct the republican war effort. All groups believed that it was necessary to establish a unified command, yet the communists were the only ones who offered a programme that appeared realistic enough to attain this end. As we have seen, the anarchosyndicalists lacked a concrete military strategy for unifying even their own civilian militia units, and they did not wield enough power on their own to assume supreme command of the republican troops. POUM was the least likely group to act in a leadership role as its

---

11. According to Burnett Bolloten, this figure must be qualified: the right-wing historian Ramón Salas Larrazábal claims that the total number of men enrolled in the regiment never exceeded 30,000. Burnett Bolloten, *The Spanish Civil War*, p. 270.

strength and influence were largely confined to Catalonia and parts of Aragón.

Part of the success of the communists' military units lay in their internal organization: their overall infrastructure was welded together by a network of commissars under communist control. As in the Russian Civil War (1917–21), when they were introduced into Trotsky's Red Army, the role of the commissars was both to ensure the loyalty of regular officers and to indoctrinate the troops with the proper political perspective. In Spain this was accomplished by feeding troops with a steady diet of communist propaganda and keeping most in ignorance of the political differences that actually existed within the republican camp. This is evidenced by the fact that most of the periodicals and newspapers that the men received at the front were communist or pro-communist publications. According to a young anarchist militaman interviewed by the American anarchist Emma Goldman, at military training schools the excessive proselytism of the communists was so blatant that they even attempted to prevent the distribution of CNT-FAI newspapers – although where the anarchosyndicalists were strong enough, this sort of censorship had limited success.

Creating a traditional army at a time when most of the troops were opposed to it was no easy task. But it soon became apparent that the communists' methods were highly successful: in a matter of a few short months they managed, among other things, to assemble an efficient military organization based on mixed brigades; an achievement that, according to the conservative Spanish historian Ricardo de la Cierva, had not even been accomplished in the Francoist zone where the battalion continued to serve as the basic military unit.[12]

Even so, the political commissariat system was not without its defects. According to Tomás Mora, himself a communist inspector of the Army of the East, the commissars tended to abrogate too much authority from the military commanders, who were themselves fearful of being branded as fascist sympathizers. Commissars exercised even greater control over the activities of the rank-and-file troops. But even the most dedicated communist recruit was not always blind or indifferent to the autocratic nature of the commissariat system. Later, when the commissariat system was extended to the International Brigades, the rigid and insensitive discipline enforced by the commanders rankled with foreign troops who were not accustomed to such draconian military measures. Writing to Virginia Woolf about his first-hand observations of the military situation, Stephen Spender, a devoted communist at the time, remarked: 'The political commissars . . .

---

12. See Ricardo de la Cierva's article in *The Republic and the Civil War in Spain*, ed. by Raymond Carr (London, 1971).

bully so much that even people who were quite enthusiastic Party Members have been driven into hating the whole thing.'[13]

In the course of the war the communist-defined techniques of military organization greatly contributed to the republicans' ability to withstand Nationalist attacks, but they did not dramatically improve their offensive strategy. This may have been due to the communists' unwavering determination to pursue their military objectives largely by conventional means. Guerrilla warfare, which had been used to such great effect during the French occupation between 1806 and 1814, was never fully developed as an alternative military strategy even though this may have proved an effective way of fighting a civil war. Ironically, the idea of employing guerrilla units was first promoted by foreigners. In a letter sent to then premier Largo Caballero, Stalin himself recommended the tactic, and the Soviet NKVD operative Alexander Orlov was placed in charge of organizing a network of guerrilla groups behind Nationalist lines. For all their efforts, however, left-wing guerrillas never posed a serious problem to the Nationalists. Reflecting on the failure of the guerrilla campaign, another key *apparatchik* in Spain, the Italian Palmiro Togliatti, later wrote that guerrilla warfare might well have been successful in Spain as much of the territory conquered by the rebels was populated by pro-leftist peasants and workers who could have been used to destabilize the rearguard.[14]

The communists' efforts to bring about the reorganization of the republican army were given an enormous boost by the arrival in mid-October 1936 of Soviet arms and supplies as well as the first units of the Comintern's volunteer army, the now legendary International Brigades. The Comintern's intervention in Spain was calculated not only to support a war against fascism, but also to advance the diplomatic aims of the Soviet Union. To achieve these ends, the communists sought to direct the course of the Republican war effort. In this respect, one of the primary functions of the International Brigades was to help the communists in Spain consolidate and extend their influence in military matters. Thus the Comintern was mobilizing volunteers for the International Brigades just as the Spanish communist Party (PCE) was launching its plans to inject some order into the Republican army. That the communists regarded the brigades as an integral component in their ever-expanding network of power and influence is borne out by the fact that the volunteers were directed by some of the Comintern's most seasoned *apparatchiks*: André Marty, a French

13. Quoted in *Spanish Front: Writers on the Civil War*, ed. by Valerie Cunningham (Harmondsworth, 1980), pp. 307–9.
14. See Fraser's articles in *Revolution and War in Spain*, ed. by Paul Preston (London, 1984), p. 241, and Barton Whaley, *Guerrillas in the Spanish Civil War* (Cambridge, Massachusetts, 1969).

communist, headed military operations at Albacete, and he was ably assisted by the Italian communists Luigi Longo (known as 'Gallo') and Giuseppe de Vittorio (known as 'Nicoletti').

COMMUNISTS AND THE INTERNATIONAL BRIGADES

Since it ended over fifty years ago, one of the most enduring legacies of the Spanish Civil War has been the dramatic story of the international volunteers who went to Spain to serve in the International Brigades of the Republican army. The outbreak of civil war and revolution in Spain in July 1936 immediately fired the political idealism of liberal and left-wing circles in Europe and the Americas. Writers, social activists, and ordinary working-class men and women rallied to the Republican cause by enlisting in the International Brigades.[15] In the course of the war, some 59,380 participants from 53 countries served in the International Brigades of the Republican army.

This diverse group of foreigners freely offered their services because they saw in the Spanish war a reflection of the left-right ideological conflict that seemed to be intensifying daily in Europe and elsewhere around the world. Though their political motives were mixed, the vast majority of volunteers joined the Spanish struggle primarily because they were convinced that, if Franco, Hitler and Mussolini were defeated in Spain the anti-fascist cause would emerge triumphant and another world war could be averted. This is not to deny the important role personal reasons played in inspiring many of the volunteers. In some instances, such as for Jews and African-Americans, ethnicity was intimately bound up with this globally-based confrontation. To African-Americans European fascism represented the same form of racialist oppression they had been subjected to at home (a view that was reinforced when Italy forcibly annexed Haile

---

15. Since the war, the story of the International Brigades has received considerable public attention: their exploits have been immortalized in dozens of movies, fictional works and histories. This is hardly surprising, for it is about a remarkable group of men and women who exhibited considerable courage and self-sacrifice in the course of a long and bitterly fought contest. But because their experiences were inextricably linked to the ideological movements that dominated the world affairs between the wars it is not surprising that the historiography of the IBs has been largely shaped and coloured by the political debates of the 1930s. Their harshest critics have portrayed the volunteers as agents of the international communist movement whose principal reason for going to Spain was to advance Soviet foreign policy objectives. Violently repudiating this charge, loyal defenders of the IBs have asserted that their sole mission in Spain was to 'fight fascism' by defending the democratically-elected republic. Both viewpoints are misleading.

Selassie's Ethiopia) whereas some Jews believed that going to Spain offered them an opportunity to take a stand against the forces of anti-semitism.[16]

ORIGINS OF THE INTERNATIONAL BRIGADES

The Republican government was initially opposed to the idea of foreign intervention of any kind, including the participation of individuals acting on their own initiative.[17] Yet in the confusion that reigned during the early weeks of the Civil War it was nearly impossible for the authorities to prevent foreigners (especially those who already happened to be in Spain) from being caught up in the sweep of events. This was particularly true of groups with strong political convictions, such as the scores of anarchists, socialists, and liberals who flocked to the Spanish arena only a few days after the military rising on 17 July 1936. By August, several hundred antifascists – mainly left-wing French trade unionists and political refugees from Italy, Germany, and Central and Eastern Europe – were fighting alongside Republican troops. The first non-Spanish units to see action were the French Paris Battalion, which participated in the defence of Irún, the Polish General Wroblewski Battalion, the Italian *Giustizia e Libertá* (Justice and Liberty) Column, and the German Ernst Thaelmann Centuria, which had grown to battalion strength by the end of September. These organized groups of foreign volunteers in the Republican camp arose spontaneously and were not part of a coordinated movement to bring anti fascists into Spain. But this situation did not last for long.

The idea of using organized groups of foreign volunteers to fight for the republican side first materialized in late July 1936 in Paris, France. Among those actively promoting this plan were such prominent members of the communist International or Comintern as Maurice Thorez, head of the French communist Party; Palmiro Togliatti, chief of the Italian communist Party in exile; and the Yugoslav communist leader Josip Broz (the future 'Tito').

16. Approximately 90 African-Americans fought in Spain, and the Abraham Lincoln Battalion became the first fully-integrated military unit in US history. During the war, Oliver Law became the first African-American to command a predominantly white military unit. On the participation of the African-Americans see D. D. Collum, *African-Americans in the Spanish Civil War* (New York, 1992); and James Yates, *From Mississippi to Madrid: memoir of a Black American in the Abraham Lincoln Brigade* (Seattle, Washington, 1989). On British Jews see Henry Srebrnik, 'Jewish Community Activism in London on Behalf of the Spanish Republic', *Michigan Academician*, Spring 1984, pp. 371–81.
17. This section on the International Brigades is based on my article which appeared in *Historical Dictionary of Modern Spain, 1700–1988*, ed. by Robert W. Kern (Westport, Connecticut, 1990), pp. 267–73.

With the backing of the Soviet Union, which had not yet defined for itself a role in the Spanish conflict, the Comintern launched in September a formal campaign to recruit an international corps of volunteers. In the following weeks, thousands of prospective candidates were interviewed by Communist Party officials, and those selected were funnelled through the Comintern's well-organized international network. How the volunteers reached their destination depended on their country of origin: the French, who constituted about a quarter of the total number of brigaders, the Germans (the second largest national group) and the Italians and others who were already living in exile in France were the easiest to transport across the Spanish frontier. However, for legal reasons, volunteers from countries like Canada, Great Britain and the United States were obliged to operate clandestinely. As a rule, they were first escorted to Paris, issued false documents, and then smuggled over the Spanish border.

Apart from a handful of middle-class professionals (mostly teachers and clerks), the vast majority of volunteers serving in the IBs were of working-class extraction. A large number of them were sailors, shipyard workers, industrial labourers and miners. For many years, however, the true composition of the volunteer units was obscured by the publicity surrounding the famous artists, poets and writers identified with the conflict. The fact that such internationally-known figures as Ernest Hemingway, Langston Hughes, Stephen Spender, George Orwell, Arthur Koestler, and André Malraux went to Spain gave rise to the popular but mistaken notion that most of the foreigners in Republican Spain, including members of the International Brigades, were middle-class poets and writers. This was especially true in Great Britain, France, and the United States, where events in Spain attracted the attention of an impressive number of eminent public figures.[18] And even though very few of these celebrities actually went to Spain to fight, their reputations overshadowed the fact that they constituted only a fraction of the overall number of individuals who took a stand on the war.

The first contingent of volunteers began arriving towards the end of September, and by mid-October a base of operations had been established at Albacete. In view of the growing number of foreign troops in Republican territory, the Republican government finally overcame its reluctance to the idea of using non-Spanish combatants by the end of the month. Because the International Brigades were to be used as shock troops, the volunteers were required to undergo a rigorous induction process at Albacete. The

---

18. An informal survey sponsored by *Left Review* and published in 1937 with the title *Authors Take Sides on the Spanish War*, revealed that, with few exceptions, members of the British intellectual and artistic community had strong views about the war. We shall return to a discussion of the role of those and other writers in Chapter 12.

older volunteers, especially those who had had previous military experience, predominated in the ruling cadres, whereas the younger men – most of whom were raw recruits – were subjected to an intensive basic training programme. The instructional period of the volunteers was usually kept to a minimum, largely because fresh troops were desperately needed on the fronts.

Thanks to the arrival of Soviet arms and supplies and to the efficiency of the commissariat system, the average soldier in the International Brigades was much better equipped and trained than his Spanish counterpart. In fact, the International Brigade units were soon regarded by the Spaniards as models of military efficiency and discipline. Given the diverse nationalities represented in the brigades, it was expedient, whenever possible, to divide the volunteers into linguistic groups. French was the most widely used language, followed by German, Italian, and English. Before June 1937, these lines of demarcation were not always clearcut and it was not uncommon for, say, an English-speaking unit to be attached to a German or French battalion. Only five International Brigades (the Eleventh to the Fifteenth) were formed during the war, although it often appeared to foreign observers that there were many more than this. Most likely this is because each Brigade was composed of a bewildering array of battalions and smaller army units, some of which – like the Thaelmann, Dombrowsky, and Abraham Lincoln battalions – were better known than the Brigades to which they were attached. The International Brigades were warmly received by the Spanish people and by most of the Republican parties. On the other hand, they were cautiously greeted by the POUM and by the anarchosyndicalists of the CNT-FAI. For their part, the libertarians feared that troops under Comintern control could be used to strengthen the official communists' hand at the expense of the revolutionary groups. Their suspicions, which were later borne out by events, prevailed throughout the war. Even so, it is interesting to note that once the foreign volunteers had the opportunity to demonstrate their valour and military skills on the battlefield, some anarchosyndicalist commanders came to admire and even respect the International Brigades.

There is insufficient evidence to establish a precise profile of the political affiliations of most volunteers. Nevertheless, judging from the large volume of memoir literature, official documents, and other first-hand sources that have come to light since the war, it is reasonable to assume that well over half of the volunteers were either communist or sympathetic to the official Communist Party line. Those who chose to enlist in the International Brigades were forced either to accept communist leadership or face severe punishment. In this connection it is essential to point out that a small number of participants on the republican side, such as the British novelist

George Orwell (Eric Blair) and the French writer and philosopher Simone Weil, regarded themselves as left-wing but anti-Stalinist. Orwell himself served in the militia of the independent communist POUM (Partido Obrero de Unificación Marxista), the Spanish equivalent of the British Independent Labour Party (ILP).

In the event, it became immediately apparent to the newly inducted volunteers that their individual political beliefs were of secondary importance. This is because the communists played a central role in defining and determining the fate of all those serving in the International Brigades. Not only was the Comintern in charge of recruitment but, through its extensive network of advisors and military strategists, it exercised considerable control over all the essential operations of the Brigade units. For example, the greater part of the Political Commissariat system – the organizational framework of the International Brigades – was dominated by communists like the Englishman Bill Alexander, who served as Political Commissar of the Anti-Tank Battery and, later in the war, as Commander of the British Battalion.

The role of the IB commissar was clearly defined in the instructional handbook of the Fifteenth Brigade: 'The Commissars are an integral part of the Army. Their role is to inspire their unit with the highest spirit of discipline and loyalty to the Republican cause . . . The Commissar teaches the recruits that victory depends on carrying out unquestioningly and unwaveringly whatever order the military command may issue . . . The Commissar's work extends to the smallest details that contribute to the material well being and comfort of the men volunteers of the rank and file . . . "First to advance and last to retreat" is the slogan of the Commissars.'[19] At company level the political commissars were often elected or took the job by consensus of their comrades. Besides attending to the personal needs and maintaining the morale of his troops, the commissar was responsible for their political education. Among other things, this entailed regularly lecturing recruits on the 'true' significance of the war as defined by the Stalinists. Dissent, especially if it challenged the official line of the communist Party, was not tolerated, and persons suspected of being provocateurs or spies were dealt with harshly. A rigorous discipline was imposed not just to enforce a high military standard but also to ensure the political conformity of the effectives (soldiers equipped for duty). Primarily for this reason very few members of the International Brigades were exposed to other viewpoints. Not surprisingly, then, most of the volunteers never fully understood either the nature or the implications of the ideological struggles that were increasingly rending apart the various political

19. William Alexander, *British Volunteers for Liberty* (London, 1982), pp. 74–5.

parties in the Republican camp. This is illustrated by the way in which members of the International Brigades perceived the anti-Stalinist POUM and its allies on the revolutionary left. Uncritically following the official communist line, which went to preposterous lengths to discredit the POUM, the majority of International Brigade members supported the far-fetched view that *poumistas* were Trotskyist saboteurs who represented a potential 'stab in the back' to Republican Spain. Their communist training also caused them to be suspicious of the anarchosyndicalists. One American volunteer, John Tisa, betrayed this prejudice when he wrote in his memoirs that an IB official introduced him to a Spanish couple who were 'anarchists but loyal to the Republic'.[20]

In fulfilling their varied responsibilities and duties some commissars abused their position by resorting to physical threats and other forms of intimidation. Even sources sympathetic to the International Brigades have admitted that sometimes the threat of violence or, on occasion, the execution of recalcitrant Brigade members did occur. Furthermore, while punitive measures were administered to maintain discipline and for common military offences committed on the battlefield – desertion, for example – there can be little doubt that some punishments were strictly politically motivated. André Marty earned the nickname the 'butcher of Albacete' for his reputed role in cold-bloodedly eliminating suspected fascist enemies as well as communist dissidents. Estimates of the number of those who were either expelled from their units, sent on suicide missions, or summarily shot vary considerably. It may well be that the zealous actions of Marty and other commissars resulted in dozens of 'liquidations' of this kind.

Since the war, civil war scholars and IB veterans alike have fiercely debated the pros and cons of the communists' commanding role in the International Brigades. Some have argued that the strict discipline and political control exercised by the communists was a necessary 'evil' in the context of war. Others have condemned communist practices, pointing to the fact that there were men and women who left Spain profoundly disillusioned by their experiences as members of the International Brigades.

What is not in dispute is the fact that the international volunteers who fought on the republican side played a pivotal role in the war itself. It would be the fate of the International Brigades to shoulder some of the heaviest burdens of the fighting between 1937 and the time of their departure in late 1938. In fact, the first units arrived at a critical moment in the anti-Nationalist struggle. Just as the first recruits were undergoing training manoeuvres at Albacete, Franco's troops were closing in on Madrid.

20. John Tisa, *Recalling the Good Fight* (South Hadly, 1985), p. 201.

Several thousand members of the newly-formed Eleventh and Twelfth Brigade units were dispatched to the capital on 8 November, only two days after the ministers of the Republican government had fled to Valencia and while the citizens and military were barricading themselves against a massive onslaught.

SIEGE OF MADRID

Following their detour to Toledo, Nationalist troops had reached the out-skirts of Madrid by 1 November. Some 25,000 troops under the command of General Varela were preparing to cut through the Casa de Campo (formerly the royal hunting grounds) and the University City. The arrival on 6 November of German arms and military advisors undoubtedly boosted Varela's confidence of achieving a swift and resounding victory.

On the republican side, the prevailing mood was much gloomier. In the face of the relentless advance of Nationalist forces, leading republicans decided to move the seat of the government to Valencia post-haste. Refus-ing to bend to the stiff opposition from the recently appointed anarchist ministers Juan Peiró, Montseny, García Oliver and Juan López, Largo Caballero and his Air Force and Navy Minister, Indalecio Prieto, laid plans for their evacuation.

Their hasty departure left the city in the hands of civilians and the military. Under the direction of General Miaja, a *Junta de Defensa* (defence council) or provisional government composed of nearly all of the republican parties was set up to oversee the defence of the city. At the same time, daily life in the capital underwent dramatic transformations. Trenches were dug, barricades erected as men, women and children fortified themselves for a long siege. Since the pre-war political map of Madrid represented parties on both the left and right, it is not surprising that a fair number of *madrileños* were not participating in the preparations for battle. These were the infamous 'Fifth Columnists' Mola and rebel propagandists had spoken of: Nationalist sympathizers trapped in republican territory who, at the right moment, would rise up in the rearguard. Some sought refuge in the foreign embassies, while others, like Franco's brother-in-law, Ramón Serrano Suñer, took advantage of the chaotic situation to escape to the other side. An untold number of determined right-wingers stayed behind and carried out subversive activities, doing all they could to undermine the republican war effort.

Determined as he was to take Madrid, Franco had greatly under-estimated the strength of popular will among the *madrileños* as well as the military capabilities of the republican forces defending the city. Following the arrival of the first fighting units of the International Brigades (Eleventh and Twelfth) and Soviet munitions and supplies in early November – Russian Chatas and Moscas could be seen flying across the Madrid sky – the pall of defeat which earlier had descended upon the city was beginning to lift just days before Franco launched his massive frontal assault. Republican troops manning the front-line trenches were both relieved and elated at this recent turn of events and the citizens of the capital could now face the enemy with greater optimism.

The International Brigades were the first to confront the full fury of the advances into the University City. Turning back the defenders was unexpectedly difficult for the Nationalists: at every turn their movements were slowed by the sharp ripostes of the brigaders. In neighbouring sectors their actions were being reinforced by POUM militias and the famous Durruti Column, some 3,500 anarchist veteran militiamen who had just arrived in Madrid from the Aragón front.

Nearly two weeks into the siege, there were clear indications that the Nationalist drive had lost its momentum. Their ceaseless attacks against the defences in the Moncloa sectors were finally being repulsed, and republican militiamen were slowly but progressively reconquering key sections of the city. By early December a growing number of Nationalists were no longer confident that they would be celebrating Christmas in the capital.

In the months to follow, Madrid, though still under pressure from the Nationalists, settled into another pattern of activity. The hyper-activity and nervous energy that had animated the city in early November gave way to other, darker moods. The appalling loss of life, that resulted from the fighting at the fronts and the bombings carried out in the rearguard, was beginning to take its toll on the civilian population. Part of this grim reality was that everyone constantly lived under the threat of death and injury, a psychological burden that was not wholly dispelled even after the bombings tapered off. Visiting Madrid some months after the November offensive, the American writer Martha Gellhorn (Ernest Hemingway's future wife) attested to how easily the orderliness of daily routines could dissolve into nerve-shattering pandemonium:

> You would be walking down a street, hearing only the city noises of streetcars and automobiles and people calling to one another, and suddenly, crushing it all out, would be the huge stony deep booming of a falling shell, at the corner. There was no place to run, because how did you know that the next shell would not be behind you, or ahead, or to the left or right?[21]

The morale of the *madrileños* was further tested by steadily deteriorating

21. Martha Gellhorn, *The Face of War* (New York, 1988), p. 22.

161

living conditions. Food shortages were everyday experiences for the ordinary person, and incessant waves of aerial and artillery bombings had reduced many apartment buildings to heaps of rubble. Under these conditions, it is truly remarkable that the city held out against the Nationalists until March 1939.

THE FALL OF MÁLAGA

While the fighting in and around Madrid was reaching an impasse, Nationalist troops were active in the south. Their first attack was directed at the port city of Málaga, a principal target in that its capture would not only have provided Franco's army with much needed access to the Mediterrean but would also have set free large numbers of pro-insurgent troops. On 17 January, Quiepo de Llano's Army of the South advanced along the southern coast towards Málaga, and was later joined by Italian troops.[22] Arriving in early February, Italian and Nationalist troops at first encountered strong opposition from the civilian and army militias defending the city. But this resistance was deceptively powerful. Only three days after the attack had begun, republican commanders were leading a mass exodus from the city. Málaga was now under Nationalist control.

The collapse of Málaga exposed some of the fundamental weaknesses of the republican army as well as the cruelities that were to attend this civil war. In the former case, it was evident that the revolutionary civilian militias – militarization of the army had not yet occurred in the anarchist-dominated city – were no match for the mechanized forces of the Italian Black Shirts and the well-equiped Army of the South. Secondly, the Nationalists were not content with a military victory: as soon as they occupied the city a ferocious repression was unleashed. Not just militiamen but also civilians were hunted down. An estimated 4,000 people were exterminated in the first week of the occupation. Even those fleeing the city came under attack. Gunboats off the coast continued shelling the roads leading out of the city after the Nationalists had secured it, and on the road to Almería Nationalist aircraft and artillery struck again and again at the knots of refugees.

While Quiepo de Llano's army was marching on Málaga, Nationalist commanders were redeploying their troops. No longer convinced that the city was vulnerable to a frontal assault, new offensives were launched with the aim of encircling the capital. The first of these took place just outside Madrid along the Corunna highway, although this was halted when General

22. Some 10,000 had disembarked in Cádiz between December 1936 and February 1937.

Orgaz's forces met fierce resistance from the Twelfth and Thirteenth International Brigades who were supported by Russian tanks. When fighting resumed in the same sector in January the objective was to open a broad front to the south-west of Madrid, thereby severing lines of communication with Valencia. Orgaz launched a massive assault through the Jarama valley at the very moment the Republican Army of the Centre was planning to mount its own offensive in the area. The resulting collision turned out to be one of the bitterest fought battles of the war. Once again the Nationalist advance got bogged down in heavy fighting, and for the first time they felt the punishing blows of an army that, although primarily on the defensive, was prepared to counter-attack. The casualties on both sides were staggeringly high – perhaps as many as 18,000 lives were lost – and the battle itself ended in stalemate. Although not defeated, the Republicans had failed to push the Nationalists back across the Jarama River. They were also suffering from the demoralizing effects of savage combat conditions. Members of the International Brigades, who had borne the brunt of the heaviest fighting, had never faced death on this scale – nearly half of the 600-man British battalion of the Fifteenth Brigade were killed on 'Suicide hill' in one afternoon. Stunned by the sight of so many dead bodies, many recruits, including those who had became hardened to the realities of war, had lost their enthusiasm for fighting.

REPUBLICANS STRIKE BACK: THE BATTLE OF GUADALAJARA

Following their success at Málaga, Italian forces under General Roatta sought to play a greater role in the fighting. Though reluctant to relinquish his complete control over military operations, in February 1937 Franco approved an Italian-led offensive to the north-east of Madrid near the town of Guadalajara. For Mussolini and the Italians this was to be the occasion for demonstrating the invincibility of the Fascist military machine. With the support of his fully motorized units, a regular army division and three divisions of the Corpo Truppe Volontarie (CTV) Roatta attacked on 8 March.

Having broken through the republican defences, Roatta's troops surged forward until inclement weather set in. The advantage of mechanized movement was now lost: Italian lorries and tanks got bogged down in muddy roads. This gave the republicans enough time to receive reinforcements from Madrid. A counter-offensive was launched on 18 March, and this led to the defeat of the crack Black Shirt and Littorio divisions. With the capture of Brihuega, the republicans secured their first decisive triumph of the war. Because of this, the Battle of Guadalajara became more than just a military success. For the republicans it represented the first real evidence that they could defeat the Nationalists. Many, like the French writer and pilot André Malraux, saw it as proof that the 'model' Popular Army that was finally taking shape was living up to its expectations.

Despite their much-trumpeted victory at Guadalajara, the war was going badly for the republicans. Besides inflicting heavy losses on the Army of the Centre, and capturing Málaga, the Nationalists had scored a string of victories on the northern front. Near the French-Spanish border, the republican cities of Irún and San Sebastián – both anarchosyndicalist strongholds – had fallen to the Nationalists, and the republican zone in Asturias was already coming under aerial attack. As we shall see, these setbacks seriously undermined republican attempts to take the initiative in the war effort.

CHAPTER NINE

The Nationalist Zone

THE POLITICS OF THE *MOVIMIENTO*

While the consolidation of military authority in the Nationalist zone was accomplished relatively easily, there still remained the problem of unifying the political and social life of the civilian population. Given the array of political groupings representing the right this was no easy task. For, despite their common desire to defeat 'Red' Spain, the Nationalist parties were divided over a number of fundamental issues. Both the Carlists and members of Renovación Española were passionately in favour of monarchy, but they quarrelled over what form it should take. An even greater schism separated the Falange or Spanish Fascist Party from the rest of the right. Their insistence on using the modern state as an instrument for radically restructuring society, for example, was at variance with the beliefs held by the Carlists and other traditional conservatives who feared that their movements would be smothered by the machinery of an omnipotent state.

The first political casualties of the military rebellion on the right were the CEDA and the monarchist Renovación Española. As we have seen, the decomposition of the CEDA was already well under way during the last months of the Second Republic, when vast numbers of cedistas – especially the CEDA youth movement, Juventud de Acción Popular (JAP) – turned their backs on the tactic of 'legalism' and joined the Falange. With normal political activity suspended following the military uprising, the CEDA ceased to function, although its head, Gil Robles, delayed his decision to dissolve the party until February 1937.

Following the demise of the monarchy, the Alfonsine movement underwent several transformations. A few purists refused to compromise their monarchist principles, but most felt compelled to modify their political strategy. Members of Renovación Española, many of whom believed it was both possible and desirable to accommodate monarchism within the framework of an authoritarian political structure, shared with the Carlists and Falangists the conviction that the legalist policy of 'accidentalism' was a waste of time and that the liberal Second Republic had to be violently overthrown. Their goal was to establish a corporatist state that would be ruled by a military monarchy much like the one that had developed under the Dictator Miguel Primo de Rivera.

Because it was never a mass party, the Renovación Española stood little chance of realizing its goals within the context of a parliamentary system. Yet, as a political party, it could not be easily ignored. Its importance lay in the fact that the party's prominent members belonged to the economic oligarchy and privileged social and military castes that had ruled Spain for generations. As we have seen, Antonio Goicoechea, one of Renovación's founders, was at the centre of the abortive right-wing plot to overturn the Republic and restore the monarchy in 1934, and, in the crucial first week of the rebellion, he successfully secured financial and material aid from the Italians. Thus, even after the party ceased to exist during the civil war, its ideals were kept alive by the clique of highly influential monarchists who remained close to the centres of political power in the Nationalist zone.

The only two radical right parties that attracted a mass following during the civil war were the Carlist Comunión Tradicionalista, and the fascist Falange. As events began to unfold it became increasingly apparent that both of these movements were destined to play a central role in defining the political and social life of Nationalist Spain.

Never a popular cause outside its bastions in the Navarre, Catalonia, Valencia and the Basque country, Carlism had, by 1936, long outlived its political relevancy. Inveterately hostile to the idea of a secular state, the Carlists aimed to destroy the laic republic and replace it with a corporatist, decentralized clerical monarchy that traced its roots to Ferdinand VII's younger brother and pretender to the throne, Don Carlos María Isidro de Borbón.[1] But while its goal of installing a reactionary Carlist monarchy in the twentieth century was quixotic, during the Second Republic Carlists found common ground on which to cooperate with other groups on the far right. Its revival at this time owed a great deal to the movement's deep-

---

1. The fact that, in 1936, it was the childless octogenarian, Alfonso Carlos, who was the claimant to the Spanish Crown did not bode well for the movement. Alfonso Carlos was killed on 28 September 1936. His great-nephew, Prince Javier de Bourbón-Parma, was designated by him to preside as 'Regent' over Carlist affairs.

seated hatred of liberal democracy as well as its strong identification with Catholicism and other traditional Spanish values that were being assailed by the republican government. Forays into the political arena also contributed to the movement's expansion. Led by the aristocrat Conde de Rodezno, and other pragmatic members of the Carlist elite from Navarre, Carlism passed through a phase during which its public organization, the Comunión Tradicionalista, formed broad alliances with other anti-republican parties.[2]

From 1934 on, Carlism, now dominated by maximalists like Manuel Fal Conde and José Luís Zamamillo, recovered its exclusive character and the movement retracted once again. In fact, it was because Fal Conde and other intransigents seriously entertained the idea of launching their own revolt in the name of Carlism that the movement split over whether it should join the national military conspiracy that was afoot in the spring of 1936. Then, on the eve of the July rising, an understanding was reached between the Carlist moderates and General Mola which seemed to encourage the former's hegemonic designs in Navarre. Carlist support was thus assured and their volunteer militia rose in tandem with the insurgent troops. During the early months of the war Carlist contributions to the rebel cause were significant: the initial success of General Mola's Army of the North, especially on the Basque and Aragón fronts, owed much to the well-trained and highly-disciplined *tercios* (regiments) of the Requetés. All told between 70,000 and 100,000 Carlist troops saw action in the first months of fighting, mostly in the Navarre region but also in and around Seville and Madrid.

As the war progressed it became increasingly apparent that, though the moderate elements of the Navarrese leadership, including the former Carlist political chief Rodezno, were prepared to cooperate fully with the army, a significant number of Carlists saw the war as an opportunity for pursuing their historic goals. Thus while the army leadership were searching for ways of uniting the *Movimiento* under a single command, intransigent Carlists began pulling harder in a different direction. This drift culminated when Fal and his loyal followers inaugurated two major projects aimed exclusively at advancing the Carlist cause. The first, launched in November 1936, was an initiative called the *Obra Corporativa Nacional*, which was designed to lay the foundation stones for a corporatist regime organized in accordance with traditionalist beliefs and values. The second was the creation of a military academy that would be used to train both commissioned and noncommissioned officers for the Requetés.

---

2. The movement began gathering momentum in 1931 as an ever-increasing number of ardent Catholics enrolled in its national organization, Traditionalist Communion.

Given the Junta's determination to exercise complete control over military matters, it is not surprising that the Academy project – which, in theory at least, challenged the supremacy of the army – was doomed to failure. In the event, Franco was so furious at having learned that the academy was a *fait accompli* that he forced Fal to choose between a court martial or exile. With his departure to Portugal, any hopes for building a Carlist state within the Nationalist camp were all but extinguished. From then on, the collaborationist tendency headed by Rodezno regained the ascendancy and the Carlist cause was gradually absorbed into the FET – the new political party Franco cobbled together in 1937 – and Carlism lost its distinctiveness. Nevertheless, as a reward for agreeing to participate in the unification process, Franco appointed top Carlists to serve in the newly-created state apparatus and Rodezno himself became the Minister of Justice in Franco's first cabinet (1938).

SPANISH FASCISM: THE FALANGE

As we have seen, during the Second Republic fascism was a highly marginalized political movement. Apart from a small group of disaffected intellectuals, it appealed mainly to taxi drivers and certain sections of the student population. Ironically, it was the victory of the left-wing Popular Front which saved the movement from extinction. The triumph of the left caused more and more discontented middle class rightists to lose faith in the ability of the parliamentary right (such as the CEDA) to defend their interests. Thus, as their right-wing political rivals lost credibility, the Falange gained in prestige. What prevented fascist expansion at this juncture was Republican repression, in March, which put Falange leaders behind bars and forced the movement underground.

Then, in July, the outbreak of civil war created the conditions for the spectacular growth of Spanish fascism, although, significantly, the resurgent Falange Party found itself bereft of its principal leaders. The charismatic National Chief José Antonio Primo de Rivera, along with several other high ranking Falangist leaders, was in Republican hands and many other *camisas viejas* or Falangist veterans – Onésimo Redondo, for example – died in the opening moments of the struggle. As we shall see, their absence would have a profound impact on the movement.[3]

In spite of this serious handicap, the Falange soon became one of the

---

3. The division of Spain into two mutually hostile blocs also jeopardized the unity of the movement as former centres of fascist activity – Madrid, for example – were now under republican control.

principal sources of Nationalist strength. In the first few months of the war, membership of Falangist organizations soared dramatically and their volunteer militia played a significant role both at the front, where Falangists fought alongside requetés and regular army troops, and in rearguard operations, where the Falange established its own political police force.

The surge of popular support for Spanish fascism was in no small measure due to the party's dynamic and efficiently-run propaganda programme. During the war, the movement not only continued to publish its national daily, *Arriba España*, but it also maintained an extensive network of provincial publications. In addition, thanks to its well-organized Press and Propaganda Department, the Falange was able to take charge of coordinating and promoting press activities in the rebel zone.[4]

On another level, the Falangists were responsible for creating a daring modernist 'aesthetic' which was reproduced in a variety of formats. Posters, newspaper illustrations, magazines, calendars, uniforms, films and even children's toys were used to convey fascist ideas and images. Following Hitler (who devoted much thought to the technique of propaganda, learning where he could from D'Annunzio, Mussolini and others), the Spanish fascists carefully cultivated their public image. Just as the SA (Sturm Abteilungen) had appropriated the 'red' colour of the communists in the decoration of their banners, the Falangists borrowed the highly dramatic red and black standards of the CNT-FAI to indicate their social bond with the working classes.[5]

The blue shirts worn by the Falangist youth (*Flechas*) and militiamen and women also spoke of the party's ideals. In the words of Giménez Caballero, the blue shirt was a universal symbol which not only identified those who opposed Marxism but had embraced the new Catholic universality that the Falange sought to defend. It was, he affirmed in the monarchist *ABC*, not an undergarment but rather 'a *whole garment*; a totalitarian garment. Affirming and aggressive'.

The Falange's prodigious growth meant that the party now possessed a political importance it had never had before. Yet the waves of new members – many of whom were not ideological converts – had inevitably diluted the overall character of a movement which, until recently, existed as a reduced core of like-minded revolutionaries. Above all, the Falange's rapid expansion created demands on the leadership which, as we have seen, had been decimated at the outset of the war. The disappearance of José Antonio, the enormously popular National Chief who was executed on 20 Novem-

4. Sheelagh M. Ellwood, *Spanish Fascism in the Franco Era* (London, 1987) p. 35.
5. But while some Falange posters bore a striking resemblance to those being produced by the CNT-FAI, the political message echoed here and elsewhere in the Falangist media was unmistakably fascist.

ber 1936, had come as the severest blow to the movement. To resolve what they initially believed to be only a temporary problem – official word of Primo's death was not announced until one year later – the National Council of the Falange decided to create a Junta de Mando Provisional or Provisional Command Committee (PCC). Significantly, it was decided that the head of this seven-member ruling body would not fill José Antonio's shoes and become the National Chief (*Jefe*). The mantle of leadership fell to Manuel Hedilla, a former ship's mechanic who had never held a political post of national scope.

Since the task of uniting the Falangist movement and investing it with dynamism at this juncture would have been a daunting one for even the most gifted of leaders, it is hardly surprising that Hedilla, who possessed a lacklustre personality, failed to assert himself in his new role. In fact, territorial and provincial party chiefs continued to exercise more authority in the areas under their control than Hedilla was able to do.[6]

Moreover, Hedilla's claim to the top Falangist post did not go unchallenged. Although he commanded the support of the principal Falangist leaders in the northern provinces as well as the writers of the party apparatus, he was opposed by the so-called 'legitimists' who were led by José Antonio's cousin, Sancho Dávila, and the militia chief Agustín Aznar.[7] Hedilla himself tried desperately to unite the Falangist leadership, but his efforts were to no avail. On 18 April 1937 the 'legitimist' wing rose up against Hedilla, declaring him deposed. Hedilla and his backers reacted quickly, and on the evening of the same day the beleaguered fascist leader called a meeting of the Falangist National Council in order to determine José Antonio's successor. By a narrow margin Hedilla won the election, although, as things turned out, this would prove to be a hollow victory.[8]

Meanwhile, the search for a leader who could exercise both military and political authority over the Nationalist forces exacerbated the tensions within the Falange Party, and, just as Franco was at the point of becoming the supreme leader or *jefe nacional* of the *Movimiento*, these conflicts were coming to a head. Despite this important move and despite the fact that

---

6. Lacking popular support inside the movement, Hedilla was at least on good terms with General Franco throughout 1936 and the first part of 1937. Thus, when Franco moved his general military headquarters (Cuartel General del Generalísimo) from Burgos to Salamanca (on 30 September 1936), Hedilla followed suit, transferring the Falangist Command Committee there in October. The Junta de defensa Nacional was replaced in October by the Junta Técnica after Franco's designation as Head of State on 1 October 1936.
7. See Stanley G. Payne, *The Franco Regime, 1939–1975* (Madison, Wisconsin, 1987), pp. 170–1.
8. This was because, while the Falangists were squabbling, Franco and his chief advisor, Serrano Súñer, were completing their plans to bring about a fusion of the Falangists and Carlists by creating an umbrella organization, the Falange Española Tradicionalista (FET).

the creation of the Falange Española Tradicionalista (FET) de las JONS in early 1937 effectively ended the independence of the Falange, Hedilla and his faction chose instead to fly in the face of reality. When he refused to take up his position as a member of the new party's Political Committee, his own fate (and that of a number of his adherents) was sealed: Hedilla was accused of plotting against the new *caudillo* and, after a brief military hearing, he was placed in solitary confinement.[9]

FRANCO AND FASCISM

As the top military commander in the Nationalist zone Franco enjoyed considerable powers, but in order to rule effectively he needed a vehicle for exercising political power as well. Among the first to recognize this was Franco's brother, Nicolás, who had early on in the war suggested the need for the creation of a Francoist party. Though he did not see himself as a politician, Franco recognized the advantages of such a move, not least because it would allow him to establish complete unity of purpose and action in the *Movimiento*. In the early months of the war, however, the heterogeneous composition of the right-wing political parties worked against the kind of harmony that Franco and his supporters were trying to orchestrate.

In this connection, we know that Franco himself, now that he was the undisputed leader of the Nationalists, was entertaining the idea of establishing his own party. But what political character would it have? Franco recognized the danger of siding with one of the three civilian parties – the Renovación, the Comunión Tradicionalista, and the Falange – since this would inevitably splinter the forces backing the Nationalist cause. He therefore sought to create a unified system that accommodated all the major themes of the right.

But Franco was above all a military leader who knew very little about the art of politics. Thus, even though in theory he exercised absolute power, according to the historian Juan Pablo Fusi 'it is doubtful that he had any clear idea of what to do with it'. Up to this time, Franco's political perspective was decidedly unsophisticated: beyond his love for traditional monarchy and nostalgia for empire he held a resolute hatred for the left, especially Freemasonry and communism. Signficantly, before July 1936, these beliefs were at odds with his public record. During the Primo

9. See Stanley G. Payne, *Falange* (Stanford, 1961), pp. 169–71. Hedilla was actually sentenced to death for the murder of one of Dávila's bodyguards, but his sentence was commuted.

dictatorship, Franco had criticized the Dictator for wanting to pull back in Morocco, and he had served the Republic loyally despite the fact that he interpreted the Asturian rising of October 1934 as a sign of incipient communism and saw the Popular Front as the next step towards a left-wing revolution. Even when, in the spring of 1936, events appeared to be running out of control, Franco was reluctant to join the Spring conspiracy and did not commit himself wholeheartedly to the coup attempt until days before the rebellion began. Such inscrutable behaviour was the clearest indication that Franco possessed neither the temperament nor the imagination of a political architect.

Thus it remained for others to devise a blueprint that could unite the disparate elements of the *Movimiento*. The person who filled this role happened to be Franco's brother-in-law, Ramón Serrano Súñer, a former *cedista* who held pro-fascist convictions. After having eluded his republican captors in Madrid, Serrano arrived in Salamanca – Franco's GHQ – in February 1937. Not long afterwards, Serrano replaced Franco's older brother, Nicolás, as the general's closest advisor. Serrano's ties with the Falange – he had been a close friend of José Antonio – as well as his instinctive political savvy convinced Franco that his brother-in-law should be entrusted with the task of engineering the framework of an authoritarian system that would place the *caudillo* at its head. Perhaps with an eye to the strategy Hitler employed in his rise to power, Serrano sought to develop a programme that reconciled the ideals and goals of conservatism on the one hand and those of fascism on the other. Such a synthesis, he insisted, was possible because the two doctrines complemented one another: 'Though it was true that traditionalism was obviously a movement endowed with extraordinary vitality, heroism, romanticism and filled with virtues, it was nevertheless unable to find expression in political reality; on the other hand, the Falange was a party whose doctrine embodied many of the principles of traditionalism, and, beyond this, it possessed a popular social and revolutionary content that would permit Nationalist Spain to absorb ideologically Red Spain. . . .'[10]

The practical scheme for accomplishing this, which was formally issued in April 1937 as the 'Decree of Unification', called for the amalgamation not only of the two largest political forces supporting the rebellion, the Falange and the Comunión Tradicionalista, but also of all the pro-Nationalist groups, including the army, the large landowners, the Catholic Church, and the industrial bourgeoisie. Henceforth there was to be only one party

---

10. Ramón Serrano Súñer, *Entre Hendaya y Gibraltar* (Madrid, 1947), p. 31.

in Nationalist Spain, the Falange Española Tradicionalista (FET) de las JONS.[11]

The National-Syndicalist State headed by Franco was a political paradox: it was, as Serrano had anticipated, a skilful blend of conservative principles derived from the 'old right' (Catholicism, Carlism and monarchism) and the modern ideas of fascism. The result was a hybrid movement that strove to preserve the conservative elements of 'eternal' Spain within the boundaries of a social/political system that was tailored to accommodate the social and economic pressures of the modern age. To achieve this, Franco was forced to jettison and/or modify those aspects of conservatism and fascism that threatened to disrupt the balance attained in his political equation. On more than one occasion, for example, Franco made it clear that the monarchist aspirations of the conservative parties were to be subordinated to the pragmatic goals of the new state; and he made certain that the revolutionary *élan* of Falangism was sufficiently muted.

There were both practical and political reasons why the non-fascist right agreed to dissolve their own parties for the sake of constructing a monolithic one grounded on fascist principles. To be sure, the military support provided by Mussolini and Hitler had greatly enhanced the prestige of fascism, even among the Carlists and other conservatives who had long held strong reservations about fascist theory – especially its identification with modernist themes and its emphasis on *étatisme*. But, against the background of civil war and revolution, their desire to defeat the Spanish left was much stronger than their distaste for the fascistic trappings of the new regime. Moreover, as events in pre-war Spain had demonstrated, it was widely believed on the right that liberalism was dead and that fascism offered the most effective rampart against what they perceived as the ever-present threat of communism. The Spanish right as a whole was therefore willing to accept a fascist-type system as the basis of a new political, social and economic order in the West.[12]

In any case, having been purged of their leaders either through fate or by force, the civilian parties were in no position to directly challenge

11. It is true that fascism provided the structural foundation for the new state system, it does not follow from what has been said that Franco himself can be regarded as a fascist dictator. The consensus among most contemporary historians is that, while Franco himself was not a fascist, he consciously used fascist politics to establish a durable authoritarian regime.
12. It would be wrong to conclude from this that the monarchists and other non-fascist parties had no hand in giving shape to the new regime. In fact, it was their influence which helped to set the limits of its fascist character; for, as powerful as he was becoming, Franco continued to rely on the financial and moral support of the Carlist and monarchist parties.

Franco's authority.[13] Those who objected to the changes being imposed from above could only protest in private or show their dissatisfaction in subtle ways. Thus, die-hard Carlists did not take to the blue shirts of their new 'composite' uniforms, while recalcitrant Falangists would frequently stuff their red (Carlist) berets in their pockets.

The structural foundation of the Franquista system was to be anchored by the Falange syndicalist programme, the only one on the right which offered a realistic strategy for incorporating the hitherto refractory working classes into the new regime.

RIGHT-WING UNIONISM

From 1937 on, the new state party dealt with union matters and all labour programmes. Having forcibly dismantled all left-wing organizations, the Nationalists sought to replace them with a trade union structure that conformed to Falangist principles. Violently opposed to Marxism, liberalism, and an unregulated capitalist economy, Falangist ideology envisaged an 'organic' or corporatist society, wherein class divisions would be eliminated and a highly centralized state authority ruled in the name of 'Nation, Race, and Religion'. According to one of the regime's Fundamental Laws, the Fuero del Trabajo (Labour Charter), passed by the Burgos government in 1938, unions were to be used as instruments of state policy. The unions themselves were amalgamated, forming a monolithic organization called the Organización Sindical Española (OS): Spanish Syndical Organization.

Based on the principles of 'Unity, Totality, and Hierarchy', the OS grouped together both employers and employees and was initially composed of twenty-eight syndicates, corresponding to the different branches of production organized at the local, provincial and national levels. With its emphasis on the union's subservience to the state and the implied elimination of class conflict, the OS resembled the corporatist-organicist models of labour organization adopted by Portugal, Austria, Italy and Germany during the 1930s. Like them, the Falangist model was opposed to what was perceived as the chaos produced by a system where trade unions competed with one another. It therefore followed that, as all aspects of trade union activity were to be defined by the one-party state, there would be no place for independent union action. Henceforth, it was believed,

13. The fact is that the civilian sector could not produce a formidable challenger: Fal Conde, Gil Robles, and Hedilla – who, in any case, had never been more than just factional leaders – were now out of the picture and José Antonio and the two minor prophets of Spanish fascism, Ledesma Ramos and Redondo, were dead.

strikes and similar kinds of direct action tactics were to be a thing of the past.

The imposition of docility on a formerly mobilized and radicalized working class required much more than the publication of decrees. Recognizing this, the Nationalist authorities sought to impose the new labour scheme by means of repression. As we shall see, their wide-ranging programme of terror was used to liquidate leading left-wing opponents and cow the rest of organized labour into submission.

NATIONALISM AND CATHOLICISM

Franco believed that the structures of the new state would be held together not only by harmonizing all political differences but also by drawing upon the spiritual strength of Catholicism. He therefore turned to the Church, the transcendent symbol of old Spain, to help define the social content of his regime.

The relationship between Catholicism and the military revolt of July 1936 was a complicated one. Even though Catholic political parties and movements like Carlism played a central role in the conspiracy and rising partly because they believed that they were defending their faith, it cannot be said that they were fighting in the name of the Church. This was particularly true of the Falange movement. It will be recalled that, before the war, relations between the Falange and the Church were rather ambivalent. Some Falangists, most notably intellectuals such as Rafael Sánchez Mazas, Ernesto Giménez Caballero and the national leader José Antonio Primo de Rivera, stressed the Catholic underpinnings of their movement, but many others had no interest in religion *per se*.

Given the pre-war hostility between the Popular Front government and the Church and in view of the ferocious anti-clerical assault in the republican zone that took the lives of nearly 7,000 clergymen and women, it came as no surprise when the vast majority of the Spanish clergy cast in their lot with the rebellion. For top Church officials the most obvious reason for doing so was that a rebel victory held out the hope that the Catholic Church would regain its privileged position in Spanish society.

The Church hierarchy held back from endorsing the rebellion until September 1936, when the true political sympathies of the leading bishops were made clear. That month Bishop Pla y Deniel wrote a pastoral letter, *The Two Cities*, in which he attempted to justify the rebellion against the

175

legitimate Spanish government.[14] Couching his arguments in religious terms, Pla y Deniel was one of the first to contribute to the mythology that grew up around the Nationalist cause when he suggested that the rebellion marked the beginning of a modern-day holy crusade or *cruzada*. The publication of Pla's epistle was followed in July 1937 by a collective pastoral letter addressed to the outside world and which was sponsored and prepared by the primate and archbishop of Toledo, Isidro Gomá y Tomás.[15] Ostensibly its main purpose was to 'correct certain false impressions about the war' and thereby clarify the Church's role in the struggle. Insisting that the Church 'neither wished for the war nor provoked it', the bishops spoke of how it was both their religious and patriotic duty to endorse the rebel cause since the Nationalists were fighting for the true interests of the Spanish people, namely the preservation of Christian civilization against the onslaught of godless communism.[16] Far from merely dispelling misconceptions about the Church, the 'Joint Letter' served a political purpose. By issuing it the bishops intended not only to solicit support from the international Catholic community but also to declare their unqualified affirmation of the rebels' cause.[17].

By further arguing that the Church 'could not be indifferent' to the crisis, the bishops hoped to legimate their decision to intervene on behalf of the insurgents.[18] In fact, during the war their activities became increasingly intertwined with the Nationalist cause: besides attending military functions, they preached to the troops, and helped to shape the educational and social policies of the Burgos government.

Not all clergymen felt compelled to take an active part in promoting the crusade, yet a significant number seized the opportunity to purge Nationalist Spain of 'atheistic' influences and, on occasion, exact revenge from those whom they saw as the enemies of 'Christian civilization'. In a few cases, the clergy went so far as to justify elimination of the crusade's enemies. While mass executions were taking place in Córdoba, for example,

14. This reluctance stemmed partly from the fact that two predominantly Catholic Basque provinces – Vizcaya and Guipúzcoa – remained loyal to the Republican government; and partly from the fact that the revolt itself was not connected to the Church.
15. Cardinal Gomá later sought to win the Pope over to the Nationalists' 'crusade' by liaising between the Vatican and Franco.
16. Quoted in José M. Sánchez, *The Spanish Civil War as a Religious Tragedy* (Notre Dame, 1987), p. 93.
17. The Vatican's somewhat conciliatory posture in Spain rapidly changed in the wake of the anticlerical fury unleashed by the military rebellion and popular revolution. Papal recognition of the Nationalists (Burgos regime) was not formally made until May, 1938 – although informal recognition had been granted well before this date. Even so, the Pope refused to denounce the PNV and the Basque Catholics who remained loyal to the Republic.
18. See Frances Lannon, *Privilege, Persecution, and Prophecy* (Oxford, 1987), Chapter 8.

Father Jacinto, a local Capuchin friar, proclaimed that it was necessary to eradicate the 'degenerate and poisonous seed of marxism' even if this meant 'extinguishing' its advocates.[19]

More commonly, retribution was obtained by actively discriminating against those who were not participating in the crusade. Again in Córdoba, commissions for the Purging of Public Education were set up to dismiss all teachers who had had ties to the Popular Front or to the teacher's union, or who were suspected of harbouring liberal ideas. To signal the end to secularization of education, on 1 October 1936 crucifixes were ceremoniously returned to the classrooms and thousands of books deemed anti-Church were burned.

With the backing of the authorities, the clergy's campaign to reinstate Catholicism was vigorously pursued at every level of society. By the war's end in 1939, the last vestiges of the secular republic had been wiped out, and from then until the 1970s all private relationships and public rituals had to be conducted in accordance with Church doctrine. In post-war Spain, the Church reaped the dividends of its ideological support. Firmly entrenched as one of the major pillars of a system that came to be known as National Catholicism, for the next twenty years the interests of the Church and State were identified as one and the same.

The unification of the right under one umbrella, although undeniably shrewd, was neither novel nor revolutionary in the Spanish context. Franco's accomplishment was in keeping with a long-standing tradition of praetorian politics. Following in the footsteps of the Dictator Primo de Rivera, Franco had used the military as a vehicle for achieving political power, albeit with one crucial difference. According to Stanley Payne, Franco was determined to avoid Primo's mistake 'of failing to proceed to the direct institutionalization of a new system'.[20] He therefore demanded that all elements of the Movimiento be wholly integrated into the Nationalist-Syndicalist organization being erected.[21]

COUNTER-REVOLUTION AND TERROR ON THE RIGHT

As the wave of anti-clerical blood-letting and revolutionary terror was sweeping through neighbourhoods in the republican zone, rebel forces

19. F. Gómez Moreno, *La guerra civil en Córdoba, 1936–1939* (Córdoba, 1985), p. 461.
20. Stanley G. Payne, *The Franco Regime, 1936–1975* (Madison, Wisconsin, 1982) p. 167.
21. Ironically, Franco's rise to power also paralleled that of his bitterest enemy. For like the communists, who were exploiting the divisions on the left to achieve political supremacy in the republican camp, Franco played on the structural weaknesses of the right-wing parties to establish his control of the *Movimiento*.

were conducting what some referred to as the *limpieza* or rearguard 'clean-up' operations. With superior fire-power and in control of much territory where they constituted a minority, it is most likely that the Terror and repression on the right was on a grander scale than that on the left. However there is no way of telling precisely how many deaths can be attributed to the White Terror since the official registers of death for this period have either been destroyed or do not necessarily reflect the true number of those who died from 'unnatural' causes, a euphemism for summary execution. Estimates given by those on the left put the number of civilians killed by this onslaught in the range of 200,000, but a much lower number has been given by those sympathetic to the Nationalist cause. Extrapolating figures from sources mostly produced by pro-Franco historians, the American scholar Stanley Payne speculates that, from the beginning of the war until the end of Francoist repression four years afterwards, some 80,000 civilians fell victim to the White Terror; a number that is significantly higher than the figure he gives for the 'Red' Terror.[22]

It should be stressed here that, however many people died as a result of the White Terror, what is important is that the killings themselves touched the lives of nearly everyone in Spain. Furthermore, to a much greater extent than in the Republican half of Spain, repression in the Nationalist zone generated a palpable atmosphere of fear and recrimination that conditioned the behaviour of its inhabitants and persisted throughout and well beyond the civil war.

In the opening weeks of fighting, atrocities committed against civilians were simply reflex reactions to the chaotic conditions of civil war. As rebel forces conquered towns and villages, they sought out anyone who was on the left and therefore opposed to the military rising. The principal targets were workers and middle-class professionals (journalists, lawyers, and the like) who were sympathetic to the left. All the known republicans, anarchists, socialists and communists of a locality were thrown into prison, and those identified as 'enemies' of the rebellion were almost certain to be

22. In his *The Franco Regime* (p. 217), Payne accepts the number of Nationalist executions calculated by Ramón Salas Xarrazábal in his *Pérdidas de la guerra* (Barcelona, 1977), which are, according to Payne, '70,000 to 72,000 from beginning to end, almost exactly equal to the total in his computation of Republican executions during the Civil War'. The figures cited here reflect Payne's recent reading of studies which are focussed at the local level and which are more revealing of the true number of victims. See, for example, Antonio Hernández García, *La represión en la Rioja durante la guerra civil*, tomos i–iii (Logroño, 1984). Our intention in citing these estimates is not to assign greater blame to one side or the other. Repression, whether it is inspired by the right or left, should be condemned and to qualify it as fascist or communist does not make it any more or less deplorable.

executed simply because rebel leaders believed they represented a potential 'fifth-column' threat.

The ritual of killing 'traitors' was conducted much like it was in Republican towns and villages. On both sides the ghastly *paseos* took place nightly: 'Time after time the victim's own carriage serves him as his hearse, and there the dead are left at the edge of the fields or simply on the side of the road. The executioners are in a hurry. They can't waste time digging graves.'[23]

In other areas conquered by the rebels, especially where there were large numbers of urban-based groups, the violence was a one-sided continuation of the intense left-right street clashes and tit for tat killings that had reached a crescendo on the eve of the military coup. Now that civil war had erupted, however, right-wing gangs – such as the infamous 'Black Squad' in Granada – could settle old scores with impunity.

Sensationalized media images and reports of left-wing reprisals and of revolutionaries slaughtering clerics and desecrating religious buildings also incited violence on the right. Punitive expeditions were usually launched in the wake of such news – the mass execution of rebel officers by the left militia which stormed the Montaña barracks, for example – and these vengeful outbursts obviously served to reinforce the atmosphere of fear and uncertainty that had descended upon pro-republican regions that had fallen to the Insurgents.[24]

Although arising from similar conditions and motivated by similar passions the Red and White Terrors differed in several respects. Repression on the right was above all distinguished by the fact that the greater part of it was systematically carried out under the ubiquitous gaze of the recognized authorities.[25] By declaring martial law in occupied territories and proclaiming that all those opposed to the *movimiento* were in a 'state of rebellion', rebel officers tried to legitimate their rule and thus lend respectability to the hastily contrived military courts that sent thousands to the firing squads in the early months of the war. And while some military leaders – General Mola, for example – sought to impose limits on the purges being carried out against suspected traitors, this was done primarily

---

23. Concha Espina, *Retaguardia* (Córdoba, 1937), reprinted in *The Spanish Civil War*, ed. by Alun Kenwood (Providence, R.I., 1993), p. 129.

24. Ronald Fraser points out in his oral history of the war that not all the towns and villages targeted for revenge had been the scenes of left-wing inspired atrocities. See Ronald Fraser, *The Blood of Spain: An Oral History of the Spanish Civil War* (New York, 1983), p. 159.

25. Quiepo de Llano argued at the time that all violent acts on the republican side should be regarded as a criminal acts, whereas the Nationalists were, in his opinion, justified in using force since they were merely attempting to establish law and order. See Ian Gibson, *Quiepo de Llano* (Barcelona, 1986), pp. 116ff.

because of the destabilizing effects of such tactics and not because they themselves were recanting the use of violence, for the army continued to rely on repression as a 'military tactic' throughout and even beyond the war.[26]

Though the rebel army was the prime mover of the repression, its efforts to pacify the rearguard would not have succeeded without the cooperation of local authorities and civilian para-military organizations. Not uncommonly these groups would justify their role in the Terror by claiming that they were only following orders of the military tribunals. We know that in Granada, for example, the Guardia Civil, the Municipal police, as well as several civilian militias on the right (the Requeté and Falange) participated in 'cleaning up' operations and were directly responsible for numerous civilian deaths.[27]

Besides eliminating the threat of a rearguard attack, the White Terror served the Nationalists in other ways. Physical intimidation of this sort effectively stamped out all forms of social and political dissent. The pressure to submit to the new order was reinforced daily in newspaper columns that reported the latest executions and on evening radio broadcasts, such as a chilling speech delivered by Quiepo de Llano in March 1937: 'We are unfortunate enough to be forced to shoot plenty of people in Málaga, but all after trial by court martial . . . It must be borne in mind that those who are condemned to death are inexorably executed because we do not intend to imitate those weak governments of 1934!'[28]

In a similar way, violence was used by some to impose the ethical and cultural code of the *Movimiento*. The assassination in Granada of the renowned homosexual poet and playwright Federico García Lorca served no meaningful political purpose, but it did send an unequivocal message to the left and others who wanted to pursue lifestyles that did not conform to the traditionalist beliefs and values of the right.

Repression also made converts out of republicans of all political stripes. Many flocked to the rebel cause because they feared for their own lives as well as the safety of their families. Like the right-wing bourgeoisie in the republican zone who donned the '*mono azul*' in order to escape persecution, left-wingers under Nationalist rule escaped the firing squad by sporting the blue-shirt uniform of the Falange. (The flood of volunteers was so great in some areas in the south that Quiepo de Llano sarcastically

---

26. At the beginning of the war Mola is reputed to have said: 'It is necessary to spread an atmosphere of terror. We have to create an impression of mastery.'
27. See Chapter 7, 'Repression', in Ian Gibson, *The Assassination of García Lorca* (London, 1983).
28. Cited in Fraser, *Blood of Spain*, pp. 304–5.

dubbed the blue shirts 'life-jackets.')[29] Those not who did not fear death or imprisonment were still faced with the need to secure a livelihood, and, since being on the left was the surest way of losing one's job, an untold number of pro-republicans felt compelled to switch their allegiance to the Nationalist cause.

The cloud of terror that hung over Nationalist-occupied zones did not necessarily produce a negative reaction or feeling of disaffection among the civilian population. In certain areas of the Nationalist zone, executions aroused macabre sentiments: firing squads became public spectacles which drew crowds of men, women and children. For most, however, the violence done against pro-republicans was seen as a necessary evil. Even those who physically recoiled from the executions apparently adopted the army's view that they should be regarded as a 'military tactic' that was part and parcel of all wars. By viewing the Terror against the left in this way, Spaniards may have found it easier to reconcile themselves to a life under strict military rule. For, notwithstanding the grim and often sickening reality of repression, many hoped that the new regime represented the first step towards the establishment of law and order and the return to 'normal life'.

While the majority sought to rationalize the horrors of repression in these ways, the soul searching of others led them to a different conclusion. The enormity of politically-motivated killings did not escape the notice of a certain number of pro-Nationalists, who followed civilian and Church leaders like Bishop Marcelino Olaechea and the famous Spanish philosopher and literary figure Miguel de Unamuno in refusing to accept that cold-blooded assassinations could be justified on any grounds. To what extent the moral outrage of these public figures acted as a brake on the White Terror cannot be gauged empirically, but it seems to have had little impact on the military leaders, most of whom were bent on enforcing a policy of repression.

DAILY LIFE IN FRANCO'S SPAIN

The social order that was imposed upon civilians in Nationalist territory permeated every level of public life. First and foremost, the average person lived in a warlike atmosphere where everyone was subject to the rigours of a military regime. For men the reality of war meant that those who did not voluntarily enlist to fight in a militia faced the likely prospect of being conscripted. As far as the Nationalists were concerned men were to exhibit macho qualities. Accordingly, a man's place was fighting at the front or

29. See Anthony Beevor, *The Spanish Civil War* (London, 1982) p. 81.

defending the rearguard. The pressures to embrace militarism were immense, and those who refused to do so immediately fell under suspicion or ran the risk of being ridiculed for not fulfilling the duty expected of all patriotic and virile men living under the Nationalist banner.

In many respects the experiences of women in the Nationalist zone contrasted sharply with those of their counterparts on the Republican side. Earlier we spoke of how the war offered republican women, ranging from the liberal to the far left, an opportunity both to defend their social and political rights and to redefine their lifestyles by renouncing the anti-liberal values of traditional Spain. On the other hand, Nationalist women belonged to an ideologically homogeneous group which sought to uphold the image of women as defined by an exceedingly paternalistic Catholic Church. According to this, women, who were presumed to be both intellectually and physically inferior to males, were to play a supportive role in the struggle against 'Red' Spain primarily by attending to the needs of men and by upholding the sanctity of traditional social conventions like motherhood and the nuclear family.

Women were also expected to dress modestly – using lipstick and excessive make-up were frowned upon and wearing trousers was positively forbidden – and they were obliged to conduct themselves 'properly' (that is, unprovocatively) in public. Some even maintained that it was one's patriotic duty to be self-abnegating and to observe a puritanical code of behaviour:

> Women of Spain, in these grave moments for the country, your way of life cannot be that of frivolity, but austerity; your place is not in the theatres, the *paseos*, the cafés, but in the church and the hearth. . . . Your duty is not to procure for yourself an easy life, but to educate your children, sacrificing your pleasures and helping Spain.[30]

Such exacting standards, which were prescribed by the Church and strongly endorsed by the Nationalist authorities, were also meant to bring about greater social cohesion, especially among the many young women who were trying to adjust to the psychological and physical hardships brought on by wartime conditions.

Though publicly repressed, extramarital and illicit sexual activity flourished in the backstreets and bars frequented by soldiers on leave from the front. Prostitution was a serious problem in many areas but the authorities were generally helpless to curb its proliferation, not least because it was fuelled by economic necessity: the mounting number of women bereft of

---

30. From a manifesto entitled 'Spanish Woman', as quoted in Hugh Thomas, *The Spanish Civil War*, 3rd edn (London, 1977), p. 763.

friends and family were sometimes forced to sell their bodies as a means of supporting themselves.

On the other hand, the war experiences of some, while not openly challenging traditionally-defined gender roles, did allow them to participate in activities that took them far beyond the confines of family life. As was the case in the republican zone, the exigencies of war thrust a significant number of women – especially middle-class women and the widows, wives and daughters of the well-to-do – into new, non-traditional roles. Thousands of women answered the call to contribute to the war effort by pouring their energies into war-related enterprises. Ideologues tended to join organizations like the Carlist 'Margaritas', or the Falange's feminist section, Sección Femenina, (the only non-religious women's organization allowed to operate in the Nationalist zone); while others served in such associations as the Mujeres al Servicio de España (Women in the Service of Spain) and Obra de Asistencia al Frente (Work Aiding the Front) – all of which were 'volunteer' organizations that had the stamp of approval of the Burgos government.[31]

By far the largest and most important of these groups was the Falange's Sección Femenina (SF). Patterned after the Italian Fasci Femminili, the Sección Femenina was founded in 1934 in order to create a Falangist identity for women that could innoculate them against what José Antonio saw as the de-feminizing influences of the liberal Republican system. During the war SF was led by Pilar Primo de Rivera, José Antonio's younger sister.[32] Counting a mere 2,000 members in 1936, the organization expanded so prodigiously during the course of the conflict that by 1939 it had an estimated membership of some 580,000. Besides engaging in recruiting efforts and Falangist propagandistic activities, members of the Sección dedicated themselves to social work. For example, the Falangist Auxilio Social, which was founded in Valladolid by the widow of the Falangist leader Onésimo Redondo, Mercedes Sanz Bachiller, cared for orphaned children, including the sons and daughters of republicans who had fallen victim to the White Terror.[33]

It should be stressed that the varied experiences of the women who worked in the public arena did not qualitatively alter gender relations in the Nationalist zone. Women may have acquired a degree of independence,

---

31. A decree passed on 7 October 1937 made it obligatory for all single women between the ages of 17 and 35 to spend six months performing social services. See Payne, *The Franco Regime*, p. 187.
32. See Rosario Sánchez López, *Mujer Espanola, Una Sombra de Destino en lo Universal: Trayectoria histórica de Sección Femenina de Falange (1934–1977)* (Murcia, 1990).
33. To keep pace with the ever growing number of orphans created by the war, the Auxilio eventually established branches throughout Nationalist Spain. See Hugh Thomas, *The Spanish Civil War*, 3rd edn (London, 1977), p. 507.

but they did not see this as a way of challenging male dominance in society. For example, very few, if any, women felt threatened by the Burgos government's efforts to stamp out the liberal and, generally speaking, pro-feminist legacies of the Republic by repealing the Law of Divorce (2 March 1938) and suppressing co-education in Nationalist Spain. At most some wanted to enlarge the scope of woman's social activities so that it was possible for her to be more than just a housewife, mother and daughter.

Even if the prevailing social and cultural climate in the Nationalist camp was fairly sombre, it would be misleading to suggest that daily life was always dreary or wholly colourless. In fact, many civilians – especially the men – eagerly embraced the bellicose pomp of the martial regimen. One sympathetic eye-witness travelling with rebel forces captured the youthful exuberance and *esprit de corps* he sensed emanating from the Nationalist zone:

> . . . my favourites were always the Requetes or the Falangists. The first, so gay
> and dashing with their scarlet *boinas*, or berets, . . . their khaki shirts, wide open
> on the chest, their buff equipment, and their white socks neatly rolled round
> the ankle over their *espargatas*, or cord-soled shoes. The second, in their blue
> uniforms, looked so workman-like, and how they sang their Falangist hymn as
> they marched! There was much work in those early days, but also much singing,
> and 'Oriamendi' for the Requetes, the Falangist hymn, and the 'Novio de la
> la Muerte' for the Spanish Legion could be heard over the tramp of feet and
> the roar of the motor traffic on every road and in every town square of
> Nationalist Spain.[34]

Material comforts also made life in the Nationalist zone considerably more palatable than it was in Republican Spain. Compared to their republican counterparts, Nationalist civilians experienced a relatively secure and stable existence. While it is an exaggeration to depict Nationalist Spain – as some foreign observers did at the time – as a prosperous country that seemed little disturbed by the fact that war was raging in the greater part of the Iberian peninsula, it is true that, on the whole, Nationalist civilians did not suffer the hardships of those living in the Republican half of the country. People attended public functions – bullfighting, which was discouraged in most parts of the Republican camp, was popular – and restaurants were lively gathering spots.[35]

It was possible to engage in public activities of this sort not least because the majority of Nationalists were not continuously subjected to the trauma

---

34. Harold Cardozo, who was a correspondent for the *Daily Mail*, chronicles his experiences in *March of a Nation* (London, 1937), p. 58.
35. Both the Nationalists and Republicans used bullfights for political purposes, such as fundraising. When the great bullfighter Manolete took his *alternativa* in July 1939, he faced a bull which had been earlier dubbed 'Comunista' but which was now known as 'Mirador'.

of aerial and artillery bombings. These became a feature of daily life in Madrid and other cities and towns in the Republican zone from late 1936 until the end of the war, and contributed greatly to the demoralization of the civilian population in that sector.

The Nationalists' standard of living was also higher than that of the Republicans. During the time that Republicans – most of whom were cramped into densely-populated cities – were forced to ration an ever-shrinking amount of basic foodstuffs throughout the war, Nationalist civilians were never threatened by the spectre of hunger and many even managed to maintain a varied diet. Eggs, sugar, rice, potatoes, veal, bread and milk, if not abundant, were at least available in the food-producing regions of Andalucía, Castile and Galicia, and modest amounts could be purchased by most working families.[36] As the war progressed and the Nationalists enlarged their territory and hence control over more raw materials and natural resources, the food situation for the average person actually improved.

The relative prosperity enjoyed by the Nationalists attested to the stability of the economy underlying the military regime. For example, in contrast to the Republican government, which was increasingly overwhelmed by both external and internal economic problems, Nationalist leaders managed to hurdle the major financial obstacles facing them. Thus, despite the fact that they had practically no foreign currency to draw upon and virtually no gold reserves, the Nationalists found other ways of servicing their staggering war debt.

What prevented Nationalist Spain from sinking into an economic quagmire was the aid Franco received from the international capitalist community. It has been estimated that most of the $646-$713 million Franco spent abroad for war supplies during the conflict was obtained through credit.[37] In addition to using funds provided by wealthy Spaniards – most notably the Catalan financier, Juan March – the Nationalists secured *matériel* through a series of economic arrangements with Italy, Germany and international capitalist concerns. In the latter case, multinationals like Texaco (petroleum) and Firestone Rubber Company (tyres) sold their products on credit to Nationalist Spain because they had great confidence in Franco's ability to repay the loans.[38] Franco himself assured foreign firms and investors that the economy under the Burgos government was not vulnerable

---

36. These items were only obtainable through the black market in Republican cities.
37. Estimate given in Robert Whealey, 'How Franco financed his war – reconsidered', in *Spain in Conflict, 1931–1939*, ed. by Martin Blinkhorn (London, 1986), p. 255.
38. Texaco (Texas Oil) and other US oil firms were able to sell petroleum to Franco because of a loophole in the 1935 Neutrality Act: oil was not regarded as an essential war *matériel*.

to the revolutionary upheavals experienced in the Republican zone and that his regime would maintain the integrity and security of foreign investments:

> Economic life, both with respect to taxes and with respect to activities, commercial, industrial and agricultural, are developing within the frame of the laws that were in vigor before the war, and with full respect given to private property.[39]

Franco's economic relations with Germany were regulated by HISMA and ROWAK, export-import companies that were set up in 1936. Partly to facilitate the steady flow of arms and ammunition to the Nationalists and partly to place Germany's dealings with Spain on a financial footing, a German-financed transport company, *Compañía Hispano-Marroquí de Transportes (HISMA)*, was formed during the early weeks of the war. From October 1936 on, its operations were linked to those of a German export firm known as *Rohstoffe-und Waren-Einkaufsgesellschaft, ROWAK*. Together these companies served as the major conduits for the armaments and supplies shipped to Spain, thereby giving the Germans predominant control over Nationalist commerce with the outside world. Although this economic arrangement assured the steady flow of munitions and armaments into Franco's war machine, it was not in itself sufficient to overcome all the financial difficulties the Nationalists faced. No less important in this regard were the economic relations Nationalist Spain maintained with Mussolini's Italy. Thanks to continuous Italian military aid and their generous economic assistance over the course of the war – which, among other things, granted the Nationalists a rolling credit scheme and extended their repayment schedule – the Burgos government managed to reinforce the war sector of its economy.[40]

All of these sources of foreign aid contributed enormously to Franco's ability to finance his war without unduly burdening the domestic economy. Following the establishment of a one-party state in 1937, Franco's government successfully implemented a series of economic measures that effectively stabilized the internal economic infrastructure. Among other things, price controls were imposed and the production of wheat, sugar beets, olive oil, meat and other goods was placed under government control. It deserves mention that state encroachment in the economic sphere may have constituted an offence against the *petit bourgeois* entrepreneur but it did not signal a departure from the regime's commitment to capitalism,

---

39. Speech quoted in *One Year of War, 1936–1937* (no author) (New York, 1937?), p. 61.
40. On the Nationalist economy see the following: John R. Hubbard, 'How Franco Financed his War', *Journal of Modern History*, 25 December 1953, pp. 390–406, and Ángel Viñas, 'The Financing of the Spanish Civil War', in *Revolution and War in Spain, 1931–1939*, ed. by Paul Preston (London, 1984), pp. 266–82.

for the Franco government did not see the two as being mutually exclusive, especially in the context of war.

There can be little doubt that Franco's task of consolidating political and social control was rendered possible by the stability of the Nationalist economy. Equally important was the impact this had on the war effort. In contrast to the steadily deteriorating economy in the Republican zone, which acted as a constant drain on military operations, the relatively sound Nationalist financial picture allowed Franco and his chief lieutenants to devote their full attention to prosecuting the war on the battlefields.

CHAPTER TEN

The Role of Foreign Intervention

Before the military rebellion of July 1936 the political fate of Spain had caused little concern among the diplomatic circles of the Great Powers in Europe: France, Germany, Great Britain, Italy and the Soviet Union. After all, Spain was not seen as a determining factor in the new balance of power that had emerged in the post-war period. Nor, for that matter, was she generally regarded as having a major role in shaping European economic and cultural life. In the twentieth century, the decline of Spain's international importance can be traced to the 'Disaster of 1898', the brief and humiliating war which had cost her the last remnants of a once extensive empire. For over thirty years afterwards Spain had mostly stood on the sidelines of world events – as witnessed by her non-belligerent status during the First World War. Even when civil war erupted in 1936, her crisis at first seemed to be entirely unconnected to the problems of other countries. Thanks to foreign intervention this all changed. With German, Italian, and Soviet arms and supplies being openly funnelled into the Nationalist and Republican zones, other nations were forced to see the war not simply as a domestic affair but as an event that held international significance.[1]

Now that the spotlight was focussed on her, the value of Spain's strategic and economic assets was greatly enhanced. Of special strategic interest were her ports and territories along the North Atlantic coast and Mediterranean islands. Both Britain and France were well aware that, if a general war broke out between the democratic and fascist countries, the aeroplane and submarine bases in these areas would be of utmost importance; not least because German and Italian control of these facilities could endanger British and French communications in the Atlantic and western Mediterranean.

---

1. For a succinct summary of Spain's international status see Arnold Toynbee (with V. M. Boulter and Katherine Duff), *Survey of International Affairs* vol. II (London, 1938).

Though not nearly as great as her strategic assets, Spain's economic resources were also prized by the international community. Apart from olives and oranges, Spain supplied the world with several raw materials. At the time she dominated the mercury and pyrite markets, and her high-grade iron ore deposits, though not particularly abundant, were much sought after by countries like Great Britain and Germany.

But other factors were even more critical in determining foreign reaction to the Spanish situation. What was most troubling about the civil war was that the longer it lasted the greater were the chances of it spilling over into the general European arena. Because the Spanish imbroglio loomed large in the mind of the ordinary citizen, most governments deliberately pursued a policy that aimed to seal off Spain and thereby isolate the contagion they feared above all others.

While the dynamic interplay of fascism and communism on the European stage clearly played on the public's fear of war, it is essential to note that, as important as they were in defining the politics of the period, ideological questions were for all practical purposes ignored by the diplomats seeking a resolution to the Spanish crisis. Whether a diplomat was representing fascism, communism or democracy, he was above all concerned with advancing the foreign policy goals of his own country. As we shall see, the Spanish civil war demonstrated that conducting 'business as usual' often meant maintaining a dialogue with your bitterest ideological opponents.

CIVIL WAR AND THE INTERNATIONAL COMMUNITY

What, then, were the formal responses of the major powers? Although it was apparent to all the Western democracies that both the fascist and communist countries intended to use the Spanish war to further their own political agendas, no country was willing to take a resolute stand against them. Anxious to avoid any direct confrontation with the Axis powers, both France and Great Britain jointly pursued a policy of neutrality. And while Italy, Germany, Portugal and the Soviet Union publicly professed adherence to the idea of non-intervention, in practice each deliberately violated this policy throughout the course of the war.

On the other side of the Atlantic, the convulsion in Spain aroused considerable interest in the North and Latin American countries. For her part, the United States refused to break out of the isolation she had maintained since the end of the First World War. Roosevelt himself was personally inclined to aid the Republicans, but, ultimately, he yielded to domestic pressures – especially from the large and influential Catholic community – which demanded that the United States avoid any European entanglements. Nevertheless, by enforcing an arms embargo against Spain, the United States was effectively cooperating with both France and England to contain the Spanish crisis.

Given their historic ties to Spain, it is somewhat surprising that, with the exception of Mexico, the Latin American nations decided to remain aloof from Spain's troubles. But, during the 1930s, nearly all of the Latin American governments realized that they were too weighed down by the chronic social and economic problems besetting their own countries to take on any complicating foreign obligations. And despite the fact that several government leaders, including Peru's pro-fascist president Óscar Benavides and Cuba's pro-Republican leader Fulgencio Bastista, declared their respective partisanships, only the Cárdenas regime in Mexico made an effort to follow through its modest pledge to support the Republican cause.

From the outset, then, it was apparent that Spain's war was to be largely a European affair, and that the burden of defining the international community's official response to the complications arising from it resided with the Great Powers.

It is significant that none of the European countries turned to the League of Nations for a resolution of their common dilemma. Despite the fact that the Assembly of the League provided the Spanish Republic with a public forum for presenting its case to the world, the machinery of the League was never used to help bring about a cessation of hostilities.[2] Instead, those countries that were in principle committed to the idea of bringing about collective security through the League condemned it to futility by investing their faith in the Committee of Non-Intervention, an improvised body that had no formal ties to the League, and which, unlike the latter body, had no international status or powers *de jure*.[3]

In August 1936, the British and French declared their intention to refrain from intervention in the Spanish crisis. Their pledge unleashed a flurry of activity within the international diplomatic community, and, within two weeks, twenty-seven countries followed suit. Collectively these diplomatic replies came to be known as the Non-Intervention Agreement (NIA), although this was never recognized as a unified and legally binding

2. Between 1936 and April 1939, some aspect of the Spanish war was discussed at every session of the Council or Assembly.
3. On the NIC see P. A. M. van der Esch, *Prelude to War: The International Repercussions of the Spanish Civil War (1936–1939)* (The Hague, 1951), pp. 72–85.

document.[4] One month later, the Non-Intervention Committee (NIC) was set up in London, under the chairmanship of the Conservative Lord Plymouth. Its original function was to act as a watchdog body, monitoring outside interference in Spanish internal affairs. Over time, however, the NIC's main activity was limited to dealing with the endless wrangling among member nations who were accused of violating the terms of the Non-Intervention Agreement. In the event, violators of the NIA were not subject to prosecution under international law, and the NIC had no formal means of enforcing its decisions.

What the NIC did succeed in doing was to obstruct the Republican forces from securing desperately needed *matériel* from countries that might otherwise have come to their aid. Álvarez del Vayo, the Spanish Republican Foreign Minister and chief delegate representing his side at the League of Nations, vehemently denounced the policy of non-intervention as both unfair and illegal. It was wrong, Álvarez del Vayo further admonished the world community, to subject the Republicans to the same treatment as those who had rebelled against the legitimate government of Spain.[5]

Unhappy as it was with the policy of non-intervention, the Republican government nonetheless believed – at least during the early months of fighting – that a strict enforcement of the NIA would be to its advantage. Yet it, too, was helpless to do anything about it. Unable to participate in the activities of the NIC, the Republicans tried time and again to obtain more concrete results through the agencies of the League of Nations, where they were recognized as the official representatives of the Spanish people. But, considering that more than half of the Council of the League belonged to the NIC, it is hardly surprising that little came of their efforts.[6]

By the end of 1937 – especially in the wake of the Nyon conference held in September – most Republican leaders had abandoned all hope in the NIA. Angered by the brazen hypocrisy of the NIC and increasingly frustrated with the limitations of the diplomatic channels available to them, the Republicans did all they could in the remaining months of the war to bring about the complete abolition of the non-intervention system.

The Republicans' contemptuous attitude towards non-intervention was

---

4. Both Switzerland, wishing to maintain her traditional neutrality, and the United States were not signatories. Above all, the NIA aimed at stopping the export and transport of war materials to Spain. The question of sending 'volunteer' troops was not dealt with until 1937.
5. F. P. Walters, *A History of the League of Nations* (Oxford, 1952), p. 722.
6. The League eventually agreed to send a group of experts to the war zones to report on health and the food situation, but, apart from these minor humanitarian measures, the Council did nothing to resolve larger issues, such as the question of foreign intervention.

not misplaced.[7] In view of its overall performance, the NIC must be judged as an ineffectual organization that made a mockery of European diplomacy. From its inception until its formal disbandment in April 1939, the Committee's effectiveness was greatly diminished by the fact that it lacked any powers for stopping or controlling even the most obvious forms of intervention. Flagrant violations of the NIA, especially by Germany, Italy and the Soviet Union, further undermined the credibility of the Committee. Notwithstanding the claim of Anthony Eden (the British Foreign Secretary) that it was a 'leaky dam' that was better than none at all, the NIC hardly deterred foreign intervention in Iberia. Nor did its existence do much to relieve the international pressures created by the Spanish Civil War. While its defenders pointed out that at the time its actions were effectively preventing the war in Spain from triggering a larger European incident, the truth is that the NIC fell short in almost every other respect of fulfilling its original mandate. Not only did it fail to halt foreign intervention in Spain, but its existence fatally undermined the hope that international conflicts could be effectively resolved through collective negotiation.

FRANCE AND THE POLITICS OF NEUTRALITY

Despite having been one of the first countries to announce its commitment to a policy of non-intervention, France had not found it easy to detach herself from Spain's tragic circumstances. The Popular Front government of the socialist Prime Minister Léon Blum was, in fact, sympathetic to Republican Spain's appeals for aid. Hours after he received the request of José Giral (the Spanish premier) for arms and planes, Blum conferred with his top ministers, including Yvon Delbos (the Foreign Minister), Edouard Daladier (the Minister of Defence), and Pierre Cot (the Minister of Aviation). Despite opposition from both Delbos and Daladier, the cabinet quickly made arrangements to assist Republican efforts to put down the rebellion, although, owing to the political delicacy of their action, it was decided to keep the terms of the transaction secret.[8]

But the outbreak of hostilities in Spain occurred at a time when France herself was facing a series of highly disruptive domestic crises. Labour

---

7. According to Ángel Viñas, both the League of Nations and the NIC were also used by the Nationalists and their allies to thwart Republican attempts to transfer their gold reserves and make use of its countervalue. See his, 'The Financing of the Spanish Civil War', in *Revolution and War in Spain, 1931–1939*, ed. by Paul Preston (London, 1984) p. 269.
8. Just days after acceding to José Giral's request for arms and aircraft, Blum reversed his stand. On 25 July his cabinet decided not to provide Spain with any further assistance.

unrest (a massive wave of strikes and riots had rocked the country just before the Spanish war began), economic woes caused by the Depression, and the growing polarization of public opinion along ideological lines were not least of the problems the shaky Blum administration was forced to address in the summer of 1936. Above all, Blum was fearful that French involvement in the fratricidal strife in Spain would serve as a catalyst for this volatile mix of social, economic and political conditions developing in France, which threatened at any moment to boil over into civil war.

This was made abundantly clear to him within days of his cabinet secretly deciding to send aid to Spain. Returning from a diplomatic mission to London on 24 July, Blum was astonished to learn that the right-wing press had leaked the details of the agreement. Deeply impressed by the results of *L'Action Française's* and *L'Echo de Paris'* campaign to whip up public hysteria about the perils fraught with French intervention, Blum was forced to reconsider his commitment to the Spanish.

No less important were foreign policy considerations. Blum's initial hopes of developing a policy that would aid the Spanish Republic were all but abandoned when it became apparent that Britain, France's principal ally, would not support independent French action beyond the Pyrenees. Though he was well aware of the dangers a right-wing victory in Spain posed both to France and Great Britain, Blum and his advisors had a greater fear of what would happen if France were to be isolated from the rest of Europe. They therefore felt compelled to embrace non-intervention as the lesser evil. On 9 August the Blum government reluctantly suspended all exports to the Republicans, although, before the end of August, some direct aid (in the form of munitions, guns and aircraft) was delivered across the Spanish frontier.

After Blum stepped down as premier in 1938, France's commitment to non-intervention was pursued with even greater vigour by his successor, Edouard Daladier. From then until February 1939, when France joined Britain in recognizing the Franco regime, the French government turned its back on Spain's agonizing predicament.

GREAT BRITAIN: THE ARBITER OF NON-INTERVENTION

Immediately following the July rebellion, the Baldwin government (until 28 May 1937) adopted a 'wait and see' attitude. When, by the end of July, it became notorious that both Germany and Italy were openly assisting the Insurgent cause, Britain joined the French in promoting the idea of a multilateral non-intervention agreement.[9] British reaction to events in Spain was largely conditioned by the pivotal position she held in the European alliance system. From a purely diplomatic standpoint, Britain wanted to maintain Spain's territorial integrity and secure the benevolent neutrality of whichever side emerged victorious. In this way, she could be assured not only of maintaining Britain's historic position in the Mediterranean but also of protecting her considerable economic interests in Spanish investment and commerce.[10]

But the British response was also driven by ideological motives: for most members of the Conservative-dominated 'National' government then in power the idea of a 'Red' Spain was anathema, and there was a great deal of sympathy shown for the Insurgent cause in ruling circles. Even more compelling than these ideological considerations was the fact that the British government was highly alarmed at the possibility that the Spanish conflict might ignite another general European conflagration. An abiding fear of this possible outcome led successive Conservative administrations to adopt a policy of non-intervention throughout the civil war.

Another determinant of British foreign policy which served to reinforce her commitment to non-intervention arose during the last half of the Spanish civil war. After Neville Chamberlain became Prime Minister in July 1937, British relations towards Spain were also guided by the belief that it was possible to woo Italy away from Germany, thereby preventing the consolidation of a fascist bloc hostile to the West. Chamberlain's steadfast attachment to a policy of cooperation with the Italians was tested during the summer of 1937, when the British government was forced to respond to a series of submarine attacks on neutral (British, French and Soviet) commercial shipping vessels. Unwilling to compromise her neutrality and fearing an overwhelmingly negative public reaction to the use of force, the British initially opted for a policy of restraint. But some high ranking officials, particularly the Foreign Secretary, Anthony Eden, recognized the gravity of these attacks and therefore felt it was necessary for Britain to take a firmer stand.

To stop the unidentified submarines, well known to be Italian, France and Great Britain recommended the use of multinational naval patrols. At the Nyon Naval Conference (10–14 September 1937), their plan was formally adopted and, for a brief while, the sinkings stopped. The resolute

9. This did not inhibit the British government from exercising a secret embargo on arms sales to the Republic or from refusing a request early on in the war to allow Republican naval vessels to refuel in Gibraltar. See Enrique Moradiellos, *Neutralidad benévola* (Oviedo, 1990), p. 156.
10. British capital investment in Spain was approximately £40 million. See Jill Edwards, *The British Government and the Spanish Civil War, 1936–1939* (London, 1979), Chapter 3.

action taken by the British and French was hailed at the time as a diplomatic triumph. Yet this enthusiasm was misplaced, not least because the resolution reached at Nyon did not signal a fresh *démarche* on the part of any nation. In Britain this was primarily because Prime Minister Neville Chamberlain (1937–40) strongly opposed any new direction in foreign policy, especially if it threatened to upset his efforts to establish a rapprochement with the Italians. Above all, Chamberlain and his supporters energetically promoted a strategy that sought reconciliation rather than confrontation with the fascist powers. The following months witnessed the rift between the Foreign Secretary and the Prime Minister widening further. When, in February 1938, Chamberlain made further concessions to the Italians regarding the withdrawal of foreign volunteers fighting in Spain, Eden chose to resign. Predictably, his resignation gave impetus to the pro-appeasement forces in the government.

Meanwhile, on the domestic front, the civil war's greatest impact on society was to deepen existing political and class divisions. Like no other event of the period, the war managed to mobilize the forces of the left and, to a lesser extent, the right. Spain's troubles inspired countless public rallies and street demonstrations, and debates over the nature and signifi-cance of the war filled newspaper columns, books, and pamphlets.

Tensions between right and left culminated late in 1937, when it had become apparent to all but a few that non-intervention was working in favour of the Nationalists. In the autumn both the Trades Union Congress (TUC) and Labour Party, though still opposed to the idea of directly intervening in Spain, began pressuring the British government to lift its embargo on arms to the Republican forces. For its part, the National Council of Labour expressed its disapproval of non-intervention by provid-ing humanitarian aid. Food, clothing, medical supplies and other forms of assistance were generously provided by such groups as the Socialist Medical Association as well as many other organizations affiliated with the labour movement. Perhaps the most demonstrably successful relief programmes were those aimed at helping children who had been displaced by the war: the mineworkers contributed over £55,000 to the orphaned children of Asturian miners, and a public-supported adoption scheme (endorsed by Liberals, Conservatives and Labour alike) brought some 4,000 Basque orphans to England by the time the war had ended.

The Communist Party of Great Britain launched an even stronger initiative aimed at supporting Republican Spain. Obeying the Communist International's (Comintern) call for the formation of an international con-tingent to be sent to Spain, the British communists actively recruited volunteers. Thanks to their campaign, over 2,000 men and women served in the International Brigades of the Republican army.

Public interest in the fate of Spain remained high throughout 1937 and 1938, primarily because the tragedy of the Spanish war was kept alive in the printed media. The vicious and pointless destruction of the small Basque town of Guernica in 1937, for example, commanded the headlines of the British press for several weeks. Other sensationalized incidents – the Republican attack on the *Deutschland* and the German shelling of the coastal town of Almería, to name the most notable ones – brought home to the general public the immediacy of the Spanish situation.

As the prospects for a Republican victory grew dimmer and dimmer, however, passions about the civil war began to subside. By the time the British government extended official recognition to Franco's Spain in February 1939, public reaction to the news was muted.

MUSSOLINI AND SPAIN

Of all the European countries, Italy seems to have been the most eager to involve herself in Spanish affairs. On the eve of the military rebellion, Mussolini was still intoxicated by his highly successful Ethiopian adventure and he was apparently in the mood to taste another quick victory in foreign politics. Driven by his unshakeable belief that Italy was to once again become 'great, respected and feared' and confident that fascist aggression was the only means of achieving this end, Mussolini did not hesitate for long before sending Italian aid and military support to the Nationalists.

Mussolini's meddling in Spanish politics could be traced to the days of Miguel Primo de Rivera (1923–30), who had himself flattered Il Duce by modelling his civilian Unión Monárquica after the Partito Nazionale Fascisti. Several years later, in March 1934, Mussolini willingly committed Italian aid to pro-fascist rightists like Antonio Goicoechea's Alfonsine monarchists, the Carlists and others who were working to overthrow the Spanish Republic and restore the monarchy. In doing so, Mussolini's primary aim was not to foment the development of a Spanish variety of fascism but rather to reap some concrete advantages. Besides seeking to coordinate Italian and Spanish actions in all areas of mutual concern, Mussolini's government desired greater economic cooperation with her Iberian neighbour. Specifically, it was interested in obtaining Spanish support for Italy's designs in the western Mediterranean, and greater financial penetration of Spain.

Then, in July 1936, Mussolini was presented with another chance not only to shape the course of Spanish politics but, above all, to further Italian interests in the Mediterranean. In the opening days of the rebellion, requests were made for aid first by General Francisco Franco, whose troops of the Army of Africa were awaiting transport to the peninsula, and then by General Mola, whose army in northern Spain was encountering stiff resistance from republican troops. Shortly afterwards, the Italian Foreign Minister, Count Galeazzo Ciano, offered to send twelve Savoia S81 bombers to Spanish Morocco. By the end of July the first shipment of aircraft was transferred to the National zone, although it was not until 28 November that the Italian government formally pledged both political and economic assistance to the Nationalists.

Mussolini's initial decision to intervene on behalf of the Nationalists was motivated not only by a desire to crush a left-wing movement but also by an array of foreign policy considerations. Chief among these was his ambition to reinforce Italy's military and political presence in the Mediterranean. After all, his annexation of Abyssinia had given his regime a firm foothold in northern Africa, and, by aiding Spain, Italy might possibly obtain naval bases on the Balearic Islands and thereby extend her dominance in the region.

It deserves mention here that Italy's expansionist plans in the Mediterranean were meant to challenge not just Great Britain but also France. In the former case, Mussolini sought to diminish Britain's extensive control of the Mediterranean route. With a government friendly to Italy in power in Spain, this would be possible. The Italian navy would also benefit from the use of Spanish ports if it became necessary to check French troop movements from her colonies in North Africa.[11] Thus, for example, Mussolini later bragged to the then German foreign minister Joachim von Ribbentrop that 'not one negro will be able to cross from Africa to France by the Mediterranean route' as long as the Mediterranean bases remained under Italian control.

It is also true that, as far as Mussolini was concerned, Spain provided a splendid opportunity to impress the Germans with Italy's 'iron military strength'. While this was never demonstrated, Mussolini nonetheless found common ground on which to collaborate with Hitler's Germany. Despite Italy's concern over German influence in the Mediterranean, Spain represented one of the few areas in which Rome and Berlin could cooperate to further a common goal; namely, the defeat of communism. In fact, their joint actions in Spain helped to forge the links of the 'Berlin-Rome Axis' which led to the formation of the so-called 'Pact of Steel' in May, 1939.

In the course of the war, Italy claimed to have spent some L.7,500

---

11. Because the Nationalists emerged victorious, Mussolini had achieved his objective of strengthening Italy's position *vis-à-vis* France. In fact, Franco's victory effectively denied the French government the possibility of transporting troops across Spain from North Africa.

million (approximately $375 million at the time).[12] Much of this expenditure was used to support the large number of ground troops and mechanized units Italy committed to the war.[13] Although the Italian soldiers were officially referred to as 'volunteers' (the Corpo Truppe Volontarie CTV), nearly half were members of the Italian regular army, and some 3,000 volunteers were recruited by the Fascist Party to serve in the elite Black Shirt divisions. Yet the majority of young men (the average soldier was under thirty) who enlisted were not seeking glory for Italian Fascism but rather were simply interested in securing a steady income.

Whatever the reasons for which they went to Spain, the Italian forces failed to live up to their reputation as a well-oiled fascist military machine, and, on more than one occasion, they proved to be an embarrassment to Mussolini. Of all the major campaigns of the war, the Italians played a central role in only two, Málaga and Guadalajara. It was at Guadalajara that the highly regarded Black Arrow and Black Flame units, which were expected by Mussolini to achieve a 'triumph of great political as well as military bearing', suffered a demoralizing defeat at the hands of their fellow countrymen who were fighting in the International Brigades.[14]

Although Italy was not showered with glory and prestige for her participation in the war, Mussolini's timely intervention did have diplomatic dividends. Having gauged the degree to which the Western democracies were committed to a policy of appeasement, Mussolini was now confirmed in the belief that neither Britain nor France was ready to risk war over issues that fell outside her own sphere of interest. This was especially evident in the case of the British government, which had demonstrated its eagerness to reach an agreement with the Italians on several key issues – such as *de jure* recognition of Italy's position in Ethiopia. In the face of naked Italian aggression on the high seas, for example, Britain had not retaliated, and Mussolini naturally concluded from this that he could exercise a free hand in Spain.[15]

---

12. These figures, which were released by the Italian government on 27 February 1941, differ from those given in the Final Report of the Ufficio Spagna. According to this document, Italy's total cost for war material sent to Spain was around six billion lire: 4.2 billion supplied by the ministry of war and 1.8 spent by the air ministry. For a breakdown of these figures see John F. Coverdale, *Italian Intervention in the Spanish Civil War* (Princeton, 1975), pp. 392ff.
13. Out of a total of 72,827 Italian soldiers who went to fight in Spain, approximately 3,819 lost their lives, while another 10–11,000 were wounded.
14. On the Italian contribution to the fighting see Anthony Beevor, *The Spanish Civil War* (London, 1982); and Pierre Broué and Emile Témime, *The Revolution and Civil War in Spain* (London, 1970).
15. Friction between both countries was greatly diminished with the signing of the Anglo-Italian accord in 1938, which called for the gradual but complete withdrawal of Italian volunteers and *matériel*.

HITLER IN THE SPANISH ARENA

Because Nazi Germany was also preoccupied with the balance of ideological forces in Europe, Hitler had a keen interest in the outcome of the left-right contest in Spain. As we shall see, Hitler's decision to aid the rebels was motivated not just by his pathological hatred of communism but also by a pragmatic reading of the Spanish situation.

While it is true that for some years Spanish rightists had cultivated friendly relations with the Nazi regime, ties of this sort had little or no bearing on Hitler's decision to aid the rebels. Thus it cannot be argued, as some have tried, that there was a Nazi conspiracy to overthrow the Republican government.[16] The truth is that Germany had not anticipated a civil war in Spain, and, when the generals rose, did so without consulting the Germans.

Only a few days after Spanish agents representing the rebels had set off for Rome to ask Mussolini for transport planes, a further request for aid was sent to Hitler through a Nazi businessman, Johannes Bernhardt, who was living in Spanish Morocco. When Franco's emissaries pleaded for arms (rifles and anti-aircraft guns) and fighter planes, Hitler spontaneously decided (apparently against the advice of his future foreign minister, Ribbentrop, and his air force chief, Hermann Goering) to launch operation *Feuerzauber* ('Magic Fire'), which was to be Germany's contribution to the fight against Bolshevism in Spain.

Hitler himself correctly saw that the Insurgents' *Movimiento* would be abortive unless troops could be transported to the mainland. He therefore dispatched twenty Junker (JU–52) transport planes to join the Italian bomber-transports sent by Mussolini. In the following months, the Germans also supplied six Heinkel–51 fighters and volunteer pilots from the Luftwaffe, although, officially speaking, 'pilots were prohibited from combat except in self-defense . . .'[17] These were followed by the arrival in December 1936 of the famed Condor Legion, which was used to great effect in the Basque campaign and enabled the Nationalists to gain air superiority in early 1937. Nevertheless, because blatant violations of the NIA were merely blinked at by the forces of non-intervention, the Germans seized the chance to use Spain as a living laboratory for their own military programme. Spanish civilians were the first Europeans to suffer the devastating conse-

16. Spaniards sympathetic to Germany were affiliated with such organizations as the Ausland-Organization (an agency promoting Nazi propaganda abroad). See, for example, a work attributed to O. K. Simon (pseudonym Otto Katz), *The Nazi Conspiracy in Spain*, trans. by Emile Burns (London, 1937).

17. Ángel Viñas, *La Alemania nazi y el 16 de Julio*, p. 353. As quoted in Burnett Bolloten, *The Spanish Civil War: Revolution and Counterrevolution* (Chapel Hill, North Carolina, 1991), p. 98.

quences of dive-bombing and carpet-bombing techniques, which German pilots perfected at Durango, Guernica and at several other towns and villages.

The flow of German military personnel increased in the following months – although, compared to the Italians' commitment to the rebel cause, Germany's was considerably more measured. Over the course of the war, some 10,000 Germans went to Spain, although many of these were not infantrymen but rather specialists and technicians who were sent expressly to train Nationalist cadres.

The principal financial reward sought by the Nazi government was to acquire greater access to Spain's mineral resources. Hitler was particularly interested in obtaining the rich deposits of iron-ores and copper under Nationalist control which could be used to bolster Germany's rearmament industry. Due to his increasing dependence on German aid, Franco was eventually forced to grant HISMA-ROWAK favourable mining concessions – although these never fulfilled Germany's expectations of recovering the costs of her contributions to the Nationalist cause.

German intervention had a twofold significance. Apart from his desire to see Franco's forces emerge victorious, Hitler wanted to exploit the crisis in Spain for foreign policy purposes. As in the case of Italy, the Spanish situation provided Germany with yet another opportunity to measure the lengths to which the democracies would go to preserve the peace of Europe. Hitler particularly took note of the fact that the only two countries that could have directly challenged Germany's meddling in Spanish affairs, France and Great Britain, chose not to do so. Sensing that neither Britain nor France was willing to risk a showdown over the Spanish conflict, the Germans were emboldened to take further steps in 1938 towards consolidating Germany's imperialistic designs in Austria and Czechoslovakia. It is therefore hardly surprising that Hitler was not particularly concerned about an early Franco victory, for, as long as the war in Spain dragged on, it was possible to enlarge the scope of his manoeuvres in Central and Eastern Europe.

Hitler also used the Spanish war to draw closer to Italy. From the beginning, the Germans deferred to their new ally, recognizing that for both political and geographical reasons Italy should be allowed to take the lead in her Spanish policy. The German Ambassador in Italy, Ulrich von Hassell, made it clear as early as December 1936 what his government hoped to gain by encouraging greater Italian involvement in the conflict: 'The struggle for dominant political influence in Spain lays bare the natural opposition between Italy and France; at the same time the position of Italy as a power in the western Mediterranean comes into competition with that of Britain. All the more clearly will Italy recognize the advisability of confronting the Western powers shoulder to shoulder with Germany – particularly when considering the desirability of a future general understanding between Western and Central Europe on the basis of complete equality.'[18]

Even if Italy had successfully implanted its system in Spanish soil, it seems as though the Germans would have had little to fear about the future of Spanish-German relations. For they were concerned above all to see the creation of a Spanish state that was free from the perceived threat of Bolshevism and, again in the words of Hassell, 'removed from the hegemony of the Western powers'.

MOSCOW'S LIGHT ON THE REPUBLIC

The military rising had also caught the Soviet Union by surprise. In the beginning, the circumstances surrounding Spain's war seemed remote to Moscow, and the Soviets were not favourably disposed to intervene. Then, with the advent of foreign intervention and the inevitable widening of the dimensions of the war, Stalin grew ever more anxious about the possibility that the upheaval in Spain could boil up into a general European war. By August the Soviet Union was presented with an acute dilemma. To remain consistent with her commitment to the Comintern's 'popular front' tactics as well as to her leadership role in the world of socialism, the Soviet Union was impelled to aid the republicans. But, for Stalin and his advisors, this obligation had to be weighed against the demands of higher diplomacy. At the time, the Soviet Union was fearful of being encircled by the fascist countries, and therefore she was seeking closer ties with the Western democracies. A step in this direction has already been taken in May 1935, when Russia concluded a pact of mutual assistance with France. But Stalin knew that becoming enmeshed in Spain's troubles might prejudice his chances of securing more anti-fascist allies, and he therefore temporized over the question of aid for as long as he could.[19]

---

18. *Documents on German Foreign Policy*, series D., vol. III (Washington DC, 1950), p. 172.
19. Why Stalin ultimately decided to come to the aid of the republicans has been the subject of numerous heated debates. For example, his critics have argued that his commitment to the republican cause was nothing more than a Machiavellian tactic, aimed not so much at aiding the Spanish but rather at advancing the foreign policy interests of the Soviet Union. Those less cynical about Stalin's motives adamantly reject this interpretation, and instead insist that his decision to aid the Republic sprang primarily from his abiding commitment to the international revolutionary movement as well as his pressing desire to stop the spread of fascism. Not surprisingly this group attaches considerable weight to the rhetoric of the period. Thus, for example, they tend to accept at face value documents such as Stalin's famous telegram to José Díaz, in which he outlined the basis for the Soviet commitment to the Republican cause: 'The toilers of the Soviet Union are only doing their duty in rendering all possible aid to the revolutionary masses of Spain. They are well aware that the liberation of Spain from the yoke of Fascist reactionaries is not the private concern of the Spanish, but the general concern of all advanced and progressive humanity.' Quoted in Jonathan Haslam, *The Soviet Union and the Struggle for Collective Security 1933–1939* (London, 1983), note 76, p. 120.

None-the-less, having decided in late August to cross the threshold of intervention, Stalin came to regard Spain as a crucial element in his foreign policy strategy. Throughout most of the war the Soviet government believed that their assistance was of value as long as it enabled them to manipulate republican relations with the democratic powers. Above all, Stalin wanted Republican Spain to induce the democratic powers to take a stand against fascism. There are two likely reasons such an outcome would have been desirable. Some contemporary observers claimed that it was because Stalin wanted the fascist and democratic powers embroiled in a major conflict. Once they had exhausted themselves in this way, Russia would emerge as the principal arbiter of a new European order. On the other hand, recent research suggests that it is highly probable that Stalin wanted to use the Spanish war as the ground on which the bourgeois democracies could cooperate more closely with the Soviet Union to check the advance of fascism.[20]

Significantly, though, the Soviets were so convinced that Great Britain and France would wake up to the threat of fascism that they underestimated the degree to which both nations were attached to the policy of appeasement.[21] Stalin's designs for building a wall around fascism through an international alliance therefore never materialized.

As in the cases of Germany and Italy, the extent of Soviet involvement in Spain modified over time. In the early weeks of the civil war, Stalin's optimism about an early Republican triumph led him to believe that the tiny amount of Russian aid — mostly money deducted from the wages of Soviet workers — he was secretly funnelling to Spain would not create any diplomatic waves. By late August, however, the possibility of a Nationalist victory could no longer be discounted, and the Soviets were forced to pursue a different tactic.

In the meantime, the rest of Europe had come round to the Anglo-French view that the most effective way of localizing Spain's problems was to support non-intervention. Rather than run the risk of being isolated, the Soviets soon followed suit. Though retaining their initial reservations about this policy, the Soviets began using the NIC and the League of Nations as their main pulpits for denouncing the brazen violations of the non-intervention pact. As Raymond Carr has written, Ivan Maisky, the Soviet Ambassador to Great Britain and Russian representative on the

---

20. See, for example, Denis Smyth, 'Soviet Policy Towards Republican Spain', in *Radicals, Rebels and Establishments*, ed. by Patrick J. Corish (Belfast, 1985).
21. According to Denis Smyth *op. cit.*, this was largely because of the 'instinctive anti-communism of British statesmen and the doctrinaire antipathy of many French policy-makers towards any Soviet connection'.

NIC, was determined to 'extract every ounce of political capital out of the "farce of non-intervention" '.

The continuous flow of German and Italian aid to the Nationalists persuaded the Soviets that, despite their public adherence to non-intervention, they should also move towards giving greater support to the Republican cause. A shipment of Soviet arms was dispatched to Spain (arriving in Alicante on 27 September) and formal assistance began on 15 October 1936, when the *Komsomol* arrived in Cartagena harbour filled with arms for the Republic.

THE PRICE OF SOVIET AID

There can be no doubt that, without the material contributions of the Soviet Union, Republican resistance would have collapsed long before 1939. In the early phase of the war, for instance, Soviet aeroplanes and tanks, which had arrived in October, were decisive factors in preventing the Nationalists from completely overrunning republican forces. This was especially true in the case of Madrid, for it was largely due to the fact that the Soviet Polikarpov fighters and Tupolev bombers were technically superior to their counterparts on the Nationalist side that the republicans managed to dominate the air during the crucial months of November and December. As indispensable as it was, though, Soviet aid arrived with certain strings attached and this had far-reaching consequences in the Republican camp.

The cementing of Soviet-Republican relations came about when republican leaders agreed in October 1936 to have Spain's considerable gold reserves transported to Russia partly to ensure that it would fall into the hands of the Nationalists but, above all, so that it could be used as credit for future arms purchases. This important transfer, estimated at the time to be around $518 million, secured the Soviet government's assistance, making them the major supplier and distributor of arms and military equipment to Republican Spain. To ensure that Soviet interests were being served, the Russians exercised their power of monopoly over these vitally important resources. In practice this took many different forms. For example, it was generally true that communist or pro-communist units could count on receiving Soviet weapons and air and tank support during military operations, whereas POUM or anarchosyndicalist militias could not.

At the same time as Soviet aid was helping the communists gain a commanding position in the Republican military apparatus, it was helping them secure a foothold in the summits of political power. The communists believed that, in order to entice the democracies to join their struggle against the Nationalists, Republican Spain could not project a 'red' image. Thus it was necessary for them to use the machinery of the central and local governments to roll back the revolutionary movement that had begun in July. The communists' efforts to establish their political hegemony affected the course of the war in a number of ways. Most of all, however, it threw the working-class revolutionary left into conflict with the moderate left and the forces representing the middle classes. The dramatic confrontation between them — which was played out in scenes like the May Events of 1937 and the Casado rising of March 1939 — greatly undermined Republican unity and thus helped to determine the outcome of the war itself.

Soviet involvement also meant transferring into the Spanish arena some of her own domestic problems. The year 1936 marked the beginning of the trials that Stalin used to eliminate his political rivals. Unfortunately, the poisonous effects of the atmosphere of hate and recrimination generated by these proceedings were imported to the Republican camp. Before the outbreak of civil war the Trotskyist-Stalinist quarrel had been an insignificant factor in Spanish politics. But because this debate had taken centre stage during the Zinoviev-Kamenev trials, the issue of Trotskyism was placed high on the communists' agenda in Spain. As we shall see, their zealous efforts to eradicate 'Trotskyism' from Spain by systematically persecuting the POUM had a profound impact on republican politics from 1937 until the end of 1938.

Soviet intervention, then, was calculated to produce, if not complete communist hegemony, at least the preponderance of communist influence in the principal nerve-centres of the Republican camp. In this way, victory, on communist terms, could be achieved. Failing this, the communists at the very least wanted to make certain that the outcome of events in Spain did not directly threaten the security of the Soviet Union.

The nagging fear that the Germans were going to attack Russia sooner rather than later also exercised a powerful influence on Stalin's thinking. After all he knew that such a confrontation would not greatly upset countries like Great Britain, which seemed willing to tolerate German expansion as long as it was directed eastwards. This helps to explain why, for example, Soviet aid to the Republican cause declined steadily from 1938 until the end of the war. For continued Soviet assistance to the faltering republican cause was increasingly conflicting with Stalin's efforts to prepare the ground for a Russo-German non-aggression pact.

FOREIGN INTERVENTION: THE BALANCE SHEET

Raymond Carr has rightly pointed out that the critical factor in the opening phases of the civil war was not 'the raising of armies but finding arms for them'. This was true most of all because the rebellion had divided Spain's war industry, rendering it impossible for either side to supply adequately their own militias. Acutely aware that the course of the war hinged on whether arms and supplies could be obtained from abroad, both the Nationalists and the Republicans exhausted every means they could to secure foreign aid.

We have seen that the assistance provided by the Axis powers proved to be of vital importance to the Nationalists. Thanks to the prompt arrival of German Junkers and Italian bombers, Franco managed to airlift his troops of the Army of Africa to the mainland, thus preventing the rebellion from completely collapsing. Additional military aid sent in the following weeks (and which continued up to the war's conclusion) meant that the Nationalists would not share the fate of the republicans, who, despite Russian aid, were generally poorly equipped and chronically starved of essential war supplies.

It is important to keep in mind here that the technical and material assistance provided by foreign powers did more than just determine the outcome of military campaigns; it also had an appreciable impact on the development of politics in both camps. In the anti-Republican zone, Franco was careful to maintain good relations with both Italy and Germany, although this did not mean that they dictated Nationalist policy. On the contrary, Franco himself stubbornly resisted any pressures of this sort being exerted by Rome and Berlin. This was not the case on the Republican side, where, as we have seen, the communists managed to exercise a great deal of power and influence because of the republicans' overwhelming dependence on Soviet aid.

Since the war, historians have attempted to weigh the contributions of the respective participating countries in order to determine the extent to which foreign aid tipped the balance against the republican side. The consensus among them is that, because the amount of German and Italian intervention was considerably greater than foreign aid received by the republicans, the Nationalists benefited most from foreign intervention.[22]

22. John F. Coverdale points out in his *Italian Intervention in the Spanish Civil War* (Princeton, 1979), p. 398, that the absence of reliable figures on the supplies that actually reached the republican side make it exceedingly difficult to assess the relative contributions of the foreign powers. Based on his own estimates, however, he concludes that 'while the Nationalists received more aid, the difference was nowhere near as great as propagandists claimed and as some historians have believed'.

Had the democratic powers, notably France, Great Britain, and the United States, assisted the republicans, the outcome of the war might not have been any different, but their intervention might have prevented Franco from achieving such a resounding victory which ultimately led to an unconditional and merciless peace settlement.

Non-Intervention, Appeasement and the Rise of Fascism

We have noted that, throughout the Spanish crisis, the Western democracies demonstrated their unwillingness to risk war, even if this meant turning a blind eye to the far-reaching political implications of foreign intervention. While the importance of Spain in the overall scheme of European affairs should not be overemphasized, we might pause for a moment to consider how the non-intervention policy of Great Britain and France contributed to the uninterrupted rise of fascism elsewhere in Europe.

It is clear that, both before and during the civil war in Spain, Hitler and Mussolini were bent on using force to challenge the European status quo. In the case of Hitler we know that he had already flouted international goodwill when he ordered German troops to reoccupy the Rhineland in March 1936. In addition, his plans to annex Austria and extend German control over the Sudetenland were drawing to a head during the war, though these goals had little to do with the origins or outcome of the Spanish conflict. Nonetheless, over the Spanish war the Axis powers managed to exercise their military prowess and, above all, to test the political will of their adversaries, which was amply illustrated by their collective failure to restrain the renegade countries – Germany and Italy and the Soviet Union – from openly intervening.

There were further ways in which the Spanish war had a bearing on international affairs. Above all else, the tragic experiences of the Spanish people reinforced pacifist sentiments in Europe, especially among the political leaders of the democratic nations. In this connection, it must be remembered that much of the pacifism of the late 1930s sprang from a fear not just of war but of its long-term consequences. It was widely believed, especially on the right, that another large-scale confrontation between the Great Powers would create the conditions for the 'Bolshevization' of Europe. And as menacing as fascism may have appeared in the mind of the ordinary person and politician, the spectre of Bolshevism seemed, in their eyes, to pose the greatest threat to the survival of Western civilization.

The Axis powers, though also reluctant to engage in another major conflict, quickly grasped the depth of pacifism in Britain and France and reacted accordingly. Thus, for example, the German Chargé de d'Affaires in France was struck by the anxiety Daladier expressed to him in a private conversation about the 'the terrible and calamitous consequences of a European war. . . .' '[From] experience gained in the Spanish and Chinese conflicts,' Daladier continued, 'a war lasts a long time and must lead to destruction on an inconceivable scale.'[23] Needless to say, similiar reports were filed by German diplomats moving among the ruling circles of Britain.

At least for Daladier, Chamberlain and their supporters, appeasement and its corollary, non-intervention, were both reasonable and necessary responses to the brinkmanship politics of Hitler and Mussolini. This was especially true at those times when it appeared as though conciliation was working. In keeping with their 'hands off' policy in Spain, the British and French governments responded to Germany's growing effrontery in 1938 by more urgently pressing for a policy of appeasement. Since most other European countries had more or less abandoned the Versailles Treaty and had lost faith in the League of Nations as an effective diplomatic instrument, the responses of the French and British leaders were, if regrettable, at least comprehensible. In the midst of the Czech crisis in September, for instance, Mussolini had worked with Britain 'to snatch the flower of peace from the jaws of war'. Chamberlain and the pro-appeasers interpreted Mussolini's behaviour as a sign that British attempts to divide Italy from Germany were not in vain. This blinded them to the disastrous consequences of appeasement, which were not fully realized until several months after the war in Spain had ended.

23. *Documents on German Foreign Policy*, series D, vol. II, pp. 712–13.

CHAPTER ELEVEN
The Dynamics of Politics in the Republican Zone

If war had provided the impetus needed to bring about the unification of the Spanish right, it brought about entirely different results on the other side. Throughout the latter part of 1936 and well into 1937 revolution and civil war continued to serve as centrifugal forces in Republican Spain, effectively preventing the republicans from achieving the degree of military unity and social cohesion attained during that same period in the Nationalist zone. We have seen that many Republican institutions disintegrated under the dual impact of military rebellion and revolution. During the summer of 1936 power in the towns and countryside remained scattered among hundreds of revolutionary or popular front committees, and regional authority resided in various types of provisional bodies – such as the Central Anti-fascist Militias Committee in Barcelona and the Council of Aragón. Even in the Basque country, which was otherwise untouched by the revolution, the creation of defence committees or juntas, which were used to put down the military rising, temporarily displaced central government authority and thereby prepared the ground for the emergence of an autonomous Basque state. Later we shall see that during the brief time the Madrid government ceased functioning the independence of the Catalan government or Generalitat evolved to the point that it behaved as though it were a separate country.[1] In many respects, then, Republican Spain during the first ten months of the war existed as a mosaic of satellite states, each possessing varying degrees of independence.

Because different republican elements were striving towards different ends, the question arose as to how they could collectively sustain a viable

---

1. In Asturias, at the opposite corner of the Republican zone, the mining villages fell under the control of revolutionary Workers' and Peasants' Committees, while the rival anarchist-dominated Gijón War Committee and the socialist Sama de Langreo Popular Front Committee ruled at the provincial level.

anti-Nationalist front. As they had done when faced with the task of organizing the military, the moderate socialists, middle-class republican parties and the communists chose to save 'Republican Spain' by conventional means. Guided by the belief that military recovery and internal efficiency relied on a centrally-directed state – albeit adapted to wartime conditions – they set about reasserting the authority of the Popular Front government. Predictably, for the CNT-FAI and POUM, establishing antifascist unity meant something altogether different. Placing great value in the constructive energies of a people in arms, the revolutionaries sought to unite the disparate elements of the republic by consolidating the strength of a revolutionary movement organized along federal lines; they therefore had no interest in resuscitating even a 'modified' bourgeois state.

Yet another model of Republican Spain was envisaged by the Basque and Catalan nationalists. Both wanted to defeat the Nationalists but neither wanted to sacrifice their independence for the sake of a resurgent central government. Thus, even though they were more inclined than the revolutionaries to participate in a Madrid-led Popular Front coalition, their cooperation largely depended on the government's ability to satisfy their demands for autonomy.

The policy of the revolutionaries failed above all because it proved especially difficult for them to prosecute the war and revolution at the same time. In the economic sphere, the problems associated with their collectivist enterprises effectively blocked them from organizing the revolution beyond a regional level. The inability of the far left to present a united front against their rivals also contributed to their predicament not least because it meant they were unable to defend the revolution against its opponents. Within the libertarian community the decision of CNT-FAI leaders to participate in the regional and national governments was critical in this regard, for the policy of collaboration deeply and irrevocably divided the movement.

The success of the nationalists policy hinged on other factors. The life of the tiny state known as Euzkadi (Basque homeland) was cut short not because of its intrinsic weaknesses but because it was physically separated from the rest of Republican Spain. Unlike the Basque country, Catalonia's separatism was bound up with the revolutionary movement. Initially overwhelmed by the power of the CNT-FAI, the Catalan government wisely decided to step aside until it could recuperate its strength. Ironically, it was the predominance of the revolutionary forces which enabled the separatists to press for greater autonomy. However, this marriage of convenience was short-lived. Once the Generalitat recovered its footing the machinery of the state was used to roll back the revolutionary movement. This led first to a 'civil war' in the region – the notorious May Events of 1937 – and ultimately to the demise of the Generalitat's independence.

For the first few months of the war no single political force was powerful enough to impose its own agenda, and therefore various strategies were tried simultaneously. For a variety of reasons, only the centralized programme of the Popular Front parties prevailed. Thanks largely to the binding sense of solidarity that arose in the initial stages of the war, the process of reconstituting state authority in Madrid was well advanced by the autumn of 1936. But given the dynamics of the anti–centralizing forces, it was evident that recovering state control would be uneven, and that it would be especially difficult to achieve the full integration of the various political entities that existed in the republican zone. In this chapter we shall see how the ascendancy of the communists in Madrid and indeed throughout Republican Spain contributed to the triumph of the Popular Front strategy.

MADRID: THE HEART OF SPAIN

From the moment the Republican government fled the capital to safer quarters in Valencia, Madrid experienced a series of changes that ultimately transformed its political and social character. We have already noted that the power vacuum created in November was filled by the Junta de Defensa, which, because it was invested with both military and civil authority, soon became the *de facto* ruling body of the city. By far the most dynamic and fastest rising force in the Junta was the communists. Having refused to abandon the capital at the eleventh hour, the PCE, its youth movement the JSU, and the communist-controlled Fifth Regiment collectively poured all their energies into the defence of the city. Work brigades were organized to build fortifications and an extensive propaganda programme was launched in order to raise morale and mobilize citizens. On the radio and at massive public rallies, communists like the fiery orator Dolores Ibarruri (better known by her sobriquet 'La Pasionaria') exhorted the civilian population to take a stand against the invaders. Her inspiring slogans, ¡No Pasarán! (They Shall Not Pass!) and 'It is better to die on your feet than to live on your knees', quickly became the watchwords of many citizens.[2] Modest in appearance – she nearly always appeared in black (a dress common to working-class women) and without make-up or flashy jewel-

---

2. Ibarruri borrowed these slogans from previous wars. The former was used to rally French morale during the First World War (principally at the Battle of Verdun), and the second was used by Emiliano Zapata and his followers during the Mexican Revolution.

lery – La Pasionaria seemed, especially to republican women, to embody the spirit of self-sacrifice that was needed at that critical moment. Thanks to her indefatigable propagandizing efforts and to the immense publicity she received in the communist and international media, La Pasionaria became not only the symbol of republican resistance but also, in the words of one communist, 'the most popular person in all Spain, an almost legendary figure'.[3]

The popularity and prestige of the communists steadily increased after the arrival of large supplies of Soviet armaments and the first units of the International Brigades. At this time, the 'Russification' of Madrid was visible everywhere: cinemas screened classics like Eisenstein's 'Potemkin' and large posters and placards drew parallels between the defence of Madrid and the Russian Revolution. Even non-Russian things appeared otherwise: the International Brigades, which, as we have noted, were not composed of Soviet troops, were cheered on by throngs of *madrileños* with shouts of ¡*Vivan los Rusos!*[4]

The sense of solidarity that arose during this preparatory period persisted throughout the early stages of the Battle of Madrid. On many fronts, anarchist and Marxist representatives of the PCE and POUM worked side by side to halt the Nationalist advances. But, once the immediate threat of a Nationalist victory had passed, the goodwill between these groups began to dissipate rapidly. Inside the Junta de Defensa itself rising tensions, especially between the pro- and anti-revolutionary parties, accelerated the dissolution of this anti-fascist coalition.

Unlike the Generalitat and the Basque government (Euzkadi), both of which had been mandated by law, the Junta was not officially recognized as an autonomous government. Nevertheless, after the Battle of Madrid, the Junta in many respects functioned as a distinct political entity in the republican camp. This was true above all because, with the republican regime ensconced in Valencia and Franco's military initiatives being directed elsewhere, Madrid ceased to be the focal point of the war. From the end of November until it was formally dissolved in April 1937, the affairs of the Junta (later renamed the Junta Delegada de Defensa de Madrid) therefore increasingly reflected the warp and woof of local politics.[5]

Following a series of reorganizations between 1 December and mid-

---

3. André Marty, *Heroic Spain* (New York, 1937), p. 30.
4. See Pierre Broué and Emile Témime, *The Revolution and Civil War in Spain* (London, 1970), pp. 246–7.
5. Much has been written about the political agenda of the Junta de Defensa, and it is not our intention here to settle the debate over the true political character of this body. Contrasting views on this matter can be found in Julio Aróstegui and J. A. Martínez, *La Junta de Defensa de Madrid* (Madrid, 1984), and Burnett Bolloten, *The Spanish Civil War: Revolution and Counterevolution* (Chapel Hill, North Carolina, 1991), Chapter 30.

January, it was apparent that the Junta would continue its pro-communist orientation. Miaja, who, it will be recalled, was placed in charge of the first Junta, stayed on as president. Whatever his real political sympathies might have been (it was rumoured that he had once belonged to the reactionary UME and some claimed he was secretly a communist), his conduct as head of the Junta clearly favoured the political line being promoted by the communists and their allies.[6] As elsewhere, the communists sought to end the dual system of authority that had emerged following the July rebellion and concentrate all power into the hands of the centralized ruling bodies. Using the considerable leverage they could exert through their cabinet posts – after 1 December they held the portfolios of Public Order, Supplies and Militias – they struck first at the revolutionary committees under POUM and CNT-FAI control. The dissolution of the Popular Committees in late November had resulted in violent clashes between the CNT forces and members of the PCE, but, by early December, the basis for unilateral administration of the Junta had been established.

The chief target of the communists was the anti-Stalinist POUM. In a series of political manoeuvres that foreshadowed what was going to happen in Barcelona in the aftermath of the May Events, the communists set out systematically to destroy the POUM. Capitalizing on the POUM's isolated position on the left – they had no firm political allies – the PCE successfully fought for the party's exclusion from the Junta. Next they forced the suspension of the POUM's mouthpieces, *POUM* and *Combatiente Rojo*, and saw to it that the POUM's headquarters were shut down. Within two months, the POUM's voice had been completely silenced.

The fact that the PCE could move so rapidly and effectively to annihilate a party that had a legitimate right to representation indicated the extent to which the communists were able to dominate the Junta. It also revealed how much power and influence Moscow was now exercising over political matters. According to one source, the Soviet Ambassador, Marcel Rosenberg, himself played a direct role in this process. The POUM leader Enrique Rodríguez was later told by the socialist Manuel Albar that: 'Ambassador Rosenberg vetoed your admission. It is of course unfair, but you should understand that the U.S.S.R. is powerful and that between Soviet help and support of the POUM there is only one possible choice. Our preference was to incline towards rejecting the POUM.'[7]

A more insidious but nonetheless corroborative sign of the communists'

6. There is still some question as to whether he was in fact a member of the PCE.
7. Quoted in Pierre Broué and Emile Témime, *La révolution et la Guerre d'Espagne* (Paris, 1961), p. 215.

growing preponderance in Madrid was the existence of their clandestine prisons (known as *chekas*), which were used as detention centres for their enemies on the left and right. It was rumoured at the time, for example, that the communists used these facilities to conceal their terrorist campaign against the anarchists. Later, when they came to dominate not only the security services in Madrid but also the republican counter-espionage apparatus known as Servicio de Investigación Militar (SIM), the communists expanded their repressive activities both below and above ground.[8]

In Valencia the ascendancy of the communists in Madrid did not escape the notice of the Premier, Largo Caballero. By this point, Largo himself was locked in a struggle with the communists and their supporters over control of the army. In particular, Largo's critics wanted him to remove his under-secretary of war, General José Asensio, a fierce opponent of the communists whose competency as a military leader was questioned following the collapse of Málaga. Sensing that the growing strength of the communists in Madrid posed a threat to his own power, Largo decreed the dissolution of the Junta on 15 April 1937. As we shall see in the next chapter, this did little to alter the political dynamics in Madrid. On the contrary, the competition among the parties intensified, finally culminating with the Casado coup attempt staged in the final weeks of the war.

THE BASQUE COUNTRY DURING THE CIVIL WAR

Because early on in the war they had been physically cut off from the rest of Republican Spain, the Basque country, Santander, Gijón and other parts of Asturias were particularly vulnerable to the Nationalists. Had Franco decided to defeat the north before taking Madrid it is highly likely that the region would have fallen much sooner. But when, in late 1936, it became apparent that the capital would not be easily taken, the Nationalists shifted their attention northward. In the early part of 1937 they succeeded in throwing up a blockade around Bilbao, the principal port in the region, and, thanks to the support of the Condor Legion, achieved air superiority. Their main target was the province of Vizcaya, the seat of Basque nationalism and one of the major centres of Spain's banking and iron and steel industries.

From July 1936 until the region fell under Nationalist control in June 1937 the political and economic environment of the Basque country bore little resemblance to the pattern of circumstances developing elsewhere in

---

8. On the creation and development of the SIM see Bolloten, *The Spanish Civil War*, Chapter 56.

Republican Spain.[9] At the beginning of the war, an alliance formed between the conservative Basque National Party (PNV) – the preponderant party in the region – socialists, communists, and other republicans had prevented any serious outbreak of violence against Church property and the clergy, and had also acted as a brake on any attempts to collectivize agriculture and industry. The anti-revolutionary trajectory of Basque politics was reinforced when the left-dominated ruling bodies – such as the Provincial Defence Juntas set up in Vizcaya and Guipúzcoa – that emerged in the wake of the rebellion were soon replaced by a moderate Basque government. With the passage of the Basque statute of autonomy in October and the ascent of the ardent nationalist José Aguirre as the President of the Basque nation, Euzkadi, the PNV quickly asserted a commanding influence over the course of events. For the short period of its existence, the Basque government managed to preserve much of the pre-war pattern of daily life. Having escaped the revolutionary changes convulsing the rest of the Republican zone, Basque citizens were not obliged to abandon familiar routines. Churches remained open and businesses, though subject to wartime government regulations, operated as usual.

While their remoteness from the rest of Spain had given the Basques the much longed for opportunity to establish their own nation, this territorial isolation meant their achievement would be short-lived. Surrounded on all sides by rebel forces, the boundaries of their homeland were constantly being eroded. By the time the autonomous government was organized in Bilbao, only the province of Vizcaya had not succumbed to the Nationalists. Attempts to defend Basque territory were hampered at every turn. Thus, even though Basque troops were eventually united under the command of the Republican army, their isolation meant that they were frequently starved of essential supplies and unable to rely on military reinforcements.

Partly for these reasons and in part because their deeply-rooted nationalistic sentiments inhibited them from becoming fully integrated into Republican affairs, the Basques opted for a largely defensive military posture during the war. To this end they constructed what was believed to be an impenetrable series of fortifications – popularly known as the 'ring of iron' (*cinturón de hierro*, literally belt of iron) – that were designed to protect the region's principal nerve-centres in and around Bilbao.

In the meantime, however, the Nationalists, having been frustrated in their all-out drive to take the capital, were concentrating their manoeuvres

9. Juan Pablo Fusi has observed that if George Orwell had gone to Bilbao instead of to Barcelona, he would not have been overwhelmed by revolutionary changes. See his article 'The Basque Question, 1931–7', in *Revolution and War in Spain, 1931–1939*, ed. by Paul Preston (London, 1984), pp. 182–201.

in the northern sectors under republican control. Towards the middle of March, General Mola launched a fresh offensive on the Vizcayan front. Arrayed against the 26,000 Nationalist troops of the sixth Division were some 27,500 Basque nationalists, communists, socialists and anarchists.[10] Yet the roughly equivalent numbers of opposing ground forces did not tell the whole story. In addition to being better trained – their forces included the formidable Navarre Brigades – and supplied, Nationalist ground troops received air support from the Italians and, above all, the German Condor Legion, which had at its disposal some sixty aircraft, including Heinkel–111 bombers and the new Messerschmidt–109 fighters. It was largely because of the effectiveness of their air force that the Nationalists achieved a relatively easy military victory in the northern campaign. In the words of the commissar of the Army of the North, aerial bombardments 'produced a vertical fall in the morale of our forces' and this cancelled out the positive effects that may have come from effective Basque resistance.[11] The devastating impact that the Nationalist air war was having on the republican side gained world-wide attention on 26 April 1937, when the small market-town of Guernica was destroyed in one afternoon.

Though it had an arms factory and provided a link in Basque communications, Guernica could not be regarded as an important military target. It was probably selected for destruction because, as the birthplace of Basque nationalism – the ancient oak of 'Gernika' stood on a small hill not far from the town's centre – it symbolized the Basque will to resist foreign domination. As it turned out, Guernica, like the Basque villages of Durango and Ochandiano which had been demolished only weeks before, provided an excellent target for the German pilots who were anxious to perfect their bombing techniques. In the event, using heavy high explosive and incendiary bombs, around forty-three aircraft from the German Condor Legion and the Italian Aviazione Legionaria nearly levelled Guernica in the space of a few hours. Amidst the burning rubble some 1,685 civilians (out of a total population of 7,000) lay dead or dying.[12] The telling irony was that no military target had been destroyed: both the arms plant and the bridge republican troops needed to make good their withdrawal were still intact. Even the famous 'Tree of Liberty' had been spared.

If the Nationalists' destruction of Guernica was calculated to achieve a psychological victory, their objective had been met: Basque morale did

---

10. For the war in the north, see José Manuel Martínez Bande, *La guerra en el Norte* (Madrid, 1969); and, in the same series, J. M. Bande, *Vizcaya* (Madrid, 1971).
11. Quoted in Raymond Carr, *The Spanish Civil War* (London, 1986), p. 186.
12. The Basque government estimated that at least 889 people had been injured in the bombing raid, though an untold number fell victim to the machine-gun strafings of Heinkel He–51s. See Paul Preston, *Franco: A Biography* (London, 1993), p. 244.

indeed plummet in the wake of the attack. But the unintended consequence of the bombing was that it generated an enormous amount of publicity which immediately scandalized world opinion. With their image stained by the blood of innocent civilians, the Nationalists desperately sought to avoid further drubbings in the media by issuing their own version of events. According to Franco's propaganda services, the foreign press agency and Radio Nacional in Salamanca, the destruction was caused by the 'red' *dinamiteros* sent in from Asturias and separatist arsonists fleeing the town. (The former was a reference to what had occurred earlier in the war at Irún, when anarchists set fire to buildings before retreating across the border. However, because of their abiding attachment to their homeland, Basque nationalists outrightly rejected any form of scorched earth policy.) Depite these efforts to salvage the Nationalists' public image, most foreigners saw through the tissue of lies. In the end, only pro-rebel sympathizers – such as the devout Catholic communities in Great Britain and the United States – accepted the official Salamanca account.[13] The affair itself would probably have died down after the war had it not been immortalized in Pablo Picasso's famous mural entitled 'Guernica'. The artist's rendering of death and destruction as a series of agonizing, grotesque figures is so evocative of the pain and suffering of Spain's civil war that the tragedy of Guernica has yet to be forgotten.

The fall of Guernica marked the beginning of a series of Nationalist advances deep into Vizcaya. With superior artillery and airpower, they broke through the 'impregnable' iron ring surrounding Bilbao in late spring and laid siege to the city. Exhausted from fighting and weakened by lack of food and supplies, the citizens of the Basque Republic held out until 19 June, when Bilbao was finally brought to its knees. Largely because of the conservative and Catholic nature of the Basque regime, the occupying troops tempered their reprisals against the vanquished. Nevertheless, resentment against Basque nationalists who had, in the eyes of the Nationalists, betrayed their religion and true fatherland, ran deep. For supporting the Basque Republic fourteen autonomist priests were executed and over 300 secular and regular clergymen were either imprisoned or exiled. In addition, a campaign was waged to eradicate all traces of the Basques' cultural identity: citizens were forbidden to teach Basque history and to speak their

---

13. Franco's Press and Intelligence Officer, Luís Bolín, was chiefly responsible for fabricating the Nationalist version of the destruction of Guernica, which was maintained well after the war had ended. See his *Spain: The Vital Years* (London, 1967), pp. 274–82. For the definitive refutation of the Franquista version see Herbert R. Southworth, *Guernica! Guernica! A Study of Journalism, Diplomacy, Propaganda and History* (Berkeley/London, 1977), and Paul Preston, *Franco* (London, 1993). Preston further points out (p. 247) that 'there can no longer be any doubt that the atrocity was carried out at the behest of the Nationalist high command, and not on the initiative of the Germans'.

ancient language. The 'hidden' victims of the Nationalist victory were the families of the 20,000 or so Basque children who had been evacuated abroad during the spring offensive. Although they were cared for by foster families in Great Britain, the Soviet Union, Belgium, Mexico, Switzerland and Denmark, many of these 'orphans' were never reunited with their relatives.[14]

Bilbao proved to be the linchpin of the northern republican defences. In the weeks following the collapse of the 'White' Basque government, the Nationalists moved their theatre of operations to the 'Red' enclaves west of Vizcaya. The coastal resort city of Santander fell to a mixed contingent of Italian and Spanish forces on 26 August, and, on 21 October, Gijón was occupied by Aranda's troops. The entire northern part of Spain, with its precious metals and iron and steel plants, was now in Nationalist hands.

POLITICS IN CATALONIA

The July revolution and civil war allowed Catalonia to experience greater autonomy than could be found anywhere else in the Republican zone. In the first few months, the separation of Catalonia from the rest of Republican Spain resulted from the transfer of power from the central government in Madrid to the hands of the revolutionary committees. A far greater degree of independence was achieved by late September, when the Generalitat reasserted its authority in the region. While this development did not signal an end to the revolutionary movement, for the strength of the social revolutionaries of the CNT-FAI and POUM was still considerable, it did give greater rein to the regionalists, who were pressing hard to erect the institutional basis for a Catalan nation.

Catalan autonomy was pushed even further during the time the Madrid government was still recovering from the shattering blows of the revolution. By the end of December, the Generalitat had already raised its own army, begun issuing its own currency notes, and begun promoting its own foreign relations with other countries. Although Catalonia was never in a position to secede from the Republic, its highly developed autonomy often compelled the central government to treat the Generalitat as an ally rather than as a regional government under its sovereignty.[15]

14. For the story of these children, see Dorothy Legarreta, *The Guernica Generation: Basque Refugee Children of the Spanish Civil War* (Reno, 1984).
15. Arnold J. Toynbee (ed.), assisted by V. M. Boulter, *The international repercussions of the war in Spain (1936–1937)*, in the series *Survey of International Affairs*, vol. II (London, 1938), pp. 94–5.

Throughout the autumn of 1936 events showed that the revolutionary state of affairs in Catalonia was rapidly giving way to a new political and social order. By early 1937 the air of excitement and spontaneity that had characterized the early days of war and revolution in the region had given place to a greyer, almost business-like climate, and revolutionary images no longer dominated the urban landscape. Returning to Barcelona several months after he first arrived in Spain, George Orwell immediately detected the new rhythm in the city's daily life:

> Everyone who has made two visits, at intervals of months, to Barcelona during the war has remarked upon the extraordinary changes that took place in it . . . the thing they said was always the same: the revolutionary atmosphere had vanished . . . The change in the aspect of the crowds was startling. The militia uniform and the blue overalls had almost disappeared . . . There were two facts that were the keynote of all else. One was that the people – the civil population – had lost much of their interest in the war; the other was that the normal division of society into rich and poor, upper class and lower class, was reasserting itself.[16]

These changes owed a great deal to the fact that the CNT-FAI and POUM's policy of collaboration, rather than advancing the revolutionary movement had brought it to a standstill. The revolutionaries proved to be ill-adapted to the world of politics and they therefore found themselves yielding step by step to the parties who were intent on restoring a centralized middle-class government. Leading this drive was the communist-controlled PSUC, which, as we have already noted, had only come into being in late July. With an initial membership of between 2,500 and 6,000, the minuscule party hardly appeared as a threat to its principal rivals, the CNT-FAI and the POUM. Yet thanks to its strong opposition to the maximalist revolutionary programme of the left – the party insisted that the war had to be won before any revolution could take place – and the power and prestige it acquired when Soviet supplies began arriving in October, the PSUC rose rapidly to become one of the principal parties in Catalonia. By 1937 party membership had surpassed the 50,000 mark, while the PSUC-dominated UGT counted nearly half-a-million members. Apart from the rank-and-file support it derived from its trade union partner, the party appealed mostly to the small peasants (*rabassaires*), small manufacturers, tradesmen, and middle- and lower-middle-class Catalans – whose interests they sought to protect by creating organizations like the GEPCI (Federación Catalana de Gremios y Entidades de Pequeños Comerciantes e Industriales), the consortium of small businessmen and manufacturers we introduced earlier.

16. George Orwell, *Homage to Catalonia* (New York, 1964), pp. 109–11.

The PSUC's ascendancy can also be attributed to its working alliance with Lluis Companys' Esquerra Republicana de Catalunya (ERC), which was seeking to establish a completely independent Catalan state. Although the two parties were striving towards different goals – the PSUC had subordinated its regionalist aspirations for the sake of a broader communist agenda – both sought to curtail the revolutionary movement.

Because of the preponderance of the CNT-FAI, early on in the war neither party wanted to take the anarchosyndicalists head on. This was especially true of the Esquerra, which, under the leadership of Companys, a former CNT lawyer, had been deferential to the CNT-FAI during the high tide of the July revolution. It will be recalled that, at this time, Companys shrewdly decided to invite the anarchosyndicalists to collaborate with other parties in the formation of the CAMC; this in the belief that, once the CNT-FAI was inside the government, it would be far easier for his party to exploit their political naïvety as well as the shortcomings of their numerous revolutionary experiments. The dissolution of the CAMC in late September and the re-establishment of the Generalitat offered concrete proof of the soundness of his strategy, for this important decision constituted the first major step towards ending dual power-sharing in the region.

Far less concerned with the subtleties of statecraft, the PSUC brazenly pursued its own agenda, and as the party grew in strength, so did its aggressive behaviour towards the revolutionaries. From the beginning the PSUC made no secret of its hatred for the POUM. To them, the POUM was more than just a renegade Marxist party, it was an eloquent and therefore dangerous critic of Stalinist policies. During the war, the PSUC and the communists went to extraordinary lengths to convince their allies that the POUM's anti-Popular Front stance should be equated with a pro-fascist position. This argument, along with the oft-repeated accusation that the POUM was a hotbed of 'Trotskyist' spies working in collusion with Franco, was later used to great effect in their campaign to liquidate the POUM.

By December the PSUC felt confident enough to challenge the POUM directly. A government crisis, provoked by the PSUC leader Joan Comorera, resulted in the expulsion of Andreu Nin, the Councillor of Justice and only POUM representative sitting in the Generalitat. The POUM bristled at this latest strategem. Shortly after Nin's dismissal, the front page of its daily, *La Batalla*, thundered: 'IT IS NOT POSSIBLE TO GOVERN WITHOUT THE POUM AND STILL LESS AGAINST IT.' Privately, however, POUM leaders were alive to the danger the PSUC posed to them and the revolutionary movement in Catalonia. Hoping to impress upon the CNT-FAI that they, too, were vulnerable to communist machinations, *La Batalla* ran the following article on 5 January 1937: 'The Soviet press expresses the hope that the cleaning up of the Spanish Anarchists and the Trotskyists [that is, the POUM] in Catalonia will be carried out with the same energy as in the USSR.' Though the authenticity of this quotation was never established – it was publicly repudiated by the Soviet Consul General, Vladimir Antonov-Ovseenko – its pointed message alarmed certain quarters of the libertarian community.[17]

MAY EVENTS OF 1937

The early months of 1937 saw the tensions between the pro- and anti-revolutionary movements in Catalonia sharpen. The highly charged political atmosphere finally exploded in May, when the opposing sides were locked in a series of bloody street skirmishes. The 'May Events', the 'war within a war' so vividly realized in Orwell's *Homage to Catalonia*, would have far-reaching political consequences. Among other things, it marked the end-point of the revolutionary drive that had begun ten months earlier and the beginning of communist hegemony in the republican camp.

Following Nin's ousting in December and the reorganization of Josep Tarradellas's administration, PSUC councillors stepped up their efforts to strip the anarchosyndicalists of the economic and political authority they exercised through their revolutionary committees and armed forces.[18] Led by Joan Comorera, the PSUC leader who held a succession of key cabinet positions between January and May, the PSUC proposed a series of measures that struck at the very heart of the revolutionary movement. Besides seeking to dissolve the CNT committees that controlled the wholesale food trades in the region, the PSUC and its ally the Catalan UGT sought to create a single police force. Among other things this meant eliminating the *patrullas de control*, the FAI Investigation Groups and the workers' armed *barrio* committees, which, as we have seen, the anarchosyndicalists had established at the outset of the revolution. In the face of these blatant

---

17. For further discussion of this controversial quotation which has been used in a pivotal way by many historians, see the exchange between Stephen Schwartz, George Esenwein and Irving Louis Horowitz in *Labor History* 'Communications', vol. XXX, no. 1, Winter 1989.
18. See Burnett Bolloten, *The Spanish Revolution: The Left and the struggle for power during the Civil War* (Chapel Hill, North Carolina, 1979).

manoeuvres, the general mood of the CNT-FAI rank and file as well as the left wing of the POUM grew increasingly belligerent. At first their disquietude was limited to a war of words, but by late spring there were more menacing signs that a showdown between the contending sides was imminent.[19]

At the end of April two tit-for-tat killings – one of the PSUC official Roldán Cortada and the other of Antonio Martín, the anarchist head of the revolutionary council in Puigcerdá – created so much tension in the region that the approaching May Day celebrations had to be cancelled. Then, on the afternoon of 3 May, the PSUC police commissioner, Eusebio Rodríguez Salas, ordered three truckloads of Assault Guards to raid the central telephone exchange (*Telefónica*), located in the Plaça de Catalunya.[20] The building served as the communication nerve-centre of the Catalan government, which the CNT had occupied since the defeat of the military in July and which they regarded as a key revolutionary conquest. In the eyes of the authorities this daring move was necessary because they wanted to end the CNT-FAI's eavesdropping (which apparently also involved some censoring) on the telephone calls of Generalitat officials. In the event, the anarchists reacted instinctively to the police provocation. Strikes followed in the wake of the news of the raid, and, by nightfall, workers had thrown up barricades in their neighbourhoods and had occupied strategic positions in and around Barcelona. With lightning speed Barcelona had been transformed into an armed camp, and the revolutionaries had become – to paraphrase Manuel Azaña – 'masters of the city'.

Behind the barricades stood the revolutionaries as represented by the POUM,[21] a handful of foreign Trotskyists who called themselves Bolshevik-Leninists, rank-and-file members of the CNT-FAI, the Libertarian Youth (*Federación Ibérica de Juventudes Libertarias*, FIJL), and a dissident anarchist organization that had been formed in early March and was known as Los

19. The FAI's *Tierra y Libertad* and the POUM daily *La Batalla* railed against the PSUC's transparent efforts to subdue the ultraleft. The literature on the May Events is extensive. Chapters 42 and 43 in Bolloten, *The Spanish Civil War*, constitute the most thoroughly documented account of the crisis in any language.

20. The fact that the orders to carry out the raid were signed by the Esquerra councillor of internal security, Artemio Aiguadé, suggests that the provocation was approved by most members of the Catalan government.

21 The creation of 'Los Amigos' coincided with the POUM's efforts to form what Juan Andrade termed a *Frente Obrero Revolucionario* or united front among the ultraradical groups which could be used to stem the momentum of the counter-revolutionary movement. And while no such alliance was formally concluded between the Marxists and anarchosyndicalists before the street-fighting broke out, during the struggle revolutionaries in both ideological camps agreed to maintain 'fraternal relations' with one another.

Amigos de Durruti ('The Friends of Durruti').[22] Opposing them were the armed forces of the Generalitat, militant members of the separatist Estat Català, and the PSUC (many of whom were holed up in the Hotel Colón, the Communist Party headquarters located across from the Plaça de Catalunya).

After the battle lines had been drawn, intermittent machine gun blasts rattled through the buildings in the major sections of the city, and exploding hand grenades and dynamite sticks could also be heard echoing throughout the militarized zones. The street-fighting continued the following morning, 4 May, and by midday it had reached an excruciating pitch.

In an effort to defuse the situation, Lluis Companys took to the airwaves, condemning Rodríguez Salas's decision to occupy the *Telefónica* and appealling for calm. His message was immediately reinforced by representatives of the CNT Regional Committee, who pleaded with the workers to lay down their arms and put a 'stop [to] this fratricidal strife'. But, upon hearing that the police had not retired from the telephone exchange, the revolutionaries refused to back down. Left with no alternative, government officials moved quickly to regain control of the situation.[23]

Despite their early successes, the revolutionaries' hold on power was tenuous. Although united in their opposition to the authorities, the radicals were unable to overcome the ideological barriers that had traditionally kept them apart. Only the militant 'Amigos de Durruti' seemed to have a concrete plan for seizing power. In the course of the fighting the 'Amigos' took on the role of a vanguard party, and, on 5 May, they began urgently appealing both to the CNT-FAI and the POUM to join forces and set up a revolutionary junta. But their calls went unanswered. When approached by a delegation from the 'Amigos', the POUM demonstrated their unwillingness to compromise with the libertarians. On the other hand, the CNT-FAI did not feel obliged to take directives either from the breakaway 'Amigos' or a Marxist party that, irrespective of its anti-Stalinism, still embraced the principles of Leninism.

22. The group named itself after Buenaventura Durruti, who had achieved martyrdom on the left after he was killed by an unknown assailant behind the lines of the Madrid Front in November 1936. (For the mysterious circumstances surrounding his death see, for example, *The Times Literary Supplement*, 24 December 1964 and January 1965). Strident critics of the collaborationist line being followed by anarchist leaders, 'Los Amigos' comprised libertarians who refused any longer to submit quietly to the counter-revolutionary measures of the central and Catalan governments. Under the charismatic leadership of Jaime Balius, the breakaway group had attracted an estimated 4,000 adherents by the time the May disturbances broke out.
23. As we have noted, except for the PSUC, the middle-class separatists of the Estat Català, the Acció Catalana, Acció Republicana and Companys's Esquerra had up to now been reluctant to challenge openly the power of the CNT-FAI. Yet this latest crisis forced them to take sides and they therefore decided to support the PSUC.

But even if a revolutionary alliance failed to materialize, it was clear that the CNT-FAI was still powerful enough to act alone. According to the FAI leader Abad de Santillán, the CNT- FAI did not press home their advantage because, even though it was possible for them to do so, toppling the middle-class government 'did not interest us, for it would have been an act of folly contrary to our principles of unity and democracy'. Whether this acccurately reflected the thinking of most anarchosyndicalists or not, the fact is that their temporizing seriously prejudiced their chances of winning the dispute.

The drama being played out in Barcelona had caught the Valencian government by surprise. Reluctant to dispatch government troops to put down the rebellion, Largo Caballero's first response was to summon the CNT ministers and UGT leaders to his office in the hope that they could work together to bring an end to the conflict. On Wednesday, 5 May, CNT-FAI ministers Federica Montseny, García Oliver and the CNT general secretary Mariano Vásquez arrived in Barcelona and joined the Catalan authorities in the Generalitat Palace in calling for a cessation of hostilities. The conciliatory pleas of the CNT-FAI leaders heard over the radio stung rather than soothed the spirits of the knots of workers still milling around the barricades. For them it was a form of treachery to allow the true *provocateurs*, the PSUC guards, to escape without just punishment.

Although order was restored on 6 May, many workers remained behind their fortifications. In the early hours of 7 May there were signs that the revolutionary ardour of the workers had finally spent itself. A feeling that it would be futile to continue the struggle had overwhelmed them, and disillusionment was widespread. When the government response finally came at 4.15 a.m., most were relieved to hear that the Generalitat had accepted the CNT-FAI's offer to end the fighting. Half an hour later the workers withdrew from the barricades and in the pre-dawn darkness they slipped back to their homes.

MAY EVENTS: THE AFTERMATH

The political repercussions of the May Events reverberated loudly throughout the republican zone. In Barcelona itself the mini-war had not only poisoned relations between the ultraleft and the moderate forces but it had caused the death of between 200 and 500 republicans.[24] With the fighting

---

24. Estimates of casualties reported at the time vary widely. The most accurate accounting of those killed can be found in J. M. Solé and J. Villarroya, 'Les Víctimes dels Fets de Maig', in *Recerques*, no 12, 1982.

over, the central government vigorously pursued a programme aimed at establishing its complete control over the political and economic life in the republican zone. As a result, in the coming weeks the Generalitat lost its semi-autonomous status: it was divested of its authority over the Catalan army and forces of public order, both of which were now the reponsibility of the government in Valencia.

At the national level the struggle had precipitated a government crisis which led to the downfall of the Prime Minister. Because he had refused to act decisively and effectively to put down the rebellion, Largo was vulnerable to the barbed criticisms of the communists and his opponents within the PSOE. When, on 13 May, he pointedly refused to accede to communist demands that the 'renegade' POUM be dissolved, Uribe and Hernández, the two communist ministers, stormed out of his cabinet. Supremely confident that he could rule without them, Largo seemed totally oblivious to the fact that the political tide had already turned against him. In recent months the moderate or *prietista* wing of the socialist movement had coalesced with the left-republicans and the communists, and, by May 1937, this new constellation of anti-Largo forces was powerful enough to depose him. Without the backing he needed to form a new government, Largo was forced to step down from his posts as war minister and premier. He was replaced on 17 May by the moderate socialist Juan Negrín, about whom we will have more to say in the next chapter.

THE ECLIPSE OF THE LEFT-SOCIALISTS

Largo's dismissal threw into sharper relief the long-standing strains and fractures within the socialist movement, especially those which were centred around the Largo/Prieto rivalry. Up till now doctrinal and tactical differences between the reformist and revolutionary wings had been kept under control, above all because of their collective desire to uphold the banner of Popular Front unity in the face of Nationalist aggression. But the more it became apparent that this commitment meant different things to the competing socialist factions, the more this unity began to break down. As far as the left-socialists were concerned, for example, Popular Frontism and the class collaboration it implied was acceptable as long as it did not mean sacrificing the social and economic gains that had been achieved during the revolutionary phase of the war. But this was not true for the moderate socialists, who made it clear in the aftermath of the May crisis that they were determined to liquidate the revolution for the sake of political expediency.

The new direction of Republican politics inevitably raised the question of whether the radical tendencies within the socialist movement would continue to support the Popular Front coalition or whether they would retaliate by directly challenging the anti-revolutionary drift of the government. For several reasons the latter alternative had little chance of succeeding. Foremost was the fact that, since July 1936, the relative strengths of the rival tendencies had been irrevocably altered. Although they maintained their numerical superiority within the socialist movement, the left-socialists increasingly found themselves unable to prevent the moderates and their friends from imposing their will on the trade unions.[25] Yet the ascendancy of the moderate socialists was not simply the result of the failure of political leadership on the left. What tipped the balance in their favour was the informal partnership that had been cobbled together between the *prietistas* and the communists.[26]

The alliance itself represented a major departure from the pre-civil war pattern of political alignments. Before the war the two groups had clashed with one another over a number of fundamental issues. The communists, for example, had been nothing less than contemptuous of Indalecio Prieto, the head of the centre faction of the PSOE who loudly condemned the PCE's efforts to build bridges between the socialist and communist movements. But relations between the two former antagonists had undergone significant changes since July 1936. Particularly in the period leading up to and immediately following the May Events of 1937, Prieto, Ramón Lamoneda and other reformist members of the PSOE executive believed that they had much to gain by cooperating with the communists. Apart from appreciating the fact that the PCE were, like themselves, enforcedly opposed to the revolutionary trajectory of Republican politics, the *prietistas* recognized that they needed another powerful ally if they ever were to dislodge the *caballeristas* from the commanding positions they held in the government and the trade unions. For their part, the communists were willing to collaborate with the moderates because this would bring them closer to realizing their own long-range hegemonic designs, which, among other things, included their desire to dominate the Spanish left by effecting a fusion of the communist and socialist movements.

Of the two partners, it was the communists who were largely responsible for systematically eroding the organizational strength and discipline of the

---

25. Largo's refusal early on in the war to embrace the revolution had cost the left dearly, but, despite his lack of resolve, he was still widely seen as the principal leader of the left-socialists.

26. Given that Negrín and the ruling parties did not rely on an electorate to hold office, the near-collapse of the PSOE's popular base did not weaken the leadership's control of the levers of government. Rather they exercised power because of the support they received from the PCE and foreign communists, who had become by this point the most powerful single political force in Republican Spain.

left-socialists. In the period immediately following the May Events they were particularly successful at whittling away at the power bases of the *caballeristas*. Thus during the summer of 1937, when Largo was still secretary of the UGT and his supporters still controlled the executive commission, the anti-Largo forces were coming to dominate the national committee by using the mostly non-industrial federations they had organized since July 1936 as springboards for opposition.[27] In the following weeks even UGT attempts to check communist penetration of the ruling cadres were effectively neutralized given that the UGT executive was itself split in its attitude towards the PCE.[28]

It soon became apparent that the more the communists applied pressure against the ramparts of the left-socialists, the more the *caballeristas* lost ground to their adversaries. Towards the end of May 1937, Largo's principal mouthpiece *Claridad* (Madrid) fell into communist hands, and shortly afterwards *Adelante*, the daily newspaper of the Largo-dominated Federación Socialista Valenciana, was forcibly taken over. In October 1937, Largo's crusade against his enemies experienced its greatest setback when the pro-communist factions of the National Committee of the UGT thwarted his attempts to expel the federations of industry that were challenging his leadership. Refusing to recognize the recent expulsions, these secessionist elements, with the backing of the Negrín government, convoked their own assembly and elected another executive. Though headed by the veteran revolutionary socialist González Peña the true orientation of the new body was reflected in the fact that all the key posts, including that held by Peña himself, were filled by *prietistas* and communists.[29]

Stubborn and defiant as ever, Largo could not accept that this latest manoeuvre had entirely undermined his leadership position. Since his access to the official channels of the UGT was now blocked, he attempted to mount a rearguard offensive by holding mass meetings. In so doing, however, he brought down on his head the wrath of the authorities. Not willing to tolerate Largo's personal campaign against his enemies, the Negrín Popular Front administration placed him under police surveillance and did everything in its power to ensure that the querulous socialist leader (and his followers) would be deprived of a public platform. The remaining public organ of the *caballeristas*, the evening paper *La Correspondencia de Valencia*, was shut down on 13 November on the grounds that it fomented a 'rebellious' (read, anti-Popular Front) attitude among the workers. Finally, on 28 November, Largo's fate was formally sealed when the government

---

27. See Stanley G. Payne, *The Spanish Revolution* (New York, 1970), p. 300.
28. Helen Graham, *Socialism and War: The Spanish Socialist Party in power and crisis, 1936–1939* (Cambridge, 1991), p. 168.
29. Peña himself was, despite his militant background, also one of Prieto's supporters.

announced its recognition of the Peña executive. Officially banished from the political stage, Largo spent the remainder of the war in near isolation.

Largo's excommunication was a resounding triumph for the Popular Frontists but it did put an end to the destructive conflicts within the socialist movement. The dispute between the rival UGT executives, for example, raged on until January 1938. Having defeated Largo, the communists decided to assuage the left-socialists by calling in the International Federation of Trade Unions to work out a 'compromise' solution. Thanks to the intervention of the French trade union leader Léon Jouhaux, it was decided on 2 January 1938 to admit four left-socialists – José Díaz Alor, Ricardo Zabalza, Pascual Tomás, and Hernández Zancajo – to the Peña executive.[30] While these appointments may have helped to calm tempers, they could hardly be regarded as a major concession on the part of the communists and moderates. For, given that the left-socialists held only four seats out of fifteen in the newly expanded executive, it was highly unlikely that they could ever challenge the dominance of their rivals.

From 1938 on there were further signs that the internal battles of the socialist movement were not over. Deeply entrenched as they were in the trade union apparatus of the UGT, die-hard *caballeristas* were loath to give up the fight against the reformist/communist bloc. This was especially true of the landworkers' federation (the FNTT), which, under the leadership of Ricardo Zabalza, actively campaigned against the PCE's aggressive anti-collectivist programmes in the countryside during the spring and summer of 1938.[31] In the next chapter we shall see that a resurgence of the socialist left in the final weeks of war revived the warfare between the pro- and anti-Popular Front forces.

REPRESSION OF THE POUM

Meanwhile, back in Catalonia, the communists and the PSUC were taking full advantage of the fact that the fulcrum of political power in the region had now shifted to Valencia. Backed by the middle-class parties of the Generalitat, they spearheaded a massive witch-hunt against the POUM and the so-called 'uncontrollable' elements of the CNT-FAI. Knowing that the POUM was a relatively easy target – in addition to being practically friendless its official publications were heavily censored – the communists began their Moscow-style purges by broadcasting over the radio anti-

30. Although also asked to join the executive, Largo adamantly refused to do so.
31. Joint committees of the FNTT-CNT challenged the PCE in this campaign. For more on the cooperation between the socialists and anarchosyndicalists see above, Chapter 7.

POUM invectives and filling their newspapers with sensational accusations. Besides broadly tarring all *poumistas* as 'Trotskyist saboteurs' and 'Fifth Columnists', *Treball, Frente Rojo* and other communist journals indicted the POUM for having undermined the unity of the anti-fascist front by allegedly inspiring the so-called 'criminal Barcelona putsch'.[32]

It did not take long for the relentless barrages of communist 'hate' propaganda to produce the desired results. On 2 June Andreu Nin, Juan Andrade, Julián Gorkín and other members of the POUM executive were arrested and, in the following weeks, *poumistas* throughout the republican camp were hounded into exile or driven underground. Nin himself was spirited away to a prison on the outskirts of Madrid, where, under torture, he was murdered by his communist captors.[33] Because his unexplained disappearance proved to be acutely embarrassing to the recently formed Negrín government, the communists attempted to cover their crime by circulating false rumours. One had Nin escaping from prison with the aid of the German Gestapo and Nationalist soldiers who had disguised themselves as International Brigaders. Even if POUM's detractors found these allegations plausible, for others the details of the story did not ring true. What made it particularly hard to swallow was the fact that Nin had a well-established reputation as a Marxist revolutionary. In addition to having dedicated most of his life to the pursuit of Marxism, Nin was known in Catalonia for his literary accomplishments, which included translations from Russian into Catalan of the works of Lenin, Plekhanov, Dostoevsky and Pilniak. At least for those on the Spanish left who knew his political background it was an act of self-deception to insist that Nin was actually a Francoist agent.[34] In the event, the fate of Nin remained an open question and the oft-repeated phrase 'Where is Andreu Nin?' continued to haunt the republican government.

Having been made the scapegoats for the May disturbances, *poumistas* were pilloried not just in the communist media but also in much of the

32. It was rumoured at the time that it was Franco's agents who, acting in collusion with the POUM, incited the May riots. Years after the war, a published memorandum of Wilhelm von Faupel, the German Ambassador to Spain, seemed to substantiate this claim (see *Documents on German Foreign Policy, 1918–1945*, series D, vol. III, p. 286). While there can be little doubt that Francoist and fascist agents were active in Barcelona, there is no conclusive evidence that they they were directly responsible for the outbreak of street-fighting. On the contrary, as we have seen, it was Rodríguez Salas's raid on the telephone exchange which ignited the conflict.

33. Until the opening of KGB files in recent years, the precise fate of Nin was not known. These records, however, confirm what was long believed by most, namely that Moscow ordered Nin's arrest and execution and that the foreign communists who carried them out were assisted by members of the PCE.

34. It was not until nearly 50 years after the war that Santiago Carrillo, Georges Soria and other leading communists admitted that Nin had been unfairly maligned.

national and international press. Only a handful of the European and American left – the most notable being Fenner Brockway, John McNair (both of the Independent Labour Party (ILP)), George Orwell, Victor Serge, V. F. Calverton, Bertram Wolfe and Sidney Hook – dared to speak out on behalf of the POUM. But their public revelations of the deeply-seated political animosities in Republican Spain as well as their documented efforts to expose the calumnies against the POUM fell mostly on deaf ears. (Against the background of Nationalist victories, this was precisely the kind of news that no one on the left wanted to hear.)

Some months later, during the POUM 'show trials' held in October 1938, the communists and their allies failed to prove conclusively that the party was acting in concert with the enemy. In fact, most of the documents used by the prosecution were so obviously faked – such as the one supposedly written in invisible ink and signed by 'N' (that is, Nin) – that the court could not bring itself to convict any *poumista* of espionage and treason. Nevertheless, Andrade, Gorkín and other POUM leaders were sentenced for their role in the May Events and imprisoned for the remainder of the war.

Although they had not been singled out for persecution, the anarchosyndicalists were also reeling from the political fallout of the May Events. The first unequivocal sign of this came on 17 May, the day when Juan Negrín announced his new cabinet. Much to the surprise and consternation of the CNT-FAI, it comprised only nine members (as opposed to eighteen in the previous administration) and, significantly, it excluded both *Caballero* socialists and anarchosyndicalists. The initial reaction in libertarian circles was hostile. The CNT and FAI press dubbed the new government 'counter-revolutionary', and, because they were suspicious of communist motives in the cabinet reshuffle, they accused the PCE of having masterminded a conspiracy to have the anarchosyndicalists ejected from the government.

However, the anarchosyndicalists' angry and rebellious mood quickly melted. On 2 June, Mariano Vásquez, representing the National Committee of the CNT, held an interview with Negrín at which he promised the Premier that the government could 'count on the material and moral support of the CNT' to defend the Republic. The reason for this sudden *volte-face* was clear. Hoping to redress the anti-revolutionary tilt of Negrín's newly formed executive, the CNT decided to reverse its stand by soliciting representation in the Popular Front government. In a minimum programme published later that week, the National Committee proposed equal representation for the Marxist, republican and libertarian sectors in all matters relating to national defence, the economy, and public order. But, considering the CNT's relatively weak bargaining position, it is small wonder that their proposal came to nothing.

Even in Catalonia, there were unmistakable signs that the power of the anarchosyndicalists had crested. Towards the end of June, the moderate leadership of the CNT suffered another humiliating rebuff by President Companys. On 29 June the provisional government formed during the May Events was replaced by a new cabinet without anarchosyndicalist representation. This demonstrated beyond a doubt that, since May, political circumstances had evolved at a rapid rate: for only two months before, a government without CNT support would have been unthinkable.

After they had been deprived of a voice in the Popular Front coalition it was natural that some leaders of the CNT wanted to draw closer to their only potential ally on the left, the Caballero socialists. An important step in this direction was taken in late July, when the still left-leaning UGT executive and the CNT signed a provisional alliance. But several stumbling blocks prevented the two organizations from immediately consummating an alliance. One had to do with the fact that forging a coherent coalition between the two unions demanded a clear direction. Experience had shown that this would be difficult since both the anarchosyndicalists and left socialists visualized their respective agendas as something at once allied to and distinct from one another. While both identified themselves with (and had a shared experience of) the revolutionary heritage of July, each understood this process differently. It would therefore take some time for them to iron out a joint strategy. An even greater obstacle to the formation of a CNT-UGT bloc, though, was the overwhelming resistance it met from moderate and pro-communist forces within the socialist movement.

As we noted above, Largo Caballero's enemies were highly successful in their efforts to divest the ageing trade union leader and his supporters of their levers of power. As a result, from the autumn of 1937 on, the idea of forming a united revolutionary front among the anarchist and socialist organizations was rendered virtually meaningless. By the time a formal pact between the CNT and UGT was finally signed on 18 March 1938, it could no longer be regarded as a culmination of the earlier initiative that sought to bring the unions together. Nor could this agreement be objectively construed as a victory for the opponents of the Negrín government. Far from consolidating the power of the revolutionaries, the pact actually subordinated the Republic's two largest unions to the will of the central government. According to the historian Helen Graham, the 'unions were,' thanks to the alliance, 'finally reduced to the role of managers of production, entirely dependent on the centralised state apparatus, an instrument for the channelling of government policy and propaganda'.[35]

No less a contributing factor to the decline of anarchosyndicalism after

35. Graham, *Socialists and War*, p. 188.

230

the May Events were the growing splits within the libertarian movement itself. It will be recalled that at the height of the crisis the pro-government stance of the CNT-FAI leaders greatly deflated the workers' revolutionary *élan*. Though temporarily repressed in the weeks that followed the May events, dissident anarchists – mostly composed of the Anarchist Youth Federation (FIJL) and the 'Amigos' – resumed their agitation for a complete reversal of official libertarian policy. Yet for a significant number of *cenetistas*, especially those who believed that unity in the anti-fascist coalition was necessary in order to defeat fascism, it was no longer feasible nor desirable to chart an alternative political course. Instead they opted for the possibilist line being advocated by Vásquez, Horatio Prieto and other prominent libertarian representatives. In the coming months, attempts to reconcile the warring factions were to no avail, and the chasm separating the pro-revolutionary elements from the collaborationists continued to widen.

CHAPTER TWELVE

The Republican Road to Defeat

The reformist socialist and communist-led Popular Front coalition that presided over the Republic for the next twenty months was more unified than any previous administration had been. And the central government benefited from this unity above all because it brought about greater consistency both to the conduct of military matters and to the execution of internal policies. Because the Republican war effort was now more dependent than ever on Soviet aid, the PCE and their foreign advisors inevitably played dominant roles in all important military operations. The communists' preponderance in the army also meant that they could virtually dictate the direction of domestic affairs. Working in close cooperation with republicans and moderate socialists like the Premier, Juan Negrín, the communists saw to it that the state consolidated its control over every aspect of social and economic life in Republican Spain. In pursuit of this goal the Popular Frontists energetically pressed forward with their plans to dismantle the surviving revolutionary and autonomous structures through which organizations like the CNT-FAI and FNTT exercised influence.

But even if the central government was now endowed with greater coherence and authority, its position was continuously undermined by its inability to overcome all the animosities, misgivings, and doubts among republican parties that had been stirred up by the war. In fact, as we shall see in this chapter, the centralizing policies and autocratic measures adopted by the Popular Front governments formed under Negrín only served to drive a wedge between those who ruled in the name of the Republic and the mass base of society.

THE POLITICS OF COUNTER-REVOLUTION

Juan Negrín, a renowned physiologist and former finance minister under Largo Caballero, assumed the crucial post of prime minister in May 1937 with relatively limited experience as a political leader. Although known as a moderate who belonged to the reformist wing of the Socialist Party, he was in many respects an inscrutable figure. A man of enormous appetites – he apparently indulged frequently in sexual and food orgies – Negrín was also an astute intellectual who, whenever he put his mind to it, was capable of working hours on end. As premier Negrín formed such a close partnership with the communists that many began questioning his true political convictions. In any case, it was this alliance which cost him the support of his former socialist colleagues and incurred the wrath of his political rivals.

Because of the controversy surrounding Negrín's relationship with the communists he has been at the centre of numerous post-Civil War historiographical debates. His defenders have characterized him as an extraordinarily brilliant politician – one historian has even likened him to the renowned seventeenth-century statesman Count Olivares – who did all he could to steer the Republic between the Scylla of communism and the Charybdis of fascism. His critics have tended to be harsh. Some have accused him of being a communist 'puppet', while others have described him as a pliable, if unwilling, accomplice to Soviet designs in Spain.[1] The truth is probably closer to the middle: Negrín was neither a communist pawn nor a great statesman. But however one assesses Negrín's political performance, it is clear from the record that in the last phases of the war he did everything possible to secure communist supremacy in the army and in key areas of the government.

To say that Negrín was the communists' principal ally and accomplice to their designs is not to deny the important role other groups played in promoting their spectacular rise to power. As we have seen, the PCE's commitment to moderation and pragmatism in social, economic and military affairs appealed not only to Negrín and his followers but also to the diverse group of non-revolutionary elements fighting on the Republican side. In addition, by late 1937 most of these groups had come round to the view that their cooperation with the communists was vitally important to the war effort. The fact that the communists proved to be more than a

---

1. For exceedingly laudatory appraisals of Negrín's political career, see Juan Marichal's article in *Triunfo* (22 June 1974); and Ángel Viñas's interview in *Tiempo de historia* (Madrid, May 1979). A highly critical assessment of the premier can be found in Burnett Bolloten, 'The Strange Case of Dr. Juan Negrín', in *Journal of Contemporary Studies*, volume VIII, no. 4, Fall/Winter, 1985.

match for their political rivals – who increasingly found themselves both divided among themselves and from each other – was also key to their success. Were it not for the convergence of all these factors, it would have been exceedingly difficult for the communists to rise so rapidly to such commanding heights in the Republican system.

Who supported the first Popular Front government under Negrín? At first it was everyone who believed, like President Azaña, that his administration would restore public order in the rear and prosecute the war at the front more vigorously than before. No doubt the moderate composition of Negrín's cabinet was the primary source of this confidence: as we have seen, neither the revolutionaries nor the *caballeristas* held portfolios. But if the *prietistas* were gloating in their victory over Largo – besides the Premiership, they occupied the Defence, Interior, and Finance Ministries – the communists were in a triumphalist mood. Although they were represented by only two seats – Uribe (Agriculture) and Hernández (Education and Health) – in the cabinet, the communists actually exercised more power than before. Above all, they maintained their predominance over the police and the military. Álvarez del Vayo stayed on as General of the Commissariat of War, and he was granted a free hand in the appointment and the political direction of the commissars.[2] In addition, several pro-communist and communist officials who had been dismissed by Largo Caballero – most notably, Antonio Cordón, Major Manuel Estrada, and Captain Eleuterio Díaz Tendero – were either reappointed or reassigned positions in the Ministry of Defence.

Some members of the Spanish Communist Party had seen the overthrow of Largo Caballero as the last major obstacle in their path to reach the summit of power, but the practical reality was that at least two major conditions had to be satisfied before they could make their final ascent.[3] In order to retain their hold over the pivotal positions they already occupied in the state apparatus and the military, it was essential that they acquire and sustain the full cooperation of the executive branch of the Popular Front government. The second, and infinitely more difficult, task was to win the support of the republican masses. In the first instance, the communists greatly benefited from the cooperation of the Popular Front governments under Juan Negrín, the person who, more than any other, helped the communists achieve political hegemony in the final year of the

2. Burnett Bolloten, *The Spanish Revolution: The Left and the struggle for power during the Civil War* (Chapel Hill, North Carolina, 1979), p. 487.
3. Despite the cunning they had shown in penetrating the military and state apparatus and despite their adroitness in exploiting the weaknesses of their political rivals, the communists did not have the supernatural powers attributed to them by some of their bitterest detractors. See, for example, Jésus Hernández, *Yo fui un ministro de Stalin* (Mexico, 1953).

war. Neither the *caballeristas* nor the anarchosyndicalists had held positions in any of the last governments – the sole exception being the pro-*negrinista* CNT politician Segundo Blanco – and there was no other faction that could effectively oppose the policies of Negrín and the communists. With few exceptions – such as Indalecio Prieto, who, as we shall see, eventually fell foul of the government – members who served in the various executive cabinets were generally supportive of the communist line. Those who were not – the left-republican José Giral, for example – lacked both the political will and the popular leverage needed to block communist ambitions.

Winning over the masses, however, was an altogether different undertaking. Notwithstanding the efforts of *apparatchiks* like Palmiro Togliatti, who recognized how critically important it was for the PCE to have the loyal backing of the working classes, the communists never achieved this goal. Earlier we saw how their union-splitting tactics within the UGT ultimately had the effect of driving the socialist rank and file further away from the PCE. The self-defeating strategy they adopted towards the anarchosyndicalists produced even more disastrous results.

Early in the war communists had actively sought to establish close relations with the anarchosyndicalists, partly because they recognized that the CNT-FAI were in touch with the revolutionary pulse of the rank and file and partly because they wanted to harness their combative spirit and creative energies to the war effort. Given their preponderance in Catalonia, Aragón and other regions, it was also strategically important for the communists to be on friendly terms with the anarchosyndicalists. The communists well knew that reaching an understanding with the CNT-FAI would afford them the opportunity to repeat what they had done in the case of the socialist youth movement: absorb them ideologically and politically. At first, the PCE's efforts to curry favour with the CNT-FAI met with some success. Relations between the two reached a high point following the arrival of the Soviet supply ship *Zyryanin* in October 1936. The ship brought thousands of tons of foodstuffs, and though there was no food shortage at this time, it was greeted by all groups with enormous enthusiasm. Shortly afterwards a gigantic public meeting was held in Barcelona to celebrate the signing of a fraternal agreement between the anarchosyndicalists and communists. To underline the symbolic importance of the occasion, the anarchist leader García Oliver is reported to have embraced the Soviet Consul, Antonov-Ovseenko, before the throng of spectators. This as well as other signs of the growing goodwill between the two historic rivals convinced some communists that the CNT-FAI could be won over.

But not all anarchosyndicalists were amenable to the PCE's friendly overtures, and it is doubtless for this reason that the communists began

235

exhibiting contradictory behaviour towards them. At the same time as the communists were holding out the olive branch to the CNT-FAI, they publicly challenged the anarchists, and when the opportunity arose they did not hesitate to subdue the refractory elements by forcible means. The communists' role in the destruction of the Council of Aragón illustrates how their aggressive policy backfired.

THE DESTRUCTION OF THE COUNCIL OF ARAGÓN

Emboldened by the fact that the power of the revolutionaries had been broken in Catalonia, in the late spring and early summer of 1937 the anti-revolutionary forces in Valencia dramatically escalated their efforts to extend centralized control over what remained of the anti-Nationalist zone. The communists played a central role in this campaign by spearheading the government's assault against the collectivization movement in Aragón, the last bastion of anarchosyndicalist strength.

It will be remembered that the Council of Aragón was an anarchist-dominated ruling body that had been set up in Caspe during the first months of the war. Because the Madrid government invested it with considerable authority – bargaining from a relatively weaker position Largo had allowed the Council to oversee the activities of its own departments – it functioned in many respects as a separate political entity. The language of its founding charter asserted that it was at one with the Republican government and that the Council was determined to 'carry out any instructions emanating from the government'. On the other hand, its libertarian creators saw it as a vehicle for imposing revolutionary order in the region.[4] Drawing support from numerous villages that were involved in collectivist experimentation as well as from their militias stationed nearby, the anarchists dominated the affairs of the Council until it was officially dissolved in the summer of 1937.

The order for its dissolution, which was issued by the anti-anarchist Prieto, was kept secret until the Eleventh Division under the communist Enrique Líster arrived in the region.[5] At this time, Líster apparently used the military might of his forces to engage in what he later referred to as a 'psychological attack'. With tanks rolling through the streets of Caspe

---

4. Julián Casanova, 'Anarchism and Revolution in Aragon, 1936–1939', *European Historical Quarterly*, vol. XVII, 1987, p. 435.
5. Prieto, long a biter foe of the anarchosyndicalists, cooperated with the communists in the plan to dissolve this semi-autonomous body because he sided with the 'Kulak' or middle-class farmers who had been conducting a beneath-the-surface war with the anarchosyndicalists since the establishment of the Council.

and the guns of artillery units trained on nearby villages, the Council collapsed on 11 August, the day when the official decree announcing its dissolution appeared in the *Gaceta de la República*. Though the Council had disappeared without a struggle, its demise was accomplished with force and against the will of the anarchosyndicalists and their supporters. According to anarchist sources, to have resisted the decree would have meant sending in anarchist militias from the front and this would have inevitably led to another 'war within a war'. Furthermore, in the following days and weeks several hundred anarchosyndicalists who were identified as 'uncontrollables' were rounded up by the authorities and thrown into prison. Force was also applied in the ensuing campaign to dismantle the collectives themselves. A number of collective farms were summarily destroyed and, in some instances, the land, farm implements, and livestock were forcibly confiscated and redistributed to their former owners. Even communists who welcomed the end of the so-called 'Anarchist dictatorship' in the region were appalled by these methods. Not long after Líster's intervention, the communist General Secretary of the Institute of Agrarian Reform, José Silva, gave the following assessment of the results of their campaign:

> It is true that the governor's aim was to repair injustices and to convince the workers of the countryside that the Republic was protecting them, but the result was just the opposite from that intended. The measure only increased the confusion, and violence was exercised, but this time by the other side.[6]

In destroying the collectives the communists may have enhanced their position among the middle-class or 'Kulak' peasants who had dominated the countryside before the war, but they drove away far greater numbers of peasants and workers. Their recognition of this lamentable fact later obliged them to try to redress the situation by calling for the restoration of some farms. But these measures could not reverse the damage already done, for the communists were never able to dispel wholly the hatred and resentment their insensate actions had generated among the pro-libertarian workers and peasants.[7]

6. Quoted in Bolloten, *The Spanish Civil War: Revolution and Counterrevolution* (Chapel Hill, North Carolina, 1991) p. 530.
7. Another blow to the CNT-FAI in this period was dealt by the Generalitat. On 15 May the revolutionary committees, which had hitherto resisted the Generalitat's decree of 9 October 1936 calling for the dissolution of anti-fascist militias committees, were declared illegal. This was followed by mass arrests and detentions of the radical elements of the CNT-FAI.

DISSENSION IN THE LIBERTARIAN MOVEMENT GROWS

The communist assault against the collectives accelerated the demise of the revolutionary forces, but it did not, by itself, render them completely impotent. As it turned out, the ultimate demise of the revolutionaries came about as a result of the growing dissent within the CNT-FAI. Ironically, it was the repression vigorously carried out by the communists that deepened the schisms within the libertarian movement. Radical groups, like the 'Friends of Durruti' in Barcelona, tried to provoke the CNT-FAI leadership into doing something about the Communist terror in the villages and towns. But their efforts were in vain. Horacio M. Prieto, Mariano Vásquez and other top officials of the anarchosyndicalist movement refused to abandon their 'possibilist' agenda because they believed that the deteriorating political situation demanded a pragmatic rather than a revolutionary response. Even more ironic was the fact that the leaders of the FAI, once the most uncompromising revolutionary group in Spain, had come round to this position. In the summer of 1937, to mark the tenth anniversary of the founding of the FAI, a plenum was held at which it was announced that the FAI was to undergo a transformation, becoming what was called the 'new organic structure' (*nueva estructura orgánica*). According to this, the nerve-centres of the FAI, the *grupos de afinidad*, were to be dissolved and in their place would be the *Agrupación* or large group consisting of some several hundred members. In effect, the FAI was to be transformed into a mass organization.

The underlying significance of the reorganization did not escape the notice of the anarchosyndicalists who were adamantly opposed to the politicization of the libertarian movement. These dissenters inveighed against the recently constituted FAI, denouncing it as a 'new government party'. In the event, given the waning importance of the anarchosyndicalists in the Popular Front coalition, it came as no surprise when these attempts to endow the CNT-FAI with political respectability were virtually ignored by the other parties.

By this time, there was little that the anarchist purists could do to reorient the political trajectory of the CNT-FAI leadership. The fragmented nature of the dissident groups (most operated clandestinely), combined with the fact that their resistance lacked focus, prevented them from forcefully challenging the upper echelons of the CNT-FAI organizations.

THE BATTLE OF BRUNETE (JULY 1937)

There can be no question that the political squabbling and social conflicts in the rearguard sapped morale and thus seriously undermined republican military efforts in the principal theatres of war. This was graphically under-scored during the Republican military campaigns launched during the spring and summer of 1937. The Nationalists' inexorable march in the north had caused considerable frustration and anxiety among the repub-lican military leaders, who were desperate for a major victory. To halt the Nationalists, Negrín and his pro-communist military advisors resorted to diversionary tactics. In May an attack led by General Domingo Moriones Larraga was launched in Segovia, but, after driving the enemy back as far as La Granja, the republicans were eventually defeated. This was followed in July by the Republican's first significant offensive of the war: the battle of Brunete.

Masterminded by the astute military commander Vicente Rojo, the operation was initially envisaged as a two-pronged attack that would not only cut the enemy's lines of communication to the west but also stop the Nationalists' planned offensive against Santander. The attack at Brunete appeared to have a good chance of succeeding in part because it was the weakest link in the Nationalist line around Madrid but also because the republican army was at the height of its fighting abilities. Reinforced by the arrival of fresh Russian supplies – which included over 140 tanks and armoured vehicles – and the greater part of all five International Brigades, a republican force of over 80,000 men was assembled. On 6 July two army corps – the Fifth led by the communist Juan Modesto and the XVIII commanded by Colonel Jurado – were sent to take an area defended by only 2,400 Nationalist troops.

Even though complete surprise was achieved in the early hours of the first assault, the Republicans met stiff resistance from the small group of defenders, who put up a fierce struggle before the town was finally overrun by the attackers. In the meantime, Nationalist forces elsewhere responded swiftly and resolutely. By 7 July the republican advance was already slowing down, and by mid-July the Nationalists, under the command of General Varela, had mustered enough reinforcements and equipment to mount a counter-offensive. Superior Nationalist air power, combined with the republicans' failure to sustain the momentum of their initial breakthrough, proved decisive. In terms of casualties the battle turned out to be one of the bloodiest contests of the war. Exposed to the extreme conditions of a boiling hot summer as well as the constant bombardment from artillery and aircraft, men on both sides were slaughtered in great numbers. By the time it ended in late July, over 25,000 republicans and 17,000 Nationalists had been killed or wounded.

While it is true that the offensive temporarily relieved the pressure on Santander – it forced Franco to call in reserves from the northern campaign – the republicans had failed to attain the victory they sorely needed. Apart from revealing the limitations of the Popular Army's offensive capabilities, Brunete demonstrated the degree to which party politics dominated military affairs in the republican camp. At the outset, the offensive had created tensions between those who opposed the ascendancy of the communists in the military and those who supported it. In the end, however, it became a communist project: communist or pro-communist commanders and military advisors dominated the planning and execution of the battle. Miaja, the head of Madrid's military command, was placed in charge of overall operations, and he was supported by several key communist units, including Juan Modesto's prestigious Fifth Corps, Enrique Líster's Eleventh Division, and Valentín González's ('El Campesino') Forty-Sixth Division.

But the failure of the Brunete offensive not only cast doubt on the efficacy of communist strategy but it also stoked the feelings of mutual recrimination throughout the ranks of the Republican army. Thus, when the republican offensive in Aragón failed a month later, the communists blamed the defeat on the indiscipline of anarchosyndicalist militias and the insubordination of the POUM. For their part, the *cenetistas* and *poumistas* were convinced that the communists were using their hegemonic position in the army to crush what remained of the revolutionary movement.

PRIETO AND THE COMMUNISTS

Of the ministers who assumed positions in Negrín's first government, none was more delighted than Prieto to see the downfall of Largo Caballero. Because of his long-standing rivalry with the veteran UGT leader, Prieto himself had supported the feud between the communists and Largo Caballero. As we have seen, at this time the then Prime Minister not only opposed communist attempts to gain control over the political commissariat of the Republican army but he also refused to back their plans to crack down on the revolutionaries of the POUM and the CNT-FAI. Then, during the May cabinet crisis, Prieto joined many others in arguing that Largo was not up to the task of running the government and the military, and thus he welcomed the opportunity to have him removed.

It did not take long, however, for Prieto's own relations with the communists to sour. Over a number of issues, including the question of whether the socialist and communist parties should be fused, Prieto found himself increasingly at odds with his opportunistic allies.[8] The first sign of friction between them surfaced soon after Prieto became Defence Minister. In May, during air raids being conducted in the war zone around the island of Ibiza, a squadron of republican planes bombed the German pocket-battleship *Deutschland*. Without warning the Germans retaliated on 31 May by having their fleet bomb the coastal town of Almería, as a result of which a number of civilians were killed and some buildings were destroyed. Apparently reasoning that a bold act was needed in order to force the hand of the Western allies, Prieto reacted to the news by calling for further Republican air attacks, but this time against all German warships in the region. Negrín and the communists thought otherwise and they therefore opted for restraint. In so doing, they had cast their first vote of no confidence in the Defence Minister.

It was Prieto's determination to check the growth of communist influence in the military that led to a final break between them. Although he had seen Largo Caballero fight a losing battle against communist efforts to dominate military affairs, Prieto believed that he was capable of curbing their unconcealed ambition to control the army. He did this by directly challenging their positions in the political commissariat system. While he failed to have this institution abolished, he took decisive steps to stop communist proselytism in the army and successfully blocked the promotion of several hundred new commissars, the majority of whom were either communists or communist sympathizers. This last measure naturally infuriated the communists and precipitated the resignation of the pro-Soviet General Commissar of War Alvarez del Vayo. For a brief moment it looked as though Prieto had paved the way for the dismemberment of the extensive communist network in the army. Yet, in the aftermath of several disastrous Republican military iniatives that took place in late 1937, Prieto's gains were completely reversed.

In the winter of 1937–38, the Republicans decided to relieve the pressure the Nationalists were exerting against Madrid by mounting an attack against the town of Teruel, a provincial capital in Aragón situated some 200 miles east of Madrid. Led by Vicente Rojo, some 77,000 Republican troops easily breached the poorly-held Nationalist lines and, by the first week in January, had captured the town. Their victory, though, had not been easy: the battle for Teruel was fought in one of the bitterest winters in recorded history and men on both sides were at the point of complete exhaustion when the fighting ended.

---

8. Before the May crisis, when his relations with the communists were friendly, Prieto apparently joined other members of the PSOE executive in calling for the fusion of the two parties. See Álvarez del Vayo, *The Last Optimist* (New York, 1950), pp. 288–9. By July, however, he had reversed his stance on this issue.

The Republican conquest had greatly wounded Franco's pride, and for this reason he decided to postpone his assault on Madrid. By mid-January the Nationalists were already concentrating their forces for a counter-attack. Bad weather once again slowed military operations, but the Nationalists nevertheless managed to press their advance steadily forward. On 22 February, after sustaining the punishing blows of a massive cavalry charge and heavy aerial attacks, Republicans were forced to abandon the town and the battle came to an end.

The defeat had staggered the Popular Army both physically and morally. Apart from having suffered heavy casualties, it had been deprived of yet another much-needed victory. Even more significant was the fact that the Nationalists were now poised to deliver a crushing blow to Republican units in the eastern sector. Sensing the acute vulnerability of his adversaries, Franco launched a huge offensive in Aragón which aimed to cut the Republican zone in two. In just six weeks of fighting his forces managed to break through all Republican defences, and they reached the Mediterranean on 15 April 1938. Republican Spain was now split into two zones.

Parallel to these developments, the communists, still smarting from the effects of Prieto's anti-communist policies, were plotting his overthrow. Although it proved too difficult for them to assign all the responsibility for the failure of Teruel and the debacle taking place in Aragón to the Defence Minister, they nevertheless argued in the light of these events that his exceedingly negative attitude was fatally undermining the morale of the army. Rumours that Prieto was encouraging capitulation to the Nationalists provoked a cabinet crisis in late March. Confronted by the communists' relentless determination to oust Prieto, Negrín dismissed his Minister of Defence on the grounds that his pessimism demoralized his colleagues. Refusing the Premier's offer to accept a minor cabinet post (Minister in charge of Public Works and Railways), Prieto subsequently resigned from the government.

Whether Negrín's decision to remove Prieto was the result of communist pressure remains in dispute. But there can be no doubt it had been made only after a great deal of agonizing. Prieto was highly respected in foreign diplomatic circles and, as the leader of the moderate wing of the Socialist Party, his presence in Negrín's government had invested it with greater authority. It was also true, however, that Prieto himself had given up hope of a Republican victory. Against the background of mounting military disasters and the unstoppable advance of the Nationalists on all fronts, Prieto had felt compelled to consider the price of resistance in human terms. Was the ceaseless slaughter of civilians and military personnel too high a price to pay for continuing the struggle? Prieto, thought so, and that is why he began calling for a cessation of hostilities. But the idea of capitulation was too abhorrent for Negrín and the communists to consider. Prieto was thus labeled a 'defeatist', and, like the obstructionist *caballeristas* and revolutionaries before him, he also fell from grace. What is beyond question is that, with his departure, there was no one left in the cabinet who could seriously challenge the communists.

WINNING THE WAR OF PROPAGANDA

As important as military engagements were in determining the outcome of the war, neither the Nationalists nor the Republicans neglected the struggle to win over the hearts and minds of the Spanish and international communities. The siege of Toledo, the Battle of Madrid and the bombing of Guernica had demonstrated the potency of propaganda and therefore each side regarded it as an indispensable weapon in the war.[9] The Spanish civil war was the first modern conflict in which propaganda was used on such a massive scale and in so many different media formats: posters (some of which made use of new techniques like the photomontage), pamphlets, photographs, film documentaries (a genre only recently developed), radio and theatre were used to promote the various ideological causes. On both sides, the production of propaganda also extended to the world of art and literature which, in the context of war, was inevitably highly politicized. In this connection it is essential to bear in mind that the Spanish war broke out during a period when the idea of 'art for art's sake' was increasingly being challenged. Therefore a literary or artistic work being labelled 'partisan' or 'propagandistic' did not necessarily carry with it a negative connotation. For many on the left and the right the idea of art being compromised so that it could be put to a political purpose was regarded as a sign of ideological commitment. Arthur Koestler recalls in his memoirs, *The Invisible Writing*, that his first efforts to write a propaganda book on Spain were criticized for being 'Too weak. Too objective' by his communist publisher Willy Muenzenberg. He, as well as others who saw the communist movement as the last great hope against fascism, willingly subordinated their work to the service of the Party.

Some of the most distinguished artists, poets, writers, movie stars,

---

9. This first became apparent during the First World War. In their efforts to rally support and mobilize civilians on a massive scale, governments on both sides found that propaganda was the most effective tool. Thousands of recruiting posters in Great Britain, for example, beckoned men to serve their country in its time of need, and these were reinforced by posters which depicted the enemy as Evil incarnate: barbarous hordes of German 'huns' threatening to devour Western civilization. Given the extent to which ideology had come to dominate the political debates of the 1930s, it would therefore have been surprising if either the Nationalists or the Republicans had regarded propaganda any differently.

musicians and intellectuals from Europe and the Americas took a stand on Spain's tragic war.[10] Though not always as forthcoming as the left about their political preferences, Nationalist supporters included the American poet Ezra Pound, the English writer Evelyn Waugh, the French poet Paul Claudel and his fellow countryman Charles Maurras. A far more impressive number of famous women and men from the world of *belles lettres* sided with the republicans. Among the writers, dramatists, and poets who became 'writer-tourists' during the war were Octavio Paz, César Vallejo, Pablo Neruda, Josephine Herbst, Malcolm Cowley, Ernest Hemingway, Theodore Dreiser, John Dos Passos, Lillian Hellman, Langston Hughes, Herbert Read, David Gascoyne, Julian Bell, Stephen Spender, and W.H. Auden.[11]

There were lesser known but in some respects equally important writers and thinkers who were drawn to Spain's revolution and anti-fascist struggle. The alternative or far left was especially well represented.[12] The Italian anarchist philosopher Camillo Berneri, who was murdered under mysterious circumstances in Barcelona during the May Events, was perhaps the most articulate and cogent critic of the libertarian policy of collaboration.[13] Similarly, the American anarchist-feminist Emma Goldman travelled to Spain as a participant observer. Later she campaigned on behalf of the Spanish revolution through her work in the International Anti-Fascist Solidarity organization based in London. The Trotskyist Surrealist poets Mary Low, Juan Brea and Benjamin Péret were also in Spain to promote the revolution. Low, for example, edited the English edition of the POUM's *The Spanish Revolution,* and worked for several months in the propaganda section of the Generalitat. But mainly because they were involved in movements about which most foreigners were ignorant or towards which

10. Among the better known artists were the British sculptor Henry Moore, Joan Miró, Pablo Picasso and Ben Nicholson, all of whom rallied to Republican Spain, not by going to Spain to fight but by painting or sculpting what the war meant to them. Famous musicians and Hollywood supporters included Benny Goodman, Joan Crawford, Errol Flynn, and Shirley Temple.

11. One has to make a clear distinction between this group of committed foreigners who came to Spain to fight or contribute their talents to the war effort and those who came because it was 'the thing to do'. The latter were celebrity 'tourists' who travelled to the front lines in Madrid and elsewhere because it offered them a 'photo opportunity' or a feature story in a leading magazine and not because they were acting on their political convictions.

12. The Spanish revolution aroused a great deal of interest in various countries. In the United States, for example, small but highly motivated groups of anarchists and Trotskyists threw their energies into organizing rallies and publishing news in support of the Spanish left. A brief summary of their activities can be found in Franklin Rosemont's entry entitled 'Spanish Revolution of 1936' in *Encyclopedia of the American Left,* Edited by Mary Jo Buhle, *et al.* (New York, 1990).

13. On the assassination of Berneri see George Esenwein's footnote to the May Events in Bolloten, *The Spanish Civil War,* pp. 875–7.

they were apathetic, their viewpoints and writings were overshadowed by communist propaganda as well as by all the publicity given to the 'celebrity' authors mentioned above.[14]

André Malraux, Gustav Regler, Ralph Bates, John Cornford, David Alfaro Siqueiros, Máté Zalka, George Orwell, Ludwig Renn, and Simone Weil were among those who went to Spain as *les hommes et les femmes engagés*, that is, those who were willing to lay down their lives for the Republican cause. The Hungarian writer Zalka, using the *nom de guerre* General Lukacz, was one of the first commanders of the International Brigades, while the French writer Malraux helped to organize a Republican air force squadron, Esquadrilla España. Except for Weil, who enlisted as a non-combatant in the POUM militia, Cornford, who was killed in action, Renn, Regler, Siqueiros, and Orwell all served either as military leaders or as foot-soldiers.

On the republican side, the production of propaganda was a complicated affair that grew increasingly problematic over the course of the war. Unlike in the Nationalist camp, where all media forms were controlled by a single authority, propaganda was for many months generated from a variety of sources. Thus (even though all forms of republican propaganda promoted the struggle against the rebels) Basques, Catalans, anarchosyndicalists, socialists, independent Marxists, Stalinists and others competed for public space in order to present their sectarian messages. The CNT-FAI extolled the revolution and gave pride of place to social messages in their poster art ('Read anarchist books and you will become human!'), PCE propaganda glorified the war effort, whereas the separatists used their literature and art to inspire patriotism among those struggling to defend their homelands against 'foreign' invasion.

This profusion of political and social messages mirrored the particularism that characterized early Republican Spain. But as different as the themes of the various parties may have been, they were not at first seen as being mutually exclusive. This, of course, changed over time. As the war dragged on Republican propaganda became less colourful and kaleidoscopic in its themes. Harrowing pictures of children mutilated by bullets and bombs, and stern messages that dwelled on the dangers of rearguard traitors, increasingly displaced the mostly positive and affirming images associated with the initial stages of the revolution and war. The lingering pall of death, destruction and military defeats contributed to this shifting emphasis,

14. Berneri's writings appeared in Italian and Spanish. See, especially, *Guerra de clases en España* (Barcelona, 1977). Emma Goldman's writings on Spain have been collected in *Vision on Fire* (New Palz, N.Y., 1983). The eye-witness testimony of Mary Low and Juan Brea, *Red Spanish Notebook* (San Francisco, 1979), still stands as one of the clearest pictures of how the revolution affected the daily lives of men and women.

but so, too, did the internecine struggles among the rival political groups. The May Events had demonstrated that political differences could easily degenerate into physical confrontations, and thus it became increasingly difficult to maintain an open arena for the production of propaganda. Because they saw the escalation of state censorship as a way of suffocating their movement, the revolutionaries chafed at having their propagandizing efforts muzzled: but from mid–1937 on, the anarchosyndicalists and POUM found themselves powerless to do anything about it. On the other hand, the communists and the moderate republican parties took satisfaction in reining in what they saw as the intemperate revolutionary media. Instead they insisted that the Popular Front forces speak with one voice both inside Spain and to the international community. To those who supported Negrín's and the communists' policies this step was of utmost importance. For they believed that unless the Western democratic societies and governments were convinced that it was in their best interests to stop fascism in Spain, the republicans stood little chance of winning the war.

As they had done in their drive to dominate the Popular Army, the communists used the leverage they were acquiring in their rise to political prominence to define and control the production of the Popular Front's propaganda programme. Over time their activities in this area followed a discernible pattern. As a rule it was true that the more they overcame opposition to their predominance the more Republican propaganda became largely a communist affair.

The communists were particularly successful at manufacturing heroes and heroines for the consumption of the popular media. Using their numerous publications, the radio and their access to international communications, they transformed republicans like General Kléber (the charismatic Soviet head of the Eleventh International Brigade who was hailed as the saviour of Madrid), 'La Pasionaria,' General Miaja and (after his murder) Buenaventura Durruti into larger-than-life figures. They also proved adept at extracting all the publicity they could from the international celebrities who came to Spain. Prominent communists and pro-communist republicans often arranged tours to selected war zones so that distinguished visitors came away with the right impressions. On the whole these chaperoned trips produced the expected results: in the company of their escorts, reporters, Hollywood stars and foreign politicians rarely got a glimpse of the revolutionary side of the republic. Instead they saw what mostly appeared to be a functioning democracy which was free of left-wing domination.

In their attempt to shape world opinion about the war, the communists also ran their own propaganda programme. The printed media was the cheapest and easiest means of putting their message across. Pamphlets were used to disseminate information about the 'true' significance of Spain's war to a wide audience. Various themes were dealt with but most portrayed Spain's war as a contest between fascism and democracy (not fascism versus communism), while others dealt with specialist topics, such as the POUM and the international fascist conspiracy. The most popular of these were translated into the major languages and distributed widely in Europe and the United States by the Comintern's international propaganda network. Among the outstanding propagandists they called upon to write were the Russian Mikhail Kolstov, *Izvestia* correspondent Ilya Ehrenburg, the British writer Ralph Bates, the American journalist Louis Fisher (the first American to enrol in the International Brigades), the Italian communist leader, Palmiro Togliatti ('Alfredo' who wrote under the *nom de plume* 'Ercole Ercoli'), the German dramatist Ernst Toller, and the French journalist Georges Soria.[15]

Inside Republican Spain, the communists also exercised a guiding hand in creating a uniform 'Popular Front' literature during the last year-and-a-half of the war. The writers and poets associated with the literary journals *Hora de España* and *El Mono Azul* – both of which were heavily influenced by the communist perspective – formed the core of this literary movement, which was represented by such well known figures as Miguel Hernández, León Felipe, Antonio Machado, Rafael Alberti, José Bergamín, and Álvarez del Vayo.[16]

It is essential to emphasize here that not all the writers and poets who belonged to the Popular Front cultural milieu were communists. Nor can it be said that they were merely communist 'dupes'. While travelling in Spain in 1937 the British (and at the time communist) poet Stephen Spender made the following observation:

> From reading the Romances of the Spanish civil war by Spanish poets, one might conclude that the whole of Spanish poetry on the Government side had adopted an uncritical, heroic attitude towards the war. Yet this is not so . . . when I spoke to Alberti, Altolaguirre and Bergamín, I found that they felt about the propagandist heroics of the war much as I did myself. Alberti, a brilliant, arrogant, passionate individualist, is himself rather isolated.[17]

Whatever they may have thought and said in private, in public they acted differently. As a group, Popular Front authors tended to accept the

---

15. Apart from his many contributions to the British and American press, Bates briefly edited the International Brigade paper *Volunteer for Liberty.*
16. In a war where lines separating art from social engagement had disappeared, literary works and artistic reproductions could also be found in the front-line newspapers of the militias.
17. Spender is referring here to the *Romancero general de la guerra*, which was a collection of Popular Front poems published in Madrid and Valencia in 1937. See his memoir *The Thirties and After* (New York, 1978), pp. 50–7.

communists' position on nearly every major issue, and, whether wittingly or not, their work was *used* by the communists in their carefully managed national and international media campaign.[18] This was demonstrated in a variety of ways but was most graphically underscored at the International Writers' Congress held in Valencia and Madrid in 1937. The event, which proved to be a showpiece of communist propaganda, drew to Republican Spain some of the best literary talents in the world. After discussing the relationship between writers and war, the vast majority of participants endorsed the notion promoted by the communists of the writer *engagé*. Miguel Hernández summarized their position when he wrote: 'All theatre, all poetry, and all art has to be, today more than ever, a weapon of war.' For those who had doubts, an appropriate example was found in the case of André Gide. For having recently spoken out against the excesses in the Soviet Union in his *Retour de l'URSS*, the French author and former communist was condemned by the Congress president Bergamín as a traitor to the anti-fascist cause. Again apropos Gide, the question of censoring literature in the name of a political cause was also taken up. Though it ran counter to their professed belief in democratic principles, the consensus among the writers was that censorship was a tool that had to be employed in the left-right dialectic.[19]

Popular Front supporters abroad also adopted the communist line *vis-à-vis* the problem of dissent. Contrary or 'politically incorrect' opinions were either ignored or outrightly condemned as undermining the Republican cause. Two important eye-witness testimonies written during the war proved that telling the truth had its price. Franz Borkenau's frank assessment of Republican politics in his *The Spanish Cockpit* went 'against the editorial policy' of the *New Statesman* in Great Britain, while Orwell's revelations that republican unity was being rent asunder by the violent quarrelling between the Stalinists and revolutionaries were, except for a handful of

18. In addition a certain number of propagandists were neither politically naive nor blinded by communist dogma. Late in the war, when they were well aware of how badly the war was going for the republicans, writers like Claude Cockburn – also known as 'Frank Pitcairn', a communist reporter for the *News Chronicle* – and the Russian Michael Kolstov privately expressed their pessimism about the prospects of victory. Their cynicism, though, did not stop them from fostering, in the words of Cockburn, the illusion that sooner or later 'the "world conscience" would be aroused . . . the "common people" in Britain and France would force their Governments to end non-intervention, and the war would be won'. Claude Cockburn, *I, Claude* (London, 1967), p. 168.
19. With their views on these issues greatly modified by the passage of time, some of the surviving literary figures returned to Spain in June 1987 to commemorate the 50th anniversary of the Second International Congress of Antifascist Writers. See, for example, Walter Haubrich, 'Letter from Valencia', *Encounter* (London, September–October, 1987), pp. 39–41; and Octavio Paz, 'The Barricades and Beyond', in *The New Republic* (New York, 9 November 1987), pp. 26–30.

independent left-wing circles, met with hostility. Orwell himself found it practically impossible to publish his highly readable, *Homage to Catalonia*, and after the book appeared it was, for political reasons, consigned to obscurity for several years.

Likewise John Dos Passos, the American novelist who had come to Spain to write about the war, was told by Ernest Hemingway that he had no business criticizing the communists, who, after all, were defending the anti-fascist cause. Even though it cost him his friendship with Hemingway, Dos Passos refused to close his eyes to the strong-handed methods of the Stalinists.[20] He later left Spain both shocked and dejected after learning that his friend José Robles Pazos had been, like Andreu Nin, arrested and murdered by communist agents.[21]

At least for the communists it was not enough to tailor republican propaganda to fit the Popular Front image they wanted to project to the outside world. In order to enhance their power and influence over Republican affairs – which was necessary if they were to serve effectively the political interests of the Soviet Union – they further endeavoured to infiltrate the government's communications media. To appreciate fully the degree to which the communists came to dominate republican communications it should be borne in mind that they ran most of the Republican government's international news agencies and/or propaganda bureaus in Paris (Agence Espagne), London (Spanish News Agency) and elsewhere in Europe and the Americas. They also occupied key media positions. In his capacity as Foreign Minister, the pro-communist Álvarez del Vayo selected Constancia de la Mora (the communist grand-daughter of Antonio Maura) as chief censor of the Foreign Press Bureau, one of the principal gateways for disseminating information to the outside world. Another communist appointee of Álvarez del Vayo, Liston Oak, briefly headed the office of propaganda for the United States and England. Years after the war, Oak admitted that he had been instructed to censor all reports that testified to the revolutionary transformations in Spain's economic system.

Though they never established 'totalitarian' control over communications, their efforts to manipulate the media were highly successful. Despite the fact that papers across the left-wing spectrum continued to be published, all were subject to the scrutinizing gaze of state censors, and,

20. Until they parted company, Dos Passos was also working with Hemingway on Joris Ivens' film, 'The Spanish Earth'.
21. What seems to have particularly disturbed Orwell, and Dos Passos, as well as a number of others who became disillusioned by their experiences in Spain, was the practice – on both the left and right – of writing history '. . . not in terms of what happened but of what ought to have happened according to the various "party lines" '. This led Orwell to comment rather cynically some years after the war that the idea of writing a truthful history had been abandoned.

with few exceptions, news that did not conform to the communist interpretation of events was deleted from press communiqués. In some instances, such as the May crisis, news reports emanating from communist sources were released to the foreign press in advance of government approval. In this way, they could better ensure that foreign coverage of the war remained consistent with their own version of events. These and numerous similar examples strongly indicate that the communists' propaganda efforts were designed to promote their own agenda, and not necessarily that of Republican Spain as a whole.

PROPAGANDA AND THE NATIONALISTS

We have already pointed out that the Falange ran the most dynamic propaganda programme in the Nationalist zone. After Franco assumed leadership of the *Movimiento*, however, this was controlled by the Burgos government. Nationalist propaganda generally assumed two forms. One was designed to reflect their commitment to an indivisible Spain imbued with a mix of fascist and traditionalist values, while the other – intended to appeal to foreign opinion – harshly condemned the barbarism of the 'Red' zone. Poster art, especially the work of Carlos Sáenz de Tejada, stirred Nationalist sentiment by linking Catholic spirituality with images of war. After 1937, Franco himself became the subject of Nationalist propaganda. His highly romanticized portrait became a central element in the iconography of the *cruzada*. As Napoleon had been elevated to the status of a roman emperor in the classical portraits of Jacques-Louis David, so Franco was frequently portrayed as the modern-day El Cid, the saviour of divided Spain.

Nationalist themes were also echoed in the poems and writings of Ernesto Giménez Caballero, José María Pemán, Ramiro de Maeztu (who was imprisoned and later killed by the republicans) and others whose works were published in journals like *Acción Española*, *Vértice*, and *Jerarquía*. Although expressed in different styles – the Falangists were partial to the experimental modernistic conventions – Nationalist authors saw their writings as a collective enterprise. They spoke with one voice about the need for hierarchical order, national unity and the preservation of the Catholic Church.

Like the republicans, the Nationalists also made use of the traveling theatre. The Burgos government set up the Teatro Ambulante de Campaña in 1938, which specialized in passion plays. By far the most effective propaganda medium was the radio, which was used to great effect by the Church and the military. The idiosyncratic Quiepo de Llano, frequently parodied in republican propaganda literature, gained widespread recognition for his lurid marathon broadcasts over Radio Sevilla.[22]

Even more so than on the other side, literature and art that was brought into the service of Nationalist propaganda was more political than it was literary. And if the writings and artistic expressions of the right emerged as being more stilted and conceptually shallower than those on the left, this can be attributed to the Nationalists' deep-seated distrust of intellectual activity, which was generally viewed as a left-wing vice. The anti-intellectualism of the right was a bitter pill for some to swallow. Miguel de Unamuno was reminded of this not long after the war had begun. At a public celebration commemorating Columbus' voyage to the New World (the fiesta of *La Raza*), Unamuno is said to have admonished the bellicose Millán Astray for shouting out the battle-cry of the Foreign Legion: ¡*Viva la muerte!* (Long live Death!) Turning to the old professor, Millán screamed in his face: '¡Mueran los intelectuales!' ('Death to intellectuals!'). Unamuno's failure to convince the Nationalists that 'might does not make right' later troubled him and others who had supported the *Cruzada* in the misplaced belief that it would save Spain from the anti-civilized forces of the left.

THE FRUITS OF VICTORY

Who won the war of propaganda? Clearly the Nationalists did not. Their chauvinistic propaganda, which was aimed at unifying the Spanish, had limited success, while their international message – that communism represented a threat not just to Spain but to the rest of the world as well – failed to make new converts. Staunch pro-Nationalists (like the demagogic Father Coughlin in the United States who excoriated Red Spain over the radio and at public meetings) never wavered in their support, but others proved to be less dogmatic. As time passed, pro-Nationalist groups abroad grew increasingly divided over the war. Following highly publicized events like Badajoz and Guernica, it was much harder to sustain the view that the Nationalists alone were defending the spirituality of Christianity and the values of Western civilization.

By comparison, the communist-led Popular Front propaganda campaign was far more successful at both the national and international levels. By 1938 it was apparent that their considerable propaganda efforts were paying off. In the United States, for example, the communists rallied support for the Popular Front government by staging mass rallies and demonstrations,

22. Alun Kenwood, *The Spanish Civil War* (Oxford, 1993), p. 29.

sponsoring fund-raising and relief activities, and coordinating extensive speaking tours that featured Popular Front propagandists like Ralph Bates, André Malraux, and José Bergamín. In the end, these campaigns swayed public opinion in the Western countries not least because the largely liberal-democratic audiences of Great Britain and the United States wanted to believe that the civil war was not about revolution or communism but rather was a contest between democracy and fascism.

The communists profited from having won the war of propaganda on the left in several ways. From a diplomatic standpoint, they were now in a better position to present the Soviet case for collective security. Against the background of Hitler's unchecked provocations in Austria and Czecho-slovakia, republicans argued more convincingly than before from the public platforms of the League of Nations and other international organizations that Republican Spain was not 'Red' and that the downfall of their democratically-elected government implicitly threatened the security of other democratic countries. Nevertheless, the impact of these efforts was mixed. The impassioned speeches of La Pasionaria, Álvarez del Vayo and other leading propagandists continued to generate popular enthusiasm for the Republic right up to the end of the war. But they did little to move foreign governments. Negrín's last major speech to the League of Nations on 21 September 1938 is a case in point. Though his offer to withdraw all foreign volunteers serving in the International Brigades was meant as a supreme gesture of the political integrity and independence of his regime, the Western powers did not find it compelling. Their attention was now focussed on Central Europe and, as we have seen, in this area they were steadfastly committed to a policy of appeasement.

Having become the principal architects of the Popular Front's propaganda programme under Negrín, the communists had also triumphed on the domestic front. Thanks to them the republican cause was no longer identified with the revolutionary elements. Instead, Spain's struggle was pictured simply as a war of national liberation against the international forces of fascism. Among other things this helped to legitimate their efforts to suppress opposition. The credibility of those who refused to accept the principles underlying Negrín's 'government of victory' and 'government of concentration' – notably, Prieto, the left socialists of the FNTT and the 'uncontrollable' elements of the anarchosyndicalists – was besmeared in the press and on the radio; critics were dubbed as 'defeatists,' or worse, saboteurs. The war would now be won or lost in the name of the Popular Front regime that ruled from mid-1937 until the end of the war.

THE POPULAR FRONT IN 1938: A GOVERNMENT OF VICTORY?

Now that the obstinate Largo Caballero and arrogant Prieto were out of the way and the revolutionary movement in Catalonia, Aragón and elsewhere had been subdued, the possibilities at last existed for the consolidation of the Spanish Popular Front programme under the Negrín government. But in the light of all that had transpired in the course of civil war and revolution, what did the Popular Front stand for? Because of the dramatic metamorphosis of Republican politics that had occurred since July 1936, the nature and purpose of the Popular Front coalition in 1938 bore little resemblance to what had come into being in February 1936. For a start, the composition of the Popular Front was radically different from before. From June 1937 until the end of the war the coalition of the republican parties cannot in any meaningful sense be regarded as pluralistic. The revolutionary left, though not rendered completely powerless, had no real voice in political affairs, and the fact that other parties represented in the government were dominated by the communists meant that they could not be counted on to act independently.

Negrín, like many other supporters of the Popular Front, seems to have genuinely believed that their strategy for winning the war – which after 1938 was known as the policy of resistance – was the only one that stood a realistic chance of working. And his actions in late 1938 can be understood only by taking this into account. Central to this policy was the belief that the Nationalists could not be defeated militarily. Negrín and the communists therefore reasoned that the republicans' only hope was to hold on to power until a general war broke out in Europe. When this happened they were confident that Spain's conflict would be subsumed into the larger one, thus giving the republicans another opportunity to overcome Franco. Given the general drift of European affairs at this time, such an outcome appeared highly probable. In fact, general war did come, but it came too late for Republican Spain.

There were further reasons why Negrín felt obliged to strengthen his alliance with the communists. In view of the overwhelmingly superior material support that the Nationalists were receiving from the fascist powers, Negrín did not want to upset the Soviets, whose material aid to the Republic was already steadily declining. Having witnessed the rise and fall of both Largo and Prieto before him, Negrín also knew that the communists were so deeply embedded in the military and political fabric of the republican zone that, even if he wanted to, it would be impossible to dislodge them completely. To do so would have involved an upheaval of major proportions, and this, of course, would have sealed the fate of

Republican Spain. In any case, Negrín was not particularly hostile to the communists or their methods. Like them he believed it was necessary to consolidate the rule of the central government, even if this meant suppressing the autonomous and revolutionary movements.

Beginning in the spring, the Premier launched the first in a series of initiatives that were designed to promote the policy of resistance to which he was now committed. At the end of April he issued the centrepiece of his campaign, the famous Thirteen War Aims Speech. Plainly intended to demonstrate Spain's independence from Moscow and thereby prevail upon the Western powers to intervene in the Spanish conflict, this important document outlined an exceedingly moderate political programme, which emphasized both the democratic nature and purpose of his régime. Among other things, it called for the full guarantee and protection of civil and political liberties, the respect of private property, and the 'free exercise of religious beliefs and practices'.[23] Like Woodrow Wilson's famous 'Fourteen Points' which helped to hasten the end of the First World War, it was hoped that Negrín's 'Thirteen Points' would provide the basis for a negotiated settlement in Spain. With Franco's forces closing in on victory and the political situation in Europe heating up, the Republicans were keenly aware that their window of opportunity for such a settlement was rapidly narrowing.

Negrín's speech was followed by an intensive publicity campaign in Europe and the Americas. The climax of this came in the autumn with the formal withdrawal of the International Brigades. At the farewell parade held in Barcelona on 15 November, thousands gathered to hear La Pasionaria, Negrín and other notable republicans pay tribute to the 10,000 or so remaining foreign volunteers. In what may well be her most memorable public address, La Pasionaria stirred the huge crowds of spectators when she waxed emotional about their achievements. She praised their self-sacrificing contributions to the Republican cause and proclaimed them heroes whose actions were 'examples of democracy's solidarity and universality'.

23. Published in *La Vanguardia*, 1 May 1938, and later issued in pamphlet form in various languages. Since no mention was made of the revolution, the radical segments of the CNT-FAI quite understandably speculated as to whether this was the government's first public announcement that the revolutionary movement would be completely 'liquidated'. But the anarchosyndicalist leadership as a whole did not interpret it as a counter-revolutionary document. Rather they followed Negrín and other *negrinistas* in seeing the proclamation as a necessary diplomatic move at a moment when the Republic had reached its greatest hour of need.

THE BATTLE OF THE EBRO AND THE FALL OF CATALONIA

In the summer of 1938, the Popular Front government decided to reinforce its diplomatic efforts and international propaganda campaign by demonstrating that the Republican army was not just staving off a complete collapse but rather was capable of achieving victory. The Republican general staff therefore laid plans for a major offensive.

It will be recalled that on 15 April Franco's forces had severed Catalonia from the rest of the Republic. But instead of conquering the now isolated Catalonia – where the seat of the central government resided – Franco decided to turn his troops towards Valencia. This was done primarily because he was fearful that the sharpening crises in Central Europe would soon erupt into war. If this were to happen, Franco could no longer count on Nazi assistance, and, in the event that France became a belligerent, his troops might be confronted with a two-front war. Besides prolonging Spain's own conflict, his decision to direct the Nationalist drive south came as the reprieve the Republican general staff were waiting for. Hoping to catch the Nationalists off guard, at the end of July they decided to launch their attack along the Ebro river. From the beginning the stakes were high: a republican triumph might well extend the war until it could become internationalized, while a defeat would spell certain doom for the Republican cause.

The Battle of the Ebro became the last great military contest of the war. Once again, the republican forces were led by Vicente Rojo and placed under communist supervision. General Modesto commanded the recently formed Army of the Ebro, and all the division commanders were also communists. The burden of defence was placed on the shoulders of the Falangist General Yagüe, the head of Nationalist forces in the northeast.

In the opening exchanges, the Republican army quickly gained the advantage, inflicting heavy casualties on Yagüe's troops. Their greatest achievement was the bridgehead they established across the river, which allowed them to push deeper into Nationalist territory. But before penetrating too far, their drive was halted towards the end of July by air attacks from the Condor Legion. At this point the battle intensified. Unwilling to relinquish their hold on the territory they had sacrificed so much to conquer, the republicans dug in against the enemy. Though badly in need of fresh supplies and reinforcements, they held out until November, when a Nationalist offensive pushed them back across the river.

Because the fighting had exhausted the Republican army of nearly all its resources, the defeat came as a terrible setback. Apart from incurring approximately 100,000 casualties – men who had been killed, wounded or taken prisoner – the army had depleted its short supply of war *matériel*, much of which had been left behind by retreating soldiers. Equally significant was the devastating impact the loss had on morale. Once again the Republican military was on the verge of victory only to have it snatched from them by an opponent that possessed superior firepower.

Hard on the heels of this latest military disaster, Negrín and his government begged the Soviets for more material assistance. But these calls for help went unanswered.[24] In fact, Soviet aid had been steadily declining in the months leading up to the Battle of the Ebro and this pattern continued until the end of the war. At the time it was difficult for the Spanish to fathom the meaning of this. After all, though their credit was overextended, Republican politicians were closely adhering to Moscow's policy of resistance.[25] What was not well known, however, was that Stalin was rapidly losing faith in the idea that France and Great Britain could be persuaded to join an anti-fascist bloc. In the diplomatic arena his cynicism had recently been validated by a succession of revealing events: Germany's annexation of Austria (March 1938), the Anglo-Italian treaty signed in April, and the Munich Crisis of September. In the latter, Chamberlain and the appeasers had caved in to Nazi aggression for, by endorsing the Munich Agreement of 30 September, they had effectively signed over the independence of Czechoslovakia. In view of these disturbing developments, Soviet diplomats began preparing the ground for an entirely different foreign policy strategy. The fruits of their efforts produced the biggest diplomatic bombshell of the inter-war years. Several months after the Spanish war had ended the German and Soviet governments announced their Pact of Non-Aggression.

As far as Spain was concerned, diplomatic events in the summer and autumn of 1938 pointed to the fact that Europe was no longer interested in her tragic struggle. With the establishment of a united front of appeasers, Negrín's policy of resistance against fascism was rendered meaningless. Perhaps because of his unshakeable belief in the efficacy of this policy or perhaps because he had closed his eyes to reality, Negrín continued to cling to the slender hope that it was not too late to reverse the course of international politics.

One month after the Battle of the Ebro, the Nationalists opened their offensive against Catalonia. With much of the Republican Army in tatters, it did not take them long to reach the capital, Barcelona. Collapse came in the last days of January 1939. In the final moments of resistance, the

24. Appeals for aid continued until the last month of the war, and though a shipment of Soviet arms reached Spain during the Catalonian offensive it arrived too late to stop Franco's onslaught.
25. In March, Negrín and his ambassador in Moscow, Marcelino Pascua, had found it difficult to obtain a credit of $70 million.

city threw all of its resources into the fray, but, without arms and munitions, there was little its inhabitants could do to defend themselves. On 23 January, Negrín and his government evacuated Barcelona and were forced temporarily to transfer the bulk of government operations to the Castle of Figueras near the Spanish-French border. The truth is that the government was in shambles and the move had only bought Negrín and his entourage a little time. Before Catalonia fell to the Nationalists in early February, the Premier, his cabinet, the sixty-four remaining deputies of the Cortes, and the politburo of the PCE had fled across the border. Just ahead of the advancing Nationalist army was an 'avalanche' of republican refugees: over 400,000 men, women and children were slowly making their way to the French frontier. The war was grinding to an end, but the Republican government steadfastly refused to surrender.

WHAT ARE THE PARTIES FIGHTING FOR?

To understand the course of events on the Republican side during the last few months of the war, it is necessary to review the positions held by the various groups under Negrín's last administration (known as the 'government of National Union'). Despite all the political wranglings on the left and the demoralizing military defeats, at first glance it appeared as though there had been no breach of the Popular Front coalition. The composition of his twelve-member cabinet formed in mid-August 1938 included representatives from the socialist, communist, left-republican, anarchist and Basque parties. Yet its diverse complexion was deceptive, for the new government did not represent a broad spectrum of opinion. A closer look at the members holding portfolios reveals that nearly all were *negrínistas*. Besides the moderate socialists, republicans, and communists, Negrín counted among his supporters Segundo Blanco, the CNT Minister of Education and Health, and Tomás Bilbao, a member of the tiny Basque Nationalist Action Party, who was a minister without portfolio. These last two appointments were clearly sops that Negrín had thrown out to his critics. In the former case, the Premier wanted to give the impression that his government was amenable to anarchist opinion; and in the latter, he wanted to demonstrate that his cabinet was not indifferent to the interests of the autonomous movements.

It was not until the reconstitution of the second Negrín administration on 5 April 1938 that the CNT re-entered the central government, but, considering that Segundo Blanco was a *negrinista*, his presence in the cabinet counted for little as far as the radical left was concerned. Far from improving the position of the anarchosyndicalists *vis-à-vis* their political rivals, the re-entry of the CNT into the government only served to drive a wedge deeper within the libertarian movement. By the time Segundo Blanco was reappointed in 1938 the libertarian community was so riven with discord over the ideological and practical consequences of governmental collaboration that it had neither the unity nor the leverage to influence the course of events. The mainstream of the movement, as represented by the National Committee of the CNT, was still decidedly pro-collabo- rationist – although few had gone as far to the right as Horacio Prieto, who was by now convinced that *apoliticismo* was dead and libertarian communism only a distant goal. But now, after nearly two years of war and the uninterrupted decline of anarchosyndicalist strength and influence, such doctrinal disputes had become patently academic to the rank and file.

Also conspicuously absent from the August government were the Esquerra and the Basque National Party, the two most important regionalist parties in Republican Spain which for several reasons had decided to distance themselves from Negrín's government. Foremost among these was the fact that both saw the centralizing policies of the national government as inimical to their autonomous aspirations. The *catalanistas* themselves had witnessed first-hand how the transfer of the central government from Valencia to Barcelona in November 1937 had inevitably led to the erosion of Catalan independence. The two parties were also both angered and disturbed by the repressive tendencies of the government, such as the flagrant abuses of the communist-dominated SIM. When, in August 1938, Negrín's cabinet approved the central government's militarization of the war industries, ports, and courts of law, the Esquerra and Basque ministers, Artemio Aiguadé and Manuel Irujo, refused to endorse the encroachment of state power any longer. A few days later they tendered their resignations, a move which signalled the withdrawal of their parties' support for Negrín's Popular Front coalition.

If the CNT-FAI, Catalans, and Basques were divided among themselves and therefore not wholly committed to Negrín's government, this could not be said of the communists. As far as they were concerned the fundamental purpose of the Popular Front strategy had always been to counter the menace of fascism in Spain and Europe in so far as it threatened the Soviet Union. That was why the communists sought at all costs to dominate the state machinery and thereby control the course of the war. Though there can be no doubt that their regard for the Soviet Union came above all other considerations, this is not to say that the PCE participated in the Popular Front coalition solely to serve Stalin. Both before and during the war the Spanish communists genuinely wanted to use the Popular Front as a vehicle for realizing social and political reforms. The problem was that this goal, though sometimes pursued with great vigour, frequently had to be subordinated to their primary agenda, which was to protect and promote the interests of the Soviet Union.[26] Those who thought or acted otherwise were constantly reminded of their mission by the ubiquitous *apparatchiks*. But for the most part Spanish communists did not need to be pressured in this way, for leaders like José Díaz and La Pasionaria were unwaveringly obedient to Moscow. Inevitably, however, their split allegiances led them to play contradictory roles during the war, and, more important, to set up a self-defeating political model. Their ambivalent relationship with the anarchosyndicalists mentioned above illustrates this, as does their inconsistent behaviour in a number of other instances. Thus, for example, at the same time as they backed agrarian reform measures meant to improve the lot of the agricultural labourer, they were championing the interests of middle-class groups – like the small businessmen who had been squeezed by collectivization – in order to undermine the power and influence of the revolutionary groups which opposed them. The difficulty of trying to appeal to two fundamentally different audiences at the same time was also apparent in Catalonia. To mark the occasion when the central government transferred its seat from Valencia to Barcelona in November 1937, the PSUC unflinchingly declared: 'Catalonia cannot be free if Fascism conquers Spain. Spain cannot be made free without the help of Catalonia.'[27] But the result of their simultaneous commitment to the idea of revolution and the practice of counter-revolution was far more serious than the production of 'doublespeak'; in the end it cost them the support of the masses.

If the principal aim of communist policy was to defend the interests of the Soviet Union, what were the major goals of the *negrinistas*? It is doubtful that, as close as he became with the communists, Negrín himself ever seriously contemplated the idea of setting up a Soviet satellite or 'client' state like those which emerged in Eastern Europe in the wake of the Second World War. The chief ambition of Negrín and his supporters late in the war was to delay a Nationalist victory for as long as possible, and it is most likely that their reliance on the support of the communists was seen as the only means of achieving this. For even after it was clear that the war was over and that Britain and France had abandoned Republican Spain, the die-hard followers of Negrín refused to renounce their commitment to the policy of resistance.

26. Thus while economic, social, and political reforms were important objectives for the communists, they were invariably pursued with the primary goal of communist hegemony in mind.
27. Cited in E. H. Carr, *The Comintern and the Spanish Civil War* (London, 1984) pp. 62–3.

THE FINAL ACT: THE CASADO COUP

With Nationalist troops poised for complete victory in February, Negrín's government lost the support of everyone except the communists. In fact, the government itself was in total disarray: although it had moved back to Madrid, President Manuel Azaña had resigned in February, and his legal successor, Martínez Barrio (President of the Cortes), refused to return to Spain. The disintegration of formal government was further hastened when Great Britain and France extended recognition to Franco's government on 27 February.

In this atmosphere of confusion and political dissolution, most socialists, republicans, and anarchists were so overwhelmed by a sense of impending disaster that they did not see the point of sacrificing any more lives in the war effort. Negrín's and the communists' refusal to accept this generated a groundswell of anger and resentment that culminated in a movement to overthrow his Popular Front regime. The final act in the republican tragedy, known as the Casado coup, was played out in March.

The head of this movement was Colonel Segismundo Casado, an officer who had started the war as the commander of Manuel Azaña's presidential guard and had, by 1938, risen through the ranks to become the commander of the Army of the Centre. Like so many others at this point in the conflict, Casado was particularly hostile to the PCE, which he saw as the real authority behind the government and whose clashes with other parties were intensifying daily. He therefore resolved in early February to launch his own initiative to end the fighting as soon as possible.[28] Joining him were the Marxist academic Julián Besteiro; the socialist Wenceslao Carrillo (the father of the communist youth leader Santiago); the anarchist military commander of the Fourth Army Corps, Cipriano Mera; and General Miaja, who was in charge of the armed forces in the central-southern zone. Together they formed the basis of a ruling junta, the National Council of Defence, which came into being on 6 March.

Just before midnight (6 March) the conspirators took over the chief government ministries and seized control of the central telephone exchange. Next, the leaders announced on the radio that a new government, the National Council of Defence, had been formed. Taking turns, Besteiro, Casado and Mera spoke of the treachery of Negrín and the communists who had, in their view, already surrendered Spain's independence to a foreign government, the Soviet Union. An honourable peace,

---

28. The unsubstantiated claim that Casado was acting in collusion with French and British agents was circulated then and later by the communists and their sympathizers. See, for example, Julio Álvarez del Vayo, 'Negrín's Plan for Spain', in *The Nation*, 21 July 1945.

they insisted, could be achieved 'through conciliation with independence and liberty' and without 'crimes'. By this time, Negrín and his advisors, who had left Madrid a few days earlier, were holed up outside Alicante in the small town of Elda. When he talked to Casado only moments later, Negrín himself was in a state of disbelief. Shortly afterwards, he made preparations to leave the country as soon as possible. Much later that same day, the Premier made good his departure to Toulouse. Not far behind were the principal leaders of the Spanish Communist Party.

Meanwhile, in Madrid, the emergence of the junta had sparked off a mini-war between the communists and the forces of the Council of Defence. By 12 March communist resistance had been broken, and the Council stepped up its efforts to reach a negotiated settlement with Franco. From the outset it was apparent that Franco had no intention of meeting their conditions for surrender. The *caudillo* had never shown any interest in negotiating with the republicans earlier in the war and now that the Republic was at the point of annihilation, he was eager to deliver the final *coup de grâce*. Two weeks later, Franco mounted his 'Ofensiva de la Victoria' or Victory Offensive. Madrid was occupied on 27 March, and on 1 April 1939 Franco proclaimed that his troops had 'achieved their last military objectives'. The war had finally ended.

PART THREE
Epilogue

Epilogue

Although the Civil War ended in April 1939, for many years circumstances as well as the concerted efforts of both victors and vanquished conspired against a progressive regeneration of Spanish society. The most obvious and fundamental reason for this was that fratricidal strife always exacts a heavy toll. Nearly everyone living in Spain during the thousand-day war lost a friend or relative, and deeply-inflicted personal wounds of this kind naturally took a long time to heal. The trauma of the Civil War was so great that it continued to shape the collective psychology of the Spanish people even fify years on; it was, in the words of Víctor Pérez Díaz, 'the moral and emotional reference point' for the politicians who achieved the country's transition to democracy during the 1970s and 1980s and for much of the Spanish people as well.[1]

In the immediate post-war years the problems of social and economic recovery were also overwhelming. With Spain's resources drained and her institutional infrastructure in shambles, the process of rebuilding proved exceedingly slow and difficult. The outbreak of the Second World War only made matters worse. Europe's greatest war of the century absorbed the attention and energies of nearly every country, and this meant that Spain, which remained neutral, was effectively denied sorely needed outside assistance. In an effort to prevent Spain from joining this Axis bloc; the United States and Great Britain provided some aid to France. But this assistance was too limited to enable Spain to overcome her enormous economic obstacles.

The peculiarities of Spain's post-war political landscape also militated against a quick recovery. The Francoist repression, the emergence of an autocratic one-party system, and the diaspora of republicans after the war

1. Víctor Pérez Díaz, *The Return of Civil Society* (Cambridge, Massachusetts, 1993) p. 25.

are among the fundamental reasons the echoes of the Civil War could be heard well into the twentieth century.

THE *NUEVO ESTADO*

The Nationalist victory ushered in a period of authoritarian rule that lasted nearly forty years. Upon assuming power, Franco took immense pride in the fact that his regime represented a complete rupture with Spain's liberal past. The *caudillo* wanted to rule Spain with an iron hand and the institutional basis of the corporatist *nuevo estado* he directed clearly manifested this ambition. The guiding principles of the Francoist system were embodied in the so-called fundamental laws, which originated with the *Fuero de Trabajo* (Labour Charter) in 1938 and which were amplified over the course of the next thirty-five years.[2] Above all, these laws reflected the Nationalists' determination to create a self-sufficient and all-encompassing one-party state system under the personal direction of Franco. While this model was never fully realized, it survived, albeit with modifications, Franco's long and durable dictatorship.

To help erect the institutional structures of this system, Franco relied on the coalition of forces – or 'families' as they were later called – that had propelled the *Movimiento*. As the victory was primarily a military one, the army was elevated to a lofty position in the immediate post-war period.[3] It was, in Franco's eyes, the true guarantor of a united Spain, and for this reason his regime retained its military character for many years. The Church, too, was assigned a prominent role in building the new order. Spain was to be morally and spiritually rehabilitated, and the Catholic Church was designated by the state to lead this movement. As it turned out, the Church's privileged relationship with Franco did not endure the entire span of his rule. For a variety of reasons, including the liberalizing effects of the Second Vatican Council, an increasing number of Catholic organizations in the late 1960s began challenging the dictatorship.

The post-war settlement among the various right-wing parties was a more complicated affair. Even before the war had ended, fissures in their united front, which had been imposed and sustained by the military, were already beginning to widen. These tensions, especially between monarchists and Falangists, continued for many years afterwards. The spoils doled out

2. The more comprehensive Seven Fundamental Laws of the State (*Fuero de los Españoles*), for example, were published in 1945 and modified periodically until Franco's death.
3. Towards the end of the regime's life, however, the army had been relegated to the status of a 'poor relation'. See Manuel González García, 'The Armed Forces: Poor Relation of the Franco Regime', in *Spain in Crisis* ed. by P. Preston (London, 1976).

by Franco mirrored the relative strengths and weaknesses of the parties. The monarchists and Carlists were rewarded with government posts for their contributions to the war. But it was clear from the outset that neither would be granted their most sought after goal, a restored (or in the case of the Carlists, newly installed) monarchy. Recognizing that their ambitions were never going to be realized within the context of Franco's authoritarian system, the Carlists decided to retreat to the background. On the other hand, the monarchists were more persistent. During the 1940s and 1950s they became a force of opposition to Franco's personal rule. Over time, Franco relented to popular demands to restore Spain's monarchy. Just before martial law finally ended in 1948 the dictator issued his famous Law of Succession, which declared Spain a monarchy with the *caudillo* as regent for life. This act did not satisfy those seeking the immediate restoration of the Bourbon line, but it did pave the way for the succession of Franco's adopted protégé, Juan Carlos, the future king of a democratic Spain.[4]

The Falange, still representing the largest single political group, predominated in many key areas of the dictatorship. Franco continued to rely on the Falange to manage the working-classes by incorporating them into their hierarchically-arranged national syndicate, the Organización Sindical Española, OSE. This monolithic trade union structure oversaw all the forces of production and was designed to ensure the 'organic' unity of labour, management and other economic and social groups.[5] The Falangists were also left in control of the media and much of the elephantine bureaucracy that was needed to administer the services of what amounted to a highly paternalistic government.

The fascist character of Franco's regime belied the fact that the Falange itself was never as politically dominant as, say, the Nazi Party was in Germany or the Fascist Party in Italy. Even so, the fact that the *caudillo's* attempts to install his regime coincided with the ascendancy of European fascism greatly contributed to the Falange's prestige. Franco's commitment to fascism waxed and waned according to the political climate. At least until 1943, when an Allied victory seemed increasingly likely, he promoted the fascist nature of his government, and though no formal alliance was ever concluded between Spain and the Axis powers, Franco cooperated with them as fully as he could without violating Spain's neutrality and endangering his own political survival.[6] In post-war Europe, however,

4. In this choice of successors, Juan Carlos' father had been bypassed. Though heir apparent to the Bourbon throne, Don Juan (who died in 1993) was too liberal for Franco's taste.
5. On the OSE during the Franco period, see especially Sebastian Balfour, *Dictatorship, Workers and the City* (Oxford, 1989).
6. For example, during the war, Franco sent 17,000 select members of his army – the famed 'Blue Division' – to fight on the Eastern front.

Franco attempted to distance himself from fascism in order to win over international opinion.

Despite its fascist underpinnings, the Falange never developed into a totalitarian party. Franco himself apparently saw the Falange as a creature of his own making.[7] In any case, it was a maxim of Franco that no 'family member' of his government should become too powerful. For this reason, throughout his dictatorship he manipulated the reins of government so that political authority was never concentrated in the hands of one party. In each of his administrations a member of one of the 'families' was represented to some degree or another. Over time, the Generalísimo's reliance on the Falange steadily declined. By the late 1950s, the largely bureaucratic Falange had been shorn of all its dynamism and it could no longer be regarded as an important independent force.

THE WAR CONTINUES

The Nationalist victory put an end to the formal fighting but, given the implacable hatred the right still had for the left, the war itself was continued by other means. Franco's war of attrition was transformed into a war of revenge; in the immediate post-war period reprisals were carried out with energy and directed against the Popular Front parties and their supporters. Without any means of effectively challenging the authority of the new state, there were no enforceable limits to the punishments being meted out. Perfunctory trials determined the guilt or innocence of the victims, and those who were convicted faced a grim future. An estimated 30,000 were executed for 'war crimes', while thousands of others ended up in prisons or prison camps. Forced labour was one of the commonest forms used to punish the 'reds' who had escaped the firing squads. Many were drafted into civil engineering projects and used for the repair and construction of roads, bridges and other public works. One of their most extravagant undertakings was to build Franco's huge monument to commemorate the Nationalist dead, the Valley of the Fallen (*Valle de los caídos*). It took 20,000 'Red' prisoners nearly twenty years to carve Franco's monument and future mausoleum out of stone.

Exacting revenge in this way was done not only to salve the hatred of the victors, but also to bind the forces of the right. The complicity of all parties in the brutal repression, metaphorically expressed as '*el pacto de la*

---

7. Raymond Carr points out that Franco viewed the Falange not as a mere party, but as a general political movement of which he was the conductor; Raymond Carr, *Spain, 1808–1975* (Oxford, 1990), p. 700. Sheelagh Ellwood details the extent to which Franco domesticated the party in her *Spanish Fascism during the Franco Era* (London, 1987).

sangre' (the pact of blood), meant that no one group could escape punishment should the political situation ever be completely reversed. But any positive benefits that the victors may have hoped to derive from these draconian policies were completely cancelled out by the negative consequences of reprisals. Physically devastated and spiritually exhausted by the ruinous effects of nearly three years of war, Spain could ill afford to lose a generation of Spaniards, whose potential contributions to rebuilding the country were snuffed out by repression. This is illustrated by the fact that a vengeful government effectively stunted the growth of Spain's cultural and social life. Because of their inveterate anti-intellectualism, the *francoists* lost the support of the greater part of Spain's once rich intellectual and artistic communities. Many of her best intellectuals, musicians and artists preferred exile to life in an authoritarian state, while the creative productions of those who remained inside the country were circumscribed by the ever vigilant – if not always competent – state censors.[8]

In many ways, then, the politics of revenge carried out in the period immediately following the war and lasting for several years signalled a continuation rather than the end of the destructive process that had been unleashed in July 1936.

REPUBLICAN EXILES

Outside the country, the agony of tens of thousands of republican refugees was also far from over. We have noted that, even before the war had ended, thousands of civilians began their slow and arduous trek across the French-Spanish border. The first major exodus came following the collapse of the northern republican sectors in 1937. Another wave came during the Nationalist offensive in Catalonia. Between January and February 1939 the continuous stream of refugees turned into a torrent. The solemn and ragged columns consisted mostly of women, the elderly, wounded soldiers, and children. Battered by appalling weather conditions and weakened by lack of food and proper shelter, the retreating masses escaped with little more than what they could carry on their backs.

Their flight was almost completely stopped in June 1938 when, under pressure from the French right and British politicians, the French government decided to seal the border against further migrations. Faced with the

---

8. This is not to deny the creative achievements of those who persevered in the otherwise sterile cultural milieu: the future Nobel laureate author Camilo José Cela (at one time a censor for the regime), Victor Erice, the director of the film 'Spirit of the Beehive' (*Espíritu de la colmena*) and the composer Joaquín Rodrigo (*Concierto de Aranjuez*) demonstrated the creative resiliency of those who remained in Franco's Spain.

likelihood that thousands of civilians would be exterminated by advancing Nationalists troops, in late January 1939 the French called for the creation of a neutral zone inside Spain. Franco, though, pointedly refused to go along with this idea. A few days after negotiations with the Nationalists fell through, the French reluctantly consented to reopen the borders on the condition that only civilians (and wounded soldiers) be allowed into France. Within days over 100,000 Spaniards had crossed the frontier, and by the second week of February the total number of refugees stood at between 350,000 and 450,000.[9]

The majority of the large and diverse exile community were forced to resign themselves to whatever fate awaited them across the Pyrenees. Many ended up in makeshift relocation camps, where they lived in abysmal conditions. Although these camps provided food and basic shelter, there was an acute shortage of medical supplies and sanitary facilities were practically non-existent. (One delegation sent to inspect the first camps found that, as a rule, drinking water was scarce and that there was no water for bathing.[10]) Luckier ones could turn to French friends (usually political contacts) or relatives, and they found work or living quarters wherever they could. Nearly all suffered the humiliations that foreign refugees often do: most did not speak the native language and they were both seen and saw themselves as outsiders.

The disagreeable plight of many refugees was made even more unbearable after war broke out in Europe. When, in 1940, France fell to Germany, exiles were forced to live under German occupation or in Vichy France, where the government was no less hostile to left-wing refugees. A number of known republican activists were rearrested and imprisoned at this time. Some, like Juan Peiró and Lluis Companys, were turned over to the Spanish authorities, who promptly arranged for their executions. Largo Caballero, the future writer Jorge Semprún and many others ended up in concentration camps.[11]

A certain number of refugees escaped these bleak fates. Republicans who remained inside France worked in the underground resistance movement and some even fought in the war. (When the Allies liberated Paris in 1944, Spanish republicans were among the first troops to enter the city.) With the assistance of the Spanish Republican Immigration Service (Servicio de Emigración para Republicanos Españoles, SERE) and similar

---

9. David Pike, *Vae victis!* (Paris, 1969), p. 13.
10. *Ibid.*, p. 44.
11. Caballero himself barely survived his wartime detention at the Nazi Mauthausen camp. Semprún, who was active in the French Resistance, was sent to Buchenwald concentration camp. See his *Communism in Spain in the Franco Era: The Autobiography of Federico Sánchez*, translated by Helen R. Lane (Brighton, 1980), p. 52.

agencies, tens of thousands of refugees managed to find homes abroad.[12] The most popular destinations were Latin America (especially Mexico and Argentina), where Juan García Oliver, Indalecio Prieto and a number of former Republican government officials landed. Some relocated elsewhere in Europe.[13] The ruling cadres of the Spanish Communist Party, including La Pasionaria, José Díaz, and José Uribe, took up residence in the Soviet Union. While the majority of the exiles never returned to Spain, a few, Abad de Santillán, Josep Tarradellas and La Pasionaria, among them, survived the dictatorship and returned to a greatly changed Spain in the late 1970s.

The diaspora of Republicans was in some respects equally damaging to Spain's spiritual and moral recovery during the 1940s and 1950s. For when the defeated Republicans fled Franco's Spain into permanent exile abroad, they transported their political prejudices and ideological disputes with them. While all were adamantly opposed to the *franquista* regime, they were nonetheless bitterly divided over who among the exile community legitimately represented the Republican government. This factional strife – which usually pitted the anti-communist left against the communists and their sympathizers – gave rise to interminable and ultimately pointless debates over who was responsible for causing the Republican defeat.

Back in Spain, the repressive Franco government effectively precluded any open dialogue concerning the origins and consequences of the war. As far as the Franco government was concerned, all one needed to know about the war could be found in its official accounts. Beginning in 1939 and continuing until the late 1960s, these state-sponsored histories served the propagandistic needs of the government. In countless pamphlets, books, magazines and documentary publications the war was kept alive in order to remind citizens of how the Nationalists had saved Spain from the evils of communism.[14] By eradicating all positive traces of the history of the Spanish left and greatly simplifying the causes and consequences of the war, the *Francoists* successfully enshrined the myth of the Crusade.

12. The SERE was founded by Juan Negrín. Prieto was in charge of another agency, Junta de Auxilio a los Republicanos Españoles (JARE).
13. On the republican exiles see especially the following: Nancy McDonald, *Homage to the Spanish Exiles*, (New York, 1987); Pike, *Vae Victis!* and *In the Service of Stalin*, (Oxford, 1993); Louis Stein, *Beyond Death and Exile*, (Harvard, 1979); and Javier Rubio, *La emigración de la guerra civil, 1936–1939*, tomos i–iii, (Madrid, 1977).
14. In publications like the widely-circulated *Causa general. La dominación roja en España* (issued in several editions by the Ministerio de Justicia, Madrid, 1944, 1961 etc.) horrifying pictures and graphic descriptions of the atrocities committed by 'los rojos' purported to expose in excruciating detail the evils wrought by the Spanish 'Reds'.

By the late sixties, however, there was little propaganda value left in these selective memories of the war. Far more important was the fact that the *franquista* system itself had to contend with the weight of its own internal contradictions. Although it was not ready to collapse – an economic boom at this time helped to buoy the regime – it was becoming increasingly apparent that the dictatorship was not responding effectively to the social and economic realities confronting Spain. Franco's death in November 1975 generated a great deal of anxiety among his die-hard supporters (the infamous 'bunker') but for most Spaniards it raised expectations for sweeping changes. In the following months, the basis for a transition to democracy was created by the centrist parties, and this led to the establishment of a constitutional monarchy. Now wholly ossified and glaringly anachronistic, *franquista* structures rapidly disintegrated in the face of the overwhelmingly popular support for democracy.

The democratization of Spain unleashed a number of social and intellectual movements including an explosion of interest in the study of the Civil War. Spaniards were anxious to understand an event which had shaped their lives but about which they had learned nothing beyond the official story for nearly forty years. In the late 1970s a highly motivated and articulate anti-*franquista* school of scholars emerged from the underground in Spain, and their work to recover Spain's troubled past was given impetus by the arrival of returning exiles, *los viejos republicanos*. What the 'new' generation of historians wanted to do was replace the *franquista* political tracts with works produced according to Western European academic standards. This generation, many of whom were trained outside of Spain, sought to ground their studies on facts, usually scrupulously culled from local archives that had hitherto been off limits to such investigations. Given that most histories produced during the Franco era lacked a proper scholarly apparatus and slavishly adhered to the régime's interpretation of events, it did not take them long to expose the shallowness and severe limitations of the *franquista* school of historians.[15]

THE WAR ENDS

The British historian Paul Preston has written that, with the death of Franco and the subsequent emergence of a new generation of academics,

15. Inside Spain, historians like Jaime Vicens Vives and José María Jover were largely responsible for maintaining the rigorous academic standards that were later put to use by the anti-*franquista* school of historians referred to here. Working in exile, the Marxist historian Manuel Túñon de Lara was also a highly influential figure.

the 'war of words' that for so long clouded our understanding of the civil war can finally be put behind us. According to him, historians both within and outside of Spain can now get on with the business of writing history without the distorting influences of ideological conflicts.[16] And, indeed, for nearly twenty years both Spanish and non-Spanish historians have produced fresh interpretations, which have collectively contributed to the process of demythologizing the Civil War. This is not to say that all the controversies surrounding the war and revolution have been laid to rest, but at least these debates can now be conducted in an open arena.[17]

What significance does the Civil War have for contemporary Spaniards? The politics of the moderate regimes of the late 1970s and 1980s built the basis for an enduring democracy, and this encouraged Spaniards to begin seeing the war as a part of their past rather than their present. For the generation of the 1930s the war is and will remain the defining moment of the twentieth century. To a certain extent this is also true of the Spaniards who grew up under Franco's dictatorship. But to the post-Franco generation which has both witnessed and participated in Spain's tremendous metamorphosis in the space of just two decades, the importance of the war has been greatly diminished. For the mostly young and increasingly apolitical population of the 1990s, the heated debates and acrimonious political feuds that have long swirled around the war are no longer relevant. This view is summed up in the following observation made during the mid–1980s by the journalist John Hooper: 'I find that whenever one refers back to the civil war or even to the Franco era, these days the reaction of young Spaniards is to shrug their shoulders and say with a smile *"Bueno, eran otros tiempos"* ('Well, those were different times.')'[18] Although it took over fifty years, the war has at last become the subject of history.

16. Not least of the reasons for this, according to Preston, is the fact that propaganda of the Francoist regime can no longer stand up to the hard evidence that has been produced by post-war scholars. In short, he believes that, with the disappearance of the censors, there are no obvious barriers to achieving a non-ideological understanding of the conflict. See his article entitled, 'War of words: the Spanish Civil War and the historian', in *Revolution and War in Spain, 1931–1939* (London, 1984), pp. 1–13.
17. George Orwell, the International Brigades, and the role of the rather enigmatic figure of Juan Negrín are subjects that still arouse considerable argument. Thus, even though great strides have been made towards 'de-politicizing' civil war literature, political partisanship is still in evidence.
18. John Hooper, *The Spaniards* (London, 1986), p. 273.

273

Select Bibliography

Since 1936 the bibliography of the Republic and Civil War has grown prodigiously: there are an estimated fifteen thousand pamphlets, monographs, memoirs, and general histories available on the subject. The following bibliography is designed primarily for an English-speaking audience and represents merely a selective list of works which we have found useful and which can serve as a point of departure for those interested in pursuing further research on the war and revolution.[1]

PART 1. THE SECOND REPUBLIC AND THE ORIGINS OF THE CIVIL WAR

General Surveys

The best historical text on modern Spain, with an emphasis on politics, is Raymond Carr, *Spain, 1808–1975* (Oxford, 1982). Richard Herr's, *An Historical Essay on Modern Spain* (Berkeley, 1971) is also useful. Although dated in many respects, Gerald Brenan's classic, *The Spanish Labyrinth* (New York, 1990; first published in 1943) is still indispensable. For a synthetic view of the social history background, see Adrian Shubert, *A Social History of Modern Spain* (London, 1990).

Two excellent accounts of Miguel Primo de Rivera's dictatorship and the immediate background to the Second Republic can be found in Shlomo Ben-Ami's, *The Origins of the Second Republic* (Oxford, 1978); and

---

1. We have filled perceived gaps in the literature with a highly selective list of non-English titles. It should also be noted that some of the titles which appear in the chapter footnotes are not repeated here.

Fascism from Above: the dictatorship of Primo de Rivera in Spain (Oxford, 1983).

The foremost general histories of the Republic are: Stanley G. Payne, *Spain's First Democracy* (Madison, 1993); Gabriel Jackson, *The Spanish Republic and the Civil War* (Princeton, 1965); and Manuel Tuñón de Lara, *La II República*, vol I–II (Madrid, 1976). Two recent collections of articles summarize research on the Republic up through the 1980s: Paul Preston, *Revolution and War in Spain* (London, 1984); and Martin Blinkhorn, *Spain in Conflict, 1931–1939* (London, 1986). The more dated essays in *Politics and Society in Twentieth-Century Spain*, ed. by Stanley G. Payne (New York, 1976) are still useful.

Republican Politics

The polarization of politics during the Republic is reflected in its historiography. Paul Heywood analyses the divergence between socialist (PSOE) ideology and practice in *Marxism and the Failure of Organized Socialism in Spain, 1879–1936* (Cambridge, 1990). Paul Preston's incisive, *The Coming of the Spanish Civil War* (London, 1978) pays close attention to the dialectics of left-right politics during the Republic; while Richard A.H. Robinson's, *The Origins of Franco's Spain: The Right, The Republic and Revolution, 1931–1936* (London, 1970) offers a sympathetic interpretation of the role of the right. Several studies focussing on the far right can be recommended: Martin Blinkhorn, *Carlism and Crisis in Spain, 1931–1939* (Cambridge, 1975); Stanley G. Payne, *Falange* (Stanford, 1961); and Sheelagh Ellwood, *Spanish Fascism in the Franco Era* (New York/London, 1987).

Church and State

On the role of the Church in Spanish society, see William J. Callahan, *Church, Society and Politics in Spain, 1750–1874* (Cambridge, Massachusetts, 1984); and France Lannon's lucid synthesis, *Privilege, Persecution and Prophecy* (Oxford, 1987). Joan C. Ullman's study of anti-clericalism in Catalonia, *The Tragic Week* (Harvard, 1968) is highly recommended, and another useful account of Church-State relations can be found in José Sánchez, *Reform and Reaction: the politico-religious background of the Spanish Civil War* (Chapel Hill, North Carolina, 1964).

Regionalism

Different aspects of the regionalist question have been explored in the following: Stanley G. Payne, *Basque Nationalism* (Reno, 1975); Marianne

Heiberg, *The Making of the Basque Nation* (New York, 1989); Pierre Vilar, 'Spain and Catalonia', in the *Review of the Fernand Braudel Centre* Spring, 1980, pp. 527–77; and Juan Pablo Fusi Aizpúrua, 'Centre and Periphery, 1900–1936: National Integration and Regional Nationalisms Reconsidered,' in *Elites and Power in Twentieth-Century Spain: Essays in Honour of Sir Raymond Carr*, ed. by Frances Lannon and Paul Preston (Oxford, 1990), pp. 33–44.

Civil-Military Relations

The best studies on civil-military relations are Stanley G. Payne, *Politics and the Military in Modern Spain* (Stanford, 1967); and Carolyn Boyd, *Praetorian Politics in Liberal Spain* (Chapel Hill, North Carolina, 1979), which is a detailed study of the role of the armed forces in the breakdown of the Restoration parliamentary system between 1917 and 1923.

Working-Class Organizations

Benjamin Martin, *The Agony of Modernization* (Ithaca, 1990) provides a balanced summary of labour relations in the nineteenth and twentieth centuries. For the early development of left-wing working-class organizations, see George Esenwein, *Anarchist Ideology and the Working-Class Movement in Spain, 1868–1898* (Berkeley, 1989) and Temma Kaplan, *Anarchists of Andalusia, 1868–1903* (Princeton, 1977). The crucial interwar years are examined in Gerald Meaker's massive volume, *The Revolutionary Left in Spain, 1914–1923* (Stanford, 1974). For a detailed study of the coal miners of Asturias, see Adrian Shubert, *The Road to Revolution in Spain* (Champaign-Urbana, 1987). The minor but nonetheless important development of right-wing unionism is the subject of Colin Winston's *Workers and the Right in Spain, 1900–1936* (Princeton, 1985).

The Agrarian Question

Edward Malefakis, *Agrarian Reform and Peasant Revolution in Spain* (New Haven, 1970) remains the classic study of the agrarian question during the Republic. Two interesting local studies written from an anthropological perspective are: George C. Collier, *Socialists of Rural Andalusia* (Stanford, 1987) and Jerome Mintz, *The Anarchists of Casas Viejas* (Chicago, 1982).

PART 2. CIVIL WAR AND REVOLUTION

General Histories

Although they employ different methodologies and represent various levels of historical sophistication the following studies of the war are particularly helpful: Anthony Beevor, *The Spanish Civil War* (London, 1982); Burnett Bolloten, *The Spanish Civil War: Revolution and Counterrevolution* (Chapel Hill, North Carolina, 1991); Pierre Broué and Emile Témime, *The Revolution and the Civil War in Spain* (Cambridge, Mass., 1970); Raymond Carr, *The Civil War in Spain* (London, 1986, a reissue of the *The Spanish Tragedy*, London, 1977); Ronald Fraser, *The Blood of Spain: An Oral History of the Spanish Civil War* (New York, 1979); Gabriel Jackson, *The Spanish Republic and the Civil War, 1936–1939* (Princeton, 1965); David Mitchell, *The Spanish Civil War* (New York, 1983); Paul Preston, *The Spanish Civil War, 1936–1939* (London, 1986); and Hugh Thomas, *The Spanish Civil War*, 3rd edn (London, 1977).

Specific topics relating to the war and revolution are treated in the following collections of historical essays: Julio Aróstegui (Coordinador), *Historia y Memoria de la Guerra Civil*, tomos 1–3 (Castilla y León, 1988); *Historical Dictionary of the Spanish Civil War, 1936–1939*, ed. by James Cortada (Westport, Connecticut, 1982); *Elites and Power in Twentieth-Century Spain*, ed. by Frances Lannon and Paul Preston (Oxford, 1990); Manuel Tuñón de Lara *et al.*, *La guerra civil española: 50 años después* (Madrid, 1985); *La guerra civil española: una reflexión moral 50 años después*, ed. by Ramón Tamames (Barcelona, 1986); and *The Republic and The Civil War in Spain*, ed. by Raymond Carr (London, 1971).

Nationalist Military Operations

For the role of the army see Ramón Salas Larrazábal, *Historia del ejército popular de la república*, vols I-IV (Madrid, 1975) and Stanley G. Payne, *Politics and Military in Modern Spain* (Stanford, California, 1967). A comprehensive overview of the military campaigns on both sides can be found in the fourteen volumes sponsored by the Servicio Histórico Militar and directed by Colonel José Manuel Martínez Bande, *Monografías de la Guerra de España* (Madrid, 1968–1985). Jesús Salas Larrazábal covers the air war in his, *Air War Over Spain* (London, 1974), while Michael Alpert's *La guerra civil española en el mar* (Mexico, D.F., 1987) is concerned with naval operations.

Right-wing Parties and Institutions

The role of the conservative right is discussed in the memoirs of the *cedista* chieftain José María Gil Robles, *No fué posible la paz* (Barcelona, 1968), while the definitive work on Carlist politics is Martin Blinkhorn's, *Carlism and Crisis in Spain, 1931–1939* (Cambridge, 1975).

Franco the man, and the movement he inspired, Francoism, have spawned an immense literature. Among the most important studies, both critical and sympathetic, are: Luís Bolín, *Spain: The Vital Years* (London, 1967); Juan Pablo Fusi, *Franco* (New York, 1987); Paul Preston, *Franco* (London/New York, 1993); Javier Tusell, *Franco en la Guerra Civil* (Barcelona, 1992); and J.W.D. Trythall, *Franco* (London, 1970). On Franco, Francoism, and their relationship to fascism the following works are highly recommended: Sheelagh Ellwood, *Spanish Fascism in the Franco Era* (London, 1987); *Fascists and Conservatives*, ed. by Martin Blinkhorn (London, 1990); Stanley G. Payne, *The Franco Regime, 1939–1975* (Madison, Wisconsin, 1987); Alberto Reig Tapia, *Ideología e historia: Sobre la represión franquista y la Guerra Civil* (Madrid, 1984); Ramón Serrano Suñer, *Entre Hendaya y Gibraltar* (Madrid, 1947); and Herbert Southworth, *El mito de la Cruzada de Franco* (Barcelona, 1986).

Two studies which shed light on the relationship between politics and Catholicism during the war are: Frances Lannon, *Privilege, Persecution, and Prophecy: The Catholic Church in Spain, 1875–1975* (Oxford, 1987) and José M. Sánchez, *The Spanish Civil War as Religious Tragedy* (Notre Dame, 1987).

Rafael Abella describes daily life under Franco in *La vida cotidiana durante la guerra civil: la España nacional (vol. I)* (Barcelona, 1973).

Republican Politics and Society

The recollections of Diego Martínez Barrio, *Memorias* (Barcelona, 1983) and Manuel Azaña's in *Obras completas*, vols III and IV (Mexico City, 1967, 1968) reflect the attitudes of two leading middle-class republican politicians.

The most illuminating studies devoted to the anarchists and anarchism during the war are: Abad de Santillán, *Por qué perdimos la guerra* (Buenos Aires, 1940); Walther Bernecker, *Colectividades y revolución social* (Barcelona, 1982); John S. Brademas, *Anarcosindicalismo y revolución en España, 1930–1937* (Barcelona, 1974); Julián Casanova, *Anarquismo y revolución en la sociedad rural aragonesa, 1936–1938* (Madrid, 1985); Noam Chomsky, *American Power and the New Mandarins* (New York, 1969), pp. 23–158; Juan Gómez Casas, *Anarchist Organization: the history of the FAI*, trans. by Abe Bluestein (Toronto, 1986); Graham Kelsey, *Anarchosyndicalism, Libertarian*

Communism and the State: The CNT in Zaragosa and Aragon, 1930–1937 (Amsterdam, 1991); Gaston Leval, *Collectives in the Spanish Revolution* (London, 1975); César Lorenzo, *Les Anarchistes Espagnols et le Pouvoir, 1868–1969* (Paris, 1969); Abel Paz, *Durruti: The People Armed* (New York, 1977); José Peirats, *Anarchists in the Spanish Revolution* (Detroit, n.d.); and Vernon Richards, *Lessons of the Spanish Revolution* (London, 1983).

There are few works about the communists that are not politically motivated. E.H. Carr's, *The Comintern and the Spanish Civil War* (London, 1984); and *The Communist International, 1919–1943*, selected and ed. by Jane Degras, vol. III: (1929–1943) (Oxford, 1965) contain useful documentary sources. Fernando Claudín's *The Communist Movement: froom Comintern to Cominform* (London, 1975) is a general survey of the international communist movement which provides a cogent analysis of the Spanish case from the point of view of an insider. The most thoroughly documented and detailed history of the communists' role in Republican politics is Burnett Bolloten's masterly, *The Spanish Civil War: Revolution and Counterrevolution* (Chapel Hill, North Carolina, 1990). Victor Alba's, *The Communist Party in Spain* (New Brunswick, New Jersey, 1983) is a biased but nonetheless valuable account of the communists' record written from a POUM perspective. A general assessment of their activities is given in David T. Cattell, *Communism and the Spanish Civil War* (Berkeley, 1955). Representative of the numerous pro-communist interpretations is Dolores Ibarruri's incomplete autobiography, *They Shall Not Pass* (New York, 1966).

The POUM's role is explained in two sympathetic studies: V. Alba and Stephen Schwartz, *Spanish Marxism vs. Soviet Communism* (New Brunswick, New Jersey, 1988) and Reiner Tosstorff's, *Die POUM im spanischen Bürgerkrieg*, (Frankfurt, 1987).

Scholars are also forced to contend with the highly contentious literature on the socialists. Richard Gillespie's, *The Spanish Socialist Party* (Oxford, 1989) is a dispassionate general study of the party, while Helen Graham's, *Socialism and War: The Spanish Socialist Party in power and crisis, 1936–1939* (Cambridge, 1991) is the best in-depth account of socialist politics during the war.

Memoirs of socialist participants, though tendentious, contain useful insights. This is especially true of Indalecio Prieto, *Convulsiones de España* (Mexico, 1967); and Francisco Largo Caballero, *Mis recuerdos* (Mexico, 1954). Although no known memoir was written by Juan Negrín, there are several accounts written from a pro-*negrinista* perspective. Julio Álvarez del Vayo defends Negrín's wartime policies in, *Freedom's Battle* (New York, 1940), *Give Me Combat* (Boston, 1973), and *The Last Optimist* (New York, 1950); and Louis Fisher's *Men in Politics* (New York, 1941) is also important.

There is a growing literature dealing with the role of republican women: Martha A. Ackelsberg, *Free Women of Spain* (Bloomington, 1991); Carmen Alcalde, *La mujer en la guerra civil española* (Madrid, 1976); Sara Berenguer, *Entre el Sol y la Tormenta* (Barcelona, 1987); Robert Low, *La Pasionaria* (London, 1992); *Mujeres y la Guerra Civil Española* (Madrid, 1991); Mary Nash, *Mujer y movimiento obrero en España, 1931–1939* (Barcelona, 1981); Geraldine M. Scanlon, *La polémica feminista en la España contemporanea* (Madrid, 1976 and 1988); and *Women of the Mediterranean*, ed. by Monique Gadant (London, 1986).

For a general account of Republican society, see Rafael Abella, *La vida cotidiana durante la Guerra Civil, vol. II* (Barcelona, 1975). On the fate of the Basque children, see Dorothy Legarreta, *The Guernica Generation* (Reno, Nevada, 1984).

For republican military policy see, Michael Alpert, *El ejército republicano en la guerra civil* (Paris, 1977); and José Martín Blázquez, *I Helped to Build an Army* (London, 1939). The final weeks of the war are chronicled in Segismundo Casado, *The Last Days of Madrid* (London, 1939).

Foreign Intervention

Survey of International Affairs, Volume II (London, 1937–1938) is the best introduction to diplomatic affairs. The diplomatic background is surveyed by Dante A. Puzzo, *Spain and the Great Powers* (Columbia, 1962).

American attitudes are covered in Douglas Little, *Malevolent Neutrality: The United States, Great Britain and the Origins of Non-Intervention* (Ithaca, 1985); T.G. Powell, *Mexico and the Spanish Civil War* (Albuquerque, 1981); and *The Spanish Civil War: American Hemispheric Perspectives*, ed. by Marc Falcoff and Frederick Pike (Nebraska, 1982).

French attitudes are discussed in John E. Dreifort, *Yvon Delbos at the Quai d'Orsay: French Foreign Policy during the Popular Front, 1936–1938* (Wichita, Kansas, 1973); Joel Colton, *Léon Blum: Humanist in Politics* (New York, 1966); Charles Micaud, *The French Right and Nazi Germany, 1933–1939* (Durham, North Carolina, 1943); David W. Pike, *Conjecture, Propaganda, and Deceit and the Spanish Civil War* (Stanford, California, 1968).

For Germany's perspective on intervention, see *Documents on German Foreign Policy, 1918–1945*, ser. D., vol. III (Washington, DC, 1950); while Nazi economic and political aims are described in Glenn T. Harper, *German Economic Policy in Spain during the Spanish Civil War, 1936–1939* (The Hague, 1967); Ángel Viñas, *La Alemania nazi y el 18 de Julio* (Madrid, 1977) and his *Guerra, Dinero, Dictablanda* (Barcelona, 1984). Robert H. Whealey, *Hitler and Spain* (Lexington, Kentucky, 1989) offers a concise summary of Hitler's role and Gerhard L. Weinberg, *The Foreign Policy of*

Hitler's Germany, 1937–1939 (Chicago, 1980) places German involvement in Spain in the broader context of Hitler's foreign policy strategy. The development of British policy is traced in *Documents on British Foreign Policy*, 2nd and 3rd Series (London, 1946, 1979–82); and Jill Edwards, *The British Government and the Spanish Civil War* (London, 1979). For non-intervention, see Enrique Moradiellos, *Neutralidad benévola: El gobierno británico y la insurrección militar española de 1936* (Oviedo, 1990). The civil war's impact on British society is the subject of Tom Buchanan's, *The Spanish Civil War and the British Labour Movement* (Cambridge, 1991) and K.W. Watkin's, *Britain Divided. The Effect of the Spanish Civil War on British Public Opinion* (London, 1963).

For Italian policy, see Count Galeazzo Ciano's, *The Ciano Diaries, 1939–1943* (Garden City, New Jersey, 1946) and *Diplomatic Papers* (London, 1948); and John F. Coverdale's authoritative study, *Italian Intervention in the Spanish Civil War* (Princeton, 1975).

On Soviet intervention see the following: David T. Cattell, *Soviet Diplomacy and the Spanish Civil War* (Berkeley, 1957); and Ivan M. Maisky, *Spanish Notebooks* (London, 1966). A general view of Soviet diplomacy during the civil war period can be found in Jonathan Haslam, *The Soviet Union and the Struggle for Collective Security in Europe, 1933–1939* (New York, 1984).

Artists, Writers, Intellectuals, and International Volunteers

Personal testaments and testimonials to the International Brigades are legion. Important eye-witness accounts are contained in Bill Alexander, *British Volunteers for Liberty* (London, 1982); Alvah Bessie, *Men in Battle* (San Francisco, 1975); Jason Gurney, *Crusade in Spain* (London, 1974); Robert G. Colodny, *The Struggle for Madrid* (New York, 1958); Steve Nelson, *Volunteers* (New York, 1953); *Our Fight: Writings by Veterans of the Abraham Lincoln Brigade, Spain 1936–1939*, ed. by Alvah Bessie and Albert Prago (New York, 1987); Gustav Regler, *The Owl of Minerva* (London, 1959); and John Tisa, *Recalling the Good Fight* (South Hadley, Massachusetts, 1985).

International Solidarity with the Spanish Republic, 1936–1939 (Moscow, 1974, 1976 printing) glorifies the exploits of the international volunteers, while critical assessments of their achievements are recorded in Cecil B. Eby, *Between the Bullet and the Lie* (New York, 1969); Verle B. Johnston, *Legions of Babel: The International Brigades in the Spanish Civil War* (University Park, Pennsylvania, 1967); Dan R. Richardson, *Comintern Army* (Lexington, Kentucky, 1982); and Robert A. Rosenstone, *Crusade of the Left* (New York, 1969).

Among the most interesting and perceptive first-hand narratives of and commentaries on the war and revolution written by foreigners are: Franz Borkenau's, *The Spanish Cockpit* (Ann Arbor, 1963); Martha Gellhorn, *The Face of War* (New York, 1988); Emma Goldman, *Vision on Fire* (New York, 1983); Mary Low and Juan Brea, *Red Spanish Notebook* (San Francisco, 1979); Ilya Ehrenburg, *Eve of War, 1933–1941* (London, 1963); Arthur Koestler, *Spanish Testament* (London, 1939); George Orwell, *Homage to Catalonia* (Harmondsworth, 1974) and the articles in his, *The Collected Essays, Journalism and Letters of George Orwell*, ed. by Sonia Orwell and Ian Angus, vol. I ('An Age Like This, 1920–1940') (New York/London, 1968).

For works that examine the role of foreign intellectuals and writers see the following: Frederick R. Benson, *Writers in Arms: The Literary Impact of the Spanish Civil War* (New York, 1967); Bernard Crick, *George Orwell: A Life* (London, 1980); Allen Guttmann, *The Wound in the Heart: America and the Spanish Civil War* (New York, 1962); Samuel Hynes, *The Auden Generation* (New York, 1976); Marilyn Rosenthal, *Poetry of the Spanish Civil War* (New York, 1975); Peter Stansky and William Abrahams, *Journey to the Frontier* (New York, 1966); Gareth Thomas, *The Novel of the Spanish Civil War* (Cambridge, 1990); and Stanley Weintraub, *The Last Great Cause* (New York, 1968).

Only a few of the numerous literary and poetical works inspired by the war are: John Dos Passos, *The Adventures of a Young Man* (New York, 1940); Ernest Hemingway, *For Whom the Bell Tolls* (New York, 1940); William Herrick, *Hermanos!* (New York, 1969); André Malraux, *Days of Hope* (London, 1968); Pablo Neruda, *Spain in the Heart* (Washington, DC, 1993); and César Vallejo, *Spain, Take This Cup From Me* (New York, 1974). A variety of shorter artistic and literary expressions have been collected in several excellent anthologies: *The Penguin Book of Spanish Civil War Verse*, ed. by Valentine Cunningham (Harmondsworth, 1980); *Spanish Front: Writers on the Civil War*, ed. by Valentine Cunningham (Oxford, 1986); *The Spanish Civil War*, ed. by Alun Kenwood (Oxford, 1993); and *Voices Against Tyranny*, ed. by John Miller (New York, 1986).

The bibliography of works by Spanish writers is huge. A sample of the better known ones are: Arturo Barea, *The Forging of a Rebel*, a memoir in literary form (New York, 1946); Camilo José Cela, *San Camilo, 1936* (Durham, 1991); José María Gironella, *One Million Dead* (New York, 1963); and Ramón Sender, *Counter-Attack in Spain* (Boston, 1937).

PART 3. POST-CIVIL WAR

There are several good case studies of the republican exile communities: Patricia W. Fagen, *Exiles and Citizens: Spanish Republicans in Mexico* (Austin, 1973); Nancy MacDonald, *Homage to the Spanish Exiles: Voices from the Spanish Civil War* (New York, 1987); David W. Pike, *In the Service of Stalin* (Oxford, 1993); and Louis Stein, *Beyond Death and Exile: The Spanish Republicans in France, 1939–1955* (Cambridge, Massachusetts, 1979). For the Franco regime see 'Right-wing Parties and Institutions' above. Spain's remarkable transition to democracy during the 1970s and 1980s is examined in: Raymond Carr and Juan Pablo Fusi, *Spain: From Dictatorship to Democracy*, 2nd edn (London, 1981); David Gilmour, *The Transformation of Spain: From Franco to the constitutional monarchy* (London, 1985); José María Maravall, *The Transition to Democracy in Spain* (London, 1982); Victor M. Pérez Díaz *The Return of Civil Society: The emergence of democratic Spain* (Cambridge, Massachusetts., 1993); and Paul Preston, *The Triumph of Democracy* (London, 1986).

Glossary (1): Political Groups and List of Abbreviations

ACNP   *Asociación Católica Nacional de Propagandistas* (The political vanguard of the legalist right associated with Catholic Action.)

ASM   *Agrupación Socialista Madrileña* (The Madrid section of the PSOE.)

BOC   *Bloc Obrer i Camperol* (Workers and Peasants Bloc; Marxist organization which fused with the *Izquierda Comunista* in 1935 to create the POUM.)

CEDA   *Confederación Española de Derechas Autónomas* (The Spanish-Confederation of Autonomous Rightist Groups; the largest political organization of the legalist right.)

CLUEA   *Consejo Levantino Unificado de la Exportación Agrícola* (Anarchosyndicalist-dominated agricultural export organization set up in Valencia during the war.)

CNCA   *Confederación Nacional Católico-Agraria* (A conservative, Catholic smallholders' organization which provided mass support for the CEDA.)

CNT   *Confederación Nacional del Trabajo* (The anarchosyndicalist trade union founded in 1910.)

DRV   *Derecha Regional Valenciana* (The Valencian component of the CEDA.)

ERC   *Esquerra Republicana de Catalunya* (The left-republican party of Catalonia.)

284

FAI   *Federación Anarquista Ibérica* (The insurrectionary vanguard of the anarchist movement.)

FE/JONS   *Falange Española y de las Juntas de Ofensiva Nacional Sindicalista* (Spanish Fascist Party created in 1934.)

FET/JONS   *Falange Española Tradicionalista* (The Nationalist party established in 1937 by Franco's unification decree.)

FIJL   *Federación Ibérica de Juventudes Libertarias* (Anarchist Youth Federation.)

FNTT   · *Federación Nacional de Trabajadores de la Tierra* (The land workers' section of the UGT.)

FOUS   *Federación Obrera de Unidad Sindical,* (POUM trade-union organization that merged with the PSUC-controlled Catalan UGT soon after the outbreak of the civil war.)

FPFR   *Federación de Propietarios de Fincas Rústicas* (A landowners' organization devoted to blocking the reforms of the Republic).

FRE   *Federación de la Región Española* (Spanish branch of the First International).

GEPCI   *Federación Catalana de Gremios y Entidades de Pequeños Comerciantes e Industriales* (Catalan federation of small businessmen and manufacturers.)

HISMA   *Hispano-Marroquí de Transportes S.L.* (The company founded in Morocco on 31 July 1936 to act as a cover for the supply of German aid to the Nationalists.)

JAP   *Juventudes de Acción Popular* (Youth movement of CEDA.)

JSU   *Juventudes Socialistas Unificadas,* (United Youth Movement formed by the merger of the Socialist Youth Federation (FJS) and the Union of Young Communists (UJC.))

ORGA   *Organización Republicana Gallega Autónoma* (Galician regionalist party founded in 1930 and fused into Azaña's *Izquierda Republicana* in 1934.)

PCE   *Partido Comunista de España* (The Moscow-orientated Communist Party founded in 1920–21.)

PNV   *Partido Nacionalista Vasco* (The Christian Democrat Basque Nationalist Party.)

POUM   *Partido Obrero de Unificación Marxista* (An amalgam of left-Communist dissidents and Trotskyists from the BOC and the *Izquierda Comunista* who united in 1935 to create a revolutionary vanguard party.)

PRC   *Partit Republicá Catalá* (The middle-class Catalan Nationalist party that was later merged into the *Esquerra* led by Lluis Companys.)

PSOE   *Partito Socialista Obrero Español* (The Spanish Socialist Workers' Party established in 1879).

PSUC   *Partido Socialista Unificat de Catalunya* (Communist-controlled Catalan Socialist Party which came into being in late July 1936.)

ROWAK   *Rohstoff-eund Waren-Einkaufsgesellschaft* (Export agency set up in Germany in October 1936 to channel German supplies to Nationalist Spain.)

SIM   *Servicio de Investigación Militar* (Communist-dominated counter-espionage agency set up in the Republican zone during the war.)

SMA   *Sindicato Minero Asturiano* (The Asturian miners' section of the UGT.)

SOV   *Solidaridad de Obreros Vascos* (The Basque workers' organization linked to the PNV.)

SUM   *Sindicato Único de Mineros* (Communist-dominated union of Asturian coal miners).

UGT   *Unión General de Trabajadores* (The trade union organization of the Socialist movement.)

UME   *Unión Militar Española* (Ultra-rightist army officers' society.)

UMRA   *Unión de Militares Republicanos Antifascistas* (Union of anti-fascist officers set up to counteract the influence of the UME.)

Glossary (2): Major Actors

REPUBLICAN ZONE

Anarchists

Abad de Santillán, Diego   prominent CNT/FAI member who served briefly in the Catalan government.

Ascaso, Francisco   famous anarchosyndicalist militant who died during the assault on the Atarazanas military barracks in Barcelona in July 1936.

Berneri, Camillo   Italian anarchist intellectual who arrived shortly after the outbreak of civil war. He was murdered during the 'May Events' of 1937 under mysterious circumstances.

Durruti, Buenaventura   anarchist militant who lead the first popular militia column to the Aragón front (Durruti column). After being killed on the Madrid front, Durruti achieved near-legendary status in the Republican camp.

García Oliver, Juan   member of the FAI who became Minister of Justice from November 1936 to May 1937.

Montseny, Federica   born into the well known anarchist family of Teresa Mañé (Soledad Gustavo) and Juan Montseny (Federico Urales), she became the first woman in Europe to occupy a ministerial post: she served as Minister of Health from November 1936 to May 1937.

Prieto, Horacio M.   'possibilist' CNT National Secretary until November, 1936.

Vásquez, Mariano reformist-minded National Secretary of CNT from November 1936 until end of war.

Communists (Independent)

Andrade, Juan former Trotskyist and ultra-leftist member of POUM executive.

Gorkín, Julián member of POUM executive. After the war he wrote a number of important works concerning the communists' role in the repression of the POUM.

Maurín, Joaquín along with Andreu Nin, he founded the anti-Stalinist Partido Obrero de Unificación Marxista (POUM) in September 1935. When war broke out in July 1936 he was trapped behind Nationalist lines; he remained in Francoist prisons until 1946.

Nin, Andreu Catalan political/literary figure. During the first weeks of the war he replaced Maurín as the leader of the POUM. He was arrested and then secretly murdered by the communists following the 'May Events' of 1937.

Communists (PCE) and Foreign

Carrillo, Santiago Secretary of the JSU, member of the PCE from November 1936 onwards. He was Secretary-General of the PCE from 1960 until 1982.

Codovila, Vitorio (alias 'Medina') Argentinian Comintern delegate.

Comorera, Joan leader of PSUC and member of the Catalan government Generalitat.

Díaz, José Secretary-General of PCE during the war.

Gerö, Ernö (alias 'Pedro') Hungarian Comintern agent who directed communist affairs in Catalonia during the Civil War.

Hernández, Jesús member of the politburo, Minister of Education from September 1936 to April 1938, Chief Political Commissar of the central army from April 1938 to April 1939.

Ibarurri, Dolores better known as 'La Pasionaria', member of the politburo. Secretary-General of the PCE from 1942 until 1960, when she was given the honorary title of 'President' of the party.

Líster, Enrique famous leader of the prestigious Fifth regiment.

Togliatti, Palmiro leading Italian communist and Comintern delegate in Spain. Variously known as 'Alfredo', 'Ercoli', etc.

Republicans

Aguirre, José Antonio Basque National Party (PNV) chief who was President of the Republic of Euzkadi from October 1936 until June 1937.

Alcalá Zamora, Niceto conservative republican who served as President of the Republic between 1931 and 1936.

Azaña, Manuel Prime Minister from 1931 to 1933 and from February to May 1936. President of the Republic until February 1939.

Casado, Segismundo Republican army officer, commander of the Central Army who formed the National Council of Defence (in opposition to the Negrín government) in March 1939.

Companys, Lluis former labour lawyer and Esquerra Catalana leader who served as the President of the Generalitat during the war.

Giral, José liberal republican, Premier from outset of war until September 1936.

Girobles, José María CEDA leader who spent the war in Portugal.

Irujo, Manuel leader of Basque National Party (PNV) who served in Negrín's government until April 1938.

Lerroux, Alejandro leader of the Radical party; Prime Minister in 1934 and 1935.

Martínez Barrio, Dieg influential conservative republican, was briefly Prime Minister at the outbreak of the civil war.

Miaja, General José Republican officier who headed the Junta de Defensa de Madrid until April 1937 and was President of the Casado National Defence Council, March 1939.

Rojo, Vicente chief of staff of the Republican army during the siege of Madrid from November 1936 to May 1937, chief of the central general staff from May 1937 to Febrary 1939. Rojo directed the principal Republican military offensives between 1937 and 1938.

Tarradellas, Josep Esquerra leader and premier of the Catalan government Generalitat.

Socialists

Álvarez del Vayo, Julio   left-socialist leader and close ally of the communists who became Minister of Foreign Affairs in the Largo Caballero and Negrín governments.

González Peña, Ramón   leader of the SMA who participated in the Asturian Revolt of 1934. He headed the UGT executive from 1937 until the end of the war.

Largo Caballero, Francisco   a moderate during the early part of his career, he became a fiery revolutionary from 1934 to 1936. His revolutionary sentiments gave way to pragmatism while he was Prime Minister and War Minister from September 1936 to May 1937.

Negrín, Juan   moderate socialist and ally of the communists, Finance Minister in the Largo Caballero administration, Prime Minister from May 1937 (Premier and Defence Minister from April 1938 on) until the end of the war.

Prieto, Indalecio   moderate socialist, Naval and Air Minister (September 1936), Defence Minister (May 1937 until April 1938).

Zabalza, Ricardo   left-socialist leader of the FNTT (Socialist Federation of Landworkers).

Zugazagoitia, Julián   moderate socialist, editor of *El Socialista* (socialist mouthpiece) until May 1937, served as Minister of Interior from May 1937 until April 1938.

NATIONALIST ZONE

Carlists, Falangists, Military Commanders, Monarchists

Fal Conde, Manuel   Carlist leader who opposed Franco's attempt to unify the right under his command. Refusing to forswear his devotion to a reconstituted monarchy, he was forced into exile during the war.

Franco, General Francisco   military commander of the Canary Islands at the beginning of the war, leader of the July rebellion in Spanish Morocco. Director of Nationalist movement from October 1936 until end of war. Head of Spanish State from 1939 until his death in 1975.

Goicoechea, Antonio   'authoritarian monarchist' who, immediately following the military rising, secured Italian assistance for the Nationalists. After the war, Franco named him head of the Bank of Spain.

Hedilla, Manuel radical Falangist of working-class origins. Following the arrest and execution of José Antonio Primo de Rivera, Hedilla was chosen as the provisional leader of the Falangist movement. His opposition to Franco's *Decree of Unification* led to his arrest and imprisonment.

Mola, General Emilio military governor of Pamplona (Navarre) and director of July military conspiracy. He died in a plane crash on 3 June 1937.

Primo de Rivera, José Antonio son of military dictator Miguel Primo de Rivera (1923–30). Founder-member and principal leader of the Spanish Falange (Spain's fascist party). Already a prisoner when the civil war broke out, José Antonio was executed by his Republican captors on 20 November 1936.

Primo de Rivera, Pilar sister of José Antonio who led the Falangist women's group Sección Femenina during and following the war.

Sanjurjo, General José having attempted to overthrow the left-republican government in August 1932, he was imprisoned and then exiled to Portugal. Selected to head the military directory that was to be established with the overthrow of the Popular Front, he died *en route* to Spain during the opening moments of the July rebellion.

Serrano Suñer, Ramón Franco's brother-in-law who helped to lay the political and ideological foundations of the *caudillo's* one-party state.

Sotelo Calvo, José leader of monarchist Renovación Española. His assassination in July 1936 sparked off military rebellion.

Varela, General José Carlist who was placed in charge of Nationalist attack on Madrid.

Yagüe, Colonel Juan Nationalist field commander during the civil war who first achieved national notoriety (the left dubbed him the 'Hyena of Asturias') when he led African troops to put down the revolt in Asturias in 1934.

Maps

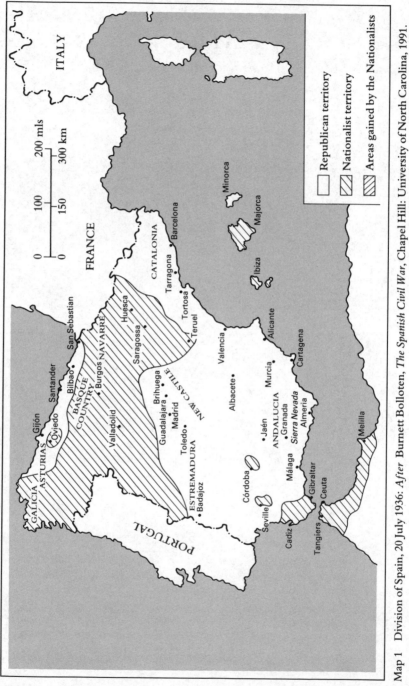

Map 1 Division of Spain, 20 July 1936: *After* Burnett Bolloten, *The Spanish Civil War*, Chapel Hill: University of North Carolina, 1991.

Republican territory

Nationalist territory

Areas gained by the Nationalists

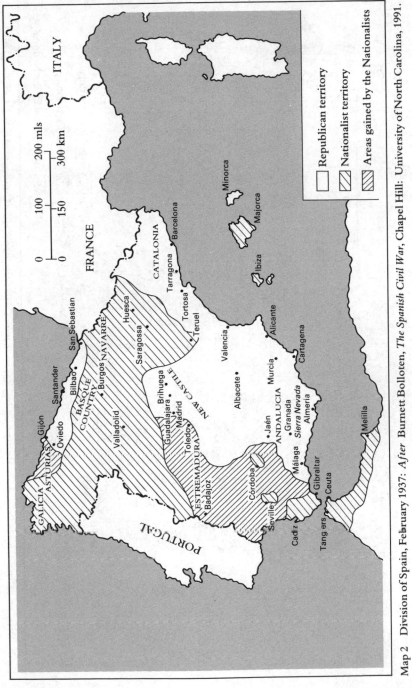

Map 2 Division of Spain, February 1937: *After* Burnett Bolloten, *The Spanish Civil War*, Chapel Hill: University of North Carolina, 1991.

Legend:
- ☐ Republican territory
- ◪ Nationalist territory
- ◪ Areas gained by the Nationalists

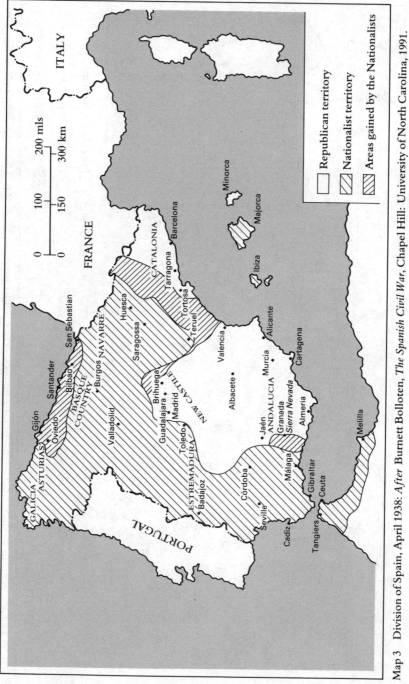

Map 3 Division of Spain, April 1938: *After* Burnett Bolloten, *The Spanish Civil War*, Chapel Hill: University of North Carolina, 1991.

□ Republican territory

▨ Nationalist territory

▨ Areas gained by the Nationalists

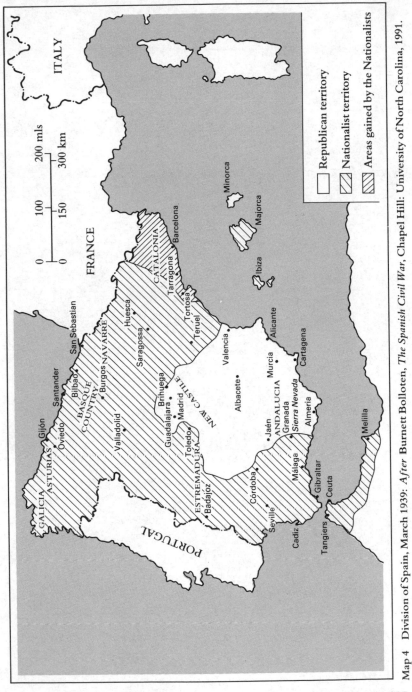

Map 4   Division of Spain, March 1939: *After* Burnett Bolloten, *The Spanish Civil War*, Chapel Hill: University of North Carolina, 1991.

Republican territory

Nationalist territory

Areas gained by the Nationalists

ITALY

FRANCE

200 mls

300 km

100

150

0

0

GALICIA

ASTURIAS

Gijón

Oviedo

Santander

San Sebastian

BASQUE COUNTRY

Bilbao

Burgos

NAVARRE

Huesca

Saragossa

CATALONIA

Barcelona

Tarragona

Tortosa

Teruel

Minorca

Majorca

Ibiza

PORTUGAL

Valladolid

Brihuega

Guadalajara

Madrid

NEW CASTILE

Toledo

ESTREMADURA

Badajoz

Valencia

Alicante

Albacete

Murcia

Cartagena

Córdoba

Seville

Cadiz

Jaén

ANDALUCIA

Granada

Sierra Nevada

Almería

Málaga

Gibraltar

Ceuta

Tangiers

Melilla

Index

Index

dictatorship, 7, 171–2
failure, 7
coup, 8, 52
and monarchist parties, 15
and nationalism, 54–5
and Morocco, 68
and CNT, 81
Asturias under, 82
and the countryside, 89
influence in Franco, 177
and Mussolini, 196
Primo de Rivera, Pilar, 183
Propaganda,
republican, 242–9
nationalist, 250–1, 273
communist, 251–2
Provisional Government,
named, 8
Socilists in, 9
comes to power, 10
school building program, 12
and the Church, 44
and Catalonia, 55
and Basque Country, 58
and agrarian reform, 90–1
Provisional Government (Basque), 61
Public Order Law, 73
Puente, Isaac, 126
Puigcerdá, 221

Queipo de Llano, Gen. Gonzalo, 104,
114, 117, 118, 119, 162, 179, 180,
250
Quintanilla, Eleuterio, 80

Rabassaires, see Law of Agricultural
Contracts
Radical Socialists (RS) (see also
Republicans), 11, 12, 17, 22, 109
Radicals (see also Lerroux), 10, 11, 17, 18,
55, 74, 91
Radio Nacional de España, 216
Radio Seville, 104, 250
Read, Herbert, 244
Recruitement and Promotion Law, 71–2
Redondo, Onésimo (see also FET-JONS),
168, 174, 183
Regler, Gustav, 244, 245
Renn, Ludwig, 244, 245
Renovación Española (see also Calvo
Sotelo), 17, 31, 32, 165–71
Republic, First, 7, 66
Republic, Second, 4, 10, 15, 16, 30, 124,
159, 165, 168, 176, 201
origins, 7
and opposing elites, 8

Provisional Government, 10
proclamation, 10
Constitution, 11
achievements, 14
and Popular Front, 23, 25
failure, 32–6
and the Church, 37–48
and nationalism, 49–63
and the military, 64–77
and social inestability, 78–9
and anarchism, 79–81
October revolution, 83–7
the agrarian problem, 87–99
internal distrust, 109
and Communists, 113
and the military rebellion, 103–20
and revolution, 121–43
and women, 127
and Foreign Intervention, 188–207
and League of Nations, 190
international support for, 243–4
abandoned by the democracies, 259
Republican Army, 119, 239, 240, 241
and militias, 144
and PCE, 150, 151–4, 246
Army of the East, 152
Army of the Center, 163, 164, 260
Army of the Ebro, 255–6
Republican-Socialist coalition (see also
Republicans and Socialists), 14, 33, 44,
45–6, 73
Republicans (see also AR, IR, PNR, RS
and UR)
and Pact of San Sebastián, 8
and municipal elections of 1931, 9
liberal republicans, 10, 22
left republicans, 14, 17, 44
right republicans, 17, 22
and Socialists, 23, 34
and Communists, 25
and Popular Front, 29
and the Church, 46
and events of 1917, 51
and Basque nationalists, 54, 58–9
in Catalonia, 55
and agrarian reform, 91
in National Union Government, 257–9
Rerum Novarum, 42
Restoration (of 1876), 49, 51, 52, 66
Retour de l'URSS, 248
Revolution, Spanish, see Anarcho-
Syndicalists, POUM and Republic
Rhineland, 206
Ribbentrop, Joachim von, 197
Ríos, Fernando de los, 10
Roatta, Gen. Mario, 163